ORGANIZATIONAL COMMUNICATION

Empowerment in a Technological Society

Patricia Hayes Andrews
Indiana University

Richard T. Herschel
University of North Carolina at Greensboro

with case studies by
John E. Baird, Jr.
Melnick, Baird, Williams, and Fisher

HOUGHTON MIFFLIN COMPANY   Boston   Toronto

Geneva, Illinois   Palo Alto   Princeton, New Jersey

Sponsoring Editor: Margaret H. Seawell
Senior Project Editor: Carol Newman
Assistant Editor: Jeanne Herring
Senior Production/Design Coordinator: Sarah Ambrose
Senior Manufacturing Coordinator: Marie Barnes
Marketing Manager: Caroline Croley

Cover designer: Diana Coe

Cover image: Variations on a Rythm-H, by Raymond Jonson. National Museum of American Art, Washington, DC/Art Resource, NY

Interior designer: Lisa DeGeorge

To those whose love has empowered us
Jim, Jennifer, Timothy, Zachary,
and Candice

CONTENTS

CHAPTER 3   *Empowering Employees Through Human Resources Management*   **66**

CHAPTER 4   *Human Relationships and Interpersonal Communication*   **100**

CHAPTER 7   *Small Group Communication in the Modern Organization   195*

CHAPTER 8   *Conflict and Organizational Communication*   **235**

CHAPTER 9   *Managing Diversity*   **269**

PREFACE

Philosophy of the Book

Nothing has changed communication in organizations more dramatically than advances in technology. It is true that scholars have studied organizations and organizational communication for the better part of this century. For more than thirty years, communication has been heralded as the lifeblood of the organization. But, much of what has been written—what we think we know about communication in organizations—has changed and will continue to change because of technological innovations. In *Organizational Communication: Empowerment in a Technological Society,* our goal is to begin to talk about the technological changes that are revolutionizing communication among employers and employees, challenging the ways that status is defined and power exercised, and, we argue, offering opportunities for empowerment. Whether such empowerment is realized will depend in large measure upon the values, attitudes, and behaviors of those in formal positions of organizational leadership.

Changes in Organizational Communication Facilitated by Technology

There is no doubt that technology has changed the way employers interact with their employees. In the past, managers who wanted to praise an employee for a job well done most likely sent a handwritten note or a typewritten memo—or stopped by the worker's office for a reinforcing chat. Today, those same managers may be more inclined to e-mail words of praise or congratulations or leave a message on the employee's voicemail. A decade ago, group meetings were held in traditional conference rooms where employees shared information and ideas, argued, and sometimes confronted each other face to face across a conference table. Now, in many organizations, electronic meeting rooms allow employees to share data and ideas, solve problems, and make decisions without necessarily using their voices. They may confront an idea by typing an argument into a computer, but they may not know for sure with whom they are arguing!

Now, more than ever, those near the bottom of the organization have access to those at the top. In most organizations a clerical worker in an obscure department can e-mail the organization's president with a complaint or a creative idea. Whether the president responds or not—or even receives e-mail

from those not named on a master list—is another matter. Today, formal bureaucratic channels can be by-passed readily as workers collaborate electronically across units, seeking solutions to today's complex problems.

Technology, Empowerment, and Organizational Change

We believe that changes in technology offer unique opportunities for worker
empowerment. Since the 1960s, management theorists have applauded empowering approaches to leadership. Given the rise in competitive pressures
that have forced organizations to adopt newer, more flexible structures, empowering employees seems especially important. Once described as the organization of the future, the knowledge-based organization, with teams of
specialists who direct and supervise their own performance, is increasingly the
organization of the present. Cross-departmental collaboration is needed to
foster entrepreneurial creativity and to realize new business opportunities. If
technology can function as a vehicle of worker empowerment as we move toward the year 2000, so much the better.

Technological advances have taken place in a context of broader changes
in the work force. For instance, the work force is more diverse with more
women and minorities in positions of leadership than ever before. As we
rapidly approach the beginning of the twenty-first century, those who forecast
work-force demographics predict even more dramatic changes in cultural,
racial, ethnic, and gender workplace diversity. Technology itself has altered the
character of the work force. Fewer people work in manufacturing; more people handle information. More people work out of their homes. Computers
have made it possible for people to access information from all over the world
and to interact electronically with people they would never have known otherwise and whom they likely will never actually meet.

In this book, we begin with the belief that empowerment is important in
the modern organization. Moreover, effective organizational communication
is at the heart of employee empowerment and productive, healthy organizational functioning. If properly understood and utilized, advancing technology
has the potential for furthering employee empowerment. Technology is far
more than a management tool. Those who master technology position themselves to be self-empowered. Indeed, in what we argue is an increasingly collaborative, team-oriented environment, managers and professionals need to
serve as integrators and facilitators rather than as formal authority figures.
Collaborative ventures bring together people who possess different attributes,
skills, and expectations. In an empowering organization, members feel free to
voice, exchange, and challenge ideas, to bargain and negotiate, and to reach
genuine consensus with their fellow workers. Technology can facilitate such
communicative exchanges.

Why This Book?

In writing this book we hope to have satisfied the need for a text that integrates our traditional understanding of organizational communication with our growing knowledge of technology. Students using the text need no particular background in organizational communication, but they should be able to understand and respond to rather complex concepts and reflect thoughtfully and analytically on the notion of empowerment—its meaning for all organizational members and the ways in which it might be realized through advances in technology.

Organizational Communication: Empowerment in a Technological Society differs from other organizational communication textbooks in its (1) thematic emphasis on technology and empowerment as an integrating conceptual framework; (2) thorough exploration of relevant organizational communication theory and research; (3) incorporation of a number of real-life cases for discussion; and (4) in-depth discussion of several timely topics, including diverse information technologies, organizational design, managing diversity (with an emphasis on gender), organizational innovation, and ethics.

Overview of the Book

The early chapters of *Organizational Communication: Empowerment in a Technological Society* establish a theoretical and conceptual foundation for an understanding of organizational communication. In the first chapter, we look at how people used to think about organizations, communication, and organizational communication, and at how they are beginning to reconceptualize these crucial concepts. We highlight the ways that technology has changed how people communicate, affording both opportunity and challenge. We stress the need for vigilance, for technology has the potential to alienate as well as to empower.

Organization theory is examined next, moving chronologically from the turn of the century to the present. We begin with the traditional schools of thought and follow their progression to more contemporary perspectives on management theory. We give special consideration to human resources management, including McGregor's Theory X/Theory Y, Hersey and Blanchard's life cycle theory, self-managing teams, and principles of Japanese management. We advance the premise that human resources theories are based on notions of empowerment.

Nearly every modern management theory stresses the importance of human relationships. Thus, in Chapter 4, we take a microscopic view of interaction in organizational settings, focusing on interpersonal relationships as the fundamental building block of the organization. We introduce a model of effective human interaction, grounded in principles of supportive communication, and we examine research on superior-subordinate communication, peer communication, and interaction in computer-mediated environments. Because human relationships are influenced significantly by the sorts of organizations in which they attempt to flourish, we move in Chapter 5 to a consideration of organizational design. We examine competing views of organizations as systems and describe diverse organizational structures and the circumstances under which each structure is most likely to be successful. Then we discuss how communication is influenced by organizational design, both at the formal and the informal level. We conclude with a consideration of the opportunities for technology within different organizational structures.

Chapter 6 focuses on leadership in the information age. Futurists have argued that notions of leadership are changing dramatically, partly in response to changing technologies. We examine that argument and compare and contrast traditional research-based perspectives on leadership. Next we consider leadership in relation to power. We discuss the meaning of power and sources of power—both personal and structural. Finally, we examine the relationship between being powerful and empowering others and the potentially empowering role of technology.

For organizational leaders, one significant way to empower is to give others a share in decision making. Using groups to make decisions is one of the most obvious ways to achieve this goal. Thus, in Chapter 7 we examine group communication. Following a discussion of our current knowledge of groups, including social influence and conformity, cohesiveness, role structure, and status and power, we explore patterns of problem-solving and decision models. Finally, we discuss the innovative ways that computers are used to assist decision-making groups in their collaborative ventures.

Next we examine conflict management, defining conflict and comparing diverse attitudes toward conflict. In Chapter 8 we explore significant sources of conflict in organizational settings and then examine styles and strategies of conflict management. We introduce a model of collaborative conflict management before considering the ways that technology may assist organizations in working through conflict situations.

Chapter 9 focuses on managing diversity. In this chapter, we consider broad diversity issues, such as changing demographics, discrimination, and sexual harassment. We give special consideration to the educational system as a foundational organizational experience which, for women and people of color, often involves discrimination. On a more positive note, we point to organizations with good track records in managing diversity. We consider gender and leadership and gender differences in communication, and we conclude the chapter by suggesting that technology might create a more equitable organizational environment, while acknowledging the potential risks.

In Chapter 10 we discuss the importance of ethics and diverse approaches to making ethical judgments. We examine several complex ethical issues, such as dealing with the tension between service and profit and making decisions about whistle blowing. The chapter also addresses employee rights, ranging from privacy to the opportunity to live a balanced personal/professional life. The chapter concludes with a large section devoted to the ethical complexities associated with advances in technology—the opportunities for enhancing productivity tempered by the potential for misuse and abuse.

The book's final chapter addresses organizational innovation and change. In it, we explore the information superhighway, including video conferencing and virtual reality technologies. Next we consider reengineering, examining its implications (both positive and negative) for organizational communication. We also explore the home as a significant new market created by advances in technology. Finally, we conclude the chapter by reflecting on the relationship among technology, empowerment, and organizational communication.

Special Features

In addition to the innovative themes of *Organizational Communication: Empowerment in a Technological Society*, we have included several features to enhance the text's pedagogical value. In particular:

- **"Focus On" boxes** spotlight innovative practices or ethical and practical problems in organizational communication.

- **Cases for Discussion** bring real world relevance to the classroom through examples of contemporary communication issues encountered by organizations and their members; discussion questions follow each case.

- *What Is the Internet?*, an appendix, introduces and briefly describes several features of the Internet, including e-mail, LISTSERVE, Telnet, FTP, Gopher, and the World Wide Web—and how to use them.

- **A Glossary of key terms** contains brief definitions of major concepts discussed within the text.

- **An extensive bibliography** following the glossary lists hundreds of articles and books pertaining to organizational communication and related themes.

An *Instructor's Resource Manual with Test Items* is available to instructors. Included in the manual are sample syllabi; chapter objectives; suggestions for how to teach the course; more than two hundred multiple-choice and fifty essay examination questions; additional cases for discussion; and suggested approaches for using cases to enhance student learning.

Acknowledgements

We are grateful to those who inspired us to write this book and who, in so many different ways, supported us along the way. First, we want to thank the wonderful staff at Houghton Mifflin for believing in us and in our work. We are especially grateful to Margaret Seawell, our sponsoring editor, who first thought the book was a wonderful idea and who has been the source of continuous encouragement, thoughtful, intelligent reactions, and kindness.

Jeanne Herring occasionally prodded us gently and pleasantly and faithfully conveyed our messages and responded to our endless inquiries. Our developmental editor, Elisa Adams, offered a perceptive reading of the first draft, and her instincts were consistently right on target. Finally, Carol Newman, our bright, persevering production editor, maintained her sense of humor while seeing us through a variety of last-minute challenges. She kept insisting that, indeed, we *were* going to meet those deadlines! And we did!

We are also grateful to those in our profession who have taught us so much about organizational communication, empowerment, and technology. In many cases, they have also taught us about friendship, caring, and ethics. Among those we count as both friends and colleagues are Mary Ellen Kranz and Valerie Sessa, Center for Creative Leadership; Michael and Suzanne Osborn, Memphis State University; Richard Johannesen, Northern Illinois University; Dennis Gouran, Penn State University; Glen Williams, Texas A&M University; J. Jeffery Auer, Robert G. Gunderson, Janet Near, and Joseph Scudder, all of Indiana University; and Jere Hershey and the entire faculty and staff in the ISOM Department at UNCG. We also extend a special thanks to John E. Baird, Jr. who developed the cases for the book based on his extensive consulting experience, and to Lisa Bates-Froiland who, while completing her doctoral studies at Indiana, made outstanding contributions to the *Instructor's Resource Manual.*

We thank our colleagues listed below, whose thoughtful and helpful critical readings guided us throughout this project.

Brenda J. Allen
University of Colorado at Boulder

Robert P. Bostrom
University of Georgia

Vikki Clawson
Independent Consultant and Trainer

Sue DeWine
Ohio University

Joey F. George
Florida State University

Sandra M. Ketrow
University of Rhode Island

Donald Lumsden
Kean College of New Jersey

Steven K. May
University of North Carolina, Chapel Hill

John C. Meyer
University of Southern Mississippi

Steven M. Ralston
East Tennessee State University

Matthew W. Seeger
Wayne State University

Shirley Willihnganz
University of Louisville

Finally, we are deeply appreciative of our families, without whose love and support this book would never have come to fruition. To them, we dedicate our book.

Patricia Hayes Andrews

Richard T. Herschel

CHAPTER

1

Organizational Communication in a Technological Age

The microprocessor . . . has suddenly brought forth PCs as powerful as main-frame computers. In the process it has destroyed hundreds of thousands of jobs, unseated CEOs at world-renowned companies, reshuffled tens of billions of dollars of shareholder value, and set off convulsions that will wrack the 50,000 companies in computing—and all their customers—through the end of the century.

Stratford Sherman "The New Computer Revolution," *Fortune,* 1993.

Organizational communication is that process wherein mutually interdependent human beings create and exchange messages, and interpret and negotiate meanings, while striving to articulate and realize mutually held visions, purposes, and goals. In the past, the processes of creating and exchanging messages were conducted primarily through verbal exchanges and handwritten or typed correspondence. Typically, it took time to transmit written information, and when such information was received, it was usually dated and frequently secondhand. Because of further processing by intermediaries, often it arrived in condensed form. As a result, organizations found that their members' understanding of visions, purposes, and goals was sometimes out of sync with the originally intended meaning.

Computers and computer networks have altered things considerably. We now live in a time when the volume of information, the means of communicating it, and the speed of message transmission have all changed dramatically. Information can be analyzed and communicated as it is being created or captured. When organizations want to inform employees of changes, they can broadcast messages simultaneously to all of their sites so that every employee receives the same complete message at the same time. Those who miss it receive the exact same message, transmitted by the exact same sender, later on videotape. With new technologies such as e-mail, messages can be created quickly and exchanged immediately. Since there are fewer intermediaries between the message source and its recipient, the probability is now greater that visions, purposes, and goals will be commonly understood.

Technology also helps organizations to overcome the limitations previously imposed by differences in time and place. Computers allow organizations to capture, analyze and share information from anywhere in the world twenty-four hours a day. These new capabilities have fostered dramatic changes in organizational processes, decision making, and organizational design. With the help of information technology, organizations have become leaner, more responsive to competitive pressures, and, unfortunately, less promising as a source of lifetime employment.

In this text we explore organizational communication from the viewpoint that many elements of such communication are continually being reshaped by rapidly changing technology. We believe that the subject of organizational communication can no longer be discussed without seriously considering how technology might impact our traditional views. Consistent with these beliefs, we incorporate technology issues in each chapter of this text.

In this first chapter we begin by considering the information age and the changing nature of work. Then, we introduce the concept of empowerment, its meaning and scope, and its relationship to the modern world in general and to technology in particular. Next, we explore both past and current perspectives on the meaning of the term *organization* before explaining our definition of organizational communication and discussing why effective communication remains a priority. We conclude by citing examples of how technology is influencing organizational communication in diverse and rapidly changing ways.

Living in an Information Age

Over thirty years ago Marshall McLuhan wrote that we live in an electronic age in which "information travels at the speed of light" (1964, p. 35). Today our emerging information age is progressively reshaping our perception of society as well as our ideas about management, organization, communication, education, and work itself. Organizations of all kinds are experiencing unprecedented change, propelled by an increasing need for information, the desire to manage that information effectively, and new technologies that offer challenge as well as opportunity.

Some have described the new age as a time of "information shock." Every two-and-a-half years the amount of available information doubles. The Sunday *New York Times* contains so much information that reading it from beginning to end would take the average reader about twenty-eight hours. The explosion of information, the ability to access nearly everything being written electronically, and the rapid and continuing distribution of computers throughout homes and offices have created a revolution. This revolution in turn is dramatically influencing the way organizations are structured, the ways people lead and attempt to share power with others, and the very nature of organizations and organizational communication.

The Changing Nature of Work

Nowhere is change more obvious than in the nature of work itself. Cetron, Rocha, and Luchins (1988) forecast a number of long-term societal trends in the labor force, work, and management for the twenty-first century. Among their predictions:

- About half of all service workers will be involved in collecting, analyzing, synthesizing, structuring, or retrieving information as a basis of knowledge by the year 2000. Half of these will work at home.
- Computer systems will issue reports and recommend actions based on data gathered electronically—all without human intervention.
- Computer competence will approach 100 percent of the population in U.S. urban areas by the year 2000.
- Five of the ten fastest-growing careers between now and 2001 will be computer-related, with the demand for programmers and systems analysts growing by 70 percent.
- The typical large business will be information-based, composed of specialists who guide themselves based on information from colleagues, customers, and top managers.

Of course, work is already in a state of rapid transition. *Forbes* magazine's latest list of the ten richest American billionaires includes seven whose fortunes were based on media, communications, or computers—software and services rather than hardware and manufacturing. In this kind of economy, labor no longer consists of working on "things," according to historian Mark Poster, but of "men and women acting on other men and women, or . . . people acting on information and information acting on people" (quoted in Toffler, 1990, p. 9). One out of every two Americans now works in some aspect of information processing. Workers today can be grouped according to the amount of information processing or "mind-work" they do, rather than their position title or whether they happen to work in a store, school, factory, or hospital.

Alvin Toffler (1990) discusses occupations in terms of a **mind-work spectrum,** that is, the balance between jobs requiring the use and creation of information and those that are strictly manual. At the top of the spectrum are research scientists, financial analysts, and computer programmers, as well as secretaries and file clerks. Although the functions and qualifications of these individuals vary and they work at vastly different levels of abstraction, their work is largely defined by the activities of moving information around and creating new information. In the middle of the mind-work spectrum exists a broad range of mixed jobs—tasks requiring the worker both to perform physical labor and to handle information. For example, the Federal Express driver handles boxes and packages but also operates a computer at his or her side. Auto mechanics at General Motors dealers still have greasy hands, but they also use a computer system designed by Hewlett-Packard to help them troubleshoot problems. The hotel clerk, the nurse, and many others may deal with people, but they also spend a considerable fraction of their time generating, getting, or giving out information. At the very bottom of the spectrum, the purely manual jobs are disappearing. Unfortunately, those whose jobs are in increasingly short supply often lack the skills that would enable them to move up the mind-work spectrum. In some industries, for example, the automobile industry, the rate of illiteracy among U.S. workers is as high as 25 percent. Not surprisingly, U.S. businesses are spending a record $210 billion for on-the-job training and education, "an effort about equal to public elementary, secondary, and higher education institutions combined" (Offerman & Gowing, 1990, p. 96).

Myths About Information

For organizations of every type, one of the greatest challenges of the twenty-first century will be the management of information. Yet several commonly held myths about information often contribute to its mismanagement (Clampitt, 1991). *The first myth is the idea that information is a kind of commodity.* Perhaps information can be purchased and sold in the marketplace, but it cannot simply be transferred outright. Instead, when information is transmitted, both sender and receiver possess it, thus making the question of information ownership more complex. *Another widely shared myth is the notion that information is power.* While information offers the potential for power, its significance depends more on how this important resource is managed. Organizations should concentrate on influencing how information is used and distributed, encouraging information sharing. Those who equate information with power may be tempted to rigidly control its dissemination, perhaps secretly hoarding information, invariably to the detriment of the organization. Yet if innovation and economic growth are to occur, sharing is essential. Peters (1987) points out that "information hoarding . . . commonplace throughout American industry, service and manufacturing alike . . . will be an impossible millstone around the neck of tomorrow's organization" (p. 10).

A third myth is based on the mistaken notion that more information is better. Yet, possessing vast quantities of information leads to many questions—how to organize it, with whom to share it, how to interpret it. The possession of too much information can be overwhelming. Nothing could more readily disempower a person than information overload and a deluge of reports, data, and fact sheets—many of them ambiguous, irrelevant, or inaccurate. More important than the quantity of information is its quality.

Still another myth is that information is value-free. On the contrary, all information is value-laden. Drucker (1988) acknowledged this when he defined information as "data endowed with relevance and purpose" (p. 46). It is gathered for certain reasons, viewed from different perspectives, and shared in specific contexts. Thus, its meaning evolves and is often negotiated over time and through repeated communicative exchanges.

A final myth is that information is knowledge. Instead, most information consists of unconnected facts or data that have been put into categories and classification schemes or arranged in other patterns. Information does not always lead to understanding. In contrast to information, knowledge goes beyond the facts, connecting and explaining them. Knowledge further refines information and seeks to reconcile seemingly disparate findings. It is knowledge, not information, that can best contribute to employee empowerment.

Empowerment

Empowerment is now a buzzword of contemporary management. Dozens of books and articles have used empowerment as their organizing framework (Block, 1987; Conger, 1986; Neilsen, 1986; Pacanowsky, 1987; Whetton & Cameron, 1991), and nearly every writer who examines power also alludes to empowerment. Some treat it as a management technique; others, perhaps more philosophically, view it as central to any motivational scheme that honors the goal of individual self-actualization through organizational affiliation.

As technology has advanced, the notion of empowerment has become especially important. Organizations are now doing the same or more work with fewer people; thus, they need to facilitate opportunities for each member to contribute maximum value to the organization and its customers, and to do so in a way that is personally compelling. In practice, the empowering process involves managers delegating and sharing resources and decision making with employees. Conceptually, empowerment has less to do with management technique and strategy and more to do with employee feelings and perceptions. To empower is to enable. As Conger and Kanungo (1988) put it, "Enabling implies creating conditions for heightening motivation for task accomplishment through the development of a strong sense of personal efficacy" (p. 474).

Several theorists have offered specific suggestions for empowering practices (and we will return to those in Chapter 6 when we discuss leadership). It is worth noting here, however, that as managers empower others, their own influence increases as well. Michael Maccoby's best seller, *The Gamesman* (1976), provides a striking illustration of how this process works. Maccoby tells the story of a manager who announced to his staff that he was going to offer a formal class after work on how to do his job. Everyone was invited to attend. Understandably, most of his staff decided to take the course. After a few months, many of them actually began picking up portions of his work. This enabled the manager to take on other, more challenging projects, which previously he had never been able to find time to do. Meanwhile, his staff felt gratified that he was encouraging them to expand their knowledge and skills— and were doing work they had selected for themselves. Over time, this group became so motivated and productive that new assignments entering the organization were channeled to them. The manager was given much credit for the group's breadth of skills, eagerness to tackle new tasks, and cooperative team spirit. As a result, he became more influential within the organization, was given more complex and interesting assignments, and rapidly ascended the organizational ladder. Consistent with Bennis and Namus's (1985) study of how empowerment makes people feel significant, committed to learning, team-spirited, and excited about their work, Maccoby's illustration demonstrates that the empowerment process is potentially valuable and motivational for all those who participate in it.

Throughout this book we will return to the concept of empowerment. Although early theories of organization and management ignored empowerment, contemporary views have embraced it. As organizations strive to become more empowering, interpersonal relationships will be affected at all levels, more teams will be used, and new views of power and leadership will emerge. Technology, too, will play a role—providing new opportunities for information access, information sharing, and decision making and thereby creating opportunities for rethinking organizational processes and design.

Of course there are no guarantees that advances in technology will be accompanied by employee empowerment. In fact, at the other extreme, technological advances can lead to substantial reductions in the work force. The most likely casualties of increasing automation are jobs in small- and medium-sized organizations. In the last decade, for example, high technology has taken over the lumber industry and is driving out small operators. New computer-driven sawmills may be pictures of precision and efficiency, but they need very few workers to operate them. Computers use electronic scanners to measure each log and decide how to cut it up into the largest amount of usable lumber. The computer chooses from among 100,000 different cutting patterns. Where does the human being fit into this picture? One operator at Lakeland Mills, Ltd. sits at a console in a glass-walled booth, flipping switches to position logs. At his side, a radio plays music all day to relieve the boredom (Bayless, 1986). In some of the most modern mills, work force reductions run as high as 80 percent (Northcraft & Neale, 1994). Thus, in some circumstances technological advances can contribute to unemployment, mindless jobs, and increasing tension between unions and management (Solomon, 1987).

On a more positive note, however, technology can also offer solutions to many problems, including worker displacement. Technological advances have altered more than the way work is done. They have also changed *training methods* for future jobs. New methods for training and retraining displaced workers provide considerably more flexibility than in the past. Computerized courses allow students to work at their own pace. These courses also change the nature of the learning process to make it less threatening (Ivey, 1988). Thus, technology must be incorporated into the workplace thoughtfully, with a balanced concern for potential pitfalls as well as unprecedented opportunities.

Before further considering the growing role of technology and its impact on organizational life, we need to examine the meaning of both *organization* and *organizational communication*. Both concepts have changed in meaning and scope over time. A foundational understanding of these concepts is important. For instance, a person who views organizational communication as a process that is largely initiated by management will think very differently about employee empowerment than one who views such communication as shared equally among all organizational participants.

Defining Organizations

Ours is an organizational society. We are born in organizations, we are educated by organizations, and we spend most of our lives working for them. We patronize organizations, play in them, and pray in them. Ultimately, most of us will die in an organization, and as the sociologist Etzioni (1964) has noted, when the time comes for burial, one of the largest and most complex organizations of all, the state, must grant official permission. We typically associate the term *organization* with large corporations, but nearly forty years ago, William Whyte, Jr., (1957) acknowledged the diversity of organizations and pointed out that we are all organizational people: "Blood brother to the business trainee off to join Du Pont is the seminary student who will end up in the church hierarchy, the doctor headed for the corporate clinic, the physics Ph.D. in a government laboratory, the engineering graduate student in the huge drafting room at Lockheed, the young apprentice in a Wall Street law factory" (p. 3).

What is an **organization**? Nearly everyone can agree that IBM is an organization, but many would argue about whether a family should be viewed as an organization. Etzioni (1964) offered a traditional view, construing organizations as social units or human groupings that are deliberately constructed and reconstructed to seek specific goals. After proposing this definition, Etzioni went on to specify corporations, churches, schools, military units, hospitals, prisons, and public interest groups as organizations while excluding families, tribes, friendship groups, and social classes. Etzioni's traditional view of organizations contains five defining elements:

1. Divisions of labor and responsibility deliberately planned to facilitate goal achievement
2. The presence of one or more centers of power whose function it is to review and direct organizational performance
3. Substitution of personnel, so that unsatisfactory personnel leaving the organization can be replaced
4. Interdependence among organizational components, so that the performance of one function affects the performance of all others
5. Coordination among organizational components, typically achieved through communication within the organization (in Baird, 1977).

Etzioni acknowledged that the social units he excluded from his definition of organizations might possess one or more of these characteristics. For example, families often divide labor, have power centers (parents), substitute personnel (through remarriage or adoption), coordinate their efforts toward common goals, and are interdependent. Etzioni argued, however, that the extent to which they do all of these things is far less typical or self-defining than in the case of IBM or General Motors, both of which have formal, documented, well-defined, and measurable goals.

Other theorists have offered more flexible definitions of organizations. Drucker (1959) succinctly noted that an organization is "an information and decision system" (p. 92). Rogers and Agarwala-Rogers (1976) described organizations as "a stable system of individuals who work together to achieve, through a hierarchy of ranks and division of labor, common goals" (p. 6). Simon (1958) highlighted the centrality of communication to the organization when he wrote that an organization is "the complex pattern of communication and other relations between human beings" (p. xvi). Finally, Putnam (1983) argued that organizations are simply "social relationships . . . interlocked behavior centered on specialized task and maintenance activities" (p. 45). Although diverse, these definitions share several common threads: *an emphasis on goal-directed behavior, coordinated actions, information sharing, decision making, and human relationships.* In turn, these elements dramatize *the importance of communication* in organizations.

In our view, organizations are socially constructed entities. As human beings organize, they come together and often interact in purposive, goal-directed ways. While many of their purposes and goals are shared, others may differ or even conflict. Organizations are dynamic, ever changing, and ever moving in new directions in response to uncertain, sometimes turbulent environments. Every organizational member is influenced by the environment but also helps to create and re-create it. As organizational members interact, they negotiate their views of the world and in so doing attempt to make their organizational lives meaningful and to discover or rediscover those things (goals, purposes, values, shared visions) that initially brought them together. Organizations do not exist as static, objective entities or "containers" into which people pour themselves and their work. Rather, organizations are interpreted by individuals, each of whom, through words, symbols, and behaviors (Putnam, 1983), may perceive a different sense of what the organization is and is becoming. Thus, the same organization (whether family or corporation) can mean different things to different people, and over time, each person may alter her or his view of organizational reality. From this perspective, organizational leaders are responsible less for dividing labor and establishing goals than for establishing shared meaning and, with the help of many others, negotiating some sense of shared purpose. In many ways, organizing and communicating are virtually interchangeable.

Organizational Types

While organizations share similarities, they are extremely diverse in function and purpose. Parsons (1963) offered a useful functional classification of organizational types. The functions are not mutually exclusive; organizations may fall into more than one category. But as Tompkins (1982) noted, we can categorize most organizations by considering their basic and primary social service or function. Parsons's typology includes these four functions:

Organizations oriented to economic production. These represent the common stereotype of organizations. Geared toward profit making, most are businesses that manufacture products and/or offer services for consumers. Economically self-sufficient, these organizations either survive or falter based on their ability to recover their expenses through the sale of their services or products.

Organizations oriented toward political goals. Generally funded and empowered by local, state, and federal governments, these organizations include government offices, legislative bodies, police and military forces, and financial institutions such as banks (the latter creating and allocating power in a business economy). They are designed to generate and distribute power within society.

Organizations oriented to integration goals. These are designed to mediate and resolve tension and discord among groups and individuals within society. Oriented toward helping solve social problems, these organizations include legal offices, the court system, public interest groups, consumer advocacy groups, and political parties.

Organizations oriented to pattern maintenance goals. These organizations promote cultural and educational goals and development within society. In general, they grow from the norms of a particular society and include families, schools, religious organizations, and diverse volunteer organizations. Health care organizations also fit into this category, since theoretically they help preserve society by diminishing and managing health problems, and by making it possible for individuals to return to normal functioning within society.

Most Americans belong to organizations that fall into each of these functional categories. They belong to families. They make their living by working for corporations or universities; they volunteer at shelters for abused women and children and organizations that promote adult literacy; they send their children to public schools, where they become active in the PTA; and they are members of churches, synagogues and mosques. They also belong to several professional societies and are registered Democrats or Republicans. These multiple organizational affiliations need not be problematic, unless the organizations to which people belong represent conflicting or inconsistent goals. Burke (1973) points out, for instance, that "the individual is composed of many 'corporate identities.' Sometimes they are concentric, sometimes in conflict" (p. 307). If people seek to maintain, as Goffman suggested, "a coherent style, sense of integrity and continuity" (quoted du Preez, 1980, p. 7), then they must coordinate their identities. Managing multiple identities can become a formidable challenge for those who belong to organizations whose interests compete or conflict in some way (Cheney & Tompkins, 1987; Pelz & Andrews, 1976). Yet by grappling with their diverse organizational identities, with all of the associated complexity and ambiguity, people discover and define their uniqueness as individuals.

Communication and the Organization

Nearly every modern work on organizations points to the importance of communication for achieving organizational objectives, furthering human relationships, making sound decisions, and so forth. Communication, however, cannot be viewed simply as an important organizational component. Rather, communication is every organization's lifeblood. Perhaps Bavelas and Barrett (1951) expressed it best in their classic article on organizational communication:

> It is entirely possible to view an organization as an elaborate system for gathering, evaluating, recombining, and disseminating information. It is not surprising in these terms that the effectiveness of an organization with respect to the achievement of its goals should be so closely related to its effectiveness in handling information . . . Communication is not a secondary or derived aspect of organization—a "helper" of the other presumably more basic functions. It is rather the essence of organized activity and is the basic process out of which all other functions derive (p. 368).

What is extraordinary about this statement is that it was made over forty years ago, long before other organizational theorists had even begun to acknowledge the integral relationship between communicating and organizing (for instance, Katz & Kahn, 1966; Putnam & Pacanowsky, 1983; Weick, 1969).

When Peters and Waterman (1982) concluded their "search for excellence" within American organizations, they asserted, "What does it all add up to? Lots of communication. All of Hewlett-Packard's golden rules have to do with communicating more. . . . The name of the successful game is rich, informal communication. The astonishing by-product is the ability to have your cake and eat it, too; that is, rich, informal communication leads to more action, more experiments, more learning, and simultaneously to the ability to stay better in touch and on top of things" (p. 124). Peters continues through the business press to admonish organizations about the critical importance of communication.

Theorists have defined **communication** in diverse ways. Regardless of the perspective taken, however, each acknowledges and incorporates several common components. Among these are *messages,* or the verbal and nonverbal cues that each communicator conveys to the other. *Senders* (those who send a message, or a generalized message source) and *receivers* (the message's destination or the person or persons who receive and decipher the message) are also involved. Since communication is a dynamic process consisting of the continuous exchange of messages, however, senders also act (often simultaneously) as receivers and receivers also serve as message sources. *Transmission,* the actual sending and receiving of verbal and nonverbal messages through designated channels, is a critical part of the message exchange process. One of the most important choices participants make in the communication process is the *channel,* the vehicle or medium through which a message travels. Channels range from light waves for nonverbal cues to memos, telephones, or computers as modes for transmitting auditory and visual messages. Ultimately, those who communicate both *encode* and *decode* (that is, create, transform, and decipher) messages; in this way they formulate *meaning* by interpreting or making sense of each other's messages. This interpretation may be facilitated through the use of *feedback* (messages sent in response to the initial message), depending upon the feedback's accuracy, timing, and tone. Finally, communication *effects,* broadly referring to the outcome or general results of the message exchange process, are of interest. Depending upon the model or perspective embraced, however, the precise definitions, emphasis, and relationships among these components may differ considerably.

Models of Communication

The earliest and simplest models of communication were **linear**. They conceptualized communication as a largely one-way process characterized by the flow of information from a source to a receiver. Berlo's model (1960), with its tidy emphasis on a source sending a message through a channel to a receiver, exemplifies the linear view of communication (see Figure 1.1). Linear models (also referred to as mechanistic and information transfer models) tend to focus on channels, so that communication is most appropriately viewed as a "conduit" through which individuals attempt to accomplish their goals and objectives.

Barriers to effective communication (that is, message fidelity) usually involve *noise,* which Berlo viewed as anything that interferes with or distorts the

FIGURE 1.1

A Linear
Model of
Communication

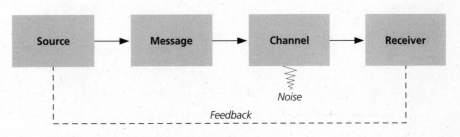

*Dotted line denotes the fact that feedback is de-emphasized in this model.

message as it is transmitted through the channel. According to Berlo, message fidelity is more than the clarity or quality of transmission. Noise, then, might involve anything from crackling telephone wires to garbage on the computer screen to the receiver's cultural background and attitudes—all of which might affect message interpretation. Finally, Berlo's model includes a feedback loop (from the receiver to the source), and in that sense is not strictly linear. Feedback, however, is not stressed in the model. Berlo viewed the source as largely originating the act of communicating and controlling it through the status or authority associated with his or her organizational role, as well as the channel chosen. He saw the receiver's role as much more passive. The linear model is quite consistent with early views of organization theory. Classical organization theorists saw managers as message sources who controlled channels; sought to eliminate noise of any kind; and sent order-oriented messages to subordinates, who responded with compliance.

A more contemporary communication model, depicted in Figure 1.2, is **transactional,** emphasizing communication as a two-way, reciprocal process of mutual message exchange. Wenburg and Wilmot (1973) described the transactional view: "All persons are engaged in sending (encoding) and receiving (decoding) messages simultaneously. Each person is constantly sharing in the encoding and decoding process and each person is affecting the other" (p. 6). The transactional perspective makes no sharp distinction between source and receiver roles, since one person plays both, and often at the same time. Feedback (both verbal and nonverbal) is central to the transactional model. An equally important component of the transactional view focuses on how meaning in a communication transaction is constructed. The linear view advances the notion that the meaning of a particular message resides with the sender, whose challenge is to use a message channel effectively and thus transmit the message's meaning clearly to some receiver or group. The transactional model is geared to the receiver, and especially to the construction of a message's meaning in her or his mind (Axley, 1984). In other words, as people

FIGURE 1.2

A Transactional Model of Communication

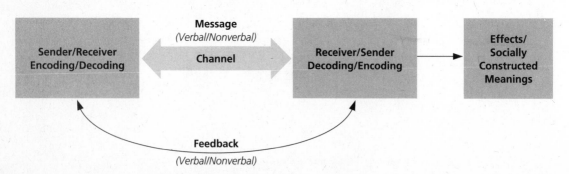

work together in organizations, they share information and experiences. Over time, they may grow to embrace similar goals and values. When they do, negotiating common interpretations of events, persons, and messages may come easily. Under less harmonious circumstances (perhaps during union-management strife, for instance), negotiating common interpretations of reality may become more demanding.

The transactional model of communication is quite compatible with several contemporary views of organizing and managing (McGregor, 1960; Pacanowsky & O'Donnell-Trujillo, 1982; Weick, 1969). Human resources theorists, for example, typically emphasize the importance of shared decision making and the centrality of feedback for healthy, empowering organizational climates.

Defining Organizational Communication

Although communication is widely regarded as crucial for organizations, definitions of **organizational communication** are diverse, growing in part from differing views of the meaning of organizations. For instance, Tortoriello, Blatt, and DeWine (1978) defined organizational communication as "the flow and impact of messages within a network of interactional relationships" (p. 3). Wilson, Goodall, and Waagen (1986) described it as "an evolutionary, culturally dependent process of sharing information and creating relationships in environments designed for manageable, cooperative, goal-oriented behavior" (p. 6). Most recently, Goldhaber (1993) noted that "organizational communication is the process of creating and exchanging messages within a network of interdependent relationships to cope with environmental uncertainty" (pp. 14–15).

Researchers have traditionally defined organizational communication from a functionalist perspective. In its most extreme form, the **functionalist** approaches the study of organizational communication as if organizations were machines, or objects to be studied. Functionalists tend to focus on outcomes rather than processes and to assume that communication behavior is an objectively observable activity—to be measured, labeled, and classified—and then related to organizational outcomes, like morale and productivity. A functionalist might study a manager's choice of certain communication channels and relate that to subordinates' compliance or resistance. The functionalist tends to embrace a unified view of an organization, seeing it as a cooperative system in pursuit of common goals. Because of its emphasis on control and goal-directed behavior, the functionalist perspective is often regarded as having a management bias (Putnam, 1983).

Another approach to studying organizational communication grows from the **interpretive** perspective, which views organizations as cultures (Pacanowsky & O'Donnell-Trujillo, 1982). Interpretive scholars conceptualize organizations as socially constructed realities. They examine communication as the process through which this social construction occurs. The interpretive view is more subjective and thinks of the organization as an array of factionalized groups with diverse purposes and goals. The interpretive researcher often focuses on metaphors, stories, rituals, and symbols and seeks the ideas of many organizational members who represent diverse perspectives.

Rather than thinking of the functionalist and the interpretive perspectives of organizations and organizational communication as competing world views, however, we might more profitably view them as offering insights into different kinds of questions. Functionalism is better suited to describing and relating variables within the communication process, for example, relating supervisors' listening skills to employee satisfaction, rigor in evaluating ideas to group decision quality, or job enrichment strategies to productivity outcomes. By contrast, interpretivism is a more appropriate perspective for seeking to understand the role of communication in members' experiences of organizational life. As Pacanowsky and O'Donnell-Trujillo (1982) put it: "We do not claim that the organizational cultural [interpretive] perspective is 'better' than any of the traditional perspectives. We do not suppose it to be more useful, nor more effective. . . . We see it as an alternative, not as a competing perspective" (p. 143).

Our notion of organizational communication acknowledges the value of both points of view. We are concerned with both processes and outcomes, with the organization as planned and expressed through the organizational chart as well as with the emerging, dynamic informal organization that could never be charted. As we recognize the reality of diversity among organizational members, and hence their differing perceptions of each other and of reality, we also believe that from that diversity must grow, through communication and negotiation, some unity of vision and purpose. Without such shared purposes organizations cannot exist. Yet those purposes are appropriately open to interpretation, scrutiny, and change.

As noted at the beginning of the chapter, it is our sense that *organizational communication is that process wherein mutually interdependent human beings create and exchange messages, and interpret and negotiate meanings, while striving to articulate and realize mutually held visions, purposes, and goals.* Organizational communication is influenced by the realities of hierarchies. Yet as organizations have become flatter, with fewer hierarchical layers, the communication challenges have changed. Managers have given up some measure of control over outcomes as they have grown to share decision-making responsibility with others. Now motivation is not just part of the supervisor's job; rather, it is also an issue for peers who collaborate on projects in teams.

Of course, changing organizational demographics present special communication challenges. For instance, from 1983 to 1993, the percentage of white male professionals and managers in the work force dropped from 55 percent to 47 percent, while the proportion of white women jumped from 37 percent to 42 percent. This diversification of the work force is likely to increase. The U.S. Department of Labor estimates that through the year 2005, half of all labor force entrants will be women, and more than one-third will be Hispanic

Americans, African Americans, and workers of other races or ethnic back-grounds (Galen, 1994). Given these and other kinds of dramatic changes, one of the greatest challenges for all organizational communicators will be to address the tensions that must be negotiated—between the desire to cooperate for the good of all and the need to compete so as to promote oneself, between one's professional demands and one's private life, between those formally called "labor" and those formally labeled "management." Although each organization is unique, in every organization the quality of the communication system will remain central to the organization's overall effectiveness. Focus On describes how changing demographics in the United States are influencing communication and human relationships in one particular kind of organizational setting, the public school.

FOCUS ON   ## U.S. Schools of the Future?

In the Los Angeles Unified School District, fewer than 10 percent of the students are white. The same is true in many suburbs of Los Angeles.

"They're the ones who are left behind," says Gerda Steel, a Pasadena-based diversity consultant who is black. "Nobody thinks about them because they're white. It's assumed they're going to survive, but they are dealing with the same things that minority kids deal with."

On many campuses today, it is the white students who stick out, who get razzed about their funny names and hair, and who have stereotypic assumptions made about their hair and their lifestyles.

Mavis Hildson, 15, a recent graduate of Roosevelt Middle School in suburban Glendale, which is 95 percent minority and immigrant, says she once asked a black classmate about Martin Luther King, Jr., and was told icily: "It's a black thing—you wouldn't know about it."

"We'd be talking about slavery, and all of a sudden the black people in class would turn around and stare at me," she recalls.

Iris Ring, 15, remembers clearly the pivotal day at age 6, when she became aware of race. She was playing at her neighborhood park in the Los Angeles-area community of La Puente, which is heavily Latino.

"Several girls came up to me and they said, 'This is a Mexican park, no white girls allowed.' I got angry and we started fighting. When I got home, I cried. I remember asking my mom, 'Why can't we be Mexican?'"

Some white students in the area say they attend mainly minority schools because of their family's progressive social beliefs. Others say their working-class parents can't afford private schools. For most of them, the issue is not race. They merely want the safest, cleanest, and best education for their kids.

This demographic situation could not have been imagined a generation ago when the dominant culture in southern California was white. Textbooks praised George Washington and Abraham Lincoln. Now, the California schools' curriculum tries to impart a more ethnically diverse and less Euro-centric view of history and literature, bringing a new set of discomforts to the classroom: California textbooks teach how white settlers killed and took land belonging to American Indians, exploited Latino farm workers, denied rights to Chinese and Japanese laborers, and enslaved blacks.

Educators hope these white students will be at the beginning of a truly diverse society, able to understand, work and play with different types of people. But, too often diversity lessons focus on the accomplishments of one group in a way that makes other groups feel uncomfortable, according to some students. The schools must also take care to present history accurately. For instance, only 6 percent of white Southerners owned slaves.

For a youngster with no racial ax to grind, navigating through charged racial encounters can be a bewildering burden. Some students chafe against what they see as a double standard that allows students of color to make white jokes but prohibits white students from joking about minorities.

Some defuse racial tension by poking fun at it. Jessica Duran, 17, a Latino at La Puente High, uses racially loaded terms with her white friend Mindy Cutler in an ironic way to mock political correctness. But she knows that her friend sometimes faces real problems because of her ethnicity.

SOURCE: Hamilton, 1994.

Effective Communication Remains a Priority

Researchers have long acknowledged the strong positive relationship between sound communication skills and individual upward mobility in organizational settings. A striking number of surveys have sought to determine those characteristics that are most valued, both for managers and for employees. For instance, Hafer and Hoth (1983) surveyed thirty-seven companies representing a broad range of industries from manufacturing to public service. They asked employment officers in those companies to rate a list of job applicants' characteristics according to the importance of those characteristics in influencing their selection decisions. Table 1.1 reports their findings.

Other researchers asked 721 chief executive officers in a number of U.S. corporations to list the qualities or skills they believed to be most significantly related to their having risen to the top of their organization (Margerison & Kakabadse, 1984). Without ranking them, the CEOs listed the following as most important: communication, managing people, delegating, patience, respect, control, understanding people, evaluating personnel, tolerance, and team spirit. Finally, Curtis, Winsor, and Stephens (1989) asked 428 members

TABLE 1.1

Job Applicant Characteristics Most Affecting Selection Decisions (Presented in Order of Importance)

1. Oral communication skills	7. Maturity
2. Motivation	8. Enthusiasm
3. Initiative	9. Punctuality
4. Assertiveness	10. Appearance
5. Loyalty	11. Written communication skills
6. Leadership	

SOURCE: Hafer & Hoth, 1983.

of the American Society of Personnel Administrators in the United States to enumerate three clusters of skills: (1) those needed to obtain employment, (2) those important for successful job performance, and (3) those needed to move up in the organization. The first cluster included verbal communication, listening, enthusiasm, written communication, technical competence, and appearance. The second cluster focused on interpersonal skills, verbal communication, written communication, persistence/determination, enthusiasm, and technical competence. The final cluster was the most extensive and included the ability to work well with others one on one, gather information and make a decision, work well in groups, listen and give counsel, give effective feedback, write effective reports, present a good image for the firm, and use computers and other business machines. This final cluster also included the need for several different areas of knowledge, such as knowledge of accounting, marketing, and finance; knowledge of the job; and knowledge of management theory.

What is striking about these and other surveys (also see Benson, 1983; Hunsicker, 1978; Luthans, Rosenkrantz, & Hennessey, 1985; and Prentice, 1984) is their consistent emphasis on communication. Each points to a variety of additional factors or skills, but all stress the importance of communicating effectively—including good interpersonal and group communication skills, listening, and written communication ability. Moreover, when the skills or characteristics are ranked, communication competencies are invariably near the top.

With ongoing changes in technology, the precise sorts of communication skills most needed will change. The manager who wants to initiate an exchange of ideas or information with her or his subordinates today must decide whether to phone them, call a meeting, stop by their offices, or send them e-mail messages. With e-mail, listening is irrelevant, and all aspects of nonverbal communication are eliminated. How might that and other new technologies change the meaning of effective communication? To what extent will the choice of communication medium become even more salient than it has been in the past? We will grapple with these issues throughout this book. However much technology may provide new opportunities and new challenges, the need for effective communication at all levels of the organization will not change.

The MIT commission (Berger, Dertouzos, Lester, Solow, & Thurow, 1989) recently concluded that the effective use of modern technology requires involved and responsible people who can develop their capabilities for planning, judgment, collaboration, and analysis of complex systems. Perhaps Kanter (1989) put it best when she argued that the "[new managerial work] involves communication and collaboration across functions, across divisions, and across companies whose activities and resources overlap. Thus, rank, title, or official charter will be less important factors in success . . . than having the knowledge, skills, and sensitivity to mobilize people and motivate them to do their best" (p. 92). Of course, organizations are changing for diverse reasons, including competitive pressures and advances in technology.

The Impact of Technology on Organizational Communication

Technology dramatically affects the way we communicate and the speed with which we transmit information to one another. Thirty years ago, support personnel in corporations dialed phones, sent telegrams, typed letters, used stencils to make copies, tabulated with adding machines, and took dictation. Now "knowledge workers" (Laudon & Laudon, 1993) use computer technology to help them access, store, analyze, and interpret data; to type their documents; to incorporate voice and images in documents; to check their spelling and grammar; to send documents via electronic mail; to get messages via voice mail (v-mail); and to call the office from the car using a cellular phone.

Technology also influences the way we collaborate. While communication involves the transmission of information, collaboration includes the use of technology to facilitate the communication of information for the purpose of shared creation and/or discovery (Schrage, 1990). Collaboration is important because today's problems, opportunities, and environments are complex. To manage this complexity, organizations need workers with specialized skills and knowledge. To create solutions and innovative products requires the collective efforts of specialists.

Technology provides new and dynamic channels for group collaboration across the dimensions of time and place. It allows us to create networks for communication and channels for cooperation that give business teams faster and broader access to information. The new team-based organization consists of "small, cross-organizational, time-driven, task-focused, cohesive work groups. Business teams are part of the evolving organization of the future that includes flatter hierarchies, network style, and international flavor" (Johansen, 1992, pp. 5–6).

Electronic collaboration technology, or "groupware," is the application of computer and network technology to the support of group work. Products of this type apply telecommunications and computing resources to support a wide range of business team communication requirements. For example, when groups meet face to face, they might use a groupware product called "group support systems" to conduct PC-based brainstorming sessions during a planning meeting. Or, when some members need to travel to remote sites, groupware technologies such as teleconferencing and video conferencing enable groups to conduct long-distance meetings. Other groupware helps teams to share electronic files, to manage schedules and projects, and to disseminate information to and from remote locations twenty-four hours a day. The goal of groupware technology is to improve group performance by facilitating team members' access to information and participation.

As groupware technology helps teams to shape their environments, it also sometimes changes the very nature of group interactions. For example, Sproull and Kiesler (1991) suggest that computer networks can create a "web of social connections that stretch across time and that exist independently of an employee's physical location or hierarchical position" (p. 116). Sproull and Kiesler believe that many electronic communication media prevent people from viewing social cues (e.g., facial expressions and body language), thereby enabling them to speak more freely than they might in person. However, the very lack of social cues may also result in the misinterpretation of messages.

Groupware technology facilitates team members' mobility. Nicholas Negroponte (1991) noted that one of the reasons workers in our society are so mobile is that they have the electronic means to stay in touch with their home base and with other team members no matter where they go. He believes that further fascinating developments will come from services that free individuals to wander by creating electronic surrogates of them on communication networks with which team members can communicate. For example, you might envision an electronic clone of yourself who is programmed on how to negotiate and resolve competing requests for appointments with you while you are swimming at the beach!

Changes in the nature of communication channels have challenged many managers who maintain that the role of management is to control and coordinate the activities of their personnel. Through technology such as e-mail or v-mail, subordinates need not consult their managers before communicating with anyone of any status in any other organizational unit. These systems provide direct, unsupervised, nonconfidential access to anyone with an account on the system. While these channels can be used to foster entrepreneurial activity and to promote computer-augmented teamwork, they also challenge managers to contend with new issues concerning information access and dissemination. For example, as we will see in later chapters, electronic channels of communication facilitate information sharing for both ethical and unethical purposes.

Changes in Technology

Technology and the communication media it shapes will continue to change and evolve. In an interview conducted by *Fortune* magazine (Schlender, 1991), Apple Computer cofounder Steven P. Jobs and Microsoft cofounder William H. Gates predicted that for the 1990s organizations should expect the following:

- Razzle-dazzle technology will emerge faster than ever. Computers will provide capabilities to read handwriting and display and edit video. Semiconductor makers will cram a PC on a single chip no bigger than a dime, making PCs cheaper and more ubiquitous than they are today.

Multimedia is fundamentally changing the nature of communication across time and place. This technology allows the combination of sound and images with text and graphics so that communication approaches the richness of face-to-face meetings. (Hotch, 1993 *Nations Business*)

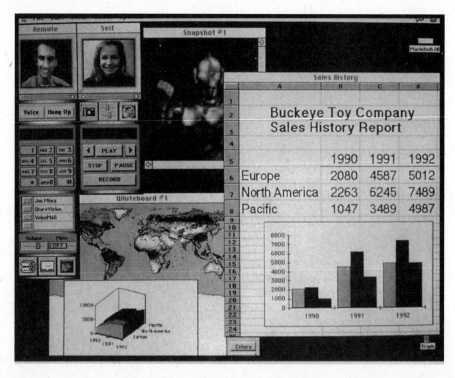

- Data networks will come of age. Face-to-face video communication will be available though one's PC from anywhere in the world, letting individuals share drawings, photos, recordings, film clips, documents, and spreadsheets on the screen as they converse.
- Users will confront a bewildering array of choices. New alliances will seek to create new personal standards. IBM and Apple, for example, have formed a joint venture to develop a successor to both the PC and the Macintosh by the end of the decade.
- Japanese electronics companies will become more of a force. They will stake out whole new markets with novel devices that bridge the gap between computers and inexpensive electronic gadgets.
- Computers will finally change the nature of organizations and office work. As a result, white-collar workers who have shown no improvement in productivity since the advent of PCs may become more efficient and find their jobs more interesting.

Looking at these predictions a few years after they were written, we can see that many of them have indeed come true. For example, Apple's Newton computer recognizes handwriting. PCs continue to decline in price as they rise in power and features. Intel Corporation is marketing low-cost video conferencing software for PCs. Power PCs from Apple and IBM have arrived, and new models are being developed. CD-ROM multimedia technology is becoming commonplace even in the home. Finally, we can observe how technology has resulted in the reengineering and downsizing of many corporations and other organizations striving to compete in an extremely competitive global marketplace.

It is possible that the impact of technology-based change may not be confined to the organizational environment. In fact, Michael Dertouzos (1991) contended that the fusion of computing and communication technologies will yield an impact as profound as the shift from an agrarian to an industrial society. He suggested that the mobile networked computer brings new freedom that will change not only business but society as a whole:

> Universal connectivity raises issues of security and personal and business privacy. It also raises the question of the distribution of power. The chasms between rich and poor could widen, for example, if the latest computing paradigm creates still more opportunities for educated people and fewer for the uneducated (p. 93).

Recent statistics show that the gap between rich and poor in the United States has indeed widened. According to the U.S. Bureau of the Census, while families in the economic top fifth bring in 44.6 percent of total U.S. income, those in the bottom fifth bring in only 4.4 percent (Bernstein, 1994). This gap translates into educational disparities as well. Seventy-six percent of young men and women from the top group go on to earn a college degree, while only 4 percent of those from the bottom group do so. As these young people seek jobs, the gap in skills and knowledge can seem insurmountable. As Labor Secretary Robert Reich wrote in his May 1994 report on rising inequality, "a society divided between the haves and the have-nots or between the well-educated and the poorly educated . . . cannot be prosperous or stable" (Bernstein, 1994). With the increasing sophistication of technology, those without education could easily be left behind.

If technology might contribute to the problem, it can also, as we noted earlier, contribute to the solution. Dertouzos (1991) assumed that change is technology-driven and that advances in computing will contribute to inequity. It is our conviction, however, that change is both technology-driven and need-driven. That is, innovation is a product of technological availability and the organizational or societal realization that an opportunity exists to employ technology in a manner that yields value. Therefore, we suggest that any potential imbalance in the distribution of power (and accompanying opportunities for empowerment) is due not just to the technology alone but also to the failure of a social system to provide technology education and access to resources in an equitable manner. The root of the potential problem is thus not the computer per se but a possible failure of U.S. society and the nation's educational system as a whole.

If technology is to empower, then managers must provide employees with relevant and necessary information, skills, and guidelines for making decisions; offer them opportunities for making decisions; and ensure that they do, in fact, participate in significant aspects of organizational life.

Summarizing Perspective

Some herald the new technologies as virtual miracles of human ingenuity. Others wonder if we have gone too far. If automation leads to unemployment, if industrialization contributes to air pollution, if chlorofluorocarbons erode the ozone layer, if group decision making using computers diminishes the opportunity to develop important interpersonal skills, should we not then carefully scrutinize the ways in which we are using technology and the values that we are communicating to others? In our view, advances in technology offer exciting challenges and unprecedented opportunities for organizations. Yet all organizational members, and especially those in positions of leadership, must be vigilant. Technology is a powerful tool that can be used either to share information and ideas or to exclude and alienate; it can be used to wield power or to empower; it can be used ethically or unethically. As Hyde (1982) put it, "the danger is not technology; rather, the danger is us—we who do not question, we who do not understand, we who do not communicate beyond the rhetoric of either/or" (p. 4). So many of the ways we use technology and the ends we seek through its use will depend upon our values—those we hold and enact every day and those we use to evaluate the words and actions of one another. Our ethical standards will be critical determinants of whether we use technology to include, to initiate dialogues, to share decision making, to empower. As Medhurst (1990) observed, "Between technology as miracle and technology as mirage lies the gray area of human choice making, human valuing" (p. xi). Thus, while we emphasize the potential contributions and value of diverse technologies throughout this book, we do so in a context of commitment to ethical, empowering organizational communication.

CASES FOR DISCUSSION

CASE 1 *Melnick, Baird, Williams, and Fisher*

The firm of Melnick, Baird, Williams, and Fisher, Inc. (MBWF) is a labor relations and organizational development consulting company. The firm has no organization chart, no president or vice presidents, and only one employee: a secretary who minds the office Monday through Friday.

The firm is actually a combination of four separate companies: HGM Enterprises (which consists of Herbert Melnick and his wife, Lisa), Baird Consulting Corporation (comprising John Baird and his wife, Linda), Robert Williams and Associates (consisting entirely of Robert Williams), and D. L. Fisher and Associates (made up of Dennis Fisher and his wife, Mary). The firm has an office near Chicago (where each of its members receives mail and telephone calls) and has published a brochure describing its services.

The firm also uses several other consultants, each of whom has his or her own company. These individuals provide their services as independent contractors and are paid on a per diem basis for the consulting work they do under the auspices of MBWF.

Billing for consulting work performed by any of the contract consultants or principals is done from the MBWF office, so that client checks are made payable to the firm. In turn, MBWF writes checks to the companies of the consultants who have performed the work (while retaining a percentage of the amounts billed for each of the independent contractors). All of the principals' companies also make monthly payments to MBWF to cover office expenses, telephone costs, the secretary's salary, and so on.

At the end of the year, any money remaining in the MBWF bank account is used to pay for a lavish holiday party (to which as many as 200 Chicago-area clients are invited), and to pay bonuses to each of the principals.

The five principals of the firm (Herb Melnick, John and Linda Baird, Bob Williams, and Dennis Fisher) coordinate their affairs through several mechanisms:

▶ They each provide the MBWF office secretary with a day-by-day rundown of the name, telephone number, and location of the organization with whom they are consulting and the hotel at which they will be staying each night. This enables the consultants to track one another down as needed.

▶ They each carry a laptop computer with a modem, so that information can be communicated to and printed by a central computer in the office.

▶ They each use the office fax machine to transmit documents between the office and field locations.

▶ They each carry a portable telephone so that they can be reached any time, any place.

The principals of the firm meet occasionally (approximately once every four to six months on the average) to discuss matters of mutual interest: who's behind in paying their share of the office rent, how each consulting project is being handled, how upcoming projects will be staffed, how better to market the firm's services, how the competition is doing, and so on.

Decisions are reached via consensus; no votes ever are taken on any matter.

Performance of the independent contractors used by the firm is discussed, both during office meetings and over the telephone. Positive and negative aspects of each contract consultant's performance are noted, and one of the principals occasionally volunteers to convey this information to the consultants individually. Often, however, these evaluations go uncommunicated.

Questions for Discussion

1. Is MBWF an "organization"? Using the definitions provided in this chapter, explain what aspects of an "organization" seem to be present and what aspects seem to be absent.

2. What problems might arise from MBWF's lack of traditional elements of "organizations"? What advantages might there be?

CASE 2 *Grappling with Globalization*

Many contemporary writers have pointed with alarm to the rapid decline of U.S. businesses in an increasingly global environment. Whetten and Cameron (1991) argued, for instance, that "with the exception of nations that have been devastated by war, it is unlikely that any country has ever experienced as extensive and as rapid an economic decline as is currently underway in the United States" (p. 1). The world marketplace has many participants, of which the United States is only one, and not necessarily the most significant. Over 100,000 American companies are doing business abroad; about one-sixth of the nation's jobs come from international business.

On the plus side, globalization brings an expanded market for products and services. The potential threats, however, are numerous. Foreign competition can erode U.S. business. American-made products are increasingly rare. Even if a product is manufactured or assembled in America, its specific parts or components probably come from around the world. Wriston (1990) offered these examples:

Today you [can] use [the] lead pencil to illustrate the impact of the globalization of business. In the first place, that old-fashioned lead pencil isn't made out of wood any more. It's made out of plastic—plastic that looks like wood, has a wood feel, and even sharpens like wood. But it's plastic nonetheless. And the plastic could have been made in a distant foreign country or it could have been made in Detroit. . . . The carbon for the lead came from another source and the eraser from a third source. And after it's all been assembled and delivered to the store and it comes time for you to buy that pencil, you don't really care where all the components came from . . . But the best example is IBM's superconductivity project. It's a global R&D exercise pioneered in Switzerland by the U.S. company working with the talents of a German scientist and a Swiss scientist. Talent doesn't carry a passport in this new age. In fact, to be successful, managers must be able to work with people who don't speak their language, who may not share their value systems, but who have the talent the business needs (pp. 80–81).

Finally, U.S. businesses are increasingly seeking the lowest possible labor costs, often turning to less expensive workers from other countries. These practices are beginning to affect white-collar as well as blue-collar employees. In many instances U.S. businesses are closing their operations at home and moving their companies abroad.

In light of this background, read the following case carefully; it is based on a true story:

A plant in northern California makes steel irons used in the home for pressing clothes. It employs approximately 800 production workers at an average wage of $10.50 an hour. This plant is owned by General Electric. Over a year ago, GE announced that it would be closing the plant and moving production to Singapore, where plastic instead of metal irons will be manufactured.

The shutdown of the plant will have a serious economic impact on the local community. Jobs at the plant were highly sought after. Workers would wait three to four years in hopes of securing a job at the GE plant, because wages and benefits were superior to those elsewhere in the community and job security at the GE plant was believed to be quite high.

The plant's closing has outraged the union. Workers are bewildered and feel that they have been cheated. GE management points out that wages in Singapore are $1.10 an hour. Moreover, in Singapore, government policy basically precludes the formation of unions. Management alleges that over the years the California union has been responsible for restrictive work rules that, in addition to decreasing efficiency and increasing costs, have been a continuing source of labor-management strife.

The union reports a willingness to negotiate "give-backs," including reduction of wages. But union leaders and many of the workers say that they are unwilling to give up everything they have fought for over these many years. Management in turn has pointed out that there is no way the California plant can compete with a plant in Singapore, given the workers' low wages there, or, for that matter, with plants in Mexico, where wages are about $2.00 an hour. The union charges that GE is callous and interested only in profit.

Questions for Discussion

1. Are the problems portrayed in this case inevitable outcomes of globalization? Why or why not?

2. If organizations are, in fact, interpreted by individuals, as noted on pages 13–14, how would those affiliated with this GE plant (managers, employees, union leaders) interpret this particular organization and its intended actions?

3. How would you describe the tension between power and empowerment demonstrated in this situation?

Foundations of Organization Theory

To say that information technology is transforming business enterprises is simple . . . But the job of actually building the information-based organization is still ahead of us—it is the managerial challenge of the future.
Peter F. Drucker, "The Coming of the New Organization," *Harvard Business Review,* 1988.

The act of organizing to accomplish something is as old as the human social experience. Communication is the social force that enables individuals to work cooperatively toward achieving their goals. The earliest civilizations developed rather sophisticated organizational systems for government, military, and economic purposes. Whenever people depended on each other to complete tasks or meet their needs, they formed organizations. When they joined together into clans and families, and when they sought survival through hunting and fishing, they organized. From the beginning, even simple organizational tasks required human beings to communicate with one another. Over time, the demands became more complex. For instance, in agricultural societies farmers developed rather complicated organizations with more complex communication needs. With farming came villages and the need to consider the welfare of the community and to govern. Later, during the Middle Ages, institutionalized religion became a dominant social and organizational force. Social class systems and notions of divine right prevailed. For centuries, during which relatively little changed (Dessler, 1980), tradition was the foundation of authority for both average citizens (feudal serfs) and their lords.

The Renaissance and, later, the Industrial Revolution extinguished the foundation of feudal life. Feudal society was based on a hierarchical system of fiefdoms ruled by kings, emperors, and lesser nobles. These fiefdoms fought for power and glory on fields of battle. Blind loyalty to peers and superiors was the order of the day (Fleming, 1975). But the Renaissance brought a new set of values. Blind loyalty was replaced by enlightened individualism. People were encouraged to develop their talents and knowledge. Patrons cultivated the arts, architecture, and science. Commerce and industry flourished. The growth of business and science during the Renaissance sowed the seeds for the Industrial Revolution and mechanized production, which flourished in the eighteenth and nineteenth centuries.

With the advent of the twentieth century, the need for new and clearer concepts of organizational behavior to address the complexities of modern society became obvious (Dessler, 1980). In the developed nations of today's world, organizations function within a complex, uncertain, and often rapidly changing economic, legal, political, and social environment. The first systematic discussions of organization theory appeared early in this century. These early, so-called classical theoretical statements envisioned organizations as social machines and emphasized formal structure and scientific management. As the century progressed, competing theories emerged, with human relations theorists arguing that organizations should focus on creating a humane and satisfying work environment.

In this chapter we will discuss each of the major theories of organization, tracing their evolution from the turn of the century to the present. Our discussion will make it clear that the early theorists had little to say about communication. They were more concerned with power and authority for those at the top of the hierarchy than with empowerment for those at the bottom. Beginning with the human relations movement in the 1950s, however, theorists and organizational leaders began to think about such communication-centered notions as leading democratically, listening to employees' ideas, working in groups, and power sharing.

In the four decades since then, every organization theory has underscored the significance of communication. The systems perspective, which became prominent in the 1960s, emphasized a dynamic view of organizations and communication as central to organizational functioning. Later theories of organizing (Weick, 1969) treated the process of organizing as virtually synonymous with the process of communicating. Others articulated a cultural view of organizations and studied emerging cultures by closely examining human communicative exchanges. Although the word *empowerment* has only become widely used in the last few years, organizational theorists have increasingly addressed questions of empowerment; and in recent years, technology has been acknowledged as a potential vehicle for empowerment.

Classical Organization Theory

The first theories of organization to be influential in the United States sought to resolve the tension between organizational and individual needs by introducing efficient operating procedures, eliminating arbitrary supervisory behavior, and motivating workers through economic rewards. An early demonstration of classical organizational thought is found in Adam Smith's *Wealth of Nations* (1937), originally published in 1776. Smith suggested that a worker completing a job alone might produce twenty pins a day. However, by dividing the task into several simple operations—such as cutting the wire, straightening it, and so on—and having one worker perform only one task, ten workers, according to Smith's observations, could produce 48,000 pins a day. This totals 4,800 pins per worker, or 240 times the amount each worker could produce by working alone! This concept of division of labor ultimately became the cornerstone of classical organizational theory.

The origins of the classical school are usually traced to the late nineteenth and early twentieth centuries, after the Industrial Revolution had taken hold. Factories were widespread, and the assembly-line technique of production was about to be implemented in the Ford automobile plants. Because so much of the technology of manufacturing was new then, and because the techniques for large-scale production were just being developed, organization theorists of the time focused on work methods as a major area in which to enhance productivity. Proponents of the classical school are widely recognized as the first to make a standardized attempt to analyze and direct organizational activities. Classical theorists emphasized the importance of organizational structure and the administrative control of organizational performance.

From a classical perspective, the organization should be viewed as a kind of social machine. In keeping with this machine analogy, classicists focused on the plan, design, and maintenance of organizational structures and activities. This mechanistic model stressed order, regularity, and rationality. Ideally, organizations, like well-constructed machines, would work reliably to accomplish predetermined goals. Given this emphasis on organizational rules, structure, and control, the classical school paid little attention to the value of the individual, viewing administrative control as a scientific venture.

Scientific Management

Perhaps the first important contributor to classical theory was Frederick Taylor, whose book *Principles of Scientific Management* (1911) was widely influential. Taylor was an American mechanical engineer who was convinced that scientific observation, analysis, and intervention should be used to improve the way tasks were accomplished in industrial settings. He was concerned with what he viewed as the sloppy, haphazard, and unsystematic operation of contemporary organizations. Taylor focused first on managers, arguing that management decisions were typically "based on hunch, intuition, past experience, or rule-of-thumb evaluations . . . [and] that workers were ineptly placed at tasks for which they had little or no ability or aptitude" (George, 1972, p. 52).

Taylor harped on the theme of unnecessary waste and inefficiency. He told managers that they would achieve productivity and efficiency only if they could find ways to get their workers to put forth their best effort. In short, Taylor believed that managers were at least as responsible as the workers for the success or failure of their organizations. By introducing science into management, he believed he could help managers achieve their goals. Trained as a mechanical engineer, Taylor found it natural to approach the task of job analysis as a scientific endeavor. His famed "time and motion" studies attempted to break down each job into its most minute components, and to match every worker with the task that individual could perform most effectively.

In his book Taylor documented the results of some of his own time-and-motion research. For instance, at the Bethlehem Steel Corporation, where he analyzed and trained workers who shoveled coal and iron ore, he was able to increase the amount of material shoveled per day from 16 to 59 tons! Even after the company paid Taylor for his work and gave the workers their incentive pay, managers found that their handling costs had been cut in half. In addition, the company was able to reduce the number of employees needed to do the shoveling by over 65 percent (Koehler, Anatol, & Applbaum, 1981). From management's point of view, these results were compelling.

Throughout his work and writing, Frederick Taylor emphasized a number of key principles. Taken together, they represent the essentials of scientific management. First, *Taylor viewed workers as essentially economic beings,* motivated by tangible economic rewards. His perceptions were no doubt colored by the fact that he was working largely with a poorly paid, unskilled work force striving to fulfill basic physiological and security needs. Taylor reasoned that it was in workers' self-interest to maximize their income while minimizing their effort. He believed that managers should determine the most efficient ways of performing tasks, train their subordinates to perform in precisely those ways, and reward them with greater income when they used the appropriate means of increasing their productivity. Thus, Taylor felt that *workers should be developed to their maximum potential.* A champion of job training and specialization, he believed that workers should be selected judiciously and then trained according to the principles of scientific management. He considered this approach to training and specialization very supportive of employees because he believed that people would be happiest under systems designed to enhance their productivity and efficiency, and thereby increase their economic rewards.

Taylor was also concerned with fairness. To that end he advocated a *competitive system,* according to which each worker would be paid based on his individual output rather than on an hourly system. Minimum standards would be established through time-and-motion studies. Managers would insist that workers meet those standards and give bonuses to those who exceeded them. Taylor believed that such a system would address a problem he referred to as "soldiering." Most of the factories of the time used a loosely structured piece-rate system. Initially, these systems worked well, and workers who produced above the standard rate received bonuses. Eventually, however, some workers became so productive that they earned significantly more than their coworkers. Employers then responded by cutting the piece rates, and as a result, workers had to work harder than ever to make the same amount of money.

Influenced by their peers, most workers responded to this situation by reducing their efforts to a minimally acceptable standard. In this way workers became "soldiers," exerting only the effort necessary to keep their jobs. Managers couldn't fire them since they met minimum criteria; however, no one really excelled and productivity languished. Taylor's system was intended to solve this problem.

Taylor envisioned a harmonious organization, growing from the clarity of the rules and procedures, the excellence of the job training, and the fairness of the reward system. Thus, he emphasized *cooperation among workers and between managers and workers.* He spoke of "close, personal, and intimate cooperation" between management and employees. His pointed insistence on maximizing productivity, however, often served to strain those relationships, as feelings of competitiveness and pressure from management brought their own share of tensions. In spite of this reality, Taylor insisted that *organizational and individual goals were compatible.* After all, if employees worked hard, the organization became more productive, and workers earned more money, wouldn't everyone be satisfied?

Although many managers appreciated Taylor's contribution to organizational productivity, some of his ideas were harshly criticized, especially by union leaders. For a brief time, some organizations achieved good labor-management relations. During the 1930s, however, this situation changed. Taylor had erroneously assumed that as organizations became more productive, their resources would expand, increasing the income "pie" for all employees. Instead, as organizations prospered, workers demanded a larger share of the pie, and managers became increasingly devious in cheating workers out of their deserved rewards. Disputes over the fair distribution of increased profits eventually reduced labor-management harmony and led to intense opposition by organized labor. Union leaders also took a dim view of the kinds of tasks employees were forced to perform, seeing them as boring, repetitive, and exploitative of workers who had no alternative but to do them or risk losing their jobs. Indeed, many objected to Taylor's approach to work, arguing that his theories were highly mechanistic and insensitive and equated people with machines whose movements could be broken down, timed, and analyzed. Neither Taylor nor those who scientifically managed their firms seemed concerned about how workers felt about the intrinsic nature of their jobs. Whenever a plant decided to hire Taylor, or use his research to support the shift to scientific management, many workers resisted with strikes and even violence. As early as 1911, the year his book was published, Taylor was forced to defend his system before a special investigative committee of Congress.

Although many questioned his system, Taylor never lost faith in scientific management. He once wrote: "Science, not rule of thumb; harmony, not discord; cooperation, not individualism; maximum output in place of restricted output; development of each man to his greatest efficiency and prosperity" (Taylor, 1911). In short, Taylor saw scientific management as beneficial, to both the individual and the organization.

Fayol's Principles of Management

Among the other writers who influenced the classical school was French mining engineer Henri Fayol, who articulated a number of basic management principles in his work *General and Industrial Management* (1949), originally published in 1916. Following a successful career in management, Fayol founded the Center for Administrative Studies in France. Through his work at the center, Fayol tried to persuade the French government to apply his management principles. As an administrative theorist concerned with larger issues of organizational design, Fayol advanced specific strategies for developing structure and order in complex organizations.

In his book Fayol proposed a number of fundamental principles of administration or management. These principles have been widely applied to organizational design and practice, and they remain influential in the design and administration of some modern industrial organizations. Fayol's principles include the following:

1. **Division of labor.** Like Taylor, Fayol stressed specialization and the careful division of work into small, specialized units. Workers should be clear about their specific responsibilities, a task made easier for managers once each job was divided into small components.

2. **Authority.** Like other classicists, Fayol emphasized the importance of authority—vested, of course, in management. He distinguished between authority that grew from one's position in the organizational hierarchy and authority based on credibility, that is, on intelligence, experience, character, and leadership ability. By making this distinction, Fayol was one of the first to argue that authority can grow from personal rather than organizational sources.

3. **Discipline.** Fayol believed in a disciplined work force, one that performed the appropriate behavior in the correct manner. Managers were held responsible for disciplining their subordinates, for they were ultimately responsible for making sure the work was completed.

4. **Unity of command.** With this principle, Fayol spoke directly to the issue of communication. In particular, he contended that orders should originate from only one superior. Orders flowing throughout the organization should be consistent with the organization's overall goals. Moreover, the chain of command should rarely be circumvented, except in the extreme case of a crisis.

5. **Scalar chain.** In describing the scalar chain, Fayol asserted that organizational members should answer directly to their superiors. The scalar chain established a clear vertical line of interaction between subordinates and superiors along the organization's hierarchical chain of command (see Figure 2.1). However, Fayol also discussed the occasional need for horizontal communication, especially in circumstances (such as emergencies) in which rapid message exchange was essential. Fayol was the only classical

FIGURE 2.1

Traditional Hierarchical Chain of Command

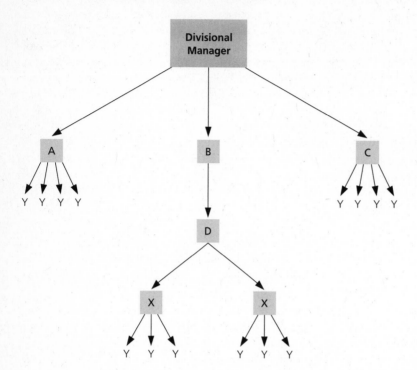

Key
A, B, C = Level III supervisors
D = Level II supervisors
X = Level I supervisors
Y = Subordinates

In a traditional hierarchy, communication flows vertically without bypassing any links in the chain of command.

theorist to acknowledge the legitimacy of horizontal communication, commonly known as "Fayol's bridge" (see Figure 2.2). He cautioned, however, that the bridge should be used sparingly and should remain strictly focused on a particular organizational task.

6. **Equity.** Fayol argued that managers could not be effective unless they were perceived as treating employees with justice and compassion. Only in circumstances in which employees perceived equity would managers reap a loyal and committed work force.

7. **Esprit de corps.** Related to his concept of unity of command, Fayol's notion of *esprit de corps* focused on the need for an organization to articulate a sense of purpose and for its members to possess a coherent understanding of that purpose. Organizational leaders should have a common understanding of organizational mission and goals and should be able to communicate that mission to those below. In general, Fayol favored direct, face-to-face interaction, arguing that misunderstandings are often further

FIGURE 2.2

Fayol's Bridge

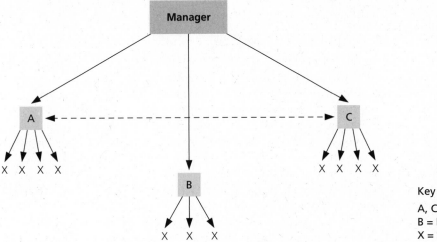

Key
A, C = Level II supervisors
B = Level I supervisors
X = Subordinates

Fayol pointed out that occasionally horizontal communication is needed, even in a traditional organization.

complicated through written exchanges. Again, Fayol was unusual in his attention to communication.

These are only a few of Fayol's principles. They demonstrate, however, the extent to which his ideas contrasted with those of Taylor, appearing to show a greater sensitivity to workers and their involvement in the organization and its purposes. In fact, Fayol went so far as to discuss the notion of initiative, or the ability to think through and execute plans, as a desirable quality at any level of the organizational hierarchy. At the same time, however, he strongly supported the subordination of individual interests to those of the organization as a whole. He instructed managers to supervise closely and constantly and discipline appropriately, which suggests that he felt somewhat ambivalent about the extent to which workers could actually be trusted to direct their own work.

Weber's Theory of Bureaucracy

Fayol was not the only European writer to influence classical theory. Perhaps the most influential work contributing to the classical tradition was *The Theory of Social and Economic Organizations* (1947) by German sociologist Max Weber. In this work Weber advanced a theoretical model of **bureaucracy,** which he defined as "a social invention that relies on the power to influence through rules, reason, and law" (p. 329). Weber was primarily interested in the relationships between a culture and its economic, political, and religious institutions. He saw similarities between societies and their organizations, for example, in the way they make decisions and go about structuring their lives and their work. Weber believed that there was a particularly good "fit" between bureaucracy as a form of organization and the cultures of Western democracies.

In his work Weber pointed to several different kinds of authority. He believed that formal, impersonal (and therefore objective) written codes of rules formed the basis of **legal authority**. Weber argued that in Western bureaucratic organizations, employees' actions could be controlled as a result of their natural willingness to obey established rules of behavior. Workers, he contended, perceive these rules as necessary and believe that the rules protect them from arbitrary, potentially harmful treatment by powerful persons who might otherwise abuse them. In other cultures, however, other forms of control are perceived as legitimate, according to Weber. Some believe that hierarchies are proper because they have always existed. Weber argued that this notion of **traditional authority** works well in stable, hierarchical cultures and organizations in which tradition and continuity are revered. He considered it less effective in cultures that are in the process of changing or abandoning their traditions.

Finally, in still other cultures, Weber argued, people respond to their leaders because they seem to have some "higher" power. This **charismatic authority** is most effective with subordinates who believe that their organizations are endowed with a mission. Weber pointed out the need for a good match between the organization's authority base and the kind of culture in which it is embedded. Similarly, there must be a good fit between the kind of tasks with which the organization is concerned and the type of authority from which it operates. For instance, charismatic authority would be an inappropriate source of influence over workers who are involved in the mundane, day-to-day tasks of running a bureaucracy. However, in other organizations, such as the Marshall Space Flight Center in the 1960s described by Tompkins (1993) in his book *Organizational Communication Imperatives: Lessons of the Space Program,* charismatic authority was exceedingly effective. In this case, the Center's director, Wernher von Braun, was "a charismatic visionary who instilled loyalty through personal magnetism" (McConnell, 1987, p. 107).

Weber also addressed the major defining characteristics of bureaucracies. He noted that a bureaucracy has *formalized rules, regulations, and procedures.* These rules articulate employee rights and responsibilities; Weber saw the two as necessarily interdependent. A bureaucracy must also have **job specialization**. Job descriptions must be carefully and clearly drawn. Managers must be clear in their expectations, to ensure that workers' behavior is predictable and leaves little to chance or interpretation. A *clearly defined hierarchy* is also critical for every bureaucracy. The authority structure must be clearly delineated, leaving little room for doubt about the proper reporting line. No one should be uncertain about who is in charge, or to whom one should go with a question or problem. In articulating these defining characteristics, Weber pointed to the importance of an organizational structure with clearly defined rules and jobs in a carefully designed hierarchy of authority.

Besides focusing on structural matters, Weber went on to articulate other principles. He argued, for instance, that **rationality** must prevail in bureaucratic organizations. While all employees should behave rationally, according to Weber, those who are in positions of leadership are especially responsible for exhibiting rationality, the basis for exerting appropriate control. Finally, Weber argued that organizational relationships must be characterized by **impersonality**. Managers should maintain considerable personal distance from their employees. Failure to do so, Weber argued, would likely result in biased judgments, leading to the unfair treatment of some workers. Weber's intention was to encourage an organizational environment in which every worker would have an equal chance of being rewarded for work well done.

Modern assessments of bureaucracy have resulted in diverse criticisms. Like other classical formulations, Weber's work emphasized the formal organizational structure, ignoring the reality of the informal organization, whose structure might or might not reinforce that of the formal organization. Critics also argued that classicists generally exaggerated the importance of strict adherence to the organizational hierarchy. Such rigid devotion to the chain of command would likely result in poor communication flow, characterized by distortion, omission, and sluggishness. Moreover, because of Weber's insistence on abundant rules and procedures, the inevitable result would be much "red tape," with its associated inefficiency. Others took issue with the assumption that managers were rational beings who controlled the actions of their workers. Conflict, the critics maintained, is an inevitable part of organizational life. People are not always rational, and conflict should not be ignored, as it commonly was by classicists. Finally, bureaucracy arguably creates an environment where the rules are so clear, and the procedures for work so carefully and clearly specified, that workers are not encouraged to think independently. Instead, they are virtually required to act as children, questioning neither the amount of work demanded of them nor the procedures specified for carrying it out. In William Whyte's words, the bureaucratic organization is the breeding ground for the "dull, gray organization man," (Whyte, 1957, p. 2) one who conforms to others' expectations and is often incapable of independent thought.

Of course, in the 1950s and 1960s, it was thought that those most adversely affected by bureaucracies were employees near the bottom of the organizational hierarchy. Later, concerns extended to those nearer the top—especially middle managers, who were so committed to making sure the organization ran by the book that they failed to question the underlying goals and their practical and ethical validity. Today, when organizations begin to falter, critics are quick to blame bureaucracy. For instance, analysts addressing IBM's unprecedented annual loss in 1992 argued, "IBM became too much of a traditional bureaucratic company in an industry that is racing into the future . . . top management failed to see the need to change its organization and focus" (Lohr, 1993).

In spite of its frequently cited disadvantages, bureaucracy offers advantages to many large, complex organizations. Among its perceived benefits are precision, clarity, speed, unity, discretion, and continuity (Tortoriello, Blatt, & DeWine, 1978). Through bureaucratic structure comes predictability and, with it, the potential for stability. Carefully articulated rules, guidelines, and procedures can help organizations cope especially well with unambiguous, simple tasks. Bureaucracy is less useful in addressing complex, ambiguous issues. Nor does it lend itself well to the demand for flexibility or creativity, as suggested by the assessment of IBM's woes.

Weber is often remembered as the "father of bureaucracy." Like many people of his time, he recognized the inevitability of bureaucracy, tracing it to the Middle Ages. In his compelling modern defense of hierarchy, Elliott Jaques wrote, "The hierarchical kind of organization we call bureaucracy did not emerge accidentally. It is the only form of organization that can enable a company to employ large numbers of people and yet preserve unambiguous accountability for the work they do. And that is why, despite its problems, it has so doggedly persisted" (Jaques, 1990, p. 127). One hundred years earlier, it was Weber who first sought to articulate the underlying rationale for bureaucracy, as well as the conditions under which a bureaucratic structure would be most appropriate and potentially effective.

Classical Theory and Communication

From a communication perspective, those who managed their organizations according to classical principles usually adopted certain communication practices. For instance, communication was almost exclusively downward. Executives issued orders and articulated plans to their managers, who in turn issued the same orders to their subordinates. These messages were almost invariably work-related. Social communication was rarely acknowledged as a legitimate part of organizational life. Not surprisingly, upward communication was virtually nonexistent. Employee suggestions were neither solicited nor appreciated. Employees rarely complained, at least officially, since complaining could lead to dismissal. Personal problems could not be discussed in exchanges with managers. While extremely rare, conflicts that did arise were handled through the chain of command, and were usually resolved through decisions made by the chief executive officer. Horizontal communication was rarely officially recognized, and certainly not encouraged. In short, communication in the classical organization moved downward, was formal in tone, and adhered rigidly to the organization's formally structured hierarchy.

Although the classical school clearly possesses disadvantages, many organizations today continue to be governed according to classical principles. In a later chapter, we will address the conditions under which bureaucracy may, in fact, be the most appropriate choice of organizational structure. The negative attributes of bureaucracy can be ameliorated in some ways by minimizing red tape and by trimming some layers from the organizational hierarchy.

Certainly the federal government, most large universities, and the military remain examples of organizations in which classical principles are widely practiced today.

The Human Relations School

Several years ago, sociologist Rosabeth Moss Kanter wrote in *The Change-masters* (1983) that ". . . the unquestioned authority of managers in the corporation of the past has been replaced by . . . the need for managers to persuade rather than to order, and by the need to acknowledge the expertise of those below" (p. 30). Kanter's statement reflected a considerable departure from the sentiments of the classical theorists. Taken from the vantage point of the 1990s, the philosophy hardly seems remarkable. Yet more than fifty years before Kanter's book was published, human relations theorists were writing about the value of workers at every level of the hierarchy and about the importance of persuading employees and involving them in the decision-making process.

The human relations movement came on the heels of World War II. It represented, in part, a reaction to the classicists' emphasis on formality and structure. At the same time, however, the human relations school was a natural outgrowth of changing socioeconomic conditions in the United States, which experienced considerable economic abundance following World War II. After the war, many veterans attended college, furthering their education and experience and later entering the work force as professionals. In earlier years, employees had either worked their way up through organizational ranks or were brought into the organization thanks to social or family relationships with those in positions of authority (a practice against which Weber had argued). But with the postwar increase in well-educated, relatively independent white-collar workers, organizations were forced to become more cognizant of workers' attributes. Hiring trained, white-collar personnel proved a costly venture. Managers soon perceived that keeping these employees satisfied (and thus ensuring that they remained members of the organization) was a task to which they should be committed. Thus, the human relations movement, with its concern for workers' needs, was in many ways a natural outgrowth of the times.

Proponents of the human relations school espoused a number of key principles or beliefs. First, in striking contrast to proponents of the classical school, human relations theorists believed that *people were essentially social beings.* Thus, their capacity for work and productivity was less likely to be determined by their physical attributes and abilities than by their social attributes and attitudes, including how they felt about the organization, their leaders, and their fellow workers. Related to this first tenet was the conviction that *noneconomic rewards play a central role* in worker motivation and satisfaction. If people are social beings, it follows that social rewards should be reinforcing and potentially fulfilling. Thus, managers should learn their employees' names, pat them on the back when they do good work, and inquire about their families' well-being. Moreover, the best way to understand and relate to employees is to look at them as members of groups. Workers do not perform their tasks in isolation in most organizations. Rather, they are connected to others through common interests, common tasks, and other social ties. Instead of encouraging competition, then, it is better to foster cooperation and to allow individuals to work on collaborative endeavors whenever possible.

By recognizing the salience of work groups within organizations, human relations advocates discovered the *informal organization*, the organization for which there is no chart. These theorists also *argued against job specialization,* claiming that higher levels of specialization by no means increased efficiency. They believed, rather, that workers would become more productive only under conditions in which they found their jobs meaningful. Finally, the human relations school *emphasized the importance of communication, participation, and democratic leadership*. Obviously, each of these notions stood in direct contrast to the contentions of the classical school. Such a bold departure from the commonly held views of the time grew in part from the results of a number of empirical investigations.

The Empirical Foundation of the Human Relations School

The empirical foundation of the human relations movement was established in the mid-1920s when the National Academy of Sciences decided to investigate the relationship between a number of environmental variables (such as lighting intensity, length of the work day, number of breaks taken) and productivity. The researchers were somewhat alarmed to discover that none of their hypothesized relationships was supported by their research. For instance, productivity increased regardless of how they adjusted the levels of lighting. The site of this investigation was near Chicago at the Hawthorne plant of Western Electric, an organization noted for its reasonable wages and considerate treatment of employees. Plant executives were troubled by the puzzling results of the study and decided to invite a team of industrial psychologists from the Harvard Graduate School of Business, under the direction of Elton Mayo, to investigate the situation. Mayo and his associates conducted studies over a period of years and found that variations in working conditions were not systematically related to worker productivity or satisfaction. The critical factor, rather, was workers' perceptions of the special attention they were receiving (Roethlisberger & Dickson, 1939). Overt observation by the Harvard research team, interviews by top company executives, and monthly checkups by the company doctor served to convince the Hawthorne plant's employees that something most unusual and no doubt important was going on—and that *they* were a significant part of it. Thus, even under conditions of poorer lighting, longer work days, and fewer rest pauses, these workers actually increased their productivity.

A final component of the investigation was an intensive study of a small group of employees who wired circuit banks. Researchers discovered that work group norms exerted considerable influence over performance standards. Employees had a very clear idea of the "appropriate" amount of output for a day's work. Thus, faster workers were actively pressured to slow down; in this way, the informal organization controlled and regulated each group member's behavior. This classic research, known as the **Hawthorne studies,** is widely regarded as the foundation of the human relations movement (Mayo, 1947).

Other scholars contributed to the movement as well. Kurt Lewin, for instance, conducted several studies during World War II. Initially interested in better understanding the nature of persuasion, Lewin discovered that people were less resistant to changing their behavior under conditions in which they were allowed to participate in groups and to discuss their feelings about impending changes. Lewin's research (1939; 1947) used diverse populations. One study tried to persuade soldiers to eat food not normally viewed as attractive, such as kidneys, hearts, and liver. Another attempted to convince mothers of the value of giving their babies cod liver oil after leaving the hospital, a practice not well received by the infants, thereby producing stress for the mothers. While the ethics of the manipulations used in these experiments are clearly questionable, the results received widespread attention in that they reinforced the value of communicating with employees and using democratic procedures in decision making. Lewin's most famous investigation, however, took place in a summer boys' camp.

Together with scholars Lippitt and White, Lewin systematically investigated three styles of leadership in a summer camp (White & Lippitt, 1960). The leaders were camp counselors trained to exhibit one of three styles of leadership: authoritarian, democratic, or laissez-faire. In this study, authoritarian leaders determined all rules and policies, dictated instructions for activities, assertively directed the behavior of the boys, and subjectively evaluated the boys as they went about their daily projects, games, and other activities. In contrast, the democratic leaders were friendly, considerate, and egalitarian. They encouraged self-direction, allowed their boys to make policy decisions, and yet were available to help when needed. Finally, the laissez-faire leaders were essentially nonleaders. They got the group started on projects and answered direct questions but otherwise did little, if anything. The boys lived in cabins with these counselors throughout the summer and engaged in a wide variety of activities, ranging from sports to crafts to games. The investigators observed their behavior, interviewed them, and took certain objective measures of their performance. Given the way the investigators defined the three styles of leadership in this study, the results were scarcely surprising.

The democratic style of leadership was found to be superior on virtually every measure. The groups led by the democratic counselors developed high levels of cohesiveness. When left unsupervised, they behaved admirably, following through on whatever project they were supposed to be pursuing. Whenever they worked on a project, the quality of their work was usually judged superior to that of other groups. Finally, the boys in these groups expressed high levels of satisfaction with the camp experience, vowing to return the following summer. In contrast, the boys who worked under the authoritarian counselors tended to require close supervision to maintain high levels of productivity. Typically, they demonstrated poor discipline when left on their own. In general, these boys suffered from low morale, and their cabin groups lacked cohesiveness. Few, if any, wanted to return to the camp in the future. When they engaged in projects, such as craft activities, they completed the work rapidly (faster than all other groups), but those judging the quality of their work often rated it as poor or sloppy. Finally, one of the most interesting findings of Lewin's research was that the boys who worked under laissez-faire leaders suffered more than either of the other groups. Their morale was extremely low. They often sought guidance from their leader, and when he refused to provide assistance of any kind, the boys reacted with frustration and anger. They did not perform well in groups, either in terms of quality of effort or productivity. Even more than the groups led by authoritarian leaders, these groups lacked cohesiveness and desired never to return to the camp.

Although Kurt Lewin's research was unusual in its choice of subjects (and highly questionable in the ethics of its procedures), many researchers of the time pursued this line of investigation. There was widespread interest in styles of leadership, and many scholars were pleased to conclude, based on their findings, that democratic leadership was superior to any other style. Much of this research was problematic, however, in that most compared the democratic style at its best with more directive and nondirective styles at their worst. In reality, directive leaders can provide structure, establish rules, and make major policy decisions without behaving as dictators. Similarly, "hands off" leadership may be appropriate in certain organizational settings where employees possess high levels of knowledge, skill, and maturity. Much of the research of this time, however, seemed bent on proving that the democratic way was superior in virtually all situations. Perhaps the nation's political climate contributed to this bias: The research was conducted in the midst of the McCarthy era when strong anti-Communist, pro-democracy sentiments prevailed.

Regardless of flaws in the research conducted during this period (Franke & Kaul, 1978), it exerted immense impact on the thinking of the human relations theorists. Thus, the human relations school championed democratic leadership—communicating with workers and involving them in the decision-making process—as the best approach for organizations to embrace. Many believed that participative decision making would invariably lead to enhanced employee satisfaction and greater organizational productivity.

Other Contributors: Barnard and Carnegie

Other writers contributed to the human relations tradition. For instance, Chester Barnard, then president of New Jersey Bell Telephone and one-time chair of the National Science Foundation, wrote *The Functions of the Executive* in 1938. In it he strongly criticized classical organization theory, arguing that it overgeneralized about workers and their needs. He stressed individual variability in organizations, pointing out that some people are more likely to be economically motivated than others. Barnard believed that good managers would strive to understand each of their worker's needs. He insisted that employees cannot be coerced. Instead, the effort they exert on behalf of organizational objectives will ultimately depend upon their willingness to cooperate. He stressed the need for managers to communicate the organization's goals, purpose, values, and mission to their subordinates and also to recognize that such goals may change over time. Finally, Barnard made communication an indispensable concept in his analysis of organizational behavior. He recognized the role of communication in group decision making and within the informal organization. In fact, he believed that it was the informal communication system that would give birth to the formal organization. Barnard believed that interpersonal networks allow workers to maintain their identities, develop a sense of self-esteem, meet many of their social needs, and exercise some control over their professional lives. Thus, the informal organization, in his view, is not something that managers should fear or ignore. Barnard's strong belief in the centrality of communication in organizations is reflected in the words for which he is perhaps best remembered: "The first function of an executive is to establish and maintain a system of communication" (Barnard, 1938).

Another writer whose work had a lasting impact on the human relations movement was Dale Carnegie. In his popular book *How to Win Friends and Influence People* (1936), Carnegie was perhaps the first writer explicitly to link communication skill with managerial skill. Like Barnard, Carnegie believed that economic incentives were completely inadequate as a form of motivation. Moreover, even formal authority could take a manager only so far. Instead, Carnegie stressed the manager's skill in interpersonal communication. He placed special emphasis on listening, showing an interest in employee concerns and problems, and striving to gain and maintain employee confidence. Dale Carnegie's writing never gained credibility among academic scholars, but his ideas were extremely influential among leaders in the business community. Carnegie died in 1955, yet his book remains in print (having sold millions of copies), and Carnegie seminars continue to be popular.

The human relations school was not without its critics. Perhaps the greatest criticism leveled against the school was that human relations advocates were manipulative and insincere. At a rhetorical level, they expressed an abiding concern for worker satisfaction. At the same time, however, they operated on the assumption that happy workers would also be productive. Thus, the "bottom line" agenda remained focused on organizational goals of productivity, with the worker having been manipulated into thinking that management really cared. Although it is impossible to judge anyone's intentions with certainty, there is little doubt that participatory decision making was a term used very loosely. In particular, employees who worked in some so-called participatory groups did little more than endorse decisions that had already been made (Coch & French, 1948). In other instances, workers were actually allowed to make decisions, but only extremely trivial ones, such as where to place the suggestion box. In addition, some union leaders argued that many managers offered employees the opportunity to help make decisions rather than to receive real rewards, such as better pay and benefits. Participatory decision making, they charged, should not be used as a substitute for tangible economic rewards. Finally, one of the key assertions underlying the human relations school, the notion that worker happiness and organization productivity go hand in hand, was never consistently verified by research. In some studies satisfaction and productivity appeared to be positively correlated; in others, no relationship was found.

Human Relations and Communication

The human relations movement was clearly not without its flaws. Nevertheless, its contributions to organization theory were substantial. The classical school had virtually ignored all but downward communication. The human relations school elevated communication to a much more important and complex role—extending to communication within groups, messages from subordinates to superiors, and interaction that stressed the good manager as listener, not just order giver. Perhaps human relations advocates went too far in stressing the role of social rewards, but such exaggerated emphasis may have been needed to remedy the inordinate classical emphasis on economic rewards. Although human relations principles could clearly be used to attempt to manipulate workers, many managers who embraced them were quite sincere in their concern for their employees' happiness. Human relations theorists advanced controversial arguments about the nature of motivation, the origins of productivity, the significance of democratic leadership, and the role of communication as a management tool. By doing so, they initiated a debate that continues today. Moreover, the movement gave birth to later schools of management theory, especially human resources (see Chapter 3), that are widely practiced by modern managers. The Scanlon plan, for instance, is often traced to the human relations movement. The plan grew out of an organizational crisis when a steel company headed by Joseph Scanlon was approaching bankruptcy. Characterized by genuine participation and a focus on significant issues, the plan built a partnership among workers, unions, and management. Since the original experiment, other organizations have tried the Scanlon plan and have found that it results in greater employee commitment and identification with the organization, as well as enhanced productivity. In general, human relations theorists sought to improve superior-subordinate communication, to acknowledge informal communication, and to encourage managers to share some decision-making power with workers. However, unlike later schools, the human relations model still viewed communication as a kind of managerial tool aimed at improving morale (Miles, 1965) rather than as the lifeblood of organizational functioning. Figure 2.3 contrasts the human relations school with the classical school.

FIGURE 2.3

**A Comparison of Classical and Human
Relations Theories of Organization**

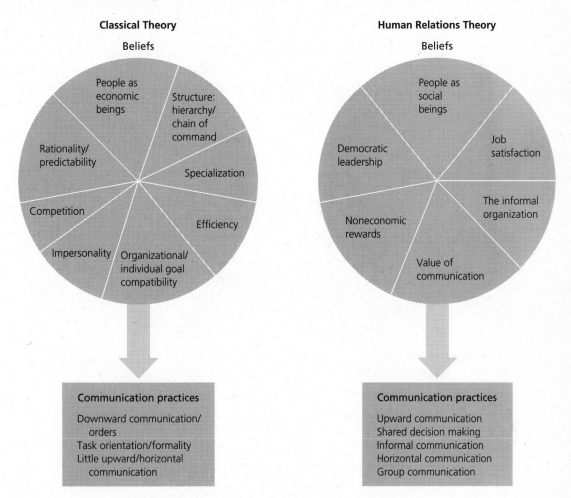

The Systems School

Another important school of organization theory, the systems school, differed from its predecessors in that it grew from a well-established theoretical framework, general systems theory. This broader theoretical view had long been influential in other fields, including logic, biology, economics, and sociology (Bertalanffy, 1956; Boulding, 1956; Lawrence & Lorsch, 1967; March & Simon, 1958). The fundamental principle of general systems theory is that the whole is equal to more than the sum of its parts. From a systems perspective, no component of an organization, a living organism, or an economic system can be viewed in isolation; rather, its **interdependence** with other parts of the entity must be recognized. Indeed, it can be understood only in a dynamic, interdependent context. Interestingly, it is through communication that interdependence is facilitated. The systems school represents a highly theoretical approach to organizations. It offers a framework for thinking about organizations rather than advancing specific principles of management.

Applying systems theory to the study of organizations has resulted in two important outcomes. First, the systems perspective acknowledges and integrates the concepts stressed by the classical and human relations schools. Systems theorists view organizations as social systems in which the chain of command, hierarchy, and structure are equal to but not more important than informal work groups, participative decision making, and democratic leadership. Thus, task-oriented and people-oriented concerns must be considered interdependently. The formal organization may best be understood by simultaneously examining the informal organization—the former representing the organizational plan for leadership and communication flow, and the latter often revealing relatively free-flowing communication patterns and fluid leadership. The reality of influence and the planned authority structure of the organization may or may not coincide. The systems theorists' view of human beings is also more complex. They believe that workers are motivated both by social incentives and by economic rewards. A failure to acknowledge either aspect results in oversimplification of human motivation. The systems school's other major contribution is its emphasis on communication as a defining element of any organization. Some systems writers have advanced the argument that organizations can best be understood from a communication perspective (Clegg, 1990; Rogers & Argawala-Rogers, 1976).

Systems Theory Applied to Organizations

Several theorists have discussed the systems approach to organizations. Perhaps the most influential among these are Daniel Katz and Robert Kahn, authors of *The Social Psychology of Organizing* (1966). Katz and Kahn conceive of *organizations as open systems*. In fact, they argue that "social organizations are flagrantly open systems in that the input of energies and the conversion of output into further energy input consist of transactions between the organization and its environment" (Katz & Kahn, pp. 16–17). Thus, a distinction is drawn between open and closed systems. The former are dynamic and especially responsive to fluctuations in the environment. The latter are static, predictable, and relatively devoid of environmental interaction. Boundaries defining the closed system are fixed, while those associated with the open system are flexible and ever permeable. Although some organizations are inherently more open than others (e.g., high-technology firms versus maximum-security prisons), all healthy organizations are characterized by some degree of openness. A few years ago, for instance, the Chrysler Corporation failed to monitor and respond to the needs of its consumer environment. Only when faced with bankruptcy did it shift its emphasis and begin producing cars that met the demands of its increasingly energy-conscious consumers.

Systems theorists believe that an organization usually develops in response to the needs of the society, culture, or environment of which it is a part. Those who create organizations believe that they can fill a void, produce a new or superior product, or contribute to a better, safer society. Organizations cannot exist without resources—raw materials, buildings, people—in short, energy. The energy the organization draws from its environment is called **input**. Automobile manufacturers require inputs of steel, rubber, plastic, machinery, and workers to produce new cars. Universities need students, libraries, buildings, faculty, and leaders to contribute to a better-educated society. In both of these examples, organizational goals are implicit. Whatever the reason for the organization's existence, whatever its goals are construed to be, the organization's **output** should reflect those goals. For organizational output to reflect the appropriate goals, energy or input must be *transformed* in some strategic way. Sometimes, unfortunately, organizations lack **accountability;** that is, they fail to produce output reflecting their goals. If a university graduates a student who cannot write or speak articulately, or is historically illiterate, it fails the accountability test. The same is true of the automobile manufacturer who produces a sports car that is unsafe, or a truck whose transmission needs to be replaced after 50,000 miles.

One of the major ways in which organizations check their accountability is by staying in touch with their environment to find out how consumers, customers, and clients are reacting to their products and services. Hotels and restaurants routinely ask their customers to complete evaluation forms. We may be more surprised, however, when the dealer who sold us a new car calls to find out how it's running, or when the dentist who just extracted our child's twelve-year molars calls to see how she is feeling. Systems theorists argue that although some organizations interact with their environments more than others, all organizations must remain relatively open to survive. As organizations strive to maintain their competitive edge, they seek to reduce the uncertainty with which they are surrounded. As markets change, as new competitors arise, as students' career interests change, the organization must acknowledge and respond to those changes. Through openness to **feedback** from the environment, organizations keep abreast of the surrounding world and monitor the extent to which their goals are being realized. Feedback may consist of output that is sent back into the system (e.g., the defective television set that has to be rewired); or it may reflect reactions, solicited and unsolicited, to something the organization has produced or an action it has taken. One of the authors recently had the experience of helping a student who had received poor advice from his academic advisor find a way to graduate on time so that he could accept a job he really wanted. A few days later, the student sent the author feedback in the form of a decorative plant for her office and a note of thanks.

As an open system, then, organizations must interact with clients, competitors, and markets outside the organization—whose interests, needs, and strategic moves must be known and understood if it is to survive. Because of the importance of openness, every organization has **boundary spanners,** those who interact extensively with those outside the organization (Adams, 1976; Aldrich & Herker, 1977; Tushman & Scanlan, 1979). Often the boundary spanner's role is strategic: to seek information the organization needs to remain competitive. Boundary spanners may do everything from consumer testing to gathering technical information for management. Ideally, they help other employees make sense of the organization's environment, reducing ambiguity and uncertainty. Occasionally, they function as gatekeepers, protecting those inside the organization from those outside who would like to influence their behavior.

Finally, boundary spanners serve as representatives of the organization, or image makers. They attempt to legitimize their organization by providing outsiders with evidence that the organization is accountable and striving to meet their needs. They may attempt to influence outsiders, persuading them to provide information or offer needed support. At major public universities, for instance, boundary spanners serve as liaisons with the state legislature. They gather information from legislators concerning available funds and priorities (e.g., for higher education, highways, health care, crime control, etc.). They arrange meetings between faculty and administrators and key legislators, so that information can be exchanged. They try to persuade the legislature that the university is serving the state with distinction in teaching and research and therefore deserves greater state support. On occasion, they try to protect administrators from a legislator's pressure, as when, for instance, a legislator's son is about to be dismissed from the university for academic reasons and the legislator is seeking special treatment. Clearly, the boundary spanner's roles are complex and important.

As an organization seeks to interact in effective ways with its environment, it must recognize that its environment is not all-inclusive. Rather, as Duncan (1972) suggested, the **relevant environment** is more profitably viewed as those physical and social factors outside the system's boundary that are directly considered in the decision making of individuals within the system. Thus, from a systems perspective, a critical decision to be made is what in fact should constitute the relevant environment? Must the local meat market compete with Kroger's? Is Harvard competing for excellent students with Ohio State, or only with the rest of the Ivy League? Can Gray's cafeteria in Mooresville, Indiana, reasonably hope to attract customers from Illinois and Kentucky, or only from within Indiana? The answers to these questions not only define the relevant environment but also suggest appropriate courses of action to be taken with advertising, pricing, and other strategic concerns. Organizations, then, do not exist in isolation; they both contribute to their environment and depend on it for survival.

Systems theorists contend that successful organizations will be clear about their purposes and will behave in appropriate, goal-directed ways. Yet within each organization are **subsystems,** each related directly or indirectly to the others, and each serving a somewhat distinct function. These subsystems often take the form of divisions or departments within the organization. Teachers are primarily concerned with student learning. Administrators are also concerned with this, but they may be preoccupied with funding, extracurricular activities, and making sure that the cafeteria serves healthy and (reasonably) attractive food. If the teachers and the administrators are to work together toward the good of the overall school system, they must understand their interdependence, recognize common goals, and reach a consensus on goal priorities. The principal who seems more interested in the school's sports record than in its students' SAT scores suffers from inappropriate goal priorities.

Finally, the systems school of organization theory views *communication as the lifeblood of the organization* (Katz & Kahn, 1966). Communication dominates the systems perspective, passing up and down formal organizational channels, moving quickly within and among small informal work groups, passing through organizational boundaries and into the environment, often to be recycled as feedback. The human relations school acknowledged

FIGURE 2.4

The Organization from a Systems Perspective

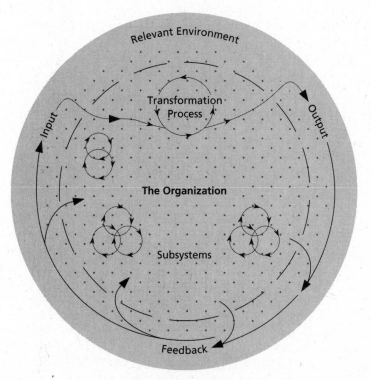

Dots = Formal and informal communication.

Communication in the organization's lifeblood from a systems perspective

the importance of communication, but the systems school embraces the view that communication is an integral part of any organization. One cannot comprehend the organization without studying its communication system and behavior. Figure 2.4 portrays an organization from a systems perspective.

Implications of the Systems School

The systems perspective on organizations is highly theoretical. Its contributors offered no views on the nature of workers, nor rules for effective management. Implicit in the systems approach, however, are several premises. First, those who lead organizations had better be clear about the organization's goals. Those goals must be communicated to others in the organization, and if their perceptions or priorities differ, those differences must be resolved. Second, everyone in the organization has an impact on many others. Interdependence is the norm since workers typically engage in activities whose impact is widely felt. If some are bored, inept, or uncommitted, eventually the organization as a whole will suffer. The manager's job is the management of interrelationships. Third, the organization must know and understand its relevant environment in order to maintain itself over time, and to fulfill some legitimate purpose within society. Its boundary spanners must be able to interact with that environment in effective ways. Finally, communication is vital, at all levels. Without communication, no organization could exist.

Weick's Theory of Organizing

Another important organization theory was advanced in the late 1960s. Like the systems school, this perspective viewed communication as central to organizational processes and outcomes. In *The Social Psychology of Organizing* Karl Weick (1969) argued that human beings organize primarily to reduce the information uncertainty with which they are confronted in their daily lives. Weick observed that life is filled with complexities. Many issues people face are difficult, unpredictable, and ambiguous. Thus, questions of how to prosper, be secure, and even survive are central to human existence. In most instances these questions present information processing problems, such as "What does this situation mean?" or "What is the most appropriate response to this problem?" Since many of these issues (like questions of survival) are so challenging, they cannot be readily resolved by individual effort. Weick argues that people organize because they need help from others in confronting, interpreting, and resolving complex problems, and accomplishing individual and group goals. Thus, Weick's theory of organizing is based on the premise that organizations develop as social systems for reducing equivocality and increasing the certainty of life. Through organizing, human beings undertake many of their most challenging and difficult tasks.

Weick's model presents a dynamic, process-oriented, and pluralistic view of organizations. From Weick's perspective, organizations do not exist as static entities; rather, they are socially constructed through human interaction. Organizations are coalitions of individuals whose priorities sometimes differ. Within organizations, people negotiate their actions, goals, and meanings to achieve a common direction. Rather than abandoning their different aims, they subjugate them to the larger needs of the group (Putnam, 1983; Weick, 1987). Communication, then, is the crucial process for creating and transforming organizations. Like systems theory, Weick's model recognizes that the complete process of organizing is more than the sum of the individual contributions or actions taken in organizing. Moreover, because people work together on each organizing endeavor, interdependence is common.

According to Weick, individuals seek order in their organizational lives. Organizational documents, like strategic plans, may function as important components in the process of creating order. They provide a sense of coherence in people's thinking, enabling them to act in the belief that their actions make sense and may be influential.

Weick also focused on the importance of organizational subsystems and their relationships to each other, thus echoing the thinking of the systems theorists. Similarly, Weick stressed the importance of the organization's environment. His view, however, is that the "environment" has little to do with the organization's physical surroundings; it is, rather, the *information* to which organizational members react. Thus, the concept of organizational environment is communication-focused. It is the **information environment** rather than the structural environment that concerns Weick. In his view people actively create the world around them through their perceptions, actions, and reactions; thus, they are not merely reacting to an objectively existing physical environment. Instead, they are *enacting* their environment as they receive information and construct its meaning. As Weick (1987) described it, "Even though organizations are built out of direct interaction, as they grow larger and more complex they are known by their inhabitants less through direct experience than through indirect images. These images both guide the construction of reality and register what is constructed. They provide explanations for what has happened and anticipations of what comes next" (p. 98).

Suppose a supervisor learns that because of a new company policy, she will not be able to replace two employees who have just retired. How will she react to this information? Her reaction will in part be determined by the sorts of inferences she makes from what she has been told. She may infer that her division is no longer highly valued. Or she may wonder whether her own management ability has been called into question, and whether giving her fewer employees to supervise represents a way of simplifying her task. She may think that the organization as a whole is downsizing—and that the future of the company could be in jeopardy. As she reacts to the information she receives, she will likely need to communicate with others, to gather more information, to question her boss about the rationale for this new policy, and to assess its implications for her and for others. Depending upon how she eventually constructs and interprets her information environment, she may behave in several different ways—by calling a staff meeting to reassure her work group that the policy is only temporary, by posting the changed policy and letting workers draw their own conclusions, by vowing to work harder, or by beginning to seek employment elsewhere.

Another critical component of Weick's model is the notion of **information equivocality**. Messages that are highly equivocal are difficult for organizational members to understand. Thus, equivocality is associated with ambiguity, complexity, and obscurity. Weick argues that organizational members attempt to process equivocal information so that they can increase predictability and respond appropriately to problems.

Organizational leaders can play an important role in reducing equivocality for their employees by carefully organizing their work assignments and clearly communicating their expectations. The manager asks her subordinate to draft a proposal, the subordinate produces the draft, and the manager reads it and provides feedback, perhaps offering praise or criticism. This process can be repeated several times. Their interaction serves to reduce equivocality for both the supervisor and the subordinate. The manager grows to understand how the employee interpreted the meaning of the assignment by evaluating the finished proposal. Similarly, the supervisor's feedback on the proposal reduces the employee's uncertainty about the adequacy of his performance. This action-response-feedback loop is a cycle repeated at all organizational levels.

The Cultural School

One of the latest schools of organization theory points to the importance of the organization's culture. Underlying the cultural approach is the desire to understand how organizational life is accomplished through communication (Pacanowsky & O'Donnell-Trujillo (1982). **Culture** can be defined in broad and inclusive terms. Pacanowsky and O'Donnell-Trujillo (1983) argued that "a culture is something an organization *is*" (p. 146). Thus, culture is not simply a characteristic an organization possesses. With culture as the root metaphor for understanding organizations, earlier conceptions of organizations as tools, instruments, or organisms become inappropriate. Instead, organizations are better understood as expressive, ideational, and symbolic processes (Smircich & Calas, 1987). In more specific terms, an organization's culture consists of "a system of shared values (what is important) and beliefs (how things work) that interacts with a company's people, organizational structures, and control systems to produce behavioral norms (the way we do things around here)" (Uttal, 1983, p. 66).

No profile for an ideal organizational culture exists. In fact, some scholars explicitly say that one organization's culture cannot be compared with another's. However, others believe that certain cultures are healthier, more productive, and more satisfying than others. Peters and Waterman (1982) reported, for instance, that the effective organizations they studied (including McDonald's, Disney, Hewlett-Packard, and the Dana Corporation) all shared certain sets of values and accompanying behaviors. In particular, Peters and Waterman identified eight themes or value sets:

1. **A bias for action.** Rather than discussing problems at length, excellent organizations acted quickly. Although careful in their problem analysis, they refused to become bogged down in an information swamp.

2. **Closeness to the customer.** Each of these organizations was committed to providing the highest level of service and viewed customer needs as paramount. Each was known for innovation, responsiveness, and reliability.

3. **Autonomy and entrepreneurship.** Employees were encouraged to be creative and take risks. Leadership was widely shared. Those who came up with excellent innovations were rewarded with enhanced responsibility and authority.

4. **Productivity through people.** These companies recognized that they could be successful only if each employee was valued and encouraged to work to his or her full potential. Artificial barriers between management and workers were discouraged.

5. **Hands-on, value-driven philosophy.** Organizational leaders made every effort to communicate clearly those values considered central to the organization's mission and identity. Everyone was committed to the organization's philosophy and values and felt part of the value-shaping process.

6. **Sticking to the knitting.** Excellent companies stayed with the businesses they knew best. They did not diversify beyond what they knew and understood.

7. **Simple form, lean staff.** These organizations were run with simple structures that emphasized decentralization and few layers of hierarchy. Self-motivation and self-management were encouraged.

8. **Simultaneous loose-tight properties.** While all members of the organization were encouraged to think and act with relative freedom and independence, basic values were widely shared and supported throughout the firm.

Thus, in the organizational cultures that Peters and Waterman deemed "excellent," leaders talked openly and freely about their values, and they sought to meet with and involve workers at all levels of the organizational hierarchy.

Types and Characteristics of Organizational Cultures

In their book *Corporate Cultures* (1982), Deal and Kennedy offered a detailed analysis of the cultures that typify contemporary organizations. They identify four basic types of organizational cultures. First, in the "tough-guy/macho culture," competitive, individualistic employees take high risks and get immediate feedback about the correctness of their actions. Investment bankers and high-level stockbrokers, for instance, start each day by gambling large sums of money and will know by the day's end whether they have made the best move. Employees tend to be young and burn out quickly. In this kind of culture, high-risk actions are considered extremely appropriate, perhaps even required. Deal and Kennedy's second cultural category is called "work hard/play hard." In this culture all organization members maintain a consistently high level of low-risk activity. They are expected virtually to merge their work and nonwork lives, with socializing revolving around friends from work; in fact, such interaction may be required. Every event has strong political overtones, and everyone is expected to be a team player. Those who sell products for Amway experience this kind of culture. Amway distributors meet regularly, talk often on the phone, attend Amway conventions together, and seek to win trips to attractive vacation spots, where they can bask in the sun with other groups of prizewinning Amway salespeople.

The third cultural type discussed by Deal and Kennedy is the "bet your company" culture, in which big-stakes decisions are made regularly and feedback comes slowly. The risks that are taken are at the organizational and policy level. Each decision made is slow and costly, requiring accurate and complex information. In many instances it will be years before the organization will know whether it has succeeded or failed. Those drug companies who chose to put other priorities on the back burner so that they might focus their full attention on AIDS research represent this kind of culture.

Finally, Deal and Kennedy noted the "process" culture, in which people focus not on what is done but on how it is done. These organizations tend to be bureaucratic and are characterized by low risks. Aimed primarily at survival, they value hierarchy, formal rank, and tangible symbols of rank and status. Of course, all these organizational types represent an oversimplification. Organizations vary over time, and different subcultures often exist within them.

Besides classifying several different types of cultures, Deal and Kennedy discussed four key attributes of organizational cultures. First are *values,* the shared views, philosophies, and beliefs of organizational members. An organization's values establish the tone, set the direction and the pace, and suggest appropriate attitudes and courses of action. Listening to the way organizational members communicate among themselves often provides some insight into their values. For instance, the 1987 film based on Peters and Waterman's *In Search of Excellence* (1982), briefly illustrates Disney's organizational culture. Disney World employees are referred to as "associates," whether they are tour guides or custodians. There are no "customers" at Disney World, only "guests"; and those who don "costumes" (not "uniforms") are "cast members." Through their insistence on using this language, Disney leaders demonstrate their respect for employees and customers and reinforce the image of Disney World as not simply an amusement park but rather a grand theatrical event where honor comes from acting each part well.

The second attribute of an organization's culture is the organizational members who personify and illuminate the organization's values, its **heroes**. Often the heroes are in positions of leadership that give them the opportunity to articulate and reflect (through language and actions) their values and their vision of what the organization is or should be. Articulating organizational mission statements is one way the leader/hero can influence the company's culture. Others will often copy the hero's language, either intentionally or unintentionally. A new academic leader may speak of the "life of the mind" in describing his or her vision of how a community of scholars should think about themselves and their mission. Of course, what is true for traditional organizational cultures also applies to other entities, such as nations. During the most recent U.S. presidential election, voters had to choose among three would-be heroes and their respective themes (reflected in nearly every major public message) of change, shared sacrifice, and trust. It is the hero who defines the allies and the enemies, who writes or sanctions the slogans, and who is highly visible during the enactment of the organization's third cultural attribute, rites and rituals.

Through **rites and rituals** organizational members celebrate and reinforce their beliefs, applaud their heroes, and share their visions of the future. In Christian religious organizations, for example, rituals abound as people marry, celebrate communion, baptize their children, and bury their dead. While these rituals are shared by many different religious denominations, each church develops distinctly different traditions for the ritual's enactment. Baptism at some churches requires complete immersion (either in the church or outdoors), whereas in other churches, the act of baptism is more symbolic—the minister sprinkles water with his or her hand or dips a rose into the baptismal font. Although differences in the ways in which rituals are enacted may sound trivial to those outside the organization, to those inside, the details often carry profound significance. Tampering with them may entail great risk, especially to those in positions of leadership.

Although rituals are of obvious significance in religious organizations, they are also evident in other kinds of organizations whose members are initiated, promoted, honored, and retired. Whatever the organization's values, members who participate in or attend formal rituals will be reminded of those values and urged to believe in or live up to them. Of course, some organizational rituals are less formal, such as getting together for coffee each morning at 10:00 A.M., or going out for pizza every Friday. The informal rituals may be less predictable, but those who avoid them may find themselves excluded from other aspects of organizational life.

The final cultural attribute discussed by Deal and Kennedy is the **communication network,** those informal channels of interaction, typically used for influencing members' perceptions of reality and indoctrinating them to hold the right attitudes and behave in appropriate ways. Networking begins even before the individual formally joins the organization. During job interviews, candidates are routinely taken out to lunch by peers who proceed to tell stories about the organization, gossip about villains and heroes, and give advice about strategies for upward mobility. This networking is likely to be particularly salient with favored candidates—giving them the "inside scoop." Having joined an organization, the new member continues to be involved in communication networks over coffee breaks, lunches, dinners, parties, and other

Even when groups have tasks to accomplish, group members often devote time to informal interaction. As individuals communicate informally, they get to know each other, and they may develop relationships that extend beyond their formal organizational roles. (Frank Siteman/Rainbow)

social events. Organizational members learn a great deal in these informal communication settings, since much information is shared that would never be mentioned in more formal meetings. Who is likely to be the leader's successor? Is there a "glass ceiling" for women or minorities in this organization? How important is it to play poker or fish or dine with the boss? How highly valued is this department within the larger organization? Is the company really serious about job sharing? In some instances conversations that are shared informally will eventually lead to formal discussions with others at work, especially if a serious problem surfaces. Many believe that one sign of a healthy organizational culture is the dynamic interchange between formal and informal communication channels. Leaders who are involved in the communication networks of the organization are more likely to be influential throughout the organization.

Implications of the Cultural School

The cultural school, like the systems school, provides no formula for structuring or managing the organization. The four attributes provide a useful perspective for examining any organization. Those doing research from a cultural perspective typically engage in long-term observation and interviewing as they seek to understand organization members' views of reality; the social knowledge with which they operate; and their practices, vocabulary, metaphors, and stories (Pacanowsky & O'Donnell-Trujillo, 1982). Others use the cultural school more prescriptively, suggesting that every organization should carefully examine and reexamine its values on a regular basis (Noller, 1991; Pacanowsky, 1987). If the basic values are not widely understood and accepted, they should be clarified or perhaps renegotiated. Questions should also be raised about those who are elevated as organizational heroes. To what extent do those who are honored or hold positions of leadership or influence truly reflect the organization's values? For instance, in universities, are the best teachers adequately rewarded? In business, are those who interact with customers with the highest concern for ethics given appropriate reinforcement? Similarly, rituals should be examined to make sure that they remain meaningful and inclusive, rather than routine and alienating. Finally, the values that are formally embraced by the organization should be reinforced, rather than denied, by words and actions in informal contexts.

Throughout this chapter we have traced the foundational schools of organization theory. We have shown how organization theory has evolved over time and how the role and place of communication has differed significantly within the framework of diverse schools of thought. Empowering workers was certainly not a concern of scientific managers. But human relations thinkers and practitioners began to engage questions of worker satisfaction, job enrichment, and democratic leadership. However crude their approach to these issues, their contributions positioned contemporary management theorists to embrace and vigorously pursue employee empowerment as a critical organizational goal.

Of course, not everyone would agree that organizations provide contexts in which employee empowerment is considered a goal. For instance, **critical theorists** view organizations as vehicles of oppression and domination. Focus On sketches critical theorists' notions about organizations. Above all, critical theory calls for vigilance and thoughtful reflection on many assumptions widely taken for granted. For example, at what level are organizational and individual values and needs consistent? Are the rules applied to all organizational members in ways that promote fairness and justice? Are leaders sincere when they speak of worker participation and empowerment? Will modern technology be used to expand employee opportunities and to better connect individuals and their collective social and task needs, or will it be used to exclude those less skilled, to monitor the performance of personnel, and to channel information and opportunities to a select few?

In this chapter's concluding section we examine the evolution of technology over time and suggest the kinds of questions that modern writers have raised about contemporary technologies and the ways in which they may be used by those in positions of power.

FOCUS ON

Critical Theory: A Brief Summary

Critical theory can be traced to the works of Karl Marx. The critical theorist views the organization as an instrument of oppression. Although the victims of organizational oppression are often thought of as those in the minority (such as women and African Americans), the critical theorist contends that all workers are oppressed by those in power.

The pivotal question for critical theorists was perhaps best captured by Robert McPhee (1985) when he asked: "How is it, given the alienated and exploitative nature of work in capitalist organizations, that workers cooperate with management, labor at their jobs, and forgo resistant stances, without the constant presence of coercion and threat?" (p. 1)

Critical theorists contend that traditional treatments of power are superficial, since most power is deeply embedded in the organizational structure. It is this deep power structure that controls the true rules by which the organization operates, or the rules by which the game is played. Getting employees to buy into those rules is critical for those in power. Theoretically, rules may be clearly articulated, but critical theorists argue that it is more likely that they will remain strategically ambiguous.

While some communication distortion is likely in any organizational hierarchy, critical theorists speak of the **systemic distortion** of communication. Such distortion is viewed as a symbolic process through which, as Tompkins and Redding have described, "the owner/manager's interests are falsely joined with those of the worker in ideological communication" (p. 27). When workers are told stories of organizational heroes or given corporate mottos embodying corporate values to "inspire and motivate," the critical theorist asks whose interests these values serve. Do they favor the elite or the ruling class while disempowering everyone else? Moreover, do the words of those in power provide the false impression that their interests are consistent with those of all workers? The critical theorist argues (1) that often those interests are inconsistent (what will make the company more productive or the customer more satisfied will *not* contribute to a more fulfilling work life for the average employee), and (2) that employees (members of dominated groups) frequently participate in their own oppression through self-deception (Mumby, 1987). They consent to the system and identify with the values, without understanding that the members of the corporate elite are basically protecting their own interests.

In short, critical theorists seek to engage scholars and practitioners in consciousness raising and to emancipate those whom they view as oppressed organizational classes. While some critical theorists' ideas may be viewed as extreme, they may at the same time point to managerial communication behaviors that serve to disempower.

Here are some questions suggested by critical theory:

1. Are there some topics or issues that managers refuse to discuss? (Warning signs: The item never appears on any meeting agenda. The group's leader

insists on a pre-established agenda and refuses to allow any new business to be introduced.)

2. Are some genuine worker concerns unjustly minimized by management? (The item appears on the agenda, but so near the end that the group never gets to it.)

3. Do managers hold fewer meetings than the legitimate business of the organization necessitates? (Warning signs: Fewer meetings are held than past practices and traditions dictate. Meetings are canceled for no stated reason.)

4. Are decision-making groups trained to use criteria (like efficiency) that primarily serve the interests of management (rather than being encouraged to develop some of their own criteria)?

5. Do managers constitute committees in such a way as to ensure promanagement outcomes? (These groups can operate as they please because the outcome is predetermined.)

6. Are employees told that their emotional reactions and feelings don't matter? ("We have to put emotions aside and move into a constructive problem-solving mode.")

7. Rather than embracing an inclusive, consensus-building management model, have leaders settled for a "majority wins" model? (Warning signs: Employees learn that the manager just wants a "working majority"—consensus is no longer the goal. Favored employees are told by managers [typically in a private setting] that certain employees will never be part of the team; they are "permanently marginalized.")

8. Do leaders use language designed to confuse or alienate those outside the inner circle? (Warning sign: During meetings, the manager begins to use words like "disambiguate" when he could have more clearly, simply, [and intelligently] used the word "clarify." Workers wonder what he is really talking about.)

These are only a few examples of communication behaviors typical of those who seek to oppress and dominate rather than empower.

Organization and Technology

A Historical Sketch

Between 1895 and 1905, the concept and structure of the modern business enterprise evolved in such a way that management was distinguished from ownership and became established as work and a task in its own right. The 1920s saw a second evolutionary change as the command-and-control organization was introduced, with its emphasis on decentralization, central service staffs, personnel management, the apparatus of budgets and controls, and the distinction between policy and operations.

During this same period, the U.S. economy had shifted from a farm economy to a manufacturing economy. In fact, the period from the Civil War until just after World War I might be characterized as a production era, a second industrial revolution wherein demand for products exceeded many manufacturers' ability to supply them. A developing oil industry provided fuel for the light, heat, and energy needed by factories. Immigration provided labor for manufacturing. Machines became the primary tools for workers, with more and more processes being simplified through mechanization and automation.

Industrial growth progressed well into the twentieth century. Henry Ford's assembly line brought the work to the worker, refined the concept of specialization, and spawned the mass production of consumer goods. Pride, Hughes, and Kapoor (1993) noted that by the 1920s the automobile industry had begun to influence the entire economy. The steel industry grew, as did the oil and gas industries. And the emerging airplane and airline industries promised new forms of transportation.

Despite the Depression and World War II, Pride et al. noted, from the end of World War I to the beginning of the Korean War in 1950, production capacity was not a major problem. What eventually did become a problem, however, was figuring out how to sell all that could be produced. After World War II, sales and marketing became issues for organizations because consumers began to have discretionary income—more income than is required to obtain the necessities of life. Whereas sales personnel had previously been expected to sell goods, regardless of product quality or whether it met consumer needs, they now faced discriminating consumers who shopped for the goods and services that they wanted and valued.

By the mid-1970s, according to Kreitner, Reece, and O'Grady (1990), five harsh realities had led to a fundamental restructuring of American business:

- the demise of the smokestack industries—steel, shipbuilding, coal, and the like—that had been the economy's backbone since the Civil War
- the shock of an oil crisis, which demonstrated how vulnerable the United States was to foreign energy suppliers
- a loss of confidence following major recessions and staggering inflation
- the astonishing discovery that foreign products could easily displace American goods, notably electronics and automobiles
- a heightened consciousness of the problems of unemployment and underemployment as a new generation with great expectations joined the work force.

The major effect of these shocks was to accelerate the growth of two new sectors of the economy: the **service sector** and the **information sector**. The service sector consists of businesses that perform work for others rather than producing goods. Education, for example, lies in the service sector, as do all the other professions. Kreitner at al. claimed that by the year 2000, an estimated 88 percent of the U.S. work force will be employed in the service sector of the economy.

Central to the service sector are those who operate the computer and information-processing technologies found in the information sector. The businesses that produce computer-related technologies are providing support for the information sector of the economy, creating what Senn (1995) has called "the Information Age."

Senn claims that the Information Age actually began in 1957, when for the first time in the United States, white-collar workers outnumbered blue-collar workers. This reconfiguration meant that the majority of workers were now involved in the creation, distribution, and application of information rather than in manufacturing or agriculture.

The Information Age can be distinguished from the Industrial Age on the basis of five characteristics:

- The Information Age came about with the rise of an information-based society, where more people work at handling information than in agriculture and manufacturing combined.

- Businesses in the Information Age depend on information technology to get their work done.

- In the Information Age, work processes are transformed to increase productivity.

- Success in the Information Age is largely determined by the effectiveness with which technology is used.

- In the Information Age, information technology is embedded in many products and services (Senn, 1995).

During the first half of the twentieth century, the impact of technology on organizations was somewhat limited. Automatic data processing based on the use of punched-card tabulating machines helped organizations grow by allowing them to be more efficient in their record keeping. However, between the mid-1930s and the early 1950s, computer technology developed to the point that the first commercially viable electronic digital computers were introduced in the mid-1950s. Between the 1950s and the 1970s, four generations of computer technology evolved. Computers went from being nearly room-size and using vacuum tubes to using integrated circuits and being so miniaturized that microprocessors now fit neatly into appliances such as microwave ovens.

The Impact of the New Technologies

The information age has had ramifications for organizational design. While the industrial age organization was typified by the rule-based, hierarchical bureaucracy, Peter Drucker (1988) heralded the coming of a new type of organization for the information age, with an information-based structure. By doing so, Drucker suggested an organization not of functional bureaucratic specialists but of knowledge specialists who create or process information for the firm so that the organization will learn and survive in a potentially hostile, turbulent, and competitive environment.

Knowledge workers might be thought of as individuals with highly specialized training and education who work primarily with information. Unlike the bureaucratic perspective, which viewed organizations as hierarchical, pyramid-like structures, Drucker's view is of the information-based organization as assuming a flatter structure—with knowledge no longer concentrated at the top, but at the bottom, in the minds of knowledge specialists who engage in different work (mental rather than physical) and who direct themselves.

Drucker sees technology as the critical enabler for changes in organizational design. Technology is seen as a mechanism for transforming decision structures and management structures, and as a means for changing the way work gets done. For example, e-mail eliminates knowledge worker telephone tag, while voice mail allows both the storing and forwarding of spoken messages across telecommunications networks. Electronic meeting systems, called "group support systems," employ specialized computer software that allows groups of knowledge workers to efficiently generate, consolidate, and evaluate ideas when they meet face to face. Teleconferencing technology allows knowledge workers at differing locations to communicate and share their information and ideas, thereby reducing travel requirements. Database technology provides knowledge workers with access to both internal and external sources of information. Decision support systems, office automation systems, and other technologies enhance analysis, decision making, coordination activities, and the reporting of information; and telecommunications networks bring information to where knowledge workers need it, when they need it.

Technology also changes the way firms communicate and do business with one another. For example, electronic data interchange (EDI) allows the direct computer-to-computer exchange of standard business transaction documents, such as purchase orders and invoices, between separate organizations. EDI saves money and time because transactions are transmitted electronically, eliminating the printing and handling of paper at one end and the input of data at the other. In addition to reducing personnel costs and transcription errors, EDI can provide strategic benefits by "locking in" suppliers and/or customers (Laudon & Laudon, 1993).

For the new organization to perform well, it must be organized as a set of interrelating teams in which each knowledge worker acts as a responsible decision maker (Drucker, 1992). In this scenario, groupware technologies function as an integral organizational enabler. Information technology, especially telecommunications, provides teams with a variety of channels with which to communicate, negotiate, and collaborate across time and space.

Teamwork in organizations is not necessarily a novel way to coordinate interdependent activities among separate units or groups of specialists in an organization. What *is* new, as Rockart and Short (1989) noted, is that "electronic mail, computer conferencing, and videoconferencing now facilitate this process"

(p. 13). Alavi and Keen (1989) contended that the current popularity of teams in organizations is, in fact, largely due to developments in information technology that now allow teams to work together when they cannot meet face to face. In the next chapter, we will consider self-managing teams in greater detail.

In sum, then, new technologies "enable corporations to flatten organizations, yoke together teams across the barriers of specialty, rank, and geography, and forge closer strategic relationships with customers and suppliers" (Sherman, 1993, p. 58). For teams and technology to generate organizational change, however, the organizational culture must emphasize the empowerment of the knowledge worker. This means that knowledge workers should be able actively to identify impediments to getting tasks done, seek and implement ideas for improving the way work is done, and take action to work with others to remedy problems.

Organizations are now under tremendous pressure to examine how best to design their processes so that their products or services provide maximum value to their internal and external customers. Technology and teams of knowledge workers provide the organization with the necessary intellectual capacity and technical resources to be creative and identify and implement new ways of working. Continuous innovation and improvement are essential to organizational survival. As Sherman (1993) noted, "Those who seize the opportunities inherent in this [computer] revolution are capturing important competitive advantages. Those who lag behind are forced to scramble breathlessly in a race to catch up, or die" (p. 56).

There is some evidence to support Drucker's prognosis for organizations. Many have pointed to the success of Wal-Mart as an example of the "coming organization." Incorporating the use of computers and networking technology and a flat organizational structure early on, upstart Wal-Mart was able to make dramatic inroads into a retail business once dominated by giants named Sears and K-Mart, which were organized along more traditional, bureaucratic lines. Wal-Mart, for instance, effectively uses technology in an inventory management system that integrates information from suppliers, stores and warehouses. This information flow allows the company to respond quickly to changing consumer behavior, even enabling them to tailor shipments to the particular needs of each of its two thousand stores. The idea is "to run each store as if it's the only one you have" (Sherman, 1993, p. 66).

However, technology will not guarantee success for the "coming organization." Benjamin and Blunt (1992) reported that research from the Massachusetts Institute of Technology Management in the 1990s program indicates that the benefits of technology implementation have been slow in coming because organizational change is often not adequately managed. As organizations attempt to change from bureaucratic to flatter structures, ongoing changes in technology make the process of organizational change that much more difficult. When this happens, Benjamin and Blunt suggested, organizational resistance to change in turn becomes that much more pronounced. They concluded that ". . . companies are likely to find that people's inability to change, not technology, is the limiting factor in transforming organizations" (p. 16).

Summarizing Perspective

The major organizational theories presented in this chapter demonstrate how managers and theorists have articulated strikingly different perspectives on organizational structure, behavior, and communication during this century. In some instances altered views of organizations could be attributed to changing socioeconomic conditions. At other times the findings of empirical research persuaded organizational leaders to reconceptualize their views of organizations and organizational communication. Classical views of organizations emphasized formal authority, structure, and rationality. Later, the human relations school focused on the informal organization and celebrated the social nature of all organizational members.

In more recent years, theorists have taken a broader, more eclectic view—conceptualizing organizations as open systems, with communication as a defining element. Indeed, every organizational theory since 1960 has integrated the concept of "organizing" with the concept of "communicating." While some theories are more prescriptive than others, each offers a vantage point for considering the significance of the act of joining together to create organizations; the sense of purpose or mission associated with such endeavors; and the relationship between organizing and leading, between holding power and empowering.

Now that new technologies are changing the way in which people interact in organizational contexts, they are in turn influencing the way in which theorists view organizational structure, power/empowerment, and the nature of human relationships. In the next chapter, we move to an examination of contemporary theories associated with human resources management. In diverse and interesting ways, each of these theories grapples with the question of empowerment.

CASES FOR DISCUSSION

CASE 1   *Organizational Culture at 3M*

One of America's most innovative organizations is 3M (Minnesota Mining & Manufacturing). The following paragraphs briefly describe its history and culture:

3M was founded not by scientists or inventors but by a doctor, a lawyer, two railroad executives, and a meat market manager. At the turn of the century these five bought a plot of heavily forested land on the shores of Lake Superior. They planned to mine corundum, an abrasive used by sandpaper manufacturers to make the paper scratchy. These entrepreneurs sought new investors, purchased machinery, hired workers, and started mining. Only then did they discover that their corundum was not, in fact, corundum at all—but a worthless mineral that the sandpaper industry wanted no part of.

At first the company tried selling its own sandpaper using corundum shipped in from the East, but it got battered by the competition. Thus, the company that is known today for its tolerance of failure was founded on a huge failure. 3M was forced to innovate or die. It was then that one of the founders, Francis G. Okie, developed a waterproof sandpaper that became a staple of the automobile industry because it produced a better exterior finish and created less dust than conventional papers. It was 3M's first blockbuster.

Today, the innovation process at 3M works like this: Someone comes up with an idea for a new product. He or she forms an action team by recruiting full-time members from technical areas, manufacturing, marketing, sales, and maybe finance. The team designs the product and figures out how to produce and market it. Then it develops new uses and line extensions. All members of the team are promoted and receive raises as the project goes from hurdle to hurdle. When sales grow to $5 million, for instance, the product's originator becomes a project manager. At sales of $20 million to $30 million, he or she becomes a department manager, and in the $75 million range, a division manager. There is a separate track for scientists who aren't interested in management.

Another practice for which 3M is famous is "bootlegging." Anyone at the company is allowed to spend up to 15 percent of the work week on anything he or she wants to, as long as it's product-related. It was bootlegging that led to the invention of Post-It notes. Arthur Fry's division was busy with other projects, so he invoked the 15 percent rule to create the adhesive for Post-Its, an idea that grew from Fry's desire to keep the bookmark from falling out of his hymn book while he sang in two services at his church. Post-Its are now a major 3M consumer business, with revenues estimated at as much as $300 million.

In general, 3M relies on a few simple rules:

1. **Keep divisions small.** Division managers must know each staff member's name. When a division becomes too large, perhaps reaching $250 to $300 million in sales, it is split up.

2. **Tolerate failure.** Encouraging experimentation and taking risks increases the chances for a new product hit. Divisions must derive 25 percent of sales from products introduced in the past five years.

3. **Motivate the champions.** When a 3M employee comes up with a product idea, that person recruits an action team to develop it. Salaries and promotions are tied to the product's progress. The champion has the chance to run his or her own product or division some day.

4. **Stay close to the customer.** Researchers, marketers, and managers visit with customers and routinely invite them to help brainstorm product ideas.

5. **Share the wealth.** Technology, wherever it is developed, belongs to everyone.

6. **Don't kill a project.** If an idea can't find a home in one of 3M's divisions, a staff member can devote 15 percent of his time to prove that it is workable. For those who need seed money, as many as ninety Genesis grants of $50,000 are awarded each year.

Questions for Discussion

1. Which organization theories seem to have most influenced the organizational climate at 3M?

2. How would you describe the company's organizational culture?

3. Would this kind of culture be appropriate or effective in other organizations? Why or why not? If so, what sorts of organizations?

SOURCE: Based on Mitchell, 1989.

CASE 2 *Employee Opinion Surveys*

Over the past ten to fifteen years, companies throughout the United States have made increasing use of employee opinion surveys. Briefly, such surveys ask employees to answer a series of questions about various aspects of their work lives: pay, benefits, promotions, supervision and management, working conditions, communication, and so on. To encourage openness and honesty, employee responses are anonymous. Summaries of survey results (typically analyzed on a group basis, such as by department or location) are communicated to senior management and, usually, to middle-level management, first-line supervisors, and nonsupervisory personnel.

During their twelve years of experience conducting employee opinion surveys for clients, Melnick, Baird, Williams, and Fisher, Inc. have heard a wide variety of reasons clients want surveys done. Here are some examples.

The manager of a manufacturing plant stated, "I want to learn how well each of my supervisors and managers are doing managing their people. No one can assess a supervisor better than the people who work for her or him, and I want to use the survey to get employees' honest opinions." When asked how he would handle those situations in which a supervisor or manager was strongly criticized, the manager replied, "I'll fire him."

The chief executive officer of a chain of Catholic hospitals, a nun, said: "People should be happy in their work. After all, they spend more of their waking time at work than they do at home. I want them to enjoy their work lives. The survey will tell me how I can make them happier to be working here."

An insurance executive observed, "Employees who are unhappy in their work lives tend to show it in their interactions with others. Unhappy people show it to their customers, just as happy people treat customers well. I want to identify problems which hurt morale and factors which can help morale, because morale will help to improve our customer service."

A bank vice president noted, "We're going to have to lay some people off in three or four months. As much as possible, I want to keep the people who like it here and get rid of the ones who don't. I know the survey is anonymous, but I think it will help me to target those areas where the layoffs should happen."

The owner of a small manufacturing company said, "My success comes from the efforts of my managers, and their success comes from the efforts of their people. The better my managers understand their people, the better they can help them to do their jobs well. I want to use the survey to help my managers understand their people, and to have them use the survey results as a tool for participative problem solving as they work with their people to make things better."

The president of a large airline commented, "Our company has two sets of customers: those outside the company, and those inside the company. We do lots of surveys of our external customers to see how they feel about the service we provide. I want to survey my internal customers to see how they feel about our company's services to them."

The American manager of a plant owned by a large Japanese manufacturing company said, "I don't really want to do a survey. The corporate office is telling us we have to do one. So, I want you to send the survey report directly to me, and I'll decide when and how I want to send all or part of it to corporate."

The manager of a large grocery store noted, "If I do a survey, then people will expect that things are going to get fixed. That should quiet them down for a while,

and when they start complaining again, I'll do another survey."

Questions for Discussion

1. What elements of the various philosophies and theories of organization described in this chapter do you see in each of the above examples?

2. If you were the employee opinion survey consultant to whom each of these remarks was made, how would you have responded in each case? Explain your answers

CHAPTER

3

Empowering Employees Through Human Resources Management

To me, the most consequential feature of the [empowering]... culture [is] that so many ... do not cower or dissemble or retreat or space out before some organizational monolith, but instead feel that they stand before their organization as an equal, as a partner, as an entity as capable of affecting their organization as of being affected by it.
Michael Pacanowsky, "Communication in the Empowering Organization," 1987.

In the early 1980s, Richard Pascale and Anthony Athos (1981) wrote in *The Art of Japanese Management,* "Most people bring three kinds of needs to their organizational existence: A need to be accepted as a unique person, a need to be rewarded for what they achieve, and a need to be appreciated not only for the function performed but also as a human being" (p. 12). With these words, Pascale and Athos articulated the assumptions about human motivation upon which the Japanese have built their modern management "art." But, they might just as readily have used the same words to introduce Douglas McGregor's seminal statement of human resources management, *The Human Side of Enterprise* (1960), published in the United States over twenty years before.

In the United States the foundation of modern management theory can be traced to the early 1960s, when it grew, in part, out of the human relations movement in business and industry. Originally articulated by McGregor of the Massachusetts Institute of Technology, *human resources management is based on several underlying assumptions.* First, McGregor (1960) and others (Likert, 1961) argued that *human beings are the organization's most valuable resource.* From that premise, they contended that the manager's fundamental task is to gain an understanding of how people can better interact and relate to one another in organizational contexts. Thus, from a human resources perspective, *the interpersonal relationship is considered the building block of the organization* (along with the communication needed to foster such relationships).

This view of management represented a dramatic departure from the human relations school's rather exclusive focus on improved employee satisfaction as a vehicle for achieving greater organizational productivity. Human resources theorists were convinced that employee morale was intrinsically valuable. Enhanced productivity might result from elevated job satisfaction—but there were no guarantees. Instead, the manager's challenge and obligation was to tap the creative energy, work ethic, and sense of responsibility already present in the work force, to nurture it, and to create an environment in which individuals might realize their own goals, in part by contributing constructively to those of the organization. Human resources managers were less interested in gaining compliance than in helping subordinates experience self-development and empowerment.

Finally, human resources management was based on a third assumption, that *self-actualization for average human beings is intrinsically linked to their organizational affiliation and identification.* No one articulated this notion more clearly than McGregor (1960), who argued that Theory Y (the theoretical foundation of human resources) was based on the notion of *integration,* "the creation of conditions such that the members of the organization can achieve their own goals best by directing their efforts toward the success of the enterprise" (p. 27).

This chapter will trace the development of human resources management over the past several decades. Although we concentrate mostly on U.S. theorists—notably McGregor, Likert, Herzberg, and Hersey and Blanchard—we will also discuss the Japanese management approach, which embraces several human resources principles while offering points of largely culture-based contrast. We are convinced that empowerment is at the heart of human resources theories of management, although each theorist approaches empowerment in different ways. Taken to an extreme, those who manage with a human resources philosophy will ultimately contribute to an organizational environment in which every man and woman manages him- or herself. Thus, we discuss self-management and show some of the potential for empowering leadership offered by modern technologies.

Human Resources Theorists

McGregor

Theories of organization and philosophies of management are often closely associated. This was especially true for Douglas McGregor, who began by examining traditional organizations, those managed according to tenets of classical organization theory. McGregor (1960) advanced the argument that traditional approaches to managing, which he labeled "Theory X", grew from the central principle of direction and control through the exercise of authority. According to McGregor, **Theory X** managers communicated in fairly predictable ways, with a distinct emphasis on downward, formal communication, no encouragement of upward communication, and an autocratic approach to decision making. McGregor believed that Theory X management practices created an organizational climate of distrust, misunderstanding, and fear. With so little information flowing upward through the hierarchy, and with the inevitable distortions that accompanied upward communication in such a negative organizational environment, managers were doomed to make decisions based on partial and often inaccurate information. In McGregor's view, then, the prospects for long-term organizational productivity under Theory X management were dim indeed.

McGregor was convinced that the Theory X manager's behavior grew from a number of unwarranted assumptions about human beings, assumptions that represented a rather dim view of workers and their potential. In the spirit of scientific management, the Theory X manager viewed—and treated—workers as economic beings who were most readily motivated by wage incentive plans and other tangible rewards. McGregor argued that this sort of manager nurtured certain unwavering beliefs about workers, summarized briefly as follows:

1. People do not like to work. Whenever possible, they will avoid it. Employees work only to make a living.

2. To get employees to exert effort on behalf of the organization, the manager must devise strategies for controlling them. Most need a highly structured environment and may have to be coerced or even threatened with punishments.

3. The average person needs direction, wants to avoid responsibility, lacks ambition, and desires security above all.

Like other theorists of his time, McGregor was strongly influenced by the work of several distinguished psychologists, including Abraham Maslow (1954). Basing his argument on Maslow's hierarchy of needs (see Figure 3.1), McGregor asserted that Theory X managers operate from an incomplete and therefore inadequate view of human needs and motivation. In particular, Theory X managers appeared to believe that subordinates were motivated only to satisfy their lower-level needs—for survival, safety, and security. They failed to recognize that subordinates, like the managers themselves, might have higher yearnings.

At the heart of any management theory are assumptions about the nature of human beings and human motivation. In formulating an alternative to the Theory X manager, McGregor articulated a different set of assumptions. Influenced by the human relations movement (discussed in Chapter 2) and its more positive socially oriented views of workers, McGregor set forth the underlying assumptions of **Theory Y**:

1. Work is a natural activity. It may even be enjoyable.

2. People are capable of self-control and self-direction, especially when they are pursuing organizational goals that they understand and to which they are committed.

FIGURE 3.1

Maslow's Hierarchy of Needs

Maslow believed that basic needs had to be satisfied before humans would seek to satisfy needs at the top of the hierarchy, especially the need for self-actualization.

3. Workers will develop commitments to organizational goals as a result of their opportunities for self-actualization. Managers must design jobs to help individuals become more fulfilled.

4. Human beings are basically responsible. Under the proper conditions, workers may actually seek out responsibility.

5. Ability, imagination, creativity, and ingenuity are widely distributed among the population. Talent is not limited to managerial ranks.

Taken together, the underlying assumptions of McGregor's Theory Y led managers to recognize the *untapped creative potential* of their employees.

Once embraced, Theory Y assumptions call for strikingly different managerial behaviors. Theory Y managers will share decision making with workers at all levels of the organizational hierarchy. They will actively encourage upward communication and listen carefully to subordinates' opinions and advice. They will offer opportunities for workers to seek greater responsibility. Because they are committed to helping workers achieve self-actualization, they will focus on job enlargement and enrichment. The Theory Y manager recognizes the full range of human needs as articulated by Maslow (see Figure 3.1) and, most important, will assume that those needs and sources of motivation are as applicable to those at the bottom as to those at the top of the organizational hierarchy.

Theory Y and Empowerment   Clearly, McGregor's Theory Y is an empowering philosophy of management. Some critics have argued that McGregor overstated the case, articulating expectations about workers that would prove unrealistic. Yet recent works have validated McGregor's views. For instance, in his book depicting the leadership philosophy and practices of Wernher von Braun, director of the Marshall Space Flight Center during the 1960s, Phillip Tompkins (1993) offered a compelling example of Theory Y in action. This is how he described von Braun's concept of "automatic responsibility":

> In practice, it meant . . . that an electrical engineer working for the Astrionics Lab, assumed automatic responsibility for any problem he perceived to fall within his area of competence, regardless of whether or not the task had been assigned to his lab. He was expected to stay with the problem until it was solved. . . . If the person who perceived a problem lacked the technical ability to see it through to its conclusion, he or she then assumed the responsibility for communicating his or her perceptions of the problem up the line so that top management, thus alerted, could direct the appropriate specialists to it (pp. 66–67).

Tompkins went on to point out that the notion of automatic responsibility is consistent with McGregor's Theory Y. He argued that although some workers may not be eager to seek out responsibility, too many organizations are designed as if no one is. Tompkins contended that the experience at the Marshall Center indicates that "large numbers of people will seek and accept responsibility for organizational problems" (Tompkins, p. 68).

Further support for human resources theories is reflected in the results of a study contrasting successful with unsuccessful corporate executives (McCall & Lombardo, 1983). Scholars at the Center for Creative Leadership identified approximately twenty executives who had risen to the top of their firms and matched them with a similar group who had failed to reach their career aspirations. In the early stages of their careers, both groups had entered their respective organizations with equal promise. There were no noticeable differences in their preparation, expertise, education, and so forth. Over time, however, the researchers found that the second group's careers had become "derailed" by a number of inadequacies: They were insensitive to others; appeared cold, aloof, and arrogant; betrayed others' trust; appeared overly ambitious; and were unable to delegate to others or to build a team. In contrast, the successful leaders had used their power to empower others and to accomplish exceptional organizational objectives. As they used their influence in positive, empowering ways, they seemed to gain even more organizational authority—hence, their upward mobility.

Some theorists have claimed that Theory Y management works best with certain kinds of workers, such as white-collar professionals, or those who in other ways find their work naturally fulfilling. McGregor, however, provided examples from his own research and consulting experiences of blue-collar workers in industrial settings who were empowered through Theory Y management. More recently, Richard Preston's (1991) book, *American Steel*, recounted the success story of Nucor, the seventh-largest steel manufacturer in the United States. Once near bankruptcy, it eventually flourished under the leadership of CEO F. Kenneth Iverson. In keeping with a Theory Y approach, Nucor's workers are organized into teams in which everyone is expected to jump in immediately to help fix any equipment that breaks down (once again, embracing the concept of automatic responsibility). One of the key elements of Iverson's leadership philosophy is encouraging participation, getting workers to offer their ideas and suggestions. With the hierarchy severely reduced, Iverson encourages peer management and self-management. Absenteeism is so low that Nucor stopped keeping figures on it. Nucor is an intriguing illustration because it shows that the Theory Y approach can be effective thirty years after McGregor first discussed it, and, equally important, that it can work in a decidedly blue-collar organizational environment.

McGregor's theory has not gone unchallenged. Some critics have argued that Theory Y demands too much of managers who cannot practice it without first embracing its underlying assumptions (and, in many cases, radically altering their beliefs). Rather than telling managers how to behave, McGregor seemed to suggest that once they develop and sustain the correct beliefs about their fellow workers, they will "naturally" come to act in empowering ways. In his later book, however, and in the face of criticism, McGregor (1967) backpedaled considerably, saying that Theory X and Theory Y offer two contrasting sets of assumptions about workers, either of which might be appropriate, depending upon the situation. Another potential problem with Theory Y is its underlying notion of integration, which assumes that individuals should be able to best meet their own needs by directing their energies toward organizational goals. Yet many workers are alienated from their jobs, and even people who enjoy their work may still feel that a great part of their self-fulfillment comes from their off-the-job lives. Finally, there is no doubt that McGregor polarized management theory, depicting an "either-or" choice, with no middle ground.

Likert

Rensis Likert was another major contributor to the human resources school of thought. Likert's extensive research program at the University of Michigan's Institute for Social Research led to several major publications (1961; 1967) in which he proposed a range of management alternatives. Likert described four different "systems" of management. As you can see in Figure 3.2, the two extremes of his categorization coincide with McGregor's Theories X and Y. Likert, however, identified considerable middle ground.

Based on his research findings, Likert identified the following four management "systems":

System 1. As with Theory X and scientific management, managers who subscribe to this approach neither trust nor have confidence in their employees. Subordinates respond by being uncommunicative with their supervisors. The organizational climate is characterized by fear, threat, punishment, and occasional rewards. Communication is mostly

FIGURE 3.2

A Comparison of Likert's and McGregor's Theories of Management

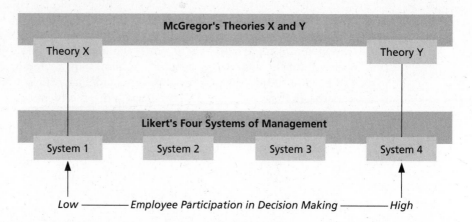

Likert offers a continuum of management styles while McGregor's theory is polarized.

downward, with upward communication limited and frequently inaccurate. Decisions are made at the top, and the emphasis is upon controlling and directing subordinates.

System 2. This approach to management retains most of the power and control at the top of the organization. However, some attempt is made to share small decisions with those lower in the hierarchy. Interaction between managers and employees is more frequent than in a system 1 organization, but the emphasis remains on downward communication, with managers extending a pretense of trust. Upward communication continues to focus on what the boss wants to hear, so negative information is suppressed. The relationship between manager and worker might be compared to that of master and servant. The manager is more benevolent than in the strictly authoritarian system 1, but the communication system remains quite restricted.

System 3. This approach might be characterized as consultative. Managers have substantial (but not complete) trust in their employees. Broad policy decisions are made at the top, but more specific decisions are made throughout the organization. Superiors and subordinates interact more frequently than in the other two systems, and both downward and upward communication are relatively open and accurate. Managers express an interest in hearing subordinates' opinions, good or bad, but subordinates approach their supervisors with some measure of caution, perhaps even suspicion. The bottom line is still clearly focused on the organization's best interests. Interestingly, Likert reported that many managers who work under this system believe themselves to be more progressive and participative than they really are.

System 4. Likert's last system directly parallels McGregor's Theory Y. Devoted to a human resources philosophy of leadership, a system 4 manager trusts subordinates implicitly and holds high expectations for their work ethic and sense of responsibility. Decision making is widely shared, even when significant matters are being addressed. The communication climate is quite interactive, with communication flowing freely and openly in all directions. Morale and productivity tend to be high. When organizational problems arise, managers and subordinates approach them collaboratively.

Likert's Notion of Participative Decision Making   At the heart of Likert's system 4 is the notion of **participative decision making**. Even though human relations and other theorists had earlier acknowledged the potential value of participative and democratic approaches to management, it was Likert who articulated the specific conditions under which genuine participative decision making could be said to occur. In particular, *Likert argued that those individuals who were most affected by a decision (that is, those who had to implement it) should be the ones to make it.* Anything less could not be viewed as participative management. Since most crucial organizational decisions involve many employees in the implementation process, this view of shared decision making called for widespread involvement by many, many workers who would in other circumstances be ignored.

Likert conducted his research in a wide variety of organizational settings. He reported that system 4 organizations had the highest level of productivity and system 1 the lowest. He also noted that many managers claimed to favor a system 4 approach and that the most successful managers tried to create a supportive climate within their organizations. However, Likert also reported that regardless of their personal preferences, the vast majority of these managers indicated that they were actually working in a less supportive organizational climate, often a system 1. Likert's studies focused largely on middle managers and lower-level supervisors. He viewed these managers as **linchpins** between executives and workers. According to Likert, the manager's job was to promote participative management by channeling worker messages up the hierarchy and executive messages down the hierarchy. In a sense, Likert viewed the manager as a communicative conduit for including workers in organizational activities. Obviously, with this kind of system, much depends on the goodwill of those conveying the messages up and down the hierarchy. If they are trusted and trustworthy, then the participative process might move smoothly. Under less ideal circumstances, however, information might be filtered, distorted, or reluctantly offered.

Some critics have argued that Likert's notion of participative decision making remains highly ambiguous, since participation can occur at many different levels and can be defined in many different ways. However, Greiner's (1973) survey of over three hundred managers (see Table 3.1) revealed a striking consensus concerning the key behavioral characteristics of the participative manager.

As a human resources theorist, Likert made significant progress in operationalizing McGregor's concept of Theory Y. Whereas McGregor focused

TABLE 3.1

A Profile of Likert's Participative Manager

- Gives subordinates a share in decision making
- Keeps subordinates informed of the true situation, good or bad, in all circumstances
- Remains aware of the state of the organization's morale and does everything possible to keep it high
- Is easily approachable
- Counsels, trains, and develops subordinates
- Communicates effectively with subordinates
- Shows thoughtfulness and consideration of others
- Is willing to make changes in the way things are done
- Is willing to support subordinates, even when they make mistakes
- Expresses appreciation when subordinates do a good job

Managers argue that these behaviors define the notion of participative management

largely on managers' *attitudes* toward workers, Likert identified specific behaviors (including *communication behaviors*) that should be part of the participative leader's daily conduct. He offered a lofty definition of participative decision making in which the system 4 participative manager must do more than possess good intentions; he or she must *behave* in empowering ways. Likert portrayed an organizational culture, much like 3M's (see Case 1 in Chapter 2), in which leaders are approachable, communication flows freely, and employees are encouraged to take risks and allowed to make mistakes. Like McGregor, Likert viewed people at all levels of the organization as potentially valuable resources, and he sought to convince managers to create participative climates in which that human potential might be realized.

Hersey and Blanchard

Other management theorists who grappled with empowering approaches to leadership were Paul Hersey and Kenneth Blanchard (1969; 1977). They based their theory on two fundamental elements of leadership: managing work and managing people. These theorists affirmed the need for a dynamic approach to leadership in which the manager's effectiveness is determined by her or his ability to assess accurately the needs and abilities of employees and subsequently to choose the most fitting leadership strategy or style. According to this view, there is no one "best" way to lead. Everything depends on the situation, and especially on the needs and skills of those being managed.

In one of their major works, *Management of Organizational Behavior: Utilizing Human Resources* (1977), Hersey and Blanchard pointed out that the manager's first responsibility is to assess his or her subordinate's *maturity*, which is defined as "the willingness and ability of a person to take responsibility for directing his or her own behavior" (p. 4). According to Hersey and Blanchard, there are two dimensions to maturity in any organizational environment: job maturity and psychological maturity. **Psychological maturity** is the employee's willingness or motivation to do something constructive, the belief that responsibility is important, and the confidence to complete tasks without extensive encouragement. In contrast, **job maturity** is the ability or competence to carry out a task—the knowledge, experience, and skill needed to carry out work without the direction of others (Hersey, Blanchard, & Hambleton, 1977). Thus, the worker's psychological maturity has to do with attitude and motivation, while job maturity focuses on job-related know-how and experience.

Hersey and Blanchard recognized that many important situational variables exist in any organizational environment, ranging from time constraints to task complexity. They remained convinced, however, that the single most powerful and important of these is *the behavior of the manager in relation to his or her individual employees.* Thus, as did other human resources theorists, Hersey and Blanchard highlighted the importance of interpersonal relations, with their focus on the superior-subordinate relationship. Based on their research, they identified four strikingly different styles of management, any one of which might be appropriate, depending upon the maturity level of the employees.

In deriving the four leadership styles, they began by arguing that there are two basic dimensions of leadership behavior, task and relationship. They defined *task behavior* as the extent to which leaders are likely to organize and define the roles of others, to explain what activities are to be undertaken as well as the procedures for undertaking them, and to establish well-defined patterns of organization and channels of communication. In contrast, they referred to *relationship behavior* as the extent to which leaders are likely to maintain personal relationships with those they supervise by opening up communication channels, providing socioemotional support, and engaging in facilitating behaviors (Hersey & Blanchard, 1977). Based on these definitions, they offered the following scheme of leadership styles, with communication taking on greater or lesser importance, depending upon the style chosen (see Figure 3.3):

1. **High task/low relationship style (telling).** This management style is characterized by one-way communication in which the manager defines roles and tells subordinates how to accomplish various tasks. According to Hersey and Blanchard, this style is most appropriate for employees who are low in both job and psychological maturity. The manager's strategy is to focus first on developing the employee's ability actually to perform the job. A middle-aged secretary who lacks computer experience and skills in an office in which technology is assuming an increasing role is likely to be psychologically unmotivated as well. However, if she is offered structure,

Hersey and Blanchard's Life Cycle Theory of Management

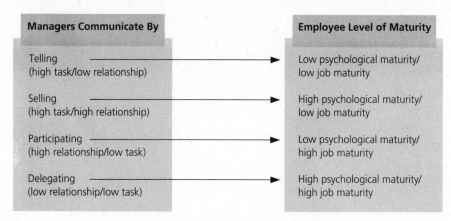

Managers Communicate By	Employee Level of Maturity
Telling (high task/low relationship)	Low psychological maturity/ low job maturity
Selling (high task/high relationship)	High psychological maturity/ low job maturity
Participating (high relationship/low task)	Low psychological maturity/ high job maturity
Delegating (low relationship/low task)	High psychological maturity/ high job maturity

According to Hersey and Blanchard, managers ought to display different styles of leadership, depending upon the characteristics/needs of their subordinates.

training, and clearly stated performance expectations, she should develop task competence, which in turn might give her a greater sense of psychological motivation. The strategy underlying this "telling" leadership style is to tackle the job maturity problem first, leaving relationship development until later.

2. **High task/high relationship style (selling).** The leader with a "selling" style remains fairly directive but encourages two-way communication and joint problem solving. Presumably, this approach works best with employees who are low in job maturity and high in psychological maturity; that is, they lack competence but want very much to do well. For instance, new employees may be eager to learn but lack any practical experience or training. Using this leadership style, the manager would provide training, interacting extensively with the subordinates in social as well as job-related settings, and praising them whenever they demonstrated progress in skill development or growth. The manager operates on the assumption that the employees' psychological maturity can be used to nurture their job maturity. This style demands much of the manager, who is providing training, guidance, and structure while functioning as a kind of cheerleader, "selling" subordinates on the importance of organizational goals.

3. **High relationship/low task style (participating).** Characterized by shared decision making, this style asks the manager to serve largely as a supportive facilitator. Employees have the knowledge and ability to complete the task; thus, they need little, if any, job-related direction or supervision. This style is most appropriate for workers who are low in psychological maturity but high in job maturity. For instance, a manager might employ this style with older employees who possess considerable skill and knowledge but have become alienated from others in the organi-

zation. In this situation, the manager's challenge is to find ways to include them in important decision making; help them see new, challenging roles they can play; and attempt to bring them back into the organizational family through supportiveness and understanding.

4. **Low relationship/low task style (delegating).** This leadership style is appropriate in situations in which employees are more or less on their own and are capable of satisfactorily completing their jobs with minimal supervision. Hersey and Blanchard believed that this style is ideally used with employees who are high in both psychological and job maturity. For instance, a group of nuclear physicists engaged in a sophisticated research program scarcely need their department head or the dean to provide guidance or emotional support. They are self-motivated and self-sufficient and likely receive most of their social support from their fellow scientists. An intriguing aspect of this delegating style is that it presents laissez-faire leadership as a viable, potentially effective, leadership option. The critical point, however, is that this style is effective or appropriate only for mature, skilled, self-motivated employees.

Life Cycle Theory of Leadership   As a situational approach to human resources management, Hersey and Blanchard's theory has been called the **life cycle theory of leadership** because it examines manager-subordinate interactions over an extended period and assumes that changes, adjustments, and growth will occur. The eager new recruit probably presents a different management challenge from that presented by the person who has been with the company for fifty years. However, it is important to recognize that Hersey and Blanchard discouraged stereotyping. They pointed out that some employees begin with high levels of job and psychological maturity and remain motivated and competent throughout their professional lives. Even the most mature subordinates, however, may experience challenges to their maturity. For instance, when mature employees are transferred into a new position, they may experience losses in both psychological and job maturity as they grapple with acquiring new skills and assuming new responsibilities. At those moments, the manager's task is to adjust her or his leadership style and to provide the kind of structure and support the employees need, later returning to a less directive style.

Like those of other theorists, Hersey and Blanchard's ideas have been subjected to considerable critical scrutiny. Some critics have argued, for instance, that Hersey and Blanchard accepted the fact that some workers will never achieve high levels of job and psychological maturity and put the burden on the manager to provide highly task-oriented leadership—through directives, close supervision, and continued efforts at training. These critics think that organizations should not be asked to tolerate such workers; nor should managers be burdened with the responsibility of ensuring that they maintain minimally acceptable levels of productivity. Hersey and Blanchard might respond that although motivating some workers may indeed be a constant challenge, the effective manager negotiates appropriate limits, extending support on the understanding that some professional growth must occur eventually. Others have questioned the value of the two leadership styles that downplay the relationship dimension of leading (i.e., telling and delegating). They believe that employees never really "mature" beyond the need for managers who demonstrate a real concern for relationships. Finally, many point out that Hersey and Blanchard's theory demands a great deal of managers. They must learn to assess and monitor employee maturity levels over time and, more important, to provide the particular kind of leadership each subordinate most needs. Is it reasonable to assume that a manager can be so versatile, or indeed equally effective, in moving between highly structured and laissez-faire leadership styles?

In spite of these acknowledged criticisms, Hersey and Blanchard's contributions to modern management thought have been substantial. Especially important are their recognition of employee differences (each worker must be approached as an individual) and their acknowledgment of changes in individual maturity over time. They were perhaps more realistic than others in recognizing that people are not perfect and organizations are less than ideal. Rather than denying the inevitability of individual variability and changes over time, they found it more profitable to identify those leadership styles that, within the constraints of reality, are potentially effective and empowering. In more recent years, these notions have received support from De Vries and Miller (1984) who argued in *The Neurotic Organization: Diagnosing and Revitalizing Unhealthy Companies,* that job satisfaction is significantly related to the stages of life. Thus, a leadership style that worked very well with the novice or the young, upwardly mobile Harvard MBA might be less effective with the same person when middle-aged and suffering from burn-out.

Like other human resources theorists, Hersey and Blanchard are committed to empowerment, but they see the manager's challenge as more complex and demanding than do some of their fellow theorists. They recognize, moreover, that empowerment is not an either/or phenomenon. Rather, the empowering process is dynamic, often subtle and intangible, and sometimes a matter of degree with a particular employee at a particular time. The life cycle theory also accepts the reality that empowerment is a reciprocal process, requiring some employee interest in growth and maturation and some willingness to work with managers toward commonly held values and shared goals.

Herzberg

Another human resources management theorist who demanded a great deal of managers was Frederick Herzberg of the University of Utah. Herzberg was especially interested in the nature of motivation, and based on his own research, he became convinced that most managers of the 1950s and 1960s had a poor understanding of human motivation. Herzberg (1966, 1968) argued that managers frequently attempted to motivate their employees to exert their efforts toward organizational objectives by manipulating the environment, or those factors external to the actual job. Herzberg labeled these external variables **hygiene factors,** maintaining that they derive their potency from the work situation or environment. He identified five sets of hygiene factors, ranging from company policy to working conditions.

Herzberg did not believe that the hygiene factors, taken by themselves, could be used to create a truly motivated work force. Rather, he argued, managers need to devote more attention to the intrinsic nature of the jobs they ask their subordinates to perform. Herzberg identified several intrinsic factors, or **motivators,** derived from the nature of work itself—including a sense of achievement, responsibility, and work itself. In Herzberg's view, effective managers must attend to motivators if they are to have any hope of creating a truly motivated work force. If workers are alienated from their work, he asked, how can they ever be satisfied? A boring, repetitive job—even if performed in a supportive environment and rewarded with a fair wage—remains uninspirational, and hence, demotivating.

From Herzberg's vantage point, hygiene factors certainly have their place in organizational settings. Clearly, working conditions must be comfortable and safe, wages must be fair, and superior-subordinate task and social relations should be positive. However, Herzberg believed that even if such factors are operating at ideal levels within an organization, they can, at most, only prevent employees from becoming dissatisfied or alienated. Herzberg was convinced that the manager's real attention and efforts should be focused on the motivators and how to use them effectively. Like Hersey and Blanchard's theory, Herzberg's ideas call for leaders to think about employee motivation in new and creative ways.

Job Enrichment: The Key to Motivation   At the heart of Herzberg's theory is the conviction that job enrichment is critically related to worker motivation. Although not the first to concern himself with job enrichment, it was Herzberg who first drew an important distinction between vertical and horizontal job loading. In traditional, horizontal approaches to job enrichment, the manager uses techniques like job rotation and job enlargement. Thus, the worker might go from turning screws to tightening bolts to pounding a nail or two. In his classic *Harvard Business Review* (1968) piece, Herzberg described **horizontal job loading** as enlarging the meaninglessness of the job. With his typical tongue-in-cheek style, he provided several examples and their probable effects:

- Challenging the employee by increasing the amount of production expected. If each tightens 10,000 bolts a day, see if each can tighten 20,000 bolts a day. The arithmetic involved shows that multiplying zero by zero still equals zero.
- Adding another meaningless task to the existing one, usually some routine clerical activity. The arithmetic here is adding zero to zero.
- Rotating the assignments of a number of jobs that need to be enriched. This means washing dishes for a while, then washing silverware. The arithmetic is substituting one zero for another.

- Removing the most difficult parts of the assignment in order to free the worker to accomplish more of the less challenging assignments. This traditional industrial engineering approach amounts to subtraction in the hope of accomplishing addition (p. 114).

To replace this type of horizontal loading, Herzberg called for **vertical job loading** and **job enrichment;** giving workers greater responsibility, assigning them more challenging and difficult tasks, including them in problem-solving sessions, and giving them opportunities to move upward and supervise others when appropriate. For instance, the worker who sees a problem with the way a tool is working should be given the opportunity to devise a better tool, or to work with others collaboratively until one is developed. This approach to job enrichment clearly approaches Tompkins's (1993) discussion of automatic responsibility (reviewed earlier in this chapter) and is quite congruent with McGregor's Theory Y and its premise that workers are inherently responsible, talented, and creative.

Extending Herzberg's theory, others have written more specifically about job enrichment. For instance, Hackman, Oldham, Janson, and Purdy (1975) argued that "of all the job-design principles, vertical loading may be the single most crucial . . ." (p. 64). They pointed out that when a job is vertically loaded, responsibilities and controls formerly reserved for managers are added to the employee's job. Here are some of their vertical loading suggestions:

- Return to the job holder greater discretion in setting schedules, deciding on work methods, checking on quality, and advising or helping to train less experienced workers.

- Grant additional authority. The objective is to advance workers from a position of no authority or highly restricted authority to positions of responsibility and perhaps, eventually, near-total authority for their own work.

- Give individual job holders the greatest possible freedom to manage their own time by allowing them to decide when to start and stop work, when to break, and how to assign priorities.

- Encourage workers to troubleshoot and resolve crises, seeking solutions on their own rather than calling immediately for the supervisor.

- Open feedback channels. The point is to make sure that individual workers and/or teams learn whether their performance is improving, deteriorating, or remaining at a constant level. In addition, this feedback should occur directly, as the worker is on the job, rather than only occasionally.

These specific suggestions demonstrate the potential effectiveness of motivators for workers in any organizational setting, including those in which many employees perform jobs that historically have been enrichment-resistant.

In the videotape based on their book *In Search of Excellence,* Peters and Waterman (1982) used the leadership style of Tom Malone, head of North American Tool and Dye to provide an extended illustration of vertical job loading. Malone attributes his success in revitalizing this organization to his unwavering belief in the work ethic and ingenuity of his blue-collar work force. Malone realizes that most of the jobs his workers perform are highly repetitive; moreover, they require tedious attention to detail and excellent co-ordination and concentration. To counter these constraints, Malone challenges the workers to find improved ways of accomplishing their tasks. The person who comes up with the most creative idea of the month is given the "Freezer Award." This title grew from the circumstances that occasioned the first award.

One of the workers, Kelly, was experiencing difficulty getting one of his tools to move into its socket. Because he had to struggle with this problem consistently, his productivity was lagging. Kelly hit upon the idea of putting the tool in the company freezer so that it would contract, decreasing in size just enough to make it slide into the socket more easily. The idea worked. Even with several daily trips to the freezer, Kelly became more productive. He was proud that he had been able to solve this nagging problem and glad to share his solution with others, who in turn were able to do their jobs a little faster. The "Freezer Award" of $50 was presented at a public gathering with much cheering and good fellowship—and it became a tradition.

The North American Tool and Dye example is especially relevant to Herzberg's work, since he was particularly interested in job enrichment in re-lation to blue-collar work. Herzberg was convinced that workers who were doomed to perform dull, meaningless jobs, with little or no hope of achieve-ment, recognition, greater responsibility, or more interesting and important work would suffer from depleted morale. While "carrot and stick" supervision might make them acceptably productive at some minimal level, their prospects for a satisfying work life were far from encouraging, and maintaining their productivity would always be a struggle. Like most of his contemporaries, Herzberg never used the word "empowerment," but it is clear that he sought an empowering organizational environment for the U.S. work force. He was concerned about worker alienation. Although he often cast his arguments in terms of the manager's interest in morale as related to enhanced productivity, he appeared equally interested in discovering ways to make organizational life more fulfilling for the average man and woman. One way of enhancing jobs is through the use of teams that manage themselves.

Self-Managing Teams

The concept of **self-managing teams** is a logical outgrowth of human re-sources management. Organizations using teams, or "superteams," as they are sometimes called (Dumaine, 1990), send powerful messages about trusting and empowering workers. Responsibilities undertaken by self-managed teams involve such traditional "management" functions as preparing an annual budget, timekeeping, recording quality control statistics, monitoring inven-tory, assigning jobs within groups, training other team members, adjusting production schedules, setting team goals, resolving internal conflicts, and evaluating team performance (Sims & Dean, 1985).

Leadership within self-managed teams usually emerges informally. Once company management has trained team members in basic problem-solving and group dynamics skills and defined the scope of the team's responsibility, the team is free to develop its own procedures and relationships. Team members most skilled in group communication processes and techniques and/or who possess a more sophisticated grasp of the team's tasks are most likely to emerge as informal leaders.

Several modern writers have discussed the significance of teams. For instance, in his widely acclaimed book *Theory Z* (1981), William Ouchi described the predominance of work teams throughout Japanese industry and argued that the teamwork approach to productivity is one of the reasons the Japanese have experienced such success over the past few decades. Ouchi writes that the "Type Z company is characterized by many cohesive and semi-autonomous work groups even though a Z company seldom undertakes any explicit attempts at teambuilding" (p. 207). Taking a slightly different approach, Edward Lawler argued in *High-Involvement Management* (1986) that entire organizations should act as teams, with every level participating to some degree in significant problem solving and decision making. This process, he claimed, entails moving knowledge, power, information, and rewards to lower levels of the organizational hierarchy. Lawler pointed out that teamwork "changes the very nature of what work is and means to everyone who works in an organization. Because it profoundly affects the jobs of everyone, it can impact the effectiveness of all work organizations" (p. 3).

Other scholars have predicted that self-managing teams will be used increasingly as organizations move toward the twenty-first century. In "The Coming of the New Organization," for instance, consultant Peter Drucker (1988) predicted:

> In the information-based organization, the knowledge will be primarily at the bottom, in the minds of the specialists who do different work and direct themselves. . . . A good deal of work will be done differently. . . . Traditional departments will serve as guardians of standards, as centers for training and the assignment of specialists; they won't be where the work gets done. That will happen largely in task-focused teams. . . . The need for a task force [team], its assignment, its composition, and its leadership will have to be decided case by case. . . . One thing is clear, though: it will require greater self-discipline and even greater emphasis on individual responsibility for relationships and for communications (p. 47).

Drucker went on to argue that self-managing teams are already quite prominent in certain industries, especially those involving research. He noted that in pharmaceuticals, telecommunications, and even paper making, the traditional research sequence (i.e., moving from research to development to manufacturing to marketing) is being replaced by *synchrony*—with specialists from each of these functions working together in teams from the beginning of a research project to the product's establishment in the marketplace.

Of course, as Lawler noted, self-managing teams are not appropriate in every organizational context. Teamwork seems especially effective when a task entails a high level of interdependency among three or more people (Dumaine, 1990). For instance, complex manufacturing processes common in the automobile, chemical, paper, and high-technology industries can benefit from teams, as can complicated service jobs in insurance, banking, and telecommunications. In most cases, simple assembly-line activities are less amenable to teamwork. Generally, the more complex the task, the better suited it is to teams. Presumably, when the right kind of task is matched with the team approach, the result will be greater problem-solving speed and effectiveness. Dumaine (1990) contrasted team efforts with the traditional approach to problem solving in a hierarchical organization: "A person with a problem in one function might have to shoot it up two or three layers by memo to a vice president who tosses it laterally to a vice president of another function who then kicks it down to the person in his area who knows the answer. Then it's back up and down the ladder again" (p. 54).

Aside from potential mismatches between task and team, some companies using teams run into another problem. With fewer middle-management positions available, the opportunities for advancement are diminished. The rewards of teamwork come instead in the form of enhanced responsibility, rewarding work, and challenge. Finally, managers must recognize that organizing teams is a long, difficult process. Everyone involved must learn to think differently about themselves and about their approach to their work and to one another. Advocates, however, are convinced that the results are worth the time and effort invested.

Practical Illustrations of the Teamwork Approach

Many U.S. organizations have already instituted various team approaches to managing and communicating. Apple Computer, for example, has long been famous for teamwork. Product innovations come from teams that work together on projects for which they feel deep commitment and enthusiasm. The Macintosh was originally developed by a team of computer specialists, engineers, and design artists. These innovators were allowed to interview and hire new team members, and every team member's name was inscribed on the inside of each new Mac—a sign of pride and commitment to excellence.

Another example of an organization sold on the value of teamwork is the Thomson Consumer Electronics plant in Bloomington, Indiana, the world's largest television assembly factory. Thomson has developed almost one thousand teams throughout its worldwide system. In the Bloomington plant, there are eighty-nine teams in the Quality Leadership Process (QLP) program. QLP allows Thomson employees to own and control the quality of their work;

anticipate and prevent problems (rather than reacting to them); know the customers and meet their expectations; and apply skills, knowledge, and experience to initiate change. Each QLP team is a multifunctional group of five employees who represent different areas of operation. Over a period of sixteen weeks, each team learns problem-solving and statistical control methods. Then the teams select a project to tackle. One team, "The Wild Five," decided to work on a picture tube problem involving improperly seated anodes. Team members found that defective washers were coming from a particular plant. They also found that certain "anode clips" in the picture tube were being damaged. The team found out how to address the washer problem and later determined how the anode clips were being deformed. They even developed a new tool, which is now used throughout the plant. This team consisted of two production operators, a quality control technician, a material groups manager, and a production trouble-shooter (Werth, 1990).

Many other companies have become more team-oriented. For example, in a General Mills cereal plant in Lodi, California, teams schedule, operate, and maintain machinery so effectively that no managers are present on the night shift. Similarly, after organizing its home office operations into teams, Aetna Life & Casualty reduced the ratio of middle managers to workers from 1:7 to 1:30, while at the same time improving customer service. During their weekly meeting, a team of Federal Express clerks identified (and eventually solved) a billing problem that had been costing the company $2.1 million a year. And at 3M, cross-functional teams tripled the number of new products produced by one division (Dumaine, 1990). Xerox CEO Paul Allaire commented, "We believe in the power of teamwork; 75 percent of all Xerox employees are actively involved in quality-improvement or problem-solving projects" (Bowles, 1990).

In some cases, teamwork can lead to enhanced labor-management relations. At the Chrysler plant in New Castle, Indiana, for instance, the president of the UAW Local 371 and a key member of the management team spend much time together. The union leader is invited to all management meetings and frequently attends. According to Zachary, the union chief, "It's been a culture change on both sides. . . . It's not union; it's not management—it's us" (Brooks, 1991). As a dramatic illustration of how effective the alliance has become, manager Ramsey points to a growing mutual respect—and to the fact that the union has actually requested *more* supervisors! The virtues of team-oriented approaches to organizing have been heralded since the human relations movement. However, more than managers and theorists of the past, contemporary teamwork advocates recognize the potential value of self-managing teams as vehicles of empowerment.

One of the keys to team building is having all group members share the same status while working on each special project. Thus, in many teams no one is appointed leader. Each person is expected to contribute to the team in diverse ways, and each has the opportunity to be equally influential within it. As self-managing teams become more prominent in U.S. business and industry, skills in providing informal leadership and working with others collaboratively to solve problems will assume even greater importance. We will address these issues in greater detail in subsequent chapters on group communication and conflict management.

New Motivational Tools

When organizations move in the direction of self-managing teams, those holding official managerial positions must focus, perhaps even more imaginatively, on the perennial question of motivation. Sociologist Rosabeth Moss Kanter (1989) tackled this question directly in her article "The New Managerial Work." Kanter discussed five "new" motivational tools, all of which are quite consistent with Herzberg's original discussion of motivators:

1. **Mission.** Help people believe in the importance of their work. Leaders must inspire others with the power and excitement of their vision, giving them a sense of purpose and pride in their work.

2. **Agenda Control.** Allow employees to take charge of their own professional lives. Leaders might provide release time for subordinates to work on pet projects, emphasize results instead of procedures, and delegate both work and the right to decide how to do it.

3. **Share of Value Creation.** Give teams a piece of the action through entrepreneurial incentives. For instance, bonuses might be given for performing excellent work that is central to the values and mission of the organization. As Kanter noted, "everyone can share the kinds of rewards that are abundant and free—awards and recognition" (p. 91).

4. **Learning.** Give subordinates the chance to learn new skills or apply them in new arenas. Continuous learning should be encouraged, especially with advances in technology. Access to training, mentors, and challenging projects may be as important as pay and benefits.

5. **Reputation.** Create conditions to motivate employees through the pride that comes with public acknowledgment of work well done. Managers can enhance their reputations by creating stars, by providing abundant public recognition and visible awards, by crediting the authors of innovation, by publicizing people outside their own departments, and by plugging people into organizational and professional networks.

Kanter's vision of self-managing teams clearly acknowledges the need for excellent leadership to inspire teams to do their best. She concluded that the new managerial work "consists of looking outside a defined area of responsibility to sense opportunities and of forming project teams drawn from any relevant sphere to address them" (p. 92).

Despite the often expressed enthusiasm for self-managing teams, and the numerous examples of their successes, their growth in the United States has been somewhat slow. Realizing the benefits of self-managed teams requires a great deal of trust between top management and employees—trust that may take years to build (and only a few moments to undo). In addition, middle managers may feel threatened by the concept, believing it will reduce their power and influence. Thus, they may openly or covertly oppose the process. In some instances middle managers simply find themselves out of work. Drucker (1988) put it succinctly, if somewhat harshly, when he wrote that ". . . both the numbers of management levels and the number of managers can be sharply cut. The reason is straightforward: it turns out that whole layers of management neither make decisions nor lead. Instead, their main, if not their only, function is to serve as 'relays'—human boosters for the faint, unfocused signals that pass for communication in the traditional organization" (p. 46). Former chair of Citicorp and Citibank, Walter B. Wriston (1990), agreed with Drucker:

> In the well-run corporations, in the corporations that will survive and create the future, layers of management are disappearing. These managers would ask the people working under them what they were doing; then they would tell the people working above them what they said. They were transmission lines. But they spun not, neither did they weave; nor did they produce anything of added value. These are the layers that are coming out (p. 79).

For those in middle management, such remarks are, at best, sobering. Finally, even if everyone concurs that the organization should move in the direction of self-managing teams, implementing the process takes a long time (eighteen months to two years is common), and training employees in self-management skills can be time-consuming and expensive. Focus On highlights several misconceptions about self-managing teams that should be avoided. In spite of potential problems, the benefits of self-management have been sufficiently dramatic, and the need to operate more efficiently so pressing, that many organizations are seriously considering and even committing to this progressive approach to human resources management.

Japanese Management

Human resources management is arguably a U.S. tradition, at least at the level of theory and research. Some believe, however, that the Japanese have surpassed many U.S. organizations in putting human resources principles into practice. Beginning in the 1970s and 1980s, many managers in the United States invested considerable time and money studying Japanese approaches to management because of the fine quality of Japanese products and the general productivity of their organizations. Comparing U.S. with Japanese management, Graham (1993) argued that the Japanese provide a better model. As he pointed out, "the cultural orientation is quite a bit different [in Japan]. They emphasize communication skills, participation skills, group decision making, and personal kinds of relationships" (p. B10). Clearly, significant differences

FOCUS ON **Misconceptions About Self-Managed Teams**

1. **Self-managed teams do not need leaders.** While such teams may not have a formal supervisor, leadership functions still must be performed by someone within the group, such as an emergent leader or elected member.

2. **Leaders lose power in the transition to teams.** While decision making within teams should be done participatively, group leaders should apply their power outward and use it to break down barriers in the organization that prevent the team from being effective.

3. **Newly formed teams are automatically self-directing.** Team development is evolutionary, and team members initially may attempt to avoid responsibility and accountability until they have learned to share leadership.

4. **All employees are waiting for opportunities to participate.** Not everyone wants to participate in making decisions; as many as 25 percent to 30 percent of all workers simply want to do their tasks and go home.

5. **Putting employees into groups automatically creates teamwork.** Groups must go through developmental processes and learn to function as a team; they do not automatically perform as teams.

SOURCE: Causron, 1993.

exist between Japanese and U.S. cultures; nevertheless, a number of Japanese management practices appear quite consistent with principles of human resources management.

Basic Principles of Japanese Management

Echoing the views of Likert, for instance, the Japanese embrace the notion of **bottom-up decision making,** with the conviction that change and initiative within an organization should come from those closest to the problem. Thus, as Ouchi (1981) pointed out, when an important decision needs to be made, every employee who will feel its impact becomes involved in making it. For instance, if a new plant is to be built, perhaps as many as sixty to eighty employees will participate in making the decision. Through team interaction, with representatives moving between and among groups, up and down the organization, the level of employee involvement is very high. This bottom-up process is quite time-consuming.

The Japanese justify the time spent by contending that a solution reached through this kind of *consensus-building process* is likely to enjoy widespread support. More important, they argue, worker understanding and support may supersede the absolute content of the decision because many competing alternatives undoubtedly possess both strengths and weaknesses. If a technically superior decision is made, but it lacks the support of those who must implement it, its implementation is unlikely to be successful. Finally, they believe that bottom-up decision making is intrinsically superior to other methods of reaching decisions, since it is those closest to the organization's problems who are best able to understand them. Moreover, lower-level employees offer a unique perspective on the problem, decision, or opportunity that managers can ill afford to ignore.

The **quality control circle** began in Japan in the early 1960s and is a logical extension of the Japanese emphasis on bottom-up decision making. In these groups individuals assemble voluntarily and share some area of responsibility. Generally, they meet on a weekly basis to discuss, analyze, and propose solutions to problems of quality that affect the area for which they are responsible. Quality control circles are taught group discussion skills, quality strategies, and measurement and problem-analysis techniques. They are further encouraged to draw on the resources of the company's personnel to help them solve their problems. In short, as Hirokawa (1981) noted, "quality control circles represent carefully trained problem-solving work groups who are given the responsibility of solving their own problems and generating their own evaluation procedures" (p. 37).

The Japanese philosophy of leadership is also consistent with human resources management. The Japanese view *top management as facilitators.* Japanese executives know that theirs is a limited view of the organization. Others may see problems differently and may, in fact, perceive problems that upper management cannot see or imagine. Thus, anyone in the organization who introduces a proposal for change or action, regardless of department or level, is treated with great respect. Managers neither accept nor reject ideas when they are first introduced. Instead, they tactfully and politely ask questions, make subtle suggestions, and provide encouragement. In this way, the subordinate is encouraged to keep thinking and communicating with those above. The manager's job is to support initiative and assist subordinates in shaping their proposed solutions and articulating their ideas more clearly. Since most subordinates who bring their ideas to top Japanese executives are themselves *middle managers,* they are *cast in the primary role of shaper of solutions.* Junior managers are initiators who perceive problems and formulate tentative solutions in coordination with others rather than functional specialists who carry out their boss's directives. As noted above, because so much emphasis is placed on coordination and integration, solutions to problems evolve more slowly, but they are known and understood by all those who have been a part of the solution generation process. Horizontal communication is stressed as essential to the coordination of the problem-solving process.

The Japanese are also known for their *concern for their employees' total well-being.* While this principle is also consistent with human resources thinking, it manifests itself in ways that are unique to the Japanese culture. For instance, when young Japanese employees are hired by a major company, they are inducted into the organization with a formal ceremony as soon as their training is completed. These ceremonies are huge events, often held in the company's auditorium. Important representatives of the company are involved, including the training director and the president. The trainees' families are also present, and the induction is rich with tradition, ritual, and exchanges of commitments, similar to a wedding ceremony. The president, for instance, makes a formal presentation in which he welcomes the new members into the organizational family and challenges them to live up to the company's high hopes and expectations. He also addresses the parents and humbly accepts their challenge to provide honest work for their children, while recognizing the organization's obligation to nurture their complete physical, intellectual, and moral development (Ouchi, 1981).

The bonding illustrated in the Japanese induction ceremony has traditionally led to other kinds of commitments. Historically, Japanese organizations have offered their workers housing, extensive recreational facilities, and even lifetime employment. The notion of *lifetime employment* is often cited as the key to the Japanese worker's commitment to the organization (Pascale, 1978). However, it is by no means universal; approximately 35 percent of Japan's work force benefits from that kind of long-term commitment. Those who favor the notion of lifetime employment believe that it offers the perfect combination of job security for the employee and a devoted work force for the organization.

Another feature of Japanese management that stands in considerable contrast to the U.S. system is its *slow evaluation and promotion process*. Those employees who enter the organization at the same time receive exactly the same pay increment and exactly the same promotions as everyone else. Only after ten years is anyone formally evaluated, and not until then will one person receive a larger promotion than another. By U.S. standards this process is perceived as excessively slow. The Japanese argue, however, that the slowness of the process discourages short-term game playing. It is a system where short-term successes are irrelevant. What counts is long-term growth and productivity, as well as the respect of one's peers. Japanese workers are strongly encouraged to work cooperatively and to share information and ideas. The open physical layout in many Japanese organizations encourages information sharing, as well as allowing managers to observe the way everyone interacts. Over time, managers can observe whose counsel is sought out and valued and whose is ignored. Thus, peer reactions are considered crucial in the overall evaluation process. As Ouchi (1981) put it, "It is not external evaluations or rewards that matter in such a setting; it is the intimate, subtle, and complex evaluation by one's peers— people who cannot be fooled—which is paramount" (p. 25).

Also in contrast to most U.S. organizations, the Japanese have fashioned *nonspecialized career paths*. New bank employees, for example, spend their first year in management training before moving on to work with tellers and study commercial banking, retail lending, and personnel. They work for a time in all of these divisions over ten years, at the end of which they receive their first big promotion; but they continue to move around across functional divisions of the organization. This lateral movement provides a systems view of the organization as employees observe how the parts of the organization affect the whole. It also provides a powerful incentive for cooperation, since those from other divisions who request information or assistance this month may well be next year's colleagues. Moreover, rather than developing commitments to their specialty, the Japanese develop a sustained commitment to the organization as a whole. Social anthropologists have pointed out that belonging to an organization is far more important in Japan than affiliation across a horizontally structured professional field. Any member of an organization, even a professional, identifies more with the company than with his or her profession. A Sony engineer is a Sony employee first and last. As Yang (1984) noted, "In the Japanese company, employees commit themselves emotionally to the well-being of the organization, which in turn looks after their welfare" (p. 174).

Finally, the Japanese emphasize the *sharing of collective values*. Many of the principles of Japanese management grow directly from widely shared values rather than from management strategies. For instance, consensus as a way of decision making is based in part on the Japanese sense of responsibility to colleagues and to the organization. Such collective values contribute to an environment in which teamwork is natural. Ouchi (1981) told the story of a U.S. company in Japan whose managers placed suggestion boxes around the plant. Monetary rewards were to go to the individual who came up with any idea that turned a profit. After six months no one had made a single suggestion. The puzzled managers interviewed several employees trying to discover the reasons for this lack of responsiveness. One worker put it compellingly: "No one can come up with a work improvement idea alone. We work together, and any idea that one of us may have is actually developed by watching others and talking to others. If one of us was singled out for being responsible for such an idea, it would embarrass us all" (p. 54). The managers immediately converted the idea to a group bonus system and were overwhelmed by the number of constructive suggestions that were offered!

This desire to work together, to share, to take collective action and responsibility is a reflection of Japanese culture. Some have argued that the common thread in Japanese life is intimacy, or close social relations. Interestingly, over forty years ago the distinguished sociologist George Homans (1950) argued that intimacy is an essential ingredient in any healthy society. He noted that people who lose their sense of communal responsibility soon lose their general sense of community. It is through intimacy that caring, support, and disciplined unselfishness are often achieved. These qualities have surely served the Japanese well in many of their organizational endeavors.

Potential Problems with the Japanese Approach

Like any approach to management, the Japanese system is far from perfect. For instance, as noted earlier, lifetime employment does not extend to the entire work force but only to a fairly elite few: college-educated males. In Japan, women work mostly part-time or in smaller, less prestigious organizations. In addition, for those who have lifetime employment, mobility between companies is limited. Since the commitment made is intended to endure, breaking it (hence divorcing the organization) is difficult and often perceived as a disgrace, making moves to comparable jobs virtually impossible. In spite of its disadvantages, lifetime employment is expected to endure. Sociologists argue that it allows corporations to assume the paternal function so important in Japanese society. It works best in societies where the "subordination of an individual's private life to the larger group is necessary and honorable" (Yang, 1984, p. 180).

Other concerns about Japanese management center on the extent to which bottom-up decision making constitutes genuine consensus building. The *ringi process* (whereby a document is circulated among managers who have the opportunity to register their agreement by affixing their seals to it) may involve more ritual than substance. The Japanese value cooperation and harmony; thus, some have argued that even though proposals are likely to originate with lower-level managers, these managers are inclined to propose what they believe to be the wishes of their superiors. With the CEO's wishes widely known, few who embrace harmony as a value are likely to oppose ideas that they know are favored at the top. Americans who examine superior-subordinate interaction among the Japanese may mistake the absence of directives and orders for the absence of executive control. Ballon (1969) suggests that the emphasis on harmony (known as the *wa* spirit) acts as a self-regulating mechanism for controlling the actions of organizational members, as well as bringing about coordination and integration of effort without the formal sanctions of a supervisor. As noted earlier, the Japanese are far more subtle in their communication behavior than their U.S. counterparts, relying heavily on nonverbal communication and linguistic subtleties to make their preferences known. For instance, the Japanese word for *yes* (*hai*) does not necessarily indicate agreement with what has been said. Thus, the Japanese executive who responds with "hai" to someone's proposal is in no sense endorsing it; rather, he is merely indicating that he understood what was said (Takenoya, 1989). Thus, Japanese leaders often express their views and exert influence in ways that are far from obvious from a U.S. perspective.

The body of research on Japanese organizations continues to grow. Recent studies suggest that one cannot generalize about Japanese workers; males and females, young and old, differ in their decision-making styles and management preference. One study reported, for instance, that Japanese workers were far more passive than commonly thought, preferring to be persuaded of the value of a decision by their supervisor rather than making the decision themselves (Stewart, Gudykunsz, Ting-Tomey, & Nishida, 1986). However, another study (Hirokawa & Miyahara, 1986) found that Japanese managers place a far greater emphasis on corporate participation and cooperation than do their American counterparts. Thus, a consistent and coherent view of Japanese organizations does not yet exist. Moreover, as younger workers move into the Japanese work force, different needs and values are likely to emerge. As twenty-three-year-old Makoto Ueda, an employee of Toshiba, pointed out, "My father and I both work for the good of our companies, but we have different philosophies." He claimed that his father put the chemical company's needs and desires ahead of his own and his family's. Ueda argued, "But, I think I will help my company improve by improving my own abilities. So I'm approaching my career at Toshiba with my own personal goals in mind" (Thornton, 1991, p. 130).

Like their U.S. counterparts, Japanese organizations will grow and change in response to the different values of newer, younger employees; increasing globalization; an increasingly diverse work force; and advances in technology.

Technology and Empowerment: A Human Resources Management Perspective

Every organization has a culture that incorporates the unique aspects of the overall environment of the organization, including management philosophy and style, organizational mission(s) and priorities, employee policies, and the beliefs valued by the firm. The human resources perspective, especially Hersey and Blanchard's life cycle theory, suggests that managers in the organization tend to reflect the culture of their organization and the styles of executives and other highly ranked leaders. Management "style" refers to communication and leadership characteristics of the manager-to-manager, manager-to-employee, and employee-to-employee relations.

Hershey and Kizzier (1992) noted that management styles range from the highly participative consensus-building approach used by the Japanese to the autocratic style, which allows for little or no employee involvement in decision making and places a heavy reliance on policies and rules (see Table 3.2).

TABLE 3.2

The Impact of Management Style on Employee Satisfaction

Consensus Building	Very high employee participation
Democratic	High employee participation
Coordinative	Moderate employee participation
Authoritarian	Limited employee participation
Autocratic	Very little or no employee participation

SOURCE: Hershey & Kizzier, 1992.

Management styles minimizing employee participation tend to emphasize one-way communication from the bottom up (in the form of status reports) or the top down (in the form of policy statements). When employees communicate upward in the organization, their communication is expected to follow designated lines of command (for example, employee to supervisor, supervisor to manager, manager to director, director to vice president, etc.). This pattern typifies a closed communication channel, represented by the communication patterns of McGregor's Theory X manager and Likert's system 1 manager.

Management Styles and the Use of Technology

Organizational culture and management styles also affect the nature of an organization's adoption and use of technology. In the traditional organization, where the flow of information tends to be vertical, computers and computer networks are usually implemented to support the organization's primary functions, with transaction data coming in from operational units at the lowest level of the organizational pyramid. These data document production, financial and accounting, sales and marketing, and/or human resource day-to-day activities. Much of this information is massaged by management information systems and filtered upward so that middle-level managers receive summary or exception reports to help them assess whether they are meeting short-term, or tactical, performance goals. Tactical systems help middle managers supervise and coordinate the day-to-day activities of the firm. This historical information, plus intelligence gleaned from the organization's environment, can then be used to create decision support systems for the senior-level managers who establish long-range organizational strategy. Strategy issues may involve decisions about whether to create new product lines, invest in new businesses, merge with another organization, move to a new location, and so on. Strategic decisions inevitably result in the downward communication of new policies and goals for those at the middle-management and operational levels of the organization.

In the traditional hierarchical organization, management tends to emphasize the use of technology to maximize a firm's efficiency. Systems development focuses on applications that ensure the efficient and timely collection of transactions. However, these firms often also use technology to disseminate organizational policies and information quickly to their employees.

Videotex, for instance, is a technology that enables firms to distribute information throughout the organization quickly and effectively through one-way (asynchronous) broadcasts of text, graphics, and images. Videotex allows untrained or casual users of technology to receive information from and interact with the firms' information bases through a television receiver and network technology. Managers can use Videotex to deliver training, personnel information, and policies efficiently to their employees (and customers), while ensuring consistency in both the format and content of the presentation. Many corporations also use internal television broadcasts for similar purposes, allowing management to filter and report information selectively throughout the organization and outside the organization, to the press and shareholders as well. Technology thus becomes an effective medium not only for distributing information but also for communicating the values, ideals, and goals of the organization's senior management in a consistent and deliberate manner.

When two-way interpersonal technologies, such as e-mail, are implemented in traditional organizations with less participative management styles, managers typically anticipate increased efficiency, but they may ignore the technology's potential for yielding more profound changes. E-mail allows members of an organization to communicate upward, downward, or even across the organization, regardless of their organizational status or rank. Because of this capability, some managers have subsequently restricted who can send e-mail or have shut down electronic discussion groups altogether (Sproull & Kaiser, 1991).

At the other end of the continuum of management styles are organizational cultures promoting consensus building and democratic styles with more open, less formal, lines of communication. Here management styles are more participatory, placing a greater emphasis on team building and the empowerment of workers. There is less restrictiveness in the breadth and scope of communication channels available. Data and information flow freely, both vertically and horizontally. As in Drucker's "coming organization," management's goal is to empower teams of knowledge specialists. These participatory management styles are compatible with those expressed by McGregor's Theory Y manager and by Likert's system 4 manager.

For example, Nestlé, SA, the Swiss-based multinational food corporation, installed an e-mail system to connect 60,000 employees in eighty countries to facilitate information sharing. When redesigning its information systems department in London, British Petroleum installed extensive electronic information sharing systems to facilitate the implementation of a new team-based organizational structure. Hewlett-Packard relies heavily on information and communications systems such as teleconferencing to enable its widely scattered teams of employees to work together more effectively. And at the University of North Carolina at Greensboro, the dean of the Bryan School of Business and Economics routinely uses e-mail to solicit comments and input from faculty as well as to share new information with them in a timely manner.

Managers can use a number of technologies that support group work, or groupware technologies, to foster employee participation and empowerment. In fact, the whole purpose of groupware is to improve group effectiveness by providing electronic communications that overcome time and distance constraints. Groupware can help managers keep in closer touch with teams of employees and also provide opportunities for groups to manage and coordinate their own affairs.

Typically, groups schedule and hold meetings, collaborate to develop ideas and make decisions, and communicate to share knowledge or information on the work each team member is doing. When groups meet face-to-face, they can now use groupware technologies such as group support systems for brainstorming. To evaluate ideas, they can use electronic keypads for group decision making, or they may use electronic whiteboards to itemize key meeting action items. When group members are geographically dispersed, they can use teleconferencing technology to hold a meeting or technology such as Lotus Notes to share ideas with group members in other locations and time zones. When group members work different hours but share common facilities, they may often use more basic technologies such as simple, nonelectronic message boards to share news and information.

Research indicates that these technologies can facilitate team building (Herschel, Mennecke, & Wynne, 1991). They can also be used to teach empowerment since they help promote better communication and active, participatory decision making (Herschel & Andrews, 1993). Johansen (1992)

Lotus Notes is one of the main reasons that IBM purchased Lotus Development Corp. in 1995. This is one of the most widely used groupware products in the world today, allowing users to share information and documents across geographically dispersed locations. (Lotus Development Corporation)

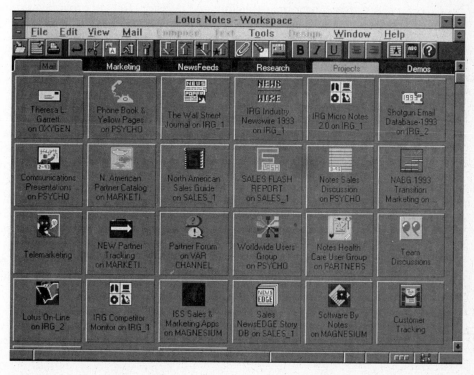

claimed that groupware technologies can be used by organizations to promote and support the basic dynamics and performance of teams. For example, such technologies can help new team members to get to know one another and to build trust. Moreover, Johansen suggested, using groupware can help all group members connect with one another and the larger organization of which they are a part.

Groupware is a means though which managers can have meaningful exchanges with their organization's employees. Indeed, Keen (1985) argued that management's very choices about the acquisition and use of information technology reflect the explicit values of the organization. Companies that resist technology promote a conservative, staid posture, which Keen believed may inevitably risk the economic and organizational health of the firm.

In surveying trends that influence the evolution of technology in the 1990s, Madnick (1991) documented the advances in information technology and the way in which they have provided opportunities for dramatically increased connectivity, enabling new forms of interorganizational relationships and enhanced group productivity. These developments have allowed organizations to change in order to seize the opportunity of globalization and withstand the impact of worldwide competition. Madnick claimed that if corporate culture and management style minimize opportunities for technology-enhanced employee participation, organizations may risk the opportunity to reengineer their thinking and decision-making processes so that they become innovative and responsive to change.

Summarizing Perspective

The approaches to management discussed in this chapter have many similarities. Each emphasizes positive relationships between managers and workers. Each recognizes the potential value of each employee and honors her or his right to seek growth and self-actualization through the organizational experience. Although there are differences among the human resources theorists (e.g., Herzberg is more job-focused, whereas Hersey and Blanchard are more relationship-oriented), all share a balanced concern for the welfare of the organization and the good of the people. All believe that the act of empowerment, though complex and elusive, is crucial for all organizational members, whether they are cast in official roles of leaders or followers. Some believe that empowerment can be realized, in part, through advances in technology.

In the next chapter, we will explore the nature of human relationships and interpersonal communication in a technological age. We shall examine how technology changes group collaboration and information sharing and investigate how technology provides new channels for interpersonal communication and new means for structuring group interaction.

CASES FOR DISCUSSION

CASE 1 *Self-Managing Teams: Hope or Hoax?*

When Pete became head of a major department in a large bank holding company, he thought he had arrived. He was proud of his title and rank, and his department was responsible for determining policy for hundreds of bank branches and those who managed them (viewed by Pete as "super-clerks"). Pete was in charge of hiring his own staff, and he sought the brightest and the best—mostly MBAs from prestigious schools. He offered them excellent salaries and the chance for quick promotions.

Then the world began to fall apart. For the first time in recent memory, the bank lost market position. In response, it decided to emphasize direct customer service at each of its branches. The people Pete considered clerks began to depart from Pete's standard policies and to tailor their services to local market conditions. The branches moved to the team concept, with self-managed teams working together to come up with ideas for improving customer service. As these teams considered their options and went about collecting data, they actually demanded services and responses from Pete's staff, and the results of these requests began to figure into performance reviews of Pete's department. In an attempt to cooperate with the branches, Pete's people began spending more and more time in the field with the branch managers and clerks and their self-managed teams.

To complicate matters further, the bank's strategy included a growing role for technology. Pete felt that because he had no direct control over the information systems department, he should not be held accountable for every facet of product design and implementation. But fully accountable he was. He had to deploy people to learn the new technology and figure out how to work with it. In addition, the bank was asking product departments like Pete's to find ways to link existing products or develop new ones that crossed traditional categories. So Pete's staff soon became involved in their own self-managing teams and were often away working with one of these cross-departmental teams just when he wanted them for an important internal assignment.

Caught between upper management's high expectations and the turbulence and uncertainty of the chaotic environment over which he supposedly presided, Pete felt confused and resentful. His superiors said that what was important was "leading, not managing," but Pete wasn't sure what that meant—especially since he seemed to have lost control over his subordinates' assignments, activities, rewards, and careers. Pete felt as if he had lost both power and status, both of which were very important to him.

Questions for Discussion

1. What are some of the potential problems with self-managing teams revealed in this case?

2. What are the implications of Pete's boss's comment about "leading, not managing"?

3. If you were in Pete's position, what constructive moves might you make to improve the situation, both for yourself and for your subordinates?

SOURCE: Kanter 1989.

CASE 2 *"Empowerment"*

A few years ago, the Joint Commission for the Accreditation of Healthcare Organizations (JCAHO) issued some new guidelines for hospitals and other health care organizations wishing to obtain or maintain accreditation. Since many types of federal funds are provided only to hospitals who have been accredited, hospital administrators were particularly anxious to learn what the new guidelines were and how they should be met.

One of the guidelines concerned quality: Every hospital and health care organization was to devise and implement a process designed to "improve quality," the JCAHO said. How "quality" was to be defined, how "improvement" was to be determined, and what "process" for quality improvement was to be used were left largely up to each hospital, but something had to be implemented.

Many hospitals decided to use some form of total quality management, a process initially devised and implemented by manufacturers years ago. In this process employees are involved in analyzing their own work, determining what factors impede "quality," and devising changes whereby quality can be improved. In short, they are "empowered" to improve the quality of the work they do.

The administration of Farmington Hospital similarly decided to implement a process they termed "QIP" (quality improvement process). Employees would be trained to participate in group problem-solving procedures and put into "QATs," (quality action teams). Those teams would be facilitated by specially trained members of management.

While the process seemed to go well in some areas of the hospital, others experienced some difficulty. One area was the fifth floor, a nursing unit headed by Ruth Robinson, the nurse manager. Peggy Cook, the vice president of Nursing, asked Ruth to come to her office to discuss the situation.

Peggy: Ruth, I hear things aren't going very well with QIP on your floor. What's the problem?

Ruth: The problem is that the nurses don't want to do it.

Peggy: What do you mean? We're asking for their input on how to make things better. Why wouldn't they want to do that?

Ruth: You just don't understand my nurses.

Peggy: What do you mean?

Ruth: Basically, I have two groups of nurses up on fifth: those who have been here for a long time, and those who have come within the past year or two. The ones who have been here a long time think things are fine the way they are. Their patients feel they get good care, the doctors are happy, and the nurses enjoy their work. Nothing needs to be changed. The newer nurses all work part-time. They're here for the money and the benefits. A lot of them have husbands who have been laid off, so they need the income and benefits to support their families. But they just want to come, do their jobs, and go home.

Peggy: And that's why they won't participate in the QATs?

Ruth: Yes. That and the scheduling problem. I don't have enough staff on the fifth floor as it is. When somebody has to leave the floor for a meeting or training session, somebody else has to pick up her patient load, or else things just don't get done until she gets back. Then she has to work doubly hard to catch up. No one wants to leave the floor during work, and no one wants to come in early or stay late.

Peggy: Ruth, you're a manager; your job is to find a way to make this thing work. The hospital is committed to QIP and to involving and empowering employees. So I don't want to hear any excuses. Just do it.

Questions for Discussion

1. What are some reasons this effort to "empower" employees might not be successful?

2. Is it possible that some employees (and managers) do not wish to be "empowered"? If so, what should be done with those individuals?

3. If you were Ruth in this case, what would you do? If you were Peggy, what would you do? Why

4

Human Relationships and Interpersonal Communication

"When you assemble a number of people to have advantage of their joint wisdom, you inevitably assemble with those people all their prejudices, their passions, their errors of opinion, their local interests, and their selfish views. From such an assembly, can perfect production be expected?"
Benjamin Franklin, speech at the Constitutional Convention, September 15, 1787.

The fundamental building block of every organization, regardless of size or structure, is the human relationship. Without good interpersonal relationships, organizations cannot flourish and human potential goes unrealized. Yet in organizational contexts, relationships are complicated by the realities of hierarchy and evaluation, the potential tensions between formal and informal channels, the collective need for cooperation, and the individual drive to succeed through competition.

Interpersonal relationships have at least three dimensions: **dominance,** the extent to which one person has power over or makes decisions that are followed by the other; **affection,** the extent to which each person likes or is attracted to the other; and **involvement,** the degree to which people identify with or interact with each other (Andrews & Baird, 1992; Schutz, 1966). These dimensions are influenced by situational variables, such as the physical environment, formal role prescriptions, and the extent to which individuals use available technologies. In group settings, for instance, relationships are affected by the task assigned to the group and the way in which the group chooses to move toward its stated goal (Bales, 1971).

This chapter is based on the premise that the way human relationships evolve, whether or not they are empowering, is intimately related to the way people interact, or communicate. We begin by advancing a model of effective human interaction, built on principles of supportive communication. Next we turn to a consideration of communication within the formal organizational hierarchy and focus on research that describes superior-subordinate communication. Then, given the increasing organizational emphasis on self-managing teams, we examine communication among peers who interact in diverse ways—and, usually, in multiple networks—at the same organizational level. Finally, since contemporary management theory and practice so heavily stress human interaction in group contexts, we conclude by examining the impact of technology, specifically of group support systems, on how people complete tasks, make decisions, and relate to one another in organizations.

Supportive Communication and Human Relationships

Although organizational relationships are influenced by a myriad of variables that may serve to make them complex, difficult, or unpredictable, most relationships flourish in supportive communication climates. **Supportive communication** relies on the accurate exchange of messages. When individuals interact supportively, their relationship is likely to be enhanced by the interchange, and their opportunities for mutual empowerment are increased. Researchers have found that organizations fostering supportive relationships enjoy higher productivity, faster problem solving, higher-quality outputs, and fewer destructive conflicts than do groups and organizations where interpersonal relationships are less positive. Hanson (1986) found, for instance, that the presence of good interpersonal relationships between managers and subordinates was three times more powerful in predicting profitability in forty major corporations over a five-year period than the four next most powerful variables (market share, capital intensity, firm size, and sales growth rate) combined.

The notion of supportive communication has appeared in the interpersonal and organizational communication literature for over three decades. In the early 1960s, for example, Carl Rogers (1961) defined effective interpersonal relationships in terms of both parties meeting several conditions:

1. coming together on a person-to person basis—setting aside constraining role relationships such as "boss" and "subordinate"
2. accurately empathizing with each other's world view and clearly communicating that understanding to one another
3. regarding each other warmly and positively, despite the behavior of either party at a particular moment
4. regarding each other unconditionally, without reservation or evaluation
5. perceiving mutually experienced acceptance, empathy, and support
6. exhibiting trusting behavior while simultaneously reinforcing feelings of security in one another

Although Rogers's definition may sound idealistic for many organizational settings, nearly every human resources theorist has in some way embraced the notion of supportiveness. Moreover, Gibb's research (1961) on interpersonal relationships in small group settings heralded the virtues of supportiveness and sought to contrast supportive with defensive climates in groups. According to Gibb, a supportive climate leads to subordinate satisfaction and accuracy in communication, whereas a defensive climate leads to distorted communication and dissatisfaction. Gibb's scheme is presented in Table 4.1.

Building upon the work of Gibb and several others, Whetton and Cameron (1991) advocated supportive communication for all sorts of interpersonal relationships in organizations. They argued that supportive communication engenders feelings of support, understanding, and helpfulness. It also helps individuals overcome two significant problems resulting from poor interpersonal communication: defensiveness and disconfirmation. *Defensiveness* results when someone feels threatened or punished by someone else's communication. Both the message and the interpersonal relationship are blocked, as the individual focuses more on self-protection and self-defense than on listening. When an individual's behavior is criticized, for example, common reactions include hostility, aggression, competitiveness, and avoidance. *Disconfirmation* occurs when individuals feel put down, ineffectual, or insignificant. Feeling that their self-worth is being questioned, they focus more on building themselves up and less on listening. Reactions may include show-

TABLE 4.1

Gibb's Communication Climates

SUPPORTIVE	DEFENSIVE
Description Presenting personal views without demanding others comply; nonjudgmental	**Evaluation** Passing judgment; blaming/praising; making moral assessments of others' motives
Problem orientation Mutually/collaboratively defining problems; avoiding blame placing	**Control** Attempting to change others' behaviors and attitudes; assuming that others are inadequate
Spontaneity Free of deception or manipulation; straightforward	**Strategy** Manipulating others; engaging in multiple/ambiguous motivations
Empathy Showing respect for others; seeing the world through others' vantage points	**Neutrality** Expressing a lack of concern for others; treating others as objects rather than human beings
Equality Participative planning without emphasizing differences in status, ability, or worth	**Superiority** Acting superior in stature, wealth, looks, intelligence, etc.; arousing feelings of inadequacy in others.
Provisionalism Presenting views with tentativeness and flexibility; willingness to change	**Certainty** Dogmatic; inflexible, argumentative/wanting to win

off behaviors, loss of motivation, and diminished respect for the offending party (e.g., the superior).

To counteract these sorts of problems, Whetton and Cameron (1991) discussed several principles of supportive communication. Their principles serve as behavioral guidelines designed to enhance interpersonal relationships in diverse organizational contexts. In many ways, supportive communication is intrinsically empowering.

Principles of Supportive Communication

Supportive Communication is Problem-Centered, Not Person-Centered. Person-oriented communication focuses on the characteristics of the individual, not on the event or the problem. It leaves the impression that the person is somehow inadequate or is to blame for a problematic situation. Although most people can change their behavior, few can change their basic personalities. Since person-oriented messages often attempt to persuade the other person that "this is how you should feel" or "this is the kind of person you are" (for instance, lazy, irresponsible, stupid, manipulative), such messages are likely to lead to defensiveness and a deterioration in the relationship. In contrast, problem-oriented communication focuses on the perceived problem and its solution rather than on someone's personal traits. The supervisor who calls a subordinate lazy or unreliable is making a person-centered judgment. The supervisor could instead use a problem-centered approach, describing the situation in terms of the worker's specific behaviors (for instance, "I've noticed you have left work early nearly every day during the past month"). In this instance, the supervisor is not claiming that the employee is lazy or irresponsible but simply describing a behavioral pattern and giving the employee the opportunity to become aware of the pattern and perhaps to explain why the behavior is occurring. Ideally, problem-oriented communication should be linked to accepted norms, rules, and standards of the organization rather than to personal opinions and tastes. Whenever possible and legitimate, problem-oriented communication should also acknowledge a desire to seek solutions collaboratively.

Supportive Communication is Based on Congruence, Not Incongruence. Several psychologists (Rogers, 1961; Dyer, 1972) have argued that the best relationships are based on **congruence,** that is, matching the communication, both verbal and nonverbal, to what the individual is thinking and feeling. **Incongruence,** on the other hand, occurs whenever there is a mismatch between what one is experiencing and what one is aware of (for example, one might unconsciously feel competitive toward a coworker without being aware of it). More directly related to supportive communication, incongruence can also occur when a person's thoughts and feelings are not accurately reflected in the accompanying verbalizations. For instance, a hostile comment may be made with a smile. Or a person may communicate anger during a meeting by tone and demeanor—but deny feeling angry. In general, supportive communication should be as congruent as possible, with true motives and feelings expressed, and with mutually reinforcing verbal and nonverbal communication. This is not to suggest that every feeling of anger, bitterness, disappointment, and aggression should be unleashed without regard for others' rights and feelings. Congruence is an important (and yet only one) element in supportive communication.

Supportive Communication is Descriptive Rather Than Evaluative.   When individuals use evaluative communication, they pass judgment or place a label on another's behavior (for instance, "You're really just being immature" or "You are being overly emotional"). The typical response to evaluative communication is defensiveness (for example, "I'm no more emotional than you are!"), and evaluative communication therefore tends to be self-perpetuating. These sorts of exchanges are counterproductive and often lead to a deterioration in the interpersonal relationship. A better alternative is to use descriptive communication, consisting of three steps:

1. Describe as objectively as possible the specific event that occurred or the behavior that needs to be modified.
2. Describe reactions to the behavior or its consequences.
3. Suggest a more acceptable alternative.

Thus, the supervisor who has observed consistent patterns of tardiness might say, "Dave, I've noticed that you've been late for every staff meeting this week. When you are late, I often start the meeting late, waiting for your arrival. Then we end up staying longer than we've planned. Also, you've got seniority over several others on the staff. When they see you arriving late, they start to think it's ok for them to do so, too. You're a role model for them. What can we do to solve this problem? I was thinking that if the time we meet is especially bad for you, one possibility might be to set the meetings at a different time. Can you think of any other ways to solve the problem?" This descriptive approach addresses the specific actions that are causing a problem rather than accusing the individual of being generally irresponsible, disorganized, or lazy. The perceived consequences are clearly spelled out. Most important, the supervisor invites the subordinate to participate in the problem-solving process—empowering him with the opportunity and responsibility of helping to suggest and shape a collaborative solution. As in this illustration, problems often "belong" to several people, and mutual changes may contribute to their solution.

Supportive Communication is Conjunctive, Not Disjunctive.   Conjunctive communication flows from previous messages or interactions, whereas disjunctive communication is disconnected from what was previously stated. **Disjunctive communication** occurs when one person interrupts another, when one person controls or dominates the conversation or meeting, or even when two or more people violate turn-taking norms and speak simultaneously. In contrast, the individual who uses **conjunctive communication** makes comments that are directly related to what others have said, waits for others to express their point of view before talking, and states his or her opinion reasonably concisely, pausing and looking at others to give them the opportunity for input. Not only is such communication viewed as supportive of others and their right to express their views, but those who communicate conjunctively are also perceived as competent communicators (Wienmann, 1977).

One critical component of conjunctive communication is being a good listener. Surveys have consistently supported the extent to which listening skills are valued. For instance, Crocker (1978) surveyed personnel directors in three hundred businesses and industries to determine what skills were considered most important to qualify as a manager. Effective listening was ranked highest. The average person spends about 45 percent of his or her time listening to others. Nevertheless, listening skills are underdeveloped; listening test results measure information recall as ranging from 25 to 50 percent in accuracy. A study of perceived listening needs of training managers in over one hundred *Fortune 500* industrial organizations revealed that poor listening, which leads to ineffective performance and low productivity (Hunt & Cusella, 1983), was one of the most important problems they faced. These training managers pointed out that listening was particularly problematic during meetings, performance appraisals, and in any context involving superior-subordinate communication. Although good, responsive listening appears to be problematic in many organizational situations, developing excellent listening skills is a critical determinant of conjunctive, supportive communication.

Supportive Communication Validates Rather Than Invalidates Individuals.

Even when communication is descriptive, it can still be destructive if it is delivered with a tone or air of superiority or judgment. For instance, the supervisor might wait until a subordinate has committed a large number of unacceptable behaviors and then proceed to describe each one in great detail and in a demeaning tone. **Invalidating communication** conveys an attitude of superiority, rigidity, or indifference (Galbraith, 1975; Sieburg, 1978). An attitude of *superiority* gives the impression of being informed while others are ignorant, adequate while others are inadequate, competent while others are incompetent, powerful while others are powerless. Those who communicate with *rigidity* can also invalidate others by portraying their own views as absolute, unequivocal, or unquestionable and by treating differing points of view as unworthy of consideration. Finally, equally invalidating is communicating an attitude of *indifference* by not acknowledging the other person's existence or value. Indifference is often communicated nonverbally by using silence, avoiding eye contact or facial expression, engaging in an unrelated activity while someone else is speaking, or frequently interrupting.

Validating communication, in contrast, helps others feel recognized, accepted, understood, and valued. First, it is *egalitarian*. The communicator conveys the impression that, whatever the difference in official organizational rank, she or he considers the other individual of equal worth as a person. Supervisors might invite subordinates to assist in problem solving and assume that they possess high levels of competence and responsibility (consistent with Theory Y). Validating communication is also *flexible*. It recognizes that alternative points of view and unknown data likely exist. Flexible communicators are open and humble, recognizing that no one person owns the truth and that few things can be known with absolute certainty. Thus, they offer personal views and assessments as opinions and tentative interpretations—open to change, challenge, and the insights of others. Implicit in this discussion is the notion that validating communication is a joint, *two-way process* in which (consistent with our discussion of communication in Chapter 1) both parties participate in sending and receiving messages in a dynamic environment of mutual exchange, commitment, and shared values. Each participant gives information and opinions; each asks questions; each listens; each knows that she or he is a valued member of the organizational community. Figure 4.1 summarizes the characteristics of supportive communication.

Supportive Communication: Some Caveats

The benefits of supportive communication seem obvious. When supervisors communicate in a supportive manner, they not only create a more satisfying work environment for their employees but are less likely to be afflicted by common distortions in upward communication, such as withholding negative information and exaggerating positive information. In addition, as role models, supportive supervisors show their subordinates how to communicate with their subordinates, furthering a generally empowering communication climate throughout the organization. However, in spite of these tangible and intangible benefits, a supportive communication climate may not result in greater productivity. Contrary to the early claims by human relations advocates that happy workers would work harder, research on the relationship between job

FIGURE 4.1

Supportive Communication

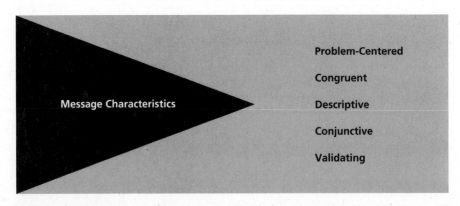

satisfaction and worker productivity has yielded strangely mixed results. Vroom (1964) reported that only 2 percent of the differences in employees' performance could be attributed to differences in job satisfaction. Iaffaldano and Muchinsky (1985) similarly concluded that only a slightly positive correlation (+0.146) existed between satisfaction and performance.

What might account for these findings? First, human motivation is complex. Individuals seek employment or choose to affiliate with others for a variety of reasons. Some will work hard just because they have embraced the Protestant work ethic—regardless of whether they are working in a supportive organization. Others find satisfaction in the act of working hard and in achieving their own objectives. Still others may be productive because they are competitive and want to achieve more than others. In each of these instances, it is internal conditions and drives that influence the choice to be productive, not supervisor behavior or organizational climate. In other instances, employees may elect not to work hard because they do not find their jobs intrinsically satisfying, or because their major sources of fulfillment in life are outside work. Or they may perceive that no matter how hard they work, they are stuck where they are in the organization (perhaps due to age, sex, disabilities, or economic realities), with no opportunities for advancement and no new challenges in the current job. No matter how supportive supervisors (or others) may be in such situations, they cannot change certain realities.

Clearly, then, supportive communication does not represent a guaranteed route to higher productivity. However, although satisfied workers may not always be more productive, dissatisfied workers are consistently less productive and are far more likely to be absent or to quit their jobs. Again, other factors influence employee absenteeism (such as dependent family members in crisis) and job turnover (such as the state of the economy). But when dissatisfied workers do discover other employment options, they frequently miss work before actually quitting, and ultimately they leave. This in turn forces the organization to recruit and train new employees—expensive and time-consuming tasks.

From an economic perspective, then, organizations benefit most from those communication practices that foster positive, satisfying organizational climates. Moreover, creating supportive (and potentially satisfying and empowering) organizational environments is intrinsically valuable. As we will discuss in detail in Chapter 10, some communication behaviors are arguably more ethical than others. Supportive communication, for instance, is quite consistent with Johannesen's views of communication as dialogue (see Table 4.2).

The value of supportive communication applies to those at all levels of the organizational hierarchy. It is just as crucial for those who interact as peers as for those who interact in unequal power or status relationships, for example, department heads and members of their staffs. However, most organizational communication research has been directed toward studying superior-subordinate interaction and interpersonal relationships. Jablin's exhaustive reviews of

TABLE 4.2

Communication as Dialogue

THE DIALOGIC COMMUNICATOR'S ATTITUDES AND BEHAVIORS	
Honest	Sincere
Trustworthy	Direct
Concerned for Others	Nonmanipulative
Open-Minded	Encourages Free Expression in Others
Empathic	Accepts Others as Persons of Intrinsic Worth

SOURCE: Johannesen, 1971.

the literature on superior-subordinate communication (1979; 1985) summarized a number of the most important research findings. In the next section we will briefly examine several of these findings.

Superior-Subordinate Communication

One of the most basic ways to examine communication is to consider its frequency. Not surprisingly, research has shown that *superior-subordinate interaction is common.* Jablin estimates that supervisors spend from one-third to two-thirds of their time communicating with their subordinates. In the past, most of this communication was verbal and occurred face-to-face (Luthans & Larsen, 1986). With changes in technology, though, these practices have begun to change; managers, for instance, are increasingly inclined to make announcements, share information, request information, and assign tasks through e-mail. About one-third of managerial communication is considered "routine" (reading and writing reports, sending and receiving requested information, and answering procedural questions).

Of course, managers also communicate with individuals external to their organizations, and most consider their interactions with outsiders, as well as interactions with their superiors, to be exciting and challenging. In fact, many prefer these upward and outward interactions to "downward" interactions with their own subordinates. Perhaps interacting with those above oneself in the hierarchy gives the individual a sense of derived status, and communicating with those outside the organization can create a feeling of connectedness with the environment.

Subordinates, too, often appreciate the opportunity to interact with their supervisors, depending on the quality of their relationship and the sorts of issues that precipitate the interaction. Not surprisingly, subordinates communicate more extensively with supervisors whom they regard as possessing high credibility. They turn to these leaders for all sorts of information, including task, political, and social (Richetto, 1969). In fact, credibility may be more important in predicting subordinate-initiated interaction with superiors than official status, even for job-related subjects.

Openness is another important aspect of superior-subordinate communication. Openness can be related to sending messages as well as receiving them. Jablin's definition of openness is conceptually consistent with the notion of supportive communication and focuses on the receiving aspect of the interaction. He noted that "both parties perceive the other interactant as a willing and receptive listener and refrain from responses that might be perceived as providing negative relational or disconfirming feedback" (p. 1204). Subordinates' views of supervisor openness and warmth are based, in part, on such nonverbal cues as eye gaze, posture, facial expression, and tone of voice (Tjosvold, 1984). For the most part, subordinate perceptions of supervisor openness correlate positively with job satisfaction, as well as reported satisfaction with the supervisor (Pincus, 1986). However, Baird and Bradley (1979) found that when openness focuses on sending rather than on receiving and is defined as including personal self-disclosure by the supervisor (for example, talking to subordinates about personal problems), some subordinates react less positively. Thus, openness, while largely beneficial, must be considered in context and carefully defined.

One of the chief problems associated with superior-subordinate communication is **upward distortion**. In general, those near the bottom of the organizational hierarchy are reluctant to communicate upward information that is unfavorable, or that in any sense reflects on them negatively. There are, however, a number of potentially mediating variables. For instance, greater distortions are likely to occur when the issue is important or when the subordinate aspires to upward mobility, is insecure, or does not really trust the supervisor. As with all subordinate communication, upward distortion is greatly influenced by the nature of the relationship between the superior and the subordinate, as well as by how the supervisor chooses to communicate downward. Fulk and Mani (1986) found that subordinates reported withholding information and generally distorting their upward communication when they perceived their supervisors as actively withholding information from them. Several scholars have argued that the critical determinant of accurate upward communication is *trust*. Read (1962) and Roberts and O'Reilly (1974) have concluded on the basis of their research that trust in a supervisor is the most important factor in accurate upward communication—more important than subordinate upward mobility aspirations or other contextual variables.

Another potential mediator of subordinate communication is the superior's perceived **upward influence,** often referred to as the "Pelz effect" (Pelz, 1952). According to this notion, subordinate satisfaction is related to *both* perceived supervisor supportiveness and the supervisor's actual ability to satisfy some of the subordinate's needs through influencing those higher in the organizational hierarchy. According to Pelz, supportiveness raises subordinates' expectations of impending rewards, but without upward influence, a superior is unable to fulfill those expectations.

Although most research has supported the Pelz effect, the relationship between subordinate satisfaction and supervisor upward influence may be curvilinear. That is, supervisors should have good relationships with those above them, but when they are perceived as too close to those near the top, they may be viewed as correspondingly less focused on promoting subordinate interests, and more concerned with furthering their own careers. Finally, Jablin (1980) found that subordinates whose supervisors were perceived as possessing great upward influence were highly satisfied with their jobs. So, too, however, were those whose supervisors were extremely supportive but lacked upward influence. Since Pelz's original work was conducted over forty years ago, perhaps employee values and expectations have simply changed. Supportiveness may be so highly valued in contemporary organizations that, whenever it is present, it may compensate for the lack of upward influence (Daniels & Logan, 1983).

Some problems with superior-subordinate communication can be attributed to a significant gap in information and understanding on certain issues that exists between supervisors and subordinates, often referred to as the **semantic information distance**. Although this problem can afflict individuals anywhere within the organization, supervisors and subordinates are especially vulnerable because of differences in their experiences, hierarchical levels, and overall perspectives on the organization (Smircich & Chesser, 1981). In fact, large gaps in understanding have been shown to exist between supervisors and subordinates on even such deceptively simple issues as the subordinate's basic job duties, performance expectations, amount and quantity of interaction, and the degree to which subordinates participate in decision making (Harrison, 1985; Dansereau & Markham, 1987). According to supervisors, subordinates underestimate the amount of positive verbal feedback they receive. Moreover, the greater the perceived gap in verbal recognition, the lower the subordinate's satisfaction with both the job and the supervisor (Hatfield, Huseman, & Miles, 1987). Jablin's (1979) review of the research came to several conclusions:

1. Superiors overestimate the frequency with which they actually communicate with their subordinates.
2. Superiors believe they communicate with subordinates more effectively than they actually do.
3. Subordinates believe that superiors are more open to communication than they actually are.
4. Subordinates believe that they possess more persuasive ability than superiors believe they do.

To some extent, a semantic information distance between superiors and subordinates can be expected because of hierarchy. However, the distance itself may be less problematic than the widely shared illusion that understanding and agreement exist.

Another goal of superior-subordinate communication research has been to identify the *communication behaviors and attitudes that distinguish effective from ineffective supervisors.* Redding (1972), for instance, endorsed the notion of a common communication style among effective leaders as depicted in Table 4.3. More recently, Robert K. Greenleaf, director of management research at AT&T and founder of the Center for Applied Ethics in Indianapolis, Indiana (a center now named for him), coined the term "servant leader" to describe his concept of effective leadership. According to Greenleaf, the servant leader exhibits "increased service to others, takes a more holistic approach to work, promotes a sense of community within an organization and between an organization and the greater community, shares power and decision making, and embraces a group-oriented approach to work" (Kelly, 1993, p. B10).

In spite of the intrinsic appeal of such profiles, others believe that no consistent profile of the communication characteristics of an effective supervisor emerges from the research (Jablin, 1979). What is effective in one situation may be ineffective in others. Situational factors influencing reactions to leader communication behaviors include organizational climate, task type, gender, and work-unit size. Moreover, as Hersey and Blanchard's life cycle theory of leadership suggests (see Chapter 3), managers may adapt their styles to suit the needs of different subordinates and may use several different styles, even with the same employee, to adapt to growth or change over time. This notion is consistent with research by Dansereau, Graen, and Haga (1975), which repudiated the concept of an "average leadership style" and pointed to the existence of varying communication relationships that differ from one superior-subordinate pair to another. We will return to the subject of leadership traits and styles in Chapter 6.

One traditional supervisor responsibility is *evaluating subordinates and providing them with feedback.* While nearly everyone endorses the notion that giving and receiving feedback is important, the best form, timing, and nature of that feedback has remained controversial. In general, subordinates tend to be more satisfied with feedback they receive from those possessing high credibility. They view the feedback as more accurate and the source as more

TABLE 4.3

Redding's Profile of the Good Supervisor

- Communication-minded; enjoys communicating.
- Approachable, willing, and empathic listener.
- Oriented toward persuading rather than demanding.
- Sensitive to the needs and feelings of subordinates.
- Open to communicating information to subordinates; willing to explain why policies and regulations are being enacted.

SOURCE: Redding, 1972.

perceptive, and they are more likely to *use* the performance suggestions offered in the feedback (Bannister, 1986). Others have argued that the extent to which subordinates *trust* their supervisors should influence their satisfaction with the feedback they receive, as well as their subsequent performance. O'Reilly and Anderson (1980) found that *quantity* of feedback is related to satisfaction when subordinates trust their superiors (that is, more feedback leads to greater satisfaction). However, when supervisors do not trust those who supervise them, *relevance* and *accuracy* of feedback (rather than quantity) promotes satisfaction.

Supervisors are often reluctant to give negative feedback, especially in face-to-face contexts and particularly when they are dealing with subordinates who are generally high performers. Those supervisors with limited authority and informal influence are unlikely to use confrontational tactics in disciplining subordinates (Beyer & Trice, 1984). A recent study by Kelly (1993) confirmed the value of extensive feedback, including specific suggestions for improvement, as a critical correlate of employee satisfaction with the overall appraisal/evaluation system. This finding seems consistent with Infante and Gordon's argument (1985) that employees thrive in a **corporatist environment,** that is, one in which individuals identify with the organization's values and find many of their most compelling needs fulfilled through their organizational experience. They pointed out that in a corporatist environment, individuals at all levels of the hierarchy are able to engage in constructive argument—to confront differences of opinion and to provide candid feedback to one another—with the goal of reaching mutual understanding. According to their research, subordinates who work in such an environment report high levels of satisfaction. As detailed in Focus On, some organizations are experimenting with "upward appraisal systems" to encourage feedback that is unencumbered by the constraints of the traditional hierarchy.

Jablin's review also pointed to the salience of *systemic organizational variables* in influencing superior-subordinate interaction. For instance, those in charge of decentralized organizations (with flatter structures) tend to reinforce and reward supervisors who support and practice information sharing and mutual goal setting by promoting them rapidly. Rewards for sharing information with subordinates are less likely to occur in centralized organizations with taller structures. In addition, organizational level appears to affect the way in which superiors interact with their subordinates. Supervisors near the top of the organizational hierarchy tend to involve their subordinates more in decision making than do those near the bottom of the organization.

Finally, technology influences superior-subordinate interaction in a variety of ways. For instance, some supervisors interact extensively "behind the scenes" through e-mail exchanges with each subordinate—asking them questions, picking their brains, and testing their reactions to ideas or proposals— all in preparation for formal face-to-face meetings. Moreover, in many organizations, technology is increasingly used to assist groups as they come together to share information, solve problems, and make decisions. In the last section of this chapter we will explore some of these technologies in detail.

FOCUS ON

Appraisal as a Two-Way Street

Performance appraisals have been traditionally used as a tool for downward communication. However, some companies are instituting upward appraisal systems as well. Here are some examples:

■ In 1992, AT&T developed a 40-question survey asking subordinates to evaluate the effectiveness with which their supervisors show respect, emphasize helping customers, promote teamwork and innovation, and maintain high standards.

■ Employees at AMOCO Corporation requested opportunities for upward appraisals, and a 135-question feedback instrument was developed as a part of a week-long mandatory training session given to middle-level managers.

■ A professional services firm, Deloitte & Touc, realizing that their service *is* their employees, instituted a process whereby those employees could express, anonymously and in writing, their satisfaction with management.

Each of these systems is based on the realization that a manager's "customers" are the people who work for him or her, and that an assessment of "customer satisfaction" is an important element of improving managerial performance.

SOURCE: Based on Romano, 1993.

Peer Interaction in Organizations

By far, most of the organizational communication research to date has focused on superior-subordinate interactions. However, equally and increasingly important (especially in the age of self-managing teams and collaboration) is peer communication. Like other organizational relationships, peer relationships have task and social dimensions. Peers can serve as valuable sources of information and social support, and, as we will elaborate in Chapter 5, informal networks of peers create norms that may enhance or inhibit morale, commitment, and productivity.

Cross-functional communication among peers is important for several reasons. First, the actual flow of work does not respect departmental boundaries. Increasingly, it has little to do with the formal structure depicted on the organizational chart. As groups of people work together to design and manufacture products, they assume group accountability. No one department is solely responsible if a product is defective. If a college freshman has an alienating experience during her first few weeks at a large university, she will not likely blame one professor or one unit but will probably feel that the overall organizational climate conspired to create a dehumanizing experience. Many individuals, across several different departments and units, were responsible.

Historically, organizations have not actively valued peer relationships. Lip service has been paid to the importance of good relationships with coworkers and the need for horizontal communication, but formal incentives have been geared more toward inspiring individual achievement and cultivating good relations with those in the upper regions of the hierarchy.

Contemporary management theories (and practices), however, have begun to reassert not only the value but the necessity of excellent peer relationships (within teams, quality circles, and groups of all kinds). Moreover, good peer relations grow in both formal and informal contexts. Thus, peer interaction can be furthered or cultivated in many ways—some of which involve informal gatherings, like picnics and sports events. In a more formal sense, peers can also supplement or replace the sorts of role relationships once viewed as exclusively reserved for superiors and their subordinates. For instance, peer relationships might creatively be used to replace mentor-protégé relationships. Like the mentoring system, peer relationships can potentially fill both career-enhancing and psychosocial functions—and they are more readily available (Fagenson, 1989; Kram, 1985; Noe, 1988). For some individuals, like women and minorities, peer relationships may offer the potential for finding a better, more flexible "fit." In hospitals, for instance, nurses have long used "peer pals" to help provide a smooth transition from the world of nursing school into the world of hospital work (Ragins, 1989).

In many ways, the qualities that individuals desire in their coworkers are not dramatically different from those they appreciate in their supervisors. Sypher and Zorn (1987), for instance, reported that preferred peers were depicted by their coworkers as considerate, personable, and possessing integrity. In some instances (especially at higher organizational levels), individuals sought relationships with peers whom they viewed as being influential. The least preferred coworkers were characterized as lacking integrity and as being self-centered and insecure.

One potential disadvantage associated with unstructured peer communication is the tendency for individuals to seek out those who are most similar to themselves. Thus, female secretaries talk with other female secretaries, female nurses with female nurses, male professors with males, and African Americans with African Americans. Managers who are concerned about managing diversity may need to focus on how to encourage individuals of diverse backgrounds to participate in informal peer communication so that dialogue that is truly enriched by diversity rather than constrained by homogeneity can begin to flourish.

Peer Networks

Often peer relationships are conceptualized within the broader domain of organizational **networks**. A network is generally regarded as a grouping of organizational members who engage in patterned interaction. As we will discuss in Chapter 7, much network research has been conducted in small group settings. Rogers and Agarwala-Rogers (1976), however, identified three levels of communication networks:

1. *Total system networks* map the patterns of communication throughout the whole organization.
2. *Clique networks* focus on groups of individuals within the organization who communicate with one another more extensively than they do with others.
3. *Personal networks* identify those individuals who most frequently interact with a particular member or members of the organization.

Those who tend to be the most empowered in organizations are those who participate actively at each of these network levels. Not only are these "well networked" individuals better informed, they also experience a greater connectedness with others and a clearer understanding of how their jobs relate to others (at a task level) and how they depend on others for their own effectiveness (in terms of interpersonal goodwill). Those who confine themselves to personal networks—communicating mostly within limited circles—may find their influence and general effectiveness diminished.

Some networks are more cohesive than others. In interlocking personal networks, strong ties exist among network members, who are often quite similar and interact extensively. However, unlike those who interact less frequently, they may not exchange a great deal of new information (Liu & Duff, 1972). Those with weaker ties, that is, who are not in constant contact, often learn a great deal from each other when they do communicate. This "theory of weak ties" reinforces the benefits of encouraging individuals to expand their peer networks and to communicate broadly across the organization, especially with those who offer differing perspectives and experiences.

Within informal communication peer networks, individuals play diverse roles (Larkin, 1980; Rice, Richards, & Cavalcanti, 1980). For instance, *isolates* have minimal contact with others, either because they desire little contact or because others seek to avoid them. Since individuals may belong to multiple networks, they may be isolated in some, yet central in others. Those who are isolated across networks usually suffer from depleted self-confidence, low morale, and reduced productivity. Networks also include *opinion leaders*, who occupy informal positions of leadership. They probably do not hold formal positions of authority, but they are quite influential nonetheless. Ensconced in the middle of the network, *gatekeepers* control the flow of information between organizational members. These individuals are potentially quite powerful because they can choose to convey or withhold information. They can decide when to communicate information, conveniently forget some messages, or prioritize the importance of information, as well as its sources and recipients. Other roles include *cosmopolites* who connect the organization to its relevant environment, *bridges* who belong to at least two groups and connect

FIGURE 4.2

**Individual Communication Roles in
Organizational Communication Networks**

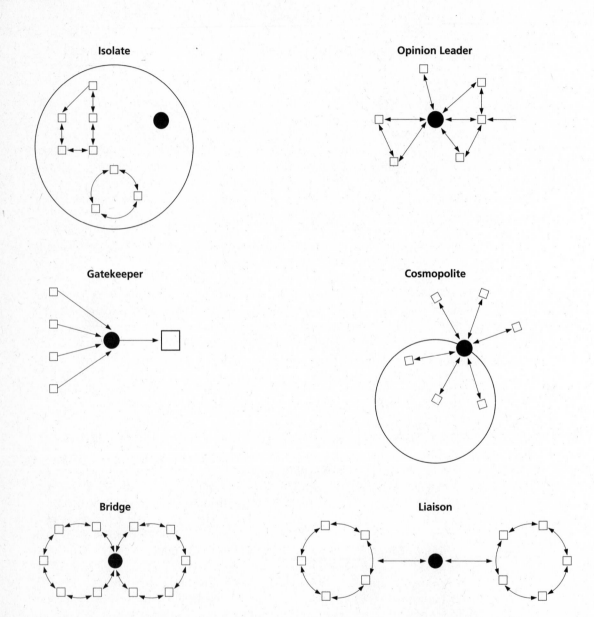

each group or clique to the other, and *liaisons* who connect two groups without belonging to either one. Figure 4.2 illustrates the different roles that individuals may play in organizational communication networks.

In both formal and informal settings, advancing technologies are playing an increasingly critical role in human relationships. In the next section we will explore the most current research on some of these technologies. Our particular focus here is upon group-related technologies, since interpersonal relationships in organizational settings (and the sense of empowerment that can grow from those relationships) so frequently evolve, flourish, or disintegrate in the context of groups.

Supportive Technologies: Groupware and Interpersonal Relationships

Most of the literature on group dynamics considers interpersonal relationships from the perspective of face-to-face interaction. In today's world, however, technology helps to create new electronic communities, in which interpersonal exchanges can occur over a wide spectrum of technology channels (e.g., videoconferencing, teleconferencing, cellular phones, electronic bulletin boards, faxes, voicemail, e-mail). Collaboration is no longer time- and place-dependent. People share information, conduct meetings, schedule activities, and discuss issues in novel ways.

What is not so obvious is that technology possesses attributes that may shape the nature of interpersonal relationships in ways that are different from the traditional means of exchange and relationship development. For example, people can meet and discuss issues over e-mail and develop an acquaintance, even a friendship, without ever having had a face-to-face encounter; this is particularly true with electronic services such as America OnLine, Prodigy, and Compuserve. The experience might be likened to having a pen-pal, except that since the exchange is technology-based, not paper-based, the dialogue can be more frequent and the exchange more immediate. Of course, the human element in the relationship is quite different from that in traditional relationships; with e-mail interactions, for example, the basis for the exchange is simply words—there is no physical contact.

When individuals engage in face-to-face interaction, they use many nonverbal cues. Much meaning (intended and unintended) is communicated through eye gaze, posture, and tone of voice. However, when the same individuals interact by using teleconferencing or e-mail, these sources of information are either diminished or completely screened out. How is this screening likely to affect the way individuals form impressions of one another, evaluate the extent of their mutual understanding, and make judgments about one another's truthfulness? The limited (mostly laboratory) research in this area suggests that much depends upon the type of information being exchanged and the relationship between the participants. Short et al. (1976), for instance, found that the recall of factual information was not influenced by the choice of communication medium. If, however, the exchange involved substantive conflict or interpersonal relations, then the medium of exchange made a considerable difference. They proposed a *theory of social presence* to account for these media effects.

According to the theory of social presence, media differ in their capacity to transmit information about facial expression, direction of gaze, attire, and other nonverbal cues. However, whether the media will have an impact on interactions depends on attitudes toward the media and on how well the media are contextually suited to the participants' goals (Culnan & Markus, 1987; Rice, 1984). For instance, if two people are using e-mail to work collaboratively on a report that must be quickly compiled and presented to their supervisor, they will likely find the rapid exchanges of information and feedback helpful. In this case, the medium serves to facilitate their shared goal of completing the job accurately and efficiently. However, if one of these individuals found it necessary to suggest that the other's contribution to the report was somehow inadequate, he or she would probably suggest a face-to-face meeting so that they might both discuss differences in a context that allows for verbal *and* nonverbal exchanges of mutual respect and the desire to maintain a positive working relationship on into the future.

Some research has also suggested that using technology to support communication may inhibit or discourage leadership emergence in a group setting. In leaderless, face-to-face groups, individuals' rates of participation are highly unequal. However, in computer conferencing, in which group members type their comments simultaneously, inequality of participation diminishes significantly (Vallee, 1984). Some have argued (e.g., Hiltz & Turoff, 1978; Rice, 1984) that anonymity reduces the need for those of lower status, minority group members, and people with communication anxiety to defer to others. These findings are important, since frequency and duration of speaking have been linked to leadership emergence in groups. In addition, those who seek leadership positions also use direction of eye gaze and eye contact as important sources of feedback and reinforcement during group meetings. Presumably using these nonverbal cues, strong individuals in one study were reported much more likely to emerge as leaders and to monopolize the discussion in face-to-face groups than in video-mediated groups (Strickland et al. 1978). The researchers argued that media appeared to reduce consensus about leadership and to increase the group members' focus on the task rather than on one another.

Technology-based communication can filter out information about the social context of the communication, such as the setting (boardroom versus office) and the hierarchical status of the participants (boss versus subordinate). Based on their review of the literature, Sproull and Kiesler (1986) argued that if a communication medium inhibits awareness of social context information, then social context will exert less influence on individuals and their communication behavior than is normal in face-to-face interactions. In their field study of electronic messaging in an office equipment manufacturing firm, these researchers found that the absence of information about social context increased uninhibited communication such as flaming (hostile exchanges), made people more self-absorbed, and neutralized status differences among participants. They found that 40 percent of the users did not know the gender and 32 percent did not know the hierarchical position of those who sent messages to them!

With the exception of the Sproull and Kiesler study, the other research discussed above took place in laboratory settings where the participants did not know one another prior to the study, were given no choice about the use of the technology, had no alternative ways of interacting with others, and were initially unfamiliar with the technology used. Moreover, they were of equal status and task knowledge.

Obviously, in actual organizations, the conditions under which individuals use technology and the choices they are allowed to make are strikingly different. In any organization, however technologically sophisticated, the use of an electronic medium will never entirely replace other means of communication. Moreover, individuals will have additional sources of information about one another and the task besides those filtered through the computer. Thus, the findings from the laboratory research (where nonverbal cues are often entirely screened and the technology is strictly controlled) portray a potentially inaccurate picture.

A number of field studies lend support to this conclusion. The use of electronic media tends to reduce the use of telephone and memos and occasionally reduces the need for meetings, but sometimes it actually increases face-to-face and written communication (Johansen, 1984; McKenney, 1985; Rice & Case, 1983). Thus, in field settings, the new technologies do not necessarily replace interpersonal communication through more traditional media but rather exist alongside them, as other options from which individuals may choose.

Supportive Communication and Technology: The Group Support Systems Example

Earlier in the chapter we discussed supportive communication and its impact on human relationships. In this section we explore how one technology, group support systems, actually fosters the principles of supportive communication, while at the same time promoting better group task performance.

Group support systems (GSS) are a technology that is rapidly being adopted and used by many corporations. GSS meeting rooms incorporate the use of a local area network, individual personal computer workstations, and GSS software to support traditional, same-time, same-place group meeting activities: generating and consolidating ideas, evaluating alternatives, and

GroupSystems from Ventana Corporation is an invaluable technology for improving meetings. Participants can brainstorm and evaluate alternatives via use of computer terminals. Unique to this process are the concepts that ideas are contributed anonymously and everyone speaks at the same time. (Ventana Corporation)

making decisions. The uniqueness of GSS lies in the way it transforms and regulates the group process.

GSS Features: Pros and Cons

GSS were designed with several specific features intended to enhance the group interaction process (Dennis, 1989). First, GSS provide group process support by allowing *parallel communication*. Because group participants brainstorm, consolidate ideas, and vote using their networked PCs, GSS allow each meeting participant to contribute simultaneously—therefore, no group member need wait for another group member to finish "speaking." Second, the computer-based GSS support *group memory* by recording all typed comments electronically, allowing participants to withdraw from the group process to think and/or type comments and then rejoin the group discussion. Third, GSS tools enable participants to contribute to the group *anonymously*, thus reducing the pressure to conform and diminishing apprehension about communication and evaluation (Herrick-Walker, 1991). Since ideas typed into the computer do not reveal the identity of the contributor, participants can evaluate the merits of an idea on the basis of its content rather than its contributor. Finally, GSS can be used *to structure and sequence a group's decision-making activities* to help maintain the group's focus on the task (DeSanctis, D'Onofrio, Sambamurthy, & Poole, 1989).

Jessup, Connolly, and Tansik (1990) contended that the third feature, anonymity, may be the most salient feature of GSS because it may change the nature of group interpersonal interactions. In the idea-generating phase of a meeting, ideas are contributed by participants anonymously, allowing the ideas to be evaluated on their inherent worth and not on the reputation or rank of their proposers. Jessup et al. (1990) have developed the *theory of anonymous interaction,* which argues that anonymity helps to reduce inner restraints on behavior by weakening immediate external social controls. For a work group using a GSS, anonymity may therefore enable members to engage in behavior that they might not display under ordinary circumstances in which their identities are known.

Nunamaker, Dennis, Valacich, Vogel, and George (1993) cautioned that using GSS can potentially help *or* hinder group productivity because of the nature of its impact on group member interaction. For example, typing comments and ideas into GSS PCs is slower than speaking, and this reduction in media speed can lessen the amount of information available to the group. Keyboarding also reduces verbal and nonverbal cues, yields slower feedback, and may actually inhibit socializing, resulting in reduced group cohesiveness and satisfaction. Finally, reduced inhibitions may encourage participants to voice negative or disruptive comments, and the size of the PC screen may cause participants to lose a global view of the task and make incomplete use of information.

On the positive side, Nunamaker et al. noted that typing comments and ideas into PCs makes for more careful and better-worded communication, and that reading is faster than listening. In addition, because GSS anonymity separates the identities of the participants from their comments and votes, group members are less self-conscious. Finally, since the PC screen typically displays only twenty-four lines of text at one time, participants may be encouraged to be more succinct, thus reducing information overload.

GSS and Supportive Communication

In terms of encouraging supportive communication, GSS appear to have features that may promote effective interpersonal relationships. For example, GSS-based anonymity and parallel communication promote the accurate exchange of typed messages in such a way that the individual is not subject to defensiveness or disconfirmation. Using GSS tends to encourage problem-centered rather than person-centered exchanges because the system helps to structure activities and channel behavior toward accomplishing the group's task. In GSS sessions, supportive communication tends to be based on congruence, not incongruence. Although message content cannot be connected to the message contributor in a GSS session due to anonymity, the group exchange benefits because people may feel less inhibited to say what they truly feel.

Of course, flaming can occur in GSS sessions, but research indicates that contributions (for example, brainstorming) are clearly more descriptive than evaluative during GSS sessions (Scudder, Herschel, & Crossland, 1994). Because of their simultaneity, GSS exchanges are free of interruption and are conjunctive, not disjunctive. Finally, using GSS tends to validate rather than invalidate individuals. GSS-based anonymity and parallel communication enable individuals to exert influence, assume leadership, or play important task-related roles by affording equal access and voice. GSS also allows individuals in groups to demonstrate their task competence and motivation to assist the group in accomplishing its task, so that they can grow to be perceived as influential.

Research generally supports the notion that using GSS promotes effective human relationships in groups. Chidambaram, Bostrom, and Wynne (1991) found, for instance, that groups using GSS over time developed higher cohesiveness and better conflict management abilities than groups not using GSS. Anson (1990) reported that groups using GSS and a meeting facilitator possessed higher cohesiveness than groups using only GSS, groups supported by only a facilitator, or groups having neither a facilitator nor the use of GSS.

In actual organizational settings, of course, groups being introduced to GSS have typically worked together in the past. Indeed, group history may be the most significant determinant of group members' feelings toward other participants in GSS sessions. Noel (1992) discovered, for instance, that attraction to the group prior to the GSS sessions was closely related to group members' attitudes about GSS processes and outcomes. He contended that one-shot use of GSS is not sufficient to moderate fully or offset negative baggage based upon prior experiences that some members bring to the group process. Thus, GSS may require repeated use before members develop an appreciation for the way in which systems can be used to decrease dysfunctional group behavior and to formulate more positive attitudes toward fellow group members.

We should also note that nontechnology elements of the GSS meeting environment may affect the nature of the group member interaction process. Because GSS meetings do not take place in anyone's office, no participants are disadvantaged by having to travel to someone else's office for the meeting, and perhaps finding themselves on something less than neutral turf. GSS same-time, same-place facilities suggest by their very design and layout a concern for equality and a commitment to task. For instance, a number of meeting rooms are organized so that participants are seated as equals. All have visual access to a large screen, which is prominently displayed at the front of the room. At times, a meeting facilitator may stand in front of the group to provide instructions or assist the group process. What is important, however, is that this kind of meeting environment promotes equitable interactions.

In traditional meeting rooms, those with higher rank or status are often advantaged, whereas those with lower rank, confidence, or skill are disadvantaged. For instance, a group member with higher status, often the group's leader, typically elects to sit at the "head" of the table, giving him or her greater visual access to others (while being the focus of everyone's attention), as well as the potential for greater influence. Studies have shown that those seated in key positions will, in fact, talk more than others and will also be perceived as more influential. At the other extreme, those with high communication apprehension (estimated by scholars to be about 10 percent of the work force) will invariably choose the most obscure seats, so that they can withdraw from communication more easily and avoid being the focus of attention. Interestingly, the GSS meeting environment neither promotes the would-be star nor provides hideouts for the apprehensive.

Summarizing Perspective

GSS and other groupware essentially facilitate collaborative communication. However, groupware cannot be used to promote interpersonal communication as long as people view possessing information as a personal competitive advantage within an organization. If the corporate culture emphasizes and reinforces individual effort and ability and does not promote cooperation and information sharing, the underlying premise, or spirit, of the groupware technology is undermined. In this situation, groupware might actually contribute to inhibiting interpersonal communication.

Wanda Orlikowski of MIT argues that for organizations accustomed to hierarchies, "the loose coupling and distributed collaboration offered by groupware require new processes, norms and ways of thinking. For such organizations, groupware is a new ball game, where the rules have not been defined. Devising a game plan under such conditions is not easy and may take time" (Wreden, 1993, p.55).

Orlikowski cautions that organizations wanting to emphasize collaboration should introduce groupware in such a way that it benefits them immediately without drastically altering the way they operate. Ronni Marshak, vice president of the Patricia Seybold Computing Group in Boston, has suggested that companies should "tell employees honestly what groupware will or will not do for them, and let them know that it may be difficult to use in the beginning. Then be sure to offer some sort of incentive to those who use groupware . . . and don't forget training. Without training, groupware is a guaranteed mess" (see Wreden, 1993, p. 55).

In Chapter 5, we explore organizational design and the impact of technology on this process. We'll see that groupware is dangerous stuff! It can have dramatic implications not only for human interaction but for organizational design and functioning as well.

CASES FOR DISCUSSION

CASE 1 *Harried Harry*

A medium-sized business recently hired a new manager, Frederick Vine. Although Fred viewed his new position as a definite step up, in that this company was more prestigious than the one for which he had previously worked, he was extremely unhappy with his new secretary, Harry. Harry preferred to think of himself as an "administrative assistant" rather than a secretary. He was quite active in the clerical union and spent many hours during the work day discussing union-related activities on the telephone. Harry also had a bad back and severe allergies and often called in sick. Fred perceived him as lazy, irresponsible, and uncooperative.

When Fred first arrived, he simply tried to go with the flow and adjust to his new secretary's habits. This proved difficult, however, because he found them so offensive and because at his previous company he had had an ideal female secretary who was sharp, motivated, and hardworking. After a short time, Fred decided he had to do something.

Fred began by summoning Harry to his office and sharing with him a lengthy document he had written on office procedures. He explained to Harry why they were important and noted that although his predecessor had not articulated such procedures, he simply could not operate without them. The procedures specified a number of work rules that affected all members of the staff—with a particular emphasis on the secretaries. Fred asked if Harry had any questions, and he responded negatively. Fred assumed, therefore, that he had made himself clear and that things would improve.

Fred was soon proven wrong. Harry's behavior did not change. In fact, about a week after he received the new set of rules, he e-mailed Fred that his back was really in bad shape and that he couldn't come to work that day. The next day he had a close friend call another secretary in the department and leave Fred a note indicating that his back was so bad that he probably would not be in for the rest of the week.

Fred was furious. He decided to take additional, more aggressive action. He began by interviewing several members of his department to discover their perceptions of the situation. He was informed of several specific examples involving instances of what he considered to be unprofessional behavior on Harry's part (like playing computer games nearly every day from 4:00 P.M. to 5:00 P.M.). Upon Harry's return, Fred began to keep a careful log of all his peculiarities that deviated from the new office procedures. Predictably, he accumulated quite a list. After several weeks, he consulted with the director of personnel to make sure he wasn't violating any company rules. Then he wrote Harry a stern three-page letter listing all of his deficiencies in specific detail. He left this letter on Harry's desk first thing on a Monday morning and then busied himself with other tasks.

Later that day, Fred called Harry in to ask if he had made himself clear. He asked if Harry understood the changes he needed to make if he were to remain gainfully employed. With teeth gritted, Harry said he did, but he also made a few comments about how difficult it was to adjust to Fred's style of leadership—a style that stood in stark contrast to that of his previous boss. Harry mentioned the fact that he was forty-five years old and had legitimate health problems. During the conversation,

Fred interrupted him several times to enquire about other sorts of issues, such as how soon Harry thought he would be able to master some newly acquired software, mail merge. As Harry attempted to respond to his questions, Fred tipped back in his chair and quietly watched him. Harry couldn't help noticing that Fred occasionally tapped his fingers on his chair arms with a subtle air of impatience.

Questions for Discussion

1. Using the supportive communication model presented in this chapter, how would you evaluate Fred's communication behavior?

2. How might Fred have communicated with Harry more supportively? Or, is supportive communication a reasonable expectation in this kind of situation?

3. What role (if any) did the choices of communication mode (face-to-face, written [the procedures and the letter], the telephone, and e-mail) play in affecting this situation? How might the varied modes have been used more effectively?

CASE 2   *Employee Layoffs*

West Metropolitan Hospital was losing money, and hospital executives knew actions had to be taken to reduce expenditures. Since a major portion of their costs were labor-related, their choice was clear: reduce staff.

A natural target for staff reduction was the fifth floor. This unit generally served elderly patients but had been less than half-full for some time. Reassigning fifth-floor patients to other units could be done easily, and closing that floor would save a significant amount of money.

Approximately forty employees worked on the fifth floor, all of them reporting to Ruth Rydek, the nurse manager. Hospital management decided that since her floor was being closed entirely, Ruth's services would no longer be needed.

There were, however, some complicating factors. First, the hospital had a policy of "reassignment" rather than "layoff" and thus had a commitment to place the fifth-floor staff in other open positions throughout the hospital for which they were qualified. While it was unclear how many of the forty displaced staff could be moved to other areas, management knew that many could be accommodated.

Second, most of the employees on the fifth floor were long-term staff who had become somewhat "set in their ways," in the view of the employees in other departments. Indeed, the fifth floor had developed a reputation for being an uncooperative group that consistently resisted even the most minor changes, and most managers felt that the quality of care provided by the fifth-floor nurses was marginal at best. Similarly, Ruth was generally regarded as the least effective of the hospital's nursing managers. As a result of all of these factors, managers in other units were extremely reluctant to accept displaced fifth-floor workers.

A series of management meetings was held to plan the closing of the fifth floor. The meetings were conducted by the assistant vice president of nursing and attended by all eleven of the hospital's nurse managers, as well as the director of personnel, the director of public relations, and a communication/labor relations consultant. Initially, management had considered omitting Ruth from those meetings but decided that it would "look better" if she were included in the planning process. During every meeting, Ruth cried openly, much to the discomfort of the others in attendance.

Everyone who participated in the meetings was sworn to secrecy; no one was to mention the closing of the fifth floor until the plan was completely developed and announced. Nevertheless, rumors quickly began to circulate that something was "in the works" and that the fifth floor specifically had been targeted by management.

Eventually, a plan was developed. On the following Wednesday morning, the vice president of nursing and the director of personnel would meet with the fifth floor staff to tell them the news and provide them with details either about their move to other units (for those for whom other positions had been found) or (for those who would be laid off) about the strikingly generous severance package the hospital was providing. Immediately afterward, this same information would be announced at a general meeting of all management; simultaneously, the hospital's chief executive officer would conduct a meeting of the medical staff. Individual letters, signed by the CEO, would be mailed to all employees' homes on Tuesday (so that most would arrive that Wednesday), and departmental meetings for employees would be conducted on Wednesday afternoon and Thursday to discuss the situation in detail with all staff. Finally, the news media would be contacted late Wednesday afternoon and provided with statements which would be broadcast on Thursday at the earliest and appear in the newspapers on Friday.

On Monday, two days before the layoffs were to occur, the group met with the chief executive officer of the hospital, Morrey Movitz, and the chief operating officer, Glen Hanson, to review their plan. Much to their dismay, Morrey and Glen both reacted extremely negatively. Both wanted to know exactly how many employees would be placed in other positions and exactly how many would be laid off. The group was unable to produce exact numbers, since the number of vacant positions fluctuated almost daily due to resignations and new hires. "Nursing never gets its numbers right!" Morrey roared in frustration. In addition, Glen strenuously objected to having the letter to employees come from the CEO: "We've got to stop passing the buck and shoving blame upward," he argued. Both demanded specific numbers and significant changes in the announcement letter drafted by the group before they would allow the plan to move forward.

At the same time, however, the organization's grapevine was functioning at full throttle. The fifth floor was going to be closed, probably this week, the rumor mill held. Indeed, fifth-floor employees themselves had apparently gotten wind of the plan: On the hospital's computer system, one fifth-floor employee typed an announcement that was communicated throughout the hospital: "We're long-service, formerly loyal employees who are about to be kicked out onto the street by the hospital. If you would like to help, we are starting a fund to help support those who will be hurt by this. Please send your contribution to (name, address of fifth floor employee)."

On Wednesday, fifth-floor employees came to work dressed in black and wearing black armbands. They covered the curtains in patient rooms with black sheets—much to the dismay and confusion of the patients in those rooms. When no one came to tell them their floor was being closed, they became all the more upset.

On Thursday, tension mounted. While senior management continued to debate the numbers involved in the layoff and the appropriateness of the communication plan, the fifth-floor employees waited for someone to tell them to go home. Eventually, the situation became unbearable. One nurse began to cry, and soon all were sobbing and hugging each other. The director of personnel called, and when she went to the fifth floor and saw what was happening, she told all of the employees just to go home. With the help of the vice president of nursing, she oversaw the hurried transfer of fifth-floor patients to other floors.

On Friday, the hospital announced that the fifth floor had been closed.

Questions for Discussion

1. What went wrong? How did existing relationships play a role in this situation?

2. What do you think the effects of this situation were on relationships among employees and managers throughout the hospital? On relations with patients? On relations with physicians?

3. Ideally, how might this situation have been handled?

CHAPTER

5

Organizational Design

*I don't think most organizations have thought about what information does
to authority, job structures, decision-making, and allocation of people's time.*
Gary Loveman in "Here Comes the Payoff from PCs," *Fortune*, March 23, 1992.

At the beginning of this book, we acknowledged the complexity and diversity of organizations. As scholars have attempted to define organizations, they have not always seen eye to eye. Some have taken traditional views, emphasizing power centers, hierarchy, and structure; others have argued that organizations are socially constructed entities, meaning different things to different people and evolving over time. For the most part, however, organizations generally emphasize goal-directed behavior, coordinated actions, information sharing, decision making, and human relationships. Central to all of these is communication.

Having acknowledged common threads, organizations can be, and often are, classified in several ways. For example, we may focus on their physical size (big or small), their profitability (rich or poor), their tax status (profit or nonprofit), their scope (local, regional, or international), the sector they serve (medical, manufacturing, or service), their stature (small business or multinational), or their membership (paid or volunteer). Organizational theorists, however, employ more sophisticated frameworks to describe how organizations differ.

As we noted in Chapter 1, Parsons (1960) provided one such scheme, identifying four different types of organizations according to their contributions to society: organizations oriented to economic production, organizations oriented toward political goals, organizations oriented to integration goals, and organizations oriented to pattern maintenance goals. Katz and Kahn (1978) offered a slightly different approach, describing organizations as being production or economic, managerial/political, maintenance, or adaptive. The distinguishing feature in this scheme is the nature of what organizations process, the orientation of their members, their organizational structure, and the means by which they use energy or resources.

From another perspective, Etzioni (1961) classified organizations in terms of compliance, or the degree to which participants lower in the organization are involved in making decisions that affect their work and are allowed to work in ways that are consistent with their values. Blau and Scott (1962) considered organizations in terms of whom they serve. In *mutual benefit* organizations, the members are the prime beneficiaries. In *businesses* the owners are the beneficiaries. Clients benefit in *service* organizations, and the public at large benefits in *commonweal* organizations.

In his classic work *The Structuring of Organizations*, Mintzberg (1979) suggested that we classify organizations by using characteristics of the organizations themselves. He differentiated organizations in terms of how they are structured to meet the various contingencies that they face:

- *Simple structures,* such as automobile dealerships, are headed by an autocrat, and supervision is direct. Technologies are not sophisticated, and the organization is usually small, existing in a dynamic environment.

- *Machine bureaucracies,* such as the postal service, are large; they exist in a stable environment, have standardized work, and are controlled by some external body.

- *Professional bureaucracies,* such as law firms or universities, have professional or highly skilled workers who perform work that is standardized through professional or craft training in an environment that is stable but in which there are no external controls on the organization.

- *Divisionalized forms,* such as large, diversified corporations, have divisions, each of which may have a simple, machine, or professional structure.

- *Adhocracies,* such as NASA, are complex organizations whose environment is dynamic and unknown and whose structure can change rapidly as events demand.

In general, descriptions of organizations depend upon one's theoretical view of the nature of organizations as systems. In this chapter we begin by considering several competing views of organizations as systems. We then examine dimensions of organizational structure and the extent to which organizational design and form is influenced by context. We move next to a consideration of organizational structure and communication channels, both formal and informal. Finally, we examine the impact of technology on organizational structure and design.

Organizations as Rational, Natural, or Open Systems

How rational are organizations? What is the relative importance of formal and informal structures within organizations? To what extent are organizations influenced by their environments in complex and dynamic ways? Basically, there are three competing schools of thought: the rational systems perspective, the natural systems perspective, and the open systems perspective.

Theorists subscribing to the **rational systems perspective** focus on systems as rational entities that seek the achievement of goals using the most rational and efficient means possible. Here managers are concerned with rules, directives, jurisdiction, coordination, and performance programs that create an effective organizational design operating with efficient processes. Goals are clearly specified, and organizational structure is seen as a rational mechanism for improving organizational performance. Particular attention is given to the formalization of roles and responsibilities, as well as to the formalization of communication flow and decision making, since a premium is placed on simplifying decisions and ensuring dependable and reliable organizational behavior. This perspective devotes little attention to the influence of the larger social, cultural, and technological context on the organization's structure.

An example of the rational systems viewpoint is the classic bureaucracy. Here communication is structured and predictable: Transactional information flows upward to inform management of progress, and policy information flows downward from the top of the hierarchy, telling people in the organization what is important and what is valued. In the rational organization, internal order and reliability of behavior are of paramount concern.

From the **natural systems perspective,** the rational systems theorist is irrational. The natural systems theorist sees an organization as a social entity whose purpose is to achieve narrowly defined goals. The focus is on organizational behavior, and on the relationship between stated and real goals, which are pursued through formal and informal organizational structures. Organizations are seen to seek stability and ongoing survival. Scott (1987) noted that where the rational systems model focuses on features of organizations that distinguish them from other social groupings, the natural systems model emphasizes commonalities among organizations and other systems. Moreover, whereas the rational model stresses the normative structure of organizations, the natural model emphasizes the behavioral structure.

In the natural systems model, interest in organizational communication focuses not just on task-related issues but also on communication relating to the activities and attitudes of individuals. Organizations are seen as dynamic and involved with the whole person, as reflected in their communication and actions. This approach differs from the rational perspective, which cares only for stability and limited, organizationally relevant, behavior.

Finally, the **open systems perspective** stresses the complexity and variability of individuals and subunits as well as the looseness of the connections among them. This model focuses less on structure and more on organizational processes that involve the arrangement of roles and responsibilities and the internal operations and boundary-spanning activities of organizations as they persist and evolve over time, adapting and changing to survive. Organizational systems and processes are diverse because of the close connection between the condition of the environment and the systems within it. That is, the organization and its environment are interdependent, and different environments place differing requirements on organizations. Organizational complexity is therefore a function of environmental complexity. Scott (1987) pointed out that the open systems model is distinctly different from the rational and natural systems models. He noted:

> Rather than overlooking the environment, as tends to be true of the rational systems perspective, or viewing it as alien and hostile, as is characteristic of the natural systems perspective, the open systems model stresses the reciprocal ties that bind and relate the organization with those elements that surround and penetrate it. The environment is perceived to be the ultimate source of materials, energy, and information, all of which are vital to the continuation of the system. Indeed, the environment is even seen to be the source of order itself (p. 91).

It is this latter model, the open systems view, that we described in greater detail in Chapter 2. The open systems perspective helps us to see, for example, that McDonald's behaves as something more than simply an efficient fast-food hamburger restaurant. Ronald McDonald and his friends are designed to help differentiate McDonald's from direct competitors such as Wendy's and Burger King. Therefore, in addition to concern for its menu, we see that McDonald's must also appeal to the nonrational aspects of social conduct, especially children's imaginations, in order to perform well in a competitive environment.

These three perspectives on organizations have important implications for students of organizational communication. Each perspective subscribes to a fundamentally different philosophy about organizations that dictates the content and flow of organizational messages. The rational systems perspective focuses on tasks, order, and procedural issues; the natural systems perspective considers both the formal and informal nature of organizational life; and the open systems perspective entertains the nature of the organization's interchange with environmental factors. Each uses differing adjectives, verbs, and metaphors to describe and define the organization. What is important is for the student of organizational communication to understand that each viewpoint prescribes and communicates a particular bias about organizational behavior.

Dimensions of Organizational Structure

Every organizational system has a structure. Why is structure necessary? Hall (1987) suggested that organizational structure serves three basic functions. First, it helps to produce organizational output and to achieve organizational goals. Second, structure is designed to minimize or at least regulate the influence of individual variations on the organization. "Structures are imposed to ensure that individuals conform to requirements of organizations and not vice versa" (p. 99). Structure is also the arena where decisions are made and where power is exercised; it is where organizational communication takes place and where organizational actions are carried out. Organizational structure therefore helps to shape communication. Hence, organizational communication is affected by the same factors that impact organizational structures: complexity, formalization, and centralization.

Complexity

Complexity is evident in almost all organizations, small or large. Even within relatively informal organizations, complexity soon becomes obvious. One of us recently served as president of a band boosters volunteer organization. One fund-raising function that proved unbelievably complex was hosting (housing and feeding) a group of several thousand bicycle enthusiasts who were in town for a 100-mile bicycle ride. Dozens of services needed to be performed (preparing chili for five thousand people, organizing piano-moving crews, dividing tasks among student and parent volunteers, and supervising parking and clean-up crews).

Organizations clearly differ in their division of labor, job titles, number of divisions and departments, number of hierarchical levels, type(s) of skills, and corporate culture. Moreover, they differ in their degree of complexity on any one of these factors. For example, those in the legal department and sales department of a large corporation may be members of the same organization, but they possess strikingly different knowledge and skills. Also, the legal division may be centrally located, while sales is distributed geographically.

Organizational complexity is often measured along four dimensions:

1. **Horizontal differentiation**   Complexity can be expressed in terms of the number of subunits in the firm, the number of occupational specialties, the range of professional activities, and the level of professional training existing in the firm.
2. **Vertical differentiation**   The greater the number of levels of hierarchy in an organization, the greater the organization's complexity.
3. **Spatial dispersion**   The more activities and personnel are dispersed by function or geography, the greater the complexity of the organization.
4. **Environment**   Organizations tend to become more complex as their activities and surrounding environment increase in complexity.

Greater structural complexity results in increasing complexity in organizational communication. When the number of organizational tasks increases, the levels of hierarchy expand; activities and personnel become dispersed, or the environment becomes differentiated and difficult to manage; and organizational communication becomes more frequent. Typically, as complexity increases, organizations seek means of communication that facilitate enhanced coordination and control of organizational subunits. Since groupware helps organizations to manage communication better between organizational units across time and place, this technology has been adopted by many organizations interested in managing organizational complexity.

Formalization

Formalization relates to the extent to which roles and relationships are specified, independently of the personal characteristics of those who occupy certain positions (Scott, 1987). Formalization also dictates the amount of control that an organization has over each individual. It is expressed in terms of the extent to which rules, policies, and procedures exist and are employed to manage organizational operations, communication, and contingencies.

Naturally, organizations vary in their degree of formalization. Hall (1987) distinguished maximal formalization from minimal formalization. *Maximal formalization* exists when there are highly formalized procedures and when the work and the methods for performing the task are necessarily precise, such as in an automobile assembly plant. *Minimal formalization* exists when a situation is unique and when there are no procedures documenting what to do. In the latter case, the situation requires discretion, intuition, inspiration, and even a trial-and-error approach. Young couples who bring their first child home from the hospital and begin the task of child rearing typically fall into this category. Similarly, three professionals who come together to try to create their own consulting firm will have few rules and procedures. Over time, more formalized procedures may develop from these situations.

Hall (1987) argued that formalization is a major defining characteristic of organizations. He concluded:

> By nature, formalization is central to the life of and in organizations. The specification of rules, procedures, penalties, and so on predetermines much of what goes on in an organization. [Organizational] behavior is not random and is directed by some degree of formalization toward a goal (p. 78).

Formalization, therefore, shapes organizational communication. Maximal formalization is indicated by strict, predictable channels of communication. Examples are company announcements, policies and procedures, organizational charts, and official company communiqués. Minimal formalization yields ad hoc committees, informal bulletin board notices, impromptu meetings, and social gatherings—all of which suggest the unstructured nature of organizational communication.

Centralization

Centralization, the third basis on which organization structures can differ, refers to how power is distributed in the organization. Hage (1980) defined centralization as "the level and variety of participation in strategic decisions by groups relative to the number of groups in the organization" (p. 65). Van de Ven and Ferry (1980) defined it as "the locus of decision making authority within an organization" (p. 399). In centralized organizational units, most decisions are made hierarchically. However, in decentralized units, significant decision making is delegated by line managers or shared with subordinates.

Centralization determines both who has the right to make decisions and the scope of their decision-making powers. In highly centralized organizations, lower-level personnel make few decisions, and decisions that are made follow clearly prescribed rules or policies; issues and/or problems not covered by procedures must generally be referred to higher-level management for a decision. In decentralized organizations, however, personnel are given discretion to make decisions, either within the framework of overarching policies, or sometimes with full discretion on issues not covered by policies.

In reviewing the relationship of centralization to other organizational properties, Hall (1987) made the following observations:

- The relationship between organizational size and centralization is paradoxical; increasing size increases the rate of delegation or decentralization.
- The greater the number of professional personnel in the organization, the greater the employee influence.
- Competition influences centralization: in an expanding economy in which competing firms are gaining, decentralization is likely; however, in a contracting economy in which one firm gains at another firm's expense, "tightening up," or centralization is a more probable outcome.
- General environmental stability is also a factor. When an organization is growing, decentralization may be the most appropriate response to turbulence, while centralization might be necessary in periods of contraction.

With centralization comes greater coordination but less flexibility. Organizationwide policies might be consistent (e.g., salary review procedures), but some of these might be ill adapted to a specific local situation (e.g., a two-person department). Decisions in centralized organizations are typically made rapidly (especially during emergencies), but employees may feel overwhelmed by the numerous rules, procedures, and decisions communicated down the hierarchical chain of command.

Above all, centralization is about power, since organizations are a major means by which power is exercised in society. In general, highly centralized organizations are less empowering for the majority of employees than those characterized by greater decentralization.

Centralization therefore has important ramifications for organizational communication. With centralization comes increased formality and extensive procedural communication. With decentralization comes a greater degree of informal, ad hoc communication, containing more decision-related information as well as important details of interactions with the organization's external environment.

Context and Organizational Design

Complexity, formalization, and centralization are useful in explaining how organizations vary, but they do not explain what factors actually shape organizational structure. For the most part, two major factors influence organizational structure: context and organizational design.

Context

Context can be viewed simply as the situation in which the organization operates. Many contemporary organizations, for instance, are attempting to operate in a context that includes downsizing, increasing competition, and a greater need to address and manage diversity.

Size can be measured in terms of the physical capacity of the organization, the number of personnel available to the organization, the number of organizational inputs or outputs, and/or the size of discretionary resources available in the form of wealth or net assets. Scott (1987) pointed to a number of empirical studies demonstrating that larger organizations are more highly differentiated and more formalized than smaller organizations. However, he also noted that these studies reveal that larger organizations "tend to be less bureaucratized and centralized in their decision-making structures. . . . Decentralization is . . . necessary, because of information overload at the top caused by increased size and differentiation, and possibly, because formalization promotes consistency of decision making" (pp. 265–266).

Research on the relationship of size to structure has produced inconsistent results. Indeed, while size is associated with structure, it ". . . may not be said to generate or to cause, structural differentiation" (Argyris, 1972, p. 12). Size is more likely to be an outcome than a cause of structure (Aldrich, 1972). Aldrich argued that more highly structured firms adopt a greater degree of specialization, formalization, and monitoring of role performance simply because they have a larger work force than less structured firms.

Technology is what organizations use to get their work done. It is the raw material that the organization manipulates (Perrow, 1967), and it affects the way the organization is structured and operated. Technology consists of machines and equipment, but it also incorporates the technical knowledge and skills of participants.

Scott (1987) distinguished three dimensions of technology: complexity, uncertainty, and interdependence. He asserted that, in general, technical complexity is associated with structural complexity and professional expertise. Technical uncertainty is associated with lower formalization and decentralized decision making. Interdependence focuses on the extent to which the items or elements upon which work is performed, or the work processes themselves, are interrelated, causing a change in one to affect another. Interdependence is associated with higher levels of coordination.

Complexity, uncertainty, and interdependence are often viewed as similar in that each increases the amount of information to be processed during the performance of a task. As a result, when these three variables increase, structural modifications need to be made that either reduce the need for information processing or improve the capacity of the information-processing system. In a crisis situation, for example, organizational communication becomes much less structured and ad hoc. Organizations may be under tremendous pressure to respond quickly, to manage, or even to shut down the demand for information by environmental constituencies. For instance, when several bottles of Tylenol were found to have been tampered with, the manufacturer, Johnson & Johnson, was taxed to provide the information needed to manage both the complexity and uncertainty of the situation. The firm mobilized existing resources in novel ways to respond as quickly as possible as new information became available. Work hours, use of information technology, and traditional roles and responsibilities were temporarily modified to provide a structure and modus operandi that were appropriate for the emergency at hand.

Technology also affects the routine and the division of work. In bureaucracies where work is highly specialized, tasks are routine, and the division of work prescribes specific roles, responsibilities, and status. However, when the organization is composed of professional personnel (lawyers, physicians, faculty), work is less routinized, and distinctions between roles and responsibilities are often less clear-cut.

Organizational decision makers are faced with making their organizational structure congruent with the demands placed on it by the *environment*. To protect themselves from environmental uncertainty, organizations create buffering units that monitor labor markets, deal with technical and scientific developments, manage different types of buyers and sellers, and oversee subcontractors and competitor behavior. As the environment becomes more diverse and competitive, organizations employ more bridging techniques (bargaining, contracting, and appropriating). Logically enough, "organizations located in more complex and uncertain environments will exhibit more complex internal structures" (Scott, 1987, pp. 250–251). Environmental demands on organizational structure therefore result in loosely coupled boundary-spanning units that act to help the organization adapt to its environment (Weick, 1976). Allowing these departments to vary independently helps the firm to detect environmental variations as it attempts to protect and buffer its vital, tightly coupled technical core operations from environmental uncertainty. Loose coupling can, for example, allow the organization to isolate any problems to affected local units, enabling them to adapt to local conditions so that the entire organization is not affected. Wendy's, for example, allows its menu to vary on a regional basis. A Carolina Burger with chili and cole slaw is offered to Wendy's customers in North Carolina but not to those in Cambridge, Massachusetts. This slight variation in condiments allows Wendy's core processes to remain constant while enabling regional units to accommodate local tastes.

Growth and mergers are also methods for managing environmental uncertainty. Their effect has been to shift many major corporations from a unitary structural form (the conventional organizational form composed of a central office and several functionally organized departments) to a multidivisional structure.

Interestingly, cultural differences appear to affect organizational structure in inconsistent ways. For example, some studies have found that host country characteristics are more important than those of the organization's country of origin in shaping its local structure. Other studies, however, have reported "culture-free" determination of structure—so that factors internal to the organization determine its structure to a greater degree than the characteristics of either the host country or the country of origin.

Organizational Design

While context suggests how an organization is shaped by its situation, organizational design describes how the organization actively *shapes* its structure. Three different theoretical perspectives on organizational design have been identified: strategic choice, member control, and institutional isomorphism. Each perspective has important ramifications for organizational communication.

The **strategic choice perspective** argues that the internal politics of an organization determine the structural form of the organization, affect the way the organization relates to environmental constituencies, and influence the choice of relevant performance standards (Child, 1972). Simon (1957) argued that the choices made by the organization are based on the concept of "bounded rationality." This means that the organization, faced with a multitude of environmental pressures, must necessarily choose a direction from among many possible choices toward one or many possible objectives. Hence, strategic choices are not always optimal ones; rather, they are those chosen from among an array of possible options through political processes within the organization.

The strategic choice perspective relates the concept of power to organizational structure. Those who have power in an organization decide what are and are not organizational issues. Those in power, the "dominant coalition," make the strategic choices with regard to the organization and its structure. Based upon their perceptions of the environment, they select strategies for dealing with it, technologies for implementing those strategies, and additional strategies for arranging roles and relationships to control and coordinate the technologies being employed.

From this perspective, organizational communication is critical to organizational design. Organizational communication incorporates negotiation, struggle, power, values, shared meaning, politics, and decisions, all of which comprise the wide array of messages that document the strategic choice process. In fact, this perspective suggests that it is the organizational communication process that yields the structural form of the organization, affects the manipulation of environmental forms, and influences the choice of relevant performance standards.

By way of contrast, the **member control perspective** is dramatically less dynamic than the strategic choice view. It argues that structure results simply from management's desire to control workers. Division of labor is caused by the desire for organizational control and the need to apply advancing technology continually to production. This perspective, fueled by Taylor's (1911) principles of "scientific management," (see Chapter 2) views control and structuring as a strictly rational process. From this vantage point, organizational communication comprises simply the formal and structured messages that document necessary coordination and control activities.

While the previous perspectives rest largely on the concept of rationality (bounded or otherwise), the **institutional isomorphism** (same shape) perspective contends that historical changes shape structures. Organizational design is not a rational process, but rather one in which external and internal pressures lead organizations in related areas to resemble one another over time. From this perspective, organizational communication may be viewed as a universal set of messages that exist across organizations of similar purpose and type. To understand fast-food organizations, for example, one would examine the common patterns of communication that prevail across the industry. The underlying notion is that an organization's communication patterns are to some extent predetermined by evolution. Among organizations of the same type, there is no significant variation.

Depending, then, upon the perspective embraced, organizational design may be viewed as politically derived and strategically determined by those in power. Here organizational messages reflect political activity. They are internally oriented, still power-based, but geared through rational considerations toward employee control and coordination, where the content of organizational messages focuses on policies and procedures. However, organizations can also be viewed as largely irrational, driven by historical and institutional forces surrounding the organization and influencing its form and fate, thus predetermining the nature of organizational communication.

Organizational Forms

Organizations, of course, come in many forms. In this section, we consider six of the most prominent: (1) the traditional, centralized structure; (2) the centralized form with decentralized management; (3) the divisional form; (4) the decentralized (holding company) structure; (5) the matrix structure; and (6) the "Type-D" organization.

The **traditional, centralized organizational form** is common in many firms, especially those in which large work systems require a high level of standardization. In the traditional centralized organization, both management and organizational work are physically centralized; activities, personnel, and management are in the same place, as, for example, in the case of most hospitals. This organizational form typically has high levels of management control, standardized procedures, uniform policies, specific titles and ranked positions, a high level of bureaucracy, and highly structured organizational communication. Its assets are related to strong control and coordination: Management and procedural communication control personnel, policies and practices are uniform, tasks are broken down into component functions, and the resulting specialization of work activities allows for greater efficiency.

The major weakness of the centralized form is its potential for creating inflexibility through its standardization. The tendency to maintain standardization and bureaucracy in the midst of a changing environment may threaten organizational survival. The hospital example is a case in point. Attempts at health care reform under the Clinton administration pointed to hospitals where rules required that numerous forms be completed and filed for each patient. While some of the forms served useful purposes, others were seen as repetitious and unnecessary. Many employees complained of drowning in a sea of paperwork. One hospital reported adding six and a half feet of new forms to its files every day!

In addition, centralized organizations are often unable to respond quickly to localized environmental demands. Procedures simply get in the way. Because of their specialization, personnel may lack the shared language and understanding to interact effectively between and among organizational units. Moreover, it may be difficult to provide employees and customers with customized and/or personalized support, since a premium is placed on standardization of functions and products (Hershey & Kizzier, 1992).

A variation on the centralized form is the situation in which senior managers choose to decentralize some lower-level management responsibilities. This **centralized organization with decentralized management** maintains top-management control over all major organizational functions (e.g., production, finance/accounting, sales/marketing, and human resources) whose operations are standardized. However, within this structure, lower-level managers may be afforded some discretion in decision making and in communication, although there may be guidelines to ensure a high degree of uniformity relative to organizational practices and policies.

For instance, most organizations have uniform affirmative action policies that govern their hiring practices. Within specific departments, however, recruiting techniques may vary considerably so long as the underlying spirit of these policies is upheld. This limited discretion provides more organizational flexibility and latitude than traditional centralization. While the major organizational structure and systems remain standardized, the possibility exists for managers to address localized or customized needs. Franchise restaurants like Chi-Chis provide a good illustration of this structure. Each restaurant looks alike and offers the same basic food, but each may differ in its choice of sponsorship for local community activities.

The **divisional structure** represents a major shift in organizational form. In this structure, the "M-Form," there is a central coordinating organizational entity, but there are also divisions with their own management structure that have direct responsibility for their organization's operation and performance. This is an extension of a hierarchical structure (see Figure 5.1); it consists of a general office and several product-based or regional divisions,

FIGURE 5.1

The Multidimensional Structure

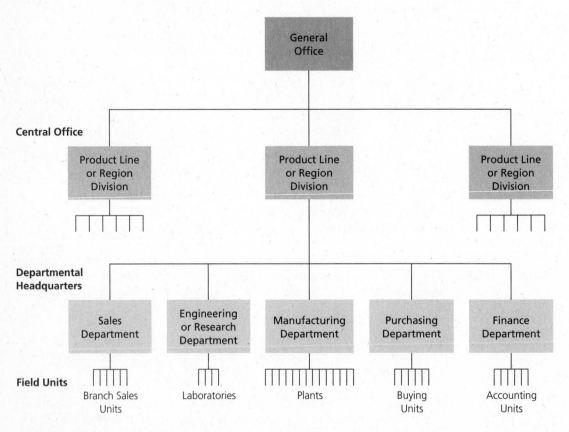

SOURCE: Chandler, 1962.

each of which contains functionally differentiated departments. These departmental units are also subdivided into work units that are distributed on a geographical basis. The divisional structures have localized authority and control structures and operate with considerable autonomy from centralized planning.

The rationale for this approach is that each division needs flexibility to meet the specialized needs of its market(s). Most communication between divisions and the central coordinating entity contains messages related to policies, procedures, and detailed transaction or summary reports. However, organizational communication may vary across divisions because each division may provide differing products and services, serve diverse clienteles, be situated in separate operating environments, and have distinct organizational cultures.

At companies like General Motors, Ford, and Chrysler, divisions within the same company may even be competitors. Different divisions within the same company may also be organized differently. However, all divisions are coordinated by and responsible to a centralized corporate entity that provides common staff functions for them all (legal, public relations, travel services, management information systems, etc.).

At the opposite end of the traditional, centralized form, as Hershey and Kizzier (1992) noted, is an extremely **decentralized approach** or holding company approach. In this structure each division may be a privately named company and operate as such. The president of the unit has total responsibility for that unit. There may be no effort to coordinate different units within the holding company. In fact, employees may not even know the overall holding company or be aware if a particular unit is sold to another holding company. Thus, for employees who work in firms owned by holding companies, there may be little assurance of security. Holding company activity was especially prevalent in the 1980s as Wall Street investors sought to make short-term gains through the acquisition and sale of companies. The nature of organizational communication in such companies will depend to a great extent on the organization's operating environment and culture.

Another organizational form, the **matrix structure,** is unlike any other. In such structures, which are sometimes temporary, vertical and lateral channels of communication and authority operate simultaneously. Vertical communication flows within functional departments, while lateral communication flows within project group or geographical area activities, where managers combine and coordinate the services of functional specialists. Figure 5.2 illustrates the matrix structure of the rocket division of a space agency. One potential problem with a matrix structure is the fact that personnel are responsible to a dual command structure. Sometimes the needs and priorities of functional and project decision makers may come into conflict. Hence, it is especially important in matrix organizations for individuals' efforts to be effectively coordinated, with ongoing communication of their commitments and schedules. Some of the problems NASA has experienced over the years may be

FIGURE 5.2

The Matrix Structure

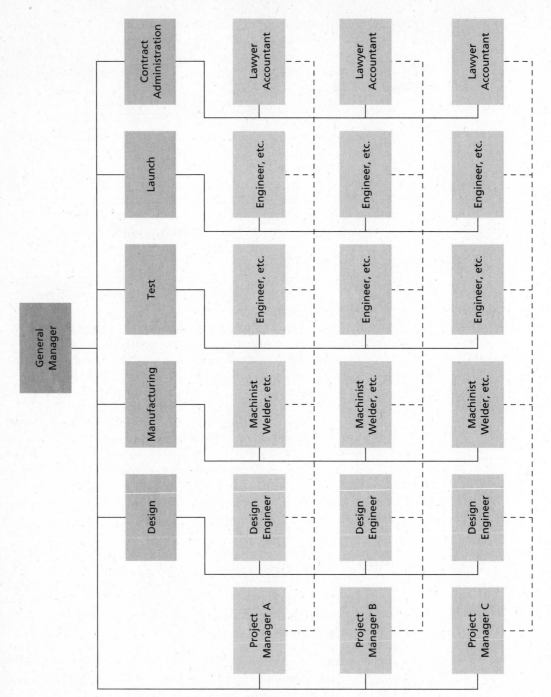

SOURCE: Steiner & Ryan, 1968.

attributed to the conflicting goals and priorities of a dual command structure that pits managers who seek to maintain launch schedules against senior engineers who uphold scientific standards based on safety.

Finally, recent developments in technology have paved the way for a new and innovative organizational form: the **type-D organization.** This is an organizational structure that supports distributed work arrangements. Such organizations exhibit two key characteristics:

1. They distribute work outside the core organization.
2. They depend heavily on information technology (Vitalari, 1990).

Type-D structures are viewed as mechanisms for adapting to environmental change or for managing shortfalls in current structures. Using this kind of structure, organizations distribute work to manage unique problems, opportunities, or circumstances. The distributed work is performed at a separate work site with its own production and social systems and links to the core organization for information transfer, control, and process coordination. The information and control linkages typically employ information technology. Type-D structures are used for

- telecommuting (working at home)
- remote/satellite offices
- mobile offices
- adhocracies (task forces and/or project teams that temporarily form around key business problems or critical business processes) (see Focus On.)

The type-D structure differs from the M-form in that it is a "loosely coupled work arrangement that is typically appended to an M-form structure to provide enhanced responsiveness to environmental demands, greater information capacity, and organizational flexibility via a decentralized setting" (Vitalari, 1990, p. 103). Moreover, a type-D structure is usually smaller in scale, consisting of one individual, a small group, or at most, an entire department. While loosely coupled, a type-D structure often has less autonomy than a division that is highly differentiated and encompasses a rather elaborate management and support structure.

Organizational Structure and Communication

As we have noted, organizational structures shape and are shaped by communication. Within organizations, communication can flow in three directions: downward, upward, or horizontally. The direction of communication flow depends somewhat on the structure of the organization; however, changes in the

FOCUS ON　The Virtual Corporation

One new trend in organizational design is something that management theorists call the *virtual corporation*. The virtual corporation is a temporary network of companies that join forces to offer goods and services to their customers. Each member company contributes what it does best. For example, one company may provide financial services, another may provide shipping and distribution support, and a third may provide product design and sales and marketing expertise. Virtual organizations are, therefore, a form of adhocracy.

The idea for this concept is not new. For example, building a house requires that many different organizations work together. Plumbing, electrical, construction, painting, fixture, appliance, and landscaping companies work with the architect and building contractor to create a product that realtors can then market to prospective customers. In many new housing developments, prospective buyers will deal with a development employee who represents the interests of all of the virtual corporation's members.

Virtual corporations usually form quickly. For example, Apple Computer asked Sony to produce one line of its PowerBook line of computers, allowing Apple to get the product to market faster than if it had to rely only on its own internal resources. In business, these alliances will exist as long as the opportunity which brought the organizations together remains profitable.

For virtual corporations to be successful, there are many legal and organizational concerns to be worked out. Issues of coordination and control are paramount, requiring trust and effective and open communication between virtual corporation members. Interorganizational communication networks must enable and facilitate the efficient and reliable transmission of information, especially information relating to product design, costs, production status, and transaction activity. Doing this ensures that the virtual corporation will be able to respond effectively to customer demands.

direction of communication flow, intentional or otherwise, can alter the shape of the organizational structure.

Downward Communication

Messages flowing from upper to lower organizational levels constitute **downward communication**. Through downward communication, organizations direct the activities of employees, instruct them in proper behaviors and work methods, persuade them to adopt certain ideas and attitudes, evaluate their performance on the job, solicit upward communication, and even provide entertainment. Katz and Kahn (1978) identified five general categories of downward communication: job instructions, rationale (for task assignments), information, feedback, and attempts to indoctrinate or motivate. For example, in centralized, bureaucratic organizations, senior management typically sets policy, while middle management focuses on tactical goals and monitoring operational activities. Once senior management makes the strategic decisions or choices, these are passed down to middle managers who must implement and administer the decisions. These managers in turn institute the changes necessary to the operational and technical levels of the organization, so that information is translated into specific job descriptions and personnel and technology requirements.

Several problems plague downward communication, particularly in highly bureaucratic organizations. For instance, sometimes the messages simply are not received: Subordinates may not read memos or announcements carefully, they may ignore bulletin boards or posted messages, and they may fail to listen at meetings. In addition, subordinates may be overloaded with downward messages—saturated, they stop paying attention. Finally, filtering and distortion can result in problems with downward communication, especially when messages are communicated orally and must work their way through several layers of hierarchy. Overreliance on oral messages by managers can exacerbate problems with downward communication.

Upward Communication

The other vertical channel of formal organizational communication is **upward communication,** the communication flowing from subordinates to superiors. According to Katz and Kahn (1978), upward communication usually assumes one of the following forms:

1. Employees' comments about themselves, their performance, and their problems.
2. Their reactions and ideas about others' behaviors and problems.
3. Their reactions to organizational practices and policies.
4. Employees' thoughts about what needs to be done and how it can be done.

Contemporary management theorists have consistently argued that encouraging upward communication is extremely important. Practitioners, too, have echoed this sentiment. For instance, Texas Instruments chairman Mark Shepherd discussed upward communication in terms of every worker being "seen as a source of ideas, not just acting as a pair of hands"; each team among the more than nine thousand people in the firm's People Involvement Program (PIP) contributes to the company's well-known productivity record by enhancing upward communication (Peters & Waterman, 1982).

In many ways, however, what is communicated upward is different from what is communicated downward in an organizational hierarchy. Those at the lower levels of the organization clearly have a lesser rank and status than those at higher levels, and this reality affects both the content of messages passed upward and employees' willingness to present them in the first place. As hierarchies are more typically associated with autocratic rather than participative or democratic styles of management, we typically find closed communication channels in hierarchical structures. Hershey and Kizzier (1992) described closed communication channels as "a situation in an organization where employee communications (requests, memos, approvals) are expected to follow designated lines of command—employee to supervisor to manager, and vice versa" (p. 773). For example, it would be inappropriate in such organizations for employees to contact their immediate supervisor's manager for requests or approvals. Similarly, official communication with superiors in other departments would likely be discouraged.

Blau and Scott (1962) noted several other dysfunctions of hierarchy for the communication process:

- Differences in status inhibit communication so that people at the same level tend to interact uninhibitedly with one another, whereas interactions with those at higher levels are politically driven, focusing on attempts to seek input and influence with those at higher levels.
- Approval is sought from superiors rather than from peers.
- Because of the reluctance of those in lower positions to criticize those in higher positions, the error-correcting function of normal social interaction is inhibited.

In hierarchies, issues of status, power, rank, and prerequisites often cloud the form and content of upward communication (as we noted in Chapter 4). Because many aspire to higher-level positions in the organizational hierarchy, there may be multiple agendas that affect and alter communication patterns. In particular, subordinates may be reluctant to communicate negative feedback—or to share information that reflects negatively on them and their work. In addition, they may not realize that they are expected to offer their opinions, ideas, or especially criticism. Thus, managers must clearly communicate their desire for such messages (and mean it).

Hierarchies typically have both formal line and staff positions. *Line positions* are responsible for core organizational functions, such as marketing and sales, finance, accounting, and manufacturing. *Staff positions* support the line and provide special kinds of expertise. They include such specialists as lawyers, engineers, medical personnel, and researchers. The formal organizational structure, depicted in an organizational chart, reflects these differing responsibilities. It is important to note that in the formal structure, staff communication is intended to feed line positions with expert advice in support of their responsibilities. Inevitably, however, responsibility for performance rests with line managers—and it is their challenge to encourage their staff members to communicate accurate, complete, and relevant information.

Horizontal Communication

The final communication channel sends messages between and among individuals on the same organizational level. **Horizontal communication** exists in two forms. The first, the interaction among subunit peers, can be either functional or dysfunctional, as discussed in Chapter 4. Groups of peers may communicate formally to coordinate a task or informally to share their problems. Indeed, group members often develop collective perspectives about their problems, which can affect both morale and performance. Contemporary managers' concerns about team effort and morale building reflect their awareness of the importance of horizontal communication within an organizational subunit.

The second form of horizontal communication occurs between and among members of different organizational subunits. Here exchanges usually use informal communication channels, which lie outside the formal organizational lines. People communicate often, usually directly and informally, about formal and informal matters. Although this can expedite information exchange and decision making, it can also result in conflict or feelings of exclusion among those not involved in these networks. For example, individuals at senior levels sometimes consult those at lower levels for advice or information. Those not so consulted may then perceive those who are as assuming influence disproportionate to their formal position and status, a perception that causes resentment and even hostile political behavior.

At the formal level, traditional bureaucratic organizations have done little to encourage horizontal communication and in some cases have actively discouraged it. The conventional wisdom was that information should pass vertically through the organization, carefully progressing up and down the hierarchy. By following such vertical flows, each message would touch all appropriate points of authority. Fayol's (1949) early statement about the need for horizontal communication carefully specified the conditions under which such lateral exchanges might be deemed acceptable (usually in situations involving crisis or emergency).

In addition to suffering from lack of official encouragement, horizontal communication also flounders in organizational environments that encourage competition rather than cooperation or where rewards and resources are scarce. Moreover, even with encouragement and rewards, specialization often serves as an additional barrier. The highly skilled machinist uses a specialized vocabulary, as do the corporate lawyer, the tax accountant, the electrical engineer, and the physical chemist. Yet many organizations bring these and other kinds of specialists together under the same professional roof, with the perhaps unrealistic expectation that they will be able to communicate effectively in their joint pursuit of organizational goals.

The Informal Organization

Within every formal organization there also exists an **informal organization**. Within this informal structure, much communication occurs, springing up whenever an individual feels a need to communicate with someone else with whom he or she is not connected by a formal organizational channel. Informal networks often develop through accidents of spatial arrangement, similarity of personalities, or compatibilities of personal skills or values. For example, employees may end up talking because they have adjacent offices, enjoy following the Indiana Hoosiers or UNCG Spartans, love jazz, or have similar political views. Of course, the interests they share at an informal level will affect the way they interact about job-related matters. Most employees are involved in several networks at the same time: Some grow from political ties, others from technical interests, and still others from social preferences (Roberts & O'Reilly, 1978).

Informal communication networks are vital in any hierarchical structure. Whereas formal structure indicates who is responsible for what and who reports to whom, the informal structure is not evident in any organizational document; it grows rather from the self-groupings that humans naturally form. Consistent with the findings of the Hawthorne studies, the informal structure can be as important as the formal structure in accomplishing the goals of the organization, especially in situations where, as Ray, Palmer, and Wohl (1991) put it, "the less precisely defined circumstances of organizational politics occur" (p. 32). For example, the staff position of assistant to the president may exist on the organizational chart, but the person most influential with the president may in fact be her spouse or secretary.

Informal communication is the dominant form of oral interaction in organizations. Deal and Kennedy (1982) have suggested that 90 percent of what goes on in an organization has nothing to do with formal events. Rather, the informal network, the "hidden hierarchy," is in reality how an organization operates. And the operation of informal networks is not necessarily bad. According to Peters and Waterman (1982):

> The excellent companies are a vast network of informal, open communication. The patterns and intensity cultivate the right people's getting into contact with each other, regularly, and the chaotic/anarchic properties of the system are kept under control simply because of the regularity of contact and its nature (e.g., peer-to-peer in quasi-competitive situations (pp. 121–22).

Top-level managers can also benefit from informal communication. Kotter, of the Harvard Business School, observed fifteen highly rated general managers in action. He concluded that they got their work done not by giving orders or churning out reports but mostly by talking to people—"asking questions, making requests, maybe prodding a bit. These conversations often consisted of nothing more than a two-minute encounter in the hallway or on the phone" (Kiechel, 1984, p. 148).

Informal communication is often referred to as the *grapevine*. When information is introduced into the grapevine, it tends to travel quickly because it is unimpeded by structural constraints. Although individuals often discredit information they receive through the grapevine, research has shown it to be amazingly (78 to 90 percent) accurate (Davis, 1973; Hellweg, 1987). However, when errors do occur in grapevine communication, the inaccuracies are sometimes quite dramatic, and the grapevine also serves as a network through which rumors (unsubstantiated and potentially damaging information) are transmitted.

The grapevine is a fact of organizational life—a natural outgrowth of human beings being together. Managers who understand that and stay in touch with the organization's informal communication networks can learn much from these networks while using them strategically to expedite the flow of information. As Davis (1973) pointed out, "if properly guided, it [the grapevine] can help build teamwork, company loyalty, and the kind of motivation that makes people want to do their best" (p. 132).

Most of the research on communication channels, both formal and informal, has focused on traditional forms of interaction. Advances in technology,

Computer networks can be used for desktop video conferencing which allows individual users to communicate visually with other employees while discussing documents or other material. (MCI International)

however, are clearly changing the way people interact within and between organizations. How the use of technology affects the way individuals communicate and relate to one another is only beginning to be understood. For instance, information overload is one common problem traditionally associated with organizational communication. Some experts argue that technology has the potential to help reduce information overload by helping managers systematically prioritize, queue, and/or filter incoming data. However, others contend that the use of computers and networks has actually exacerbated the problem by increasing the number and accessibility of communication channels.

New Challenges for Organizational Design

New factors are challenging the traditional views of organizational design. One such factor concerns the nature of the work force itself, another involves a new concept for reorganizing the workplace, and a third concerns the impact of technology.

"Workforce 2000:" Work Force Diversity and Organizational Design

In 1987 the Department of Labor published "Workforce 2000, Work and Workers for the 21st Century." That report focused national attention on the dramatic changes taking place in the economy and in the composition of the work force. Released by the Hudson Institute, the report predicted significant changes in the composition of the U.S. work force by the year 2000.

For instance, the report predicted that 85 percent of new applicants for employment over the following eight years would be women, minorities, and immigrants. Moreover, the average age of workers and the number of disadvantaged and disabled workers were also expected to rise significantly. The report's message is clear: Managing work force diversity is now critical to organizational effectiveness.

The goal of managing diversity is to create a level playing field for everyone. In many traditional bureaucracies employees have confronted a glass ceiling, or level beyond which few minorities and women have advanced; corporate strategy has not included equal employment opportunities; and recruitment practices have prevented qualified minorities and women from being considered for management positions.

The Workforce 2000 report has had important ramifications for organizational design: Work Force diversity is becoming a mediating factor in organizational design. Changes such as a decrease in the population and work force, an increase in the average age of the population and work force, and an increase in the number of women, minorities, immigrants, and contingent workers in the work force now demand a fundamental change in employment practices. Moreover, in organizations encouraging employee empowerment, decision making will now be shared by organizational members of diverse backgrounds.

Dominguez (1992) suggested a new "salad bowl" approach to corporate culture, in which the individual retains cultural identity while contributing to the richness of the team and the organization. He pointed out that successful organizational responses to work force diversity should include the following:

1. A flexible corporate culture that appreciates individual and cultural differences and incorporates this belief in its value system.
2. A mentoring system to promote the adoption and diffusion of new multicultural values.
3. Developmental programs and training.
4. Manager and employee sensitivity training.

The relevance of work force diversity to organizational design is rather straightforward. Effective organizational design allows organizations internal operating efficiency as well as the ability to respond quickly and effectively to environmental changes. Organizations that manage work force diversity are rewarded with more effective teamwork, as well as greater flexibility to adapt to the competition, because they can involve *everyone* in the enterprise. We discuss managing diversity in greater detail in Chapter 9.

Future Search Conferences and Organizational Design

Marvin Weisbord is a leader in the movement to reorganize the workplace into one that is more productive and democratic. Weisbord believes that, for the first time, the United States is about to have an entire generation of workers, managers, and supervisors who have lived through a complete change cycle. They have experienced their own resistance to new ideas, their reluctance to become involved, their conversion, and their involvement.

Galagan (1992) stated that one of Weisbord's theories, Inventing the Future: Search Strategies for Whole Systems Improvement, involves the use of future search conferences. The first premise of a future search conference is that it involves the largest possible number of people with a stake in the organization's future. Meetings usually involve a cross-section of the whole system, or company, under discussion—including employees from all levels, clients, and suppliers. Working together to improve the system as a whole, participants complete tasks such as examining the past and making action plans both for the short and the long term.

The radical aspect of this approach relative to organizational design is that it is so inclusive and empowering in its approach to structure and decision making. The organizational structure is now modified to include not only the organization itself but also its key stakeholders, who now have a voice in organizational planning and decision making. Organizational design is no longer viewed as the sole prerogative of the organization's dominant coalition. Instead it is now a shared, democratic process, whose outcome supposedly supports the needs of many interested parties.

Technology and Organizational Design and Structure

George Huber of the University of Texas at Austin has proposed a "theory of the effects of advanced information technologies on organizational design, intelligence and decision making" (1990). Huber made four predictions about the impact of technology on organizations:

1. Advanced information technology extends the range of communication and decision-making options from which potential users can choose. As technology improves task performance, the technology is more frequently used.
2. The use of advanced information technology leads to more available and more quickly retrievable information—therefore leading to increased information accessibility.
3. Increased information accessibility leads to change in organizational design. Centralized organizations will use technology to allow for greater decentralization since technologies such as groupware allow enhanced coordination and control capabilities across time and place. (However, Huber also claimed that decentralized organizations will want to become more centralized for the same reason!)
4. Increased information accessibility and changes in organizational design that increase the speed and effectiveness with which information can be converted into intelligence or intelligence into decisions lead to organizational intelligence that is more accurate, comprehensive, timely, and available. As a result, decisions improve in quality and timeliness.

Empirical evidence seems to support Huber's observations. While changes in the economics of production and transportation brought about the Industrial Revolution 150 years ago, changes today are being driven by the need for improved effectiveness in organizational coordination. Networked computer technology allows workers to work differently, to coordinate tasks more effectively, and to facilitate team member communication.

Malone and Rockart (1991) contended that computer networking furthers the development of new, coordination-intensive business structures. They suggested that a major effect of information technology is substituting such technology for human coordination. Computers are eliminating data entry personnel and order expediters and are being used to speed up the supply, processing, and distribution of goods and services. Computer networks are also helping to improve coordination and communication within organizations, allowing many companies to flatten their managerial hierarchies by eliminating layers of middle management.

Another effect of networking's reduction of coordination costs is an increase in the extent to which coordination is used. The real-time availability of databases, for example, allows for easier tracking of goods, services, orders, and accounts. For example, it helped Otis Elevator greatly improve its management of repair activities. When analyses of its databases indicate failures of certain parts, Otis can replace that part in other elevators. This improved coordination capability has allowed Otis to reduce its number of maintenance calls by 20 percent. Information is thus not only more accessible and current; it is more easily analyzed, understood, and communicated using computer software programs and networks.

A final effect associated with the reduction in coordination costs is a shift toward the use of more coordination-intensive structures. Malone and Rockart pointed out that these coordination-intensive structures promote better links between people within the same companies and make more reliable and consistent information available for decentralized decision making. Technology allows better links between companies, sometimes creating interorganizational networks among buyers, suppliers, and even potential competitors. For example, electronic data interchange (EDI) is a communication process that allows firms to share data regarding selected transactions between and among their computers. Manufacturers may receive data from their parts suppliers and send data to retailers and vice versa; they may even do their ordering and billing via EDI (as Wal-Mart does with its suppliers).

Malone and Rockart made a number of other predictions. They suggested that because of the reduction in the cost of internal and external coordination, firms may place less emphasis on vertical integration; that is, they will resort to buying product components rather than making them. They also predicted that computer networking may lead to a proliferation of smaller firms, with more electronically mediated alliances between firms and greater use of electronic markets to pick suppliers. Besides market changes, technology may also make the networked organization (the adhocracy) more common.

As noted earlier and suggested by Figure 5.1, an adhocracy differs from traditional hierarchical forms in that its communication and coordination follow nontraditional flow patterns. An adhocracy involves unpredictable amounts of lateral communication, making it extremely coordination-intensive. However, as Malone and Rockart pointed out, new media, "such as electronic mail, computer conferencing and electronic bulletin boards, can make the coordination easier and, therefore, enable the adhocracy to work more effectively. Computer networks can help find and coordinate people with diverse knowledge and skills from many parts of the organization" (p. 133).

There is little doubt that computer-based technology also enables the organization to transfer information faster, more cheaply, and more selectively, thus helping to reduce information overload. As a consequence, organizations can take in, move, digest, and respond to data more rapidly than in the past.

Summarizing Perspective

Technology is clearly expected to influence organizational design and structure. What is less certain is whether technology imperatives or traditional organizational imperatives drive organizational change. Drucker (1988) suggested a new flattened organizational structure made possible by technology. The technology imperative argues that technology shapes the choices, actions, and outcomes of decision makers, who are often uncertain of its full ramifications. Clearly, Huber's theories about the impact of technology on the organization are rooted in the technology imperative.

By way of contrast, a traditional organizational perspective contends that organizations choose how to employ technology, that managers knowingly and deliberately match technology to organizational needs. From this perspective, the manager pursuing a flattened organization of knowledge-based work teams would choose to use technologies to increase the coordination and communication of team members and to facilitate the collection and analysis of information about the organization's environment. From this vantage point, Drucker's "coming organization" was a structure waiting to happen; management recognized the need to redesign the organization, and technology facilitated the enactment of desired changes. Carlyle (1990) suggested that because of networking technologies, organizations can either centralize or decentralize as they choose—a clear message that he viewed the organizational imperative as dominant.

We argue that it is the interaction of technology and organizational factors that causes organizational change. Technology alone can not create change. Management values, choices, and policies are equally influential. Both technology and organizational factors shape organizational behavior and decision making and, hence, the structure of the organization. Managers can choose among organizational forms because the technology exists to allow them effectively to extend their span of control. However, technology also reshapes organizational communication, processes, and capabilities by automating jobs and forcing managers to consider business-process redesign and business-scope redesign. In business-process redesign, managers begin to reconsider why traditional processes are needed and whether things can be done in more efficient ways. In business-scope redesign, technology enables some companies to move into new businesses. Technological innovations may also change the nature and balance of competition, spawning new firms and terminating some organizations altogether.

When organizations adopt technology to address specific needs, they often realize both intended and unintended results. Hence, it is clear that generalized predictions about the impact of technology on organizational structure and design are, at best, tentative at this point.

CASES FOR DISCUSSION

CASE 1 *Changing Graduation Requirements*

For students pursuing a degree in the School of Business at the University of the Southern Pacific (USP), graduation requirements for undergraduates have remained unchanged for ten years. Now, however, a special faculty committee has been established to examine the current requirements and is likely to initiate some changes.

Committee members are aware of certain widely perceived problems within the current system. Among them are the following:

1. Faculty complain that even graduating seniors cannot write well.

2. Faculty perceive students' oral communication skills to be deficient.

3. Students can obtain their business degree without having been introduced to another culture or a foreign language.

4. In spite of faculty complaints about student skill deficits, grade inflation is rampant. The average grade in most classes is a B (not even a B−!).

5. Students complain that the faculty, on the whole, are not very good at teaching. Most are more interested in their research and their doctoral students.

6. Students complain that too many graduate students are used as graders, discussion leaders, and even lecturers.

The committee is also working in an organizational environment that includes the following conditions:

1. The dean of the School of Business is concerned about declining enrollments in the school. Ten years ago, 55 percent of entering freshmen declared their intention of majoring in business. That figure is now 30 percent. The dean would like to see the degree become more attractive to students.

2. With globalization an increasing reality in the business world, faculty agree that business students should be required to complete a foreign language or culture studies requirement. However, there are two complications. First, many students currently choose business to avoid the foreign language requirement of the School of Liberal Arts and Sciences. Adding such a requirement to the business degree could thus lead to further enrollment problems. In addition, foreign language departments have limited resources—and are currently having difficulty offering sufficient sections of foreign language courses for the liberal arts students who are already required to take them.

3. The state legislature (USP is a public, state-supported institution) is pressing the university to create an assessment system, in the form of a comprehensive exam to test students who have completed their course requirements on their oral, written, critical thinking, and quantitative skills. If the university does not develop its own assessment system, then the legislature is threatening to create one—and mandate its use.

4. Both the legislature and the newly elected president of USP's board of trustees are very concerned about the quality of teaching. Concerns include whether graduate students who teach (or help teach) are

appropriately trained and supervised, how much teaching faculty do, whether faculty who teach well are rewarded appropriately, and so on. The board is currently interviewing students, faculty, and administrators to explore these problems, in greater depth.

Questions for Discussion

1. Which of the systems perspectives seems most useful for assessing this situation: rational, natural, or open? Why?

2. What do you see as being the most important contextual variables affecting this university and the committee's specific task?

3. Based on your understanding of organizational structure and communication, outline some of the major problems with communication channels (both formal and informal) with which this committee will likely have to grapple.

4. How might the committee approach its task most constructively?

CASE 2 *Telecommuting*

When Steve Conroy began telecommuting—working at home several days a week rather than driving into his office—his wife and daughter interrupted him so often that he gave them his home "office" telephone number and told them to call him like everyone else.

But the interruptions did not stop there. Even in his car, Steve, a New England Telephone Co. accounts manager, was accessible. Often, he would hear the annoying buzz of his beeper, pull off the road, and find himself connecting his portable computer to his mobile phone to access the data he needed to help a coworker answer a client's billing question.

"From my home, from the car, from the tennis courts, even the golf course, I'm pretty much always available—regrettably, sometimes," said Conroy, who is one of a growing cadre of American telecommuters who work from home part-time during the normal work day, linked to the office by fax, phone, or personal computer.

Initially, the trend was viewed as a win-win situation, offering companies greater flexibility and workers extra time with children or an end to the two-hour commute. But increasingly, telecommuting is seen to have a dark side. Bosses can be mistrustful. Telecommunicators can feel out of touch. And what first appeared to be a liberating policy has the potential for creating electronic sweatshops where work drags on long after the normal workday ends.

Thomas E. Miller was working twelve- to eighteen-hour days in Manhattan but moved to Ithaca, New York, in 1982. Linked by phone line to his New York City employer, a consulting firm, he thought he would have more time to spend with his family. But his telecommuting arrangement had the opposite effect. The phone rang at all hours, meals were interrupted, and it was difficult to break away from the "office" long enough to give his children the attention they craved.

"One day my son turned to me and said, 'Dad, why can't you get a job like other kids' dads?' There I was working at the house, spending more time with my kids than my father ever spent with me and my children were saying that we were always being interrupted." Miller tackled his problem by developing a routine similar to the one he had when he was commuting. He substituted a short trip to his children's school every morning for the drive into New York City. Then, after dropping them off, he had his morning coffee and went home to work.

There is a rapidly growing number of telecommuters. Since the use of personal computers began exploding in the early 1980s, the number of telecommuters has grown 20 percent every year, reports Jack Nilles, president of the Telecommuting Advisory Council, a nonprofit organization with 120,000 members. Link Resources, a New York research firm, estimates that soon 7.6 million employees will be telecommuting to their jobs. California has become the nation's telecommuting leader, spurred on by the U.S. Clean Air Act amendments aimed at reducing automobile emissions. On the East Coast, in contrast, most telecommuters are thought of as "teleguerrillas," people who work at home without formal agreements or clearcut policies from their companies. The lack of such safeguards has led the AFL-CIO to denounce the practice of telecommuting.

"There are a lot of hidden costs that employers don't talk about, such as electricity or the cost of insuring the office and equipment or the fact that people really can't work at home when their children are around so they have to pay for day care," said Elisa Riordan, assistant to the vice president of the Communications Workers of America's New York and New England district. Although most large companies provide the equipment and installation, in 1986 eight data processors settled a $1.2 million lawsuit against California Western Life Insurance in which they allege they had been stripped of benefits, saddled with higher workloads, and told their wages would be lower after they began working at home.

A project conducted by Merrill Lynch, New York's Department of Transportation, New York Telephone Co., Banker's Trust, and the Urban Research Center showed some drawbacks to telecommuting. In addition to jealousy and griping among coworkers who feel that their telecommuting colleagues have special privileges, telecommuting can take workers away from the office when they might benefit from being there. Instead of talking to the boss, telecommuting employees are at home, tapping away. They may be twice as productive, but their supervisors might not think so unless they see them working.

Gil Gordon, author of *Telecommuting: How to Make It Work for You and Your Company,* believes that some people should not telecommute. "People who can't stay home without watching the soaps or the Oprah Winfrey show or who have to go into the refrigerator every few minutes shouldn't telecommute. People who thrive on the social dynamics of the office—singles who would rather not be alone in the condo all day, for example—are better off in the office."

To make telecommuting work, managers should (1) put telecommuting arrangements with workers in writing; (2) set clear performance goals and standards; (3) spell out when, where, and how often office meetings or conferences will be held; (4) say when the arrangement will begin and end; (5) extend the opportunity to all employees, if possible, to avoid fueling resentment by picking some employees over others; (6) limit telecommuting to a maximum of three days a week so that telecommuters will be able to meet face-to-face with office staff and the manager at least once weekly; and (7) establish how much the arrangement will affect salary, vacation, and other benefits. (For example, can telecommuters call in sick? Do they receive the same salary and bonuses as their peers?)

Telecommuters similarly should (1) find a secluded area away from the family to work, such as a room in the attic, basement, or an extra guest room; (2) maintain regular work hours but remember to take periodic breaks; (3) establish two or three telephone lines— one for the office, another for the fax machine, and a third for the personal family line; and (4) discourage relatives from "dropping in" for a visit during working hours.

SOURCE: Based on Lewis, 1993.

Questions for Discussion

1. What effects (positive and/or negative) might telecommuting have on upward, downward, and horizontal communication?

2. How might telecommuters participate in informal communication? What are the barriers? The opportunities?

3. What are the major ways in which technology influences the telecommuter's job? How do various technologies provide both opportunities and barriers for those who telecommute?

4. Examine the guidelines for managers of telecommuters presented in the case. Which ones do you find useful? Which ones might you change? Should others be added?

5. Finally, examine the guidelines for telecommuters presented here. Which of these seem sensible and useful? Are there some you would add or alter in some way?

CHAPTER

6

Organizational Leadership in the Information Age

An executive provides vision and direction, makes decisions, diagnoses and solves problems, negotiates, convinces, and selects and coaches people. All these actions depend on the executive's ability to think creatively and communicate clearly; clear communication and creative thinking can be enhanced by the use of computers.
Mary Boone, *Leadership and the Computer*, 1991, p. 3.

E veryone agrees that leadership is important. At AT&T, for instance, the company spends more than $1.5 million each year to send two hundred of its "high potential" middle managers to an intensive two-week program aimed at improving their ability to think as entrepreneurs, to adapt to change, and to work in an increasingly team-oriented environment (Gatewood, 1994). This kind of investment in leadership training means that organizations are convinced that effective leadership is vital to their futures. Hersey and Blanchard (1972) pointed out that "the successful organization has one major attribute that sets it apart from unsuccessful organizations: dynamic and effective leadership" (p. 67). But how should leadership be defined? Some think of leadership as a set of traits or skills. Others embrace the view that leadership is situation-specific; the same person may lead in one situation and not in another.

Traditionalists have long assumed that a limited number of individuals will exercise leadership within a particular organization. More recently others, as suggested by our earlier discussion of teamwork and self-management, have argued that many people should be empowered by the wide distribution of leadership functions. Advances in technology give some edge to this notion. As information is shared throughout the organizational hierarchy, traditional channels are increasingly bypassed. Insofar as information is associated with power and power with leadership, computer networks create opportunities for widespread empowerment and leadership sharing.

One way of examining the complexity of leadership is to consider the diverse ways in which it has been studied. In this chapter we will explore several different approaches to thinking about leadership; each causes us to see the relationship between communication and leadership in a different light. Then we will turn our attention to a consideration of power (and its sources), powerlessness, and empowerment. Finally, we will discuss the impact of the new technologies on organizational leadership.

Approaches to Leadership

How do we go about identifying leaders in any organization? Should we look primarily at those in official positions of authority? Or should we look for those who are wielding influence, regardless of their formal titles? How we respond to these questions will largely depend upon how we conceptualize leadership.

Throughout this century, different scholars have studied leadership in strikingly diverse ways. For the most part, the "old" ways of viewing leadership are considered less applicable to the modern, increasingly team-oriented, organization. Yet early views of leadership are not without their contemporary champions. In this section we will look briefly at each of the major approaches to thinking about leadership.

The Trait Approach

The earliest conceptualization of leadership was based on the notion that "leaders are born, not made." This theory of the "great man" first surfaced in the early writings of the Greeks and Romans, and there are still people today who subscribe to the notion that leadership is inborn and cannot be developed. This trait approach denies the potential significance of situational variables in influencing a person's ability to emerge as a leader and maintain a position of leadership. It assumes that essential leadership traits (such as courage, perseverance, and drive) are important across diverse group and organizational settings. Moreover, these critical traits are believed to separate leaders from followers.

Identifying inherent leadership traits has proven elusive. Bird (1940) conducted an extensive review of trait research prior to 1940. Although he was able to compile an extensive list of traits that apparently distinguished leaders from followers, he also reported that only 5 percent of these traits were common to four or more of the investigations. In other words, researchers didn't agree on essential leadership traits. Over thirty years later, Stogdill (1974) published an exhaustive review of leadership research conducted in diverse settings and published since 1945. He was able to identify five traits that seemed to characterize leaders: *intelligence, achievement, dependability, activity,* and *socioeconomic status.* Leaders tended to score higher than nonleaders on each of these measures; however, leadership was inhibited when a large dis-

Are leadership traits inborn? Can leadership be learned? Will any list of traits distinguish leaders from nonleaders? While scholars and practitioners rarely agree on the answers to these questions, most have little difficulty acknowledging effective leadership when they encounter it. Marian Wright Edelman, president and founder of the Children's Defense Fund, based in Washington, D.C., is a leader who seems to possess qualities that most people associate with excellent leadership, such as intelligence, honesty, and courage. (Gamma Liaison)

crepancy existed between the leader and the group. In short, the person who is too smart, too outstanding in achievement, too active, or too rich runs the risk of being perceived as more a "deviate" than a leader. Perhaps, as Gibb (1968) once put it, "the crowd prefers to be ill-governed by people it can understand."

Originally, the trait approach was personality-based and thus encountered some trouble. Personality traits are only vaguely conceived and roughly measured. No comprehensive list of personality traits currently exists, nor is there a reliable method by which those traits can be tested. In addition, the kinds of traits needed by leaders may change as organizations grow and develop. Moreover, leadership traits necessary for emerging as a leader may differ substantially from those associated with maintaining one's leadership position over time (Gouran, 1970).

In spite of expressed reservations about the trait approach, some contemporary scholars continue to construct profiles of effective leaders based on lists of leadership traits. For instance, in their book *Credibility: How Leaders Gain and Lose It, Why People Demand It,* James Kouzes and Barry Posner reported on their ongoing research in which they surveyed over fifteen thousand managers. They found that a strikingly consistent set of characteristics or attributes of "most admired leaders" emerged over time. As Table 6.1 shows, being honest, forward-looking, inspiring, and competent were especially valued.

Others have attempted to distinguish leaders from nonleaders by focusing on the characteristics of the individual's *communication behavior* rather than on her or his personality. Geier (1967), for instance, identified five negative com-

TABLE 6.1

Characteristics of Admired Leaders

Characteristic	1993 U.S. RESPONDENTS Percentage of People Selecting	1987 U.S. RESPONDENTS Percentage of People Selecting
Honest	87	83
Forward-looking	71	62
Inspiring	68	58
Competent	58	67
Fair-minded	49	40
Supportive	46	32
Broad-minded	41	37
Intelligent	38	43
Straightforward	34	34
Courageous	33	27
Dependable	32	32
Cooperative	30	25
Imaginative	28	34
Caring	27	26
Mature	14	23
Determined	13	20
Ambitious	10	21
Loyal	10	11
Self-controlled	05	13
Independent	05	10

SOURCE: Kouzes & Posner, 1993.

munication traits or behaviors that consistently prevented an individual from emerging as group leader: being uninformed, not participating, demonstrating extreme rigidity, giving orders or being authoritarian/bossy, and engaging in verbalizations offensive to others. Other researchers have focused on positive communication behaviors. For example, Russell (1970) found that appointed leaders who were able to maintain their status throughout a meeting were more agreeable and less opinionated than their unsuccessful counterparts. Since communication skills can be developed, identifying the communicative characteristics associated with leadership and other positive group and organizational outcomes is a potentially worthy venture, a promising byproduct of the trait approach.

The Stylistic Approach

Another approach to leadership focuses on what leaders *do* rather than on their personality characteristics. The stylistic approach (looking at how leadership behaviors cluster to form an identifiable "style") was first used by White and Lippitt (1960) in their often cited investigation of three different leadership styles: authoritarian, democratic, and laissez-faire. Although the study was flawed in several ways (see Chapter 2), White and Lippitt concluded that the democratic style was superior to the other two in terms of group cohesiveness, the amount of independence behavior exhibited by subjects, the quality of the groups' products, and overall member satisfaction with the experience.

The claimed superiority of the democratic style of leadership has received mixed support (see Coch & French, 1948; Galbraith, 1967; Lawrence & Lorsch, 1967; and Shaw, 1955). In addition, the results of stylistic studies are difficult to assess because of the wide differences in researchers' definitions of the various leadership styles. Democratic or participatory leadership may range from involving workers fully in all stages of the decision-making process to merely giving them the opportunity to react to an already sanctioned policy. In the study by Coch and French (1948), for instance, "participation" consisted of letting workers sit down with management and listen to explanations of why impending changes were about to occur in their factory. In other studies, leaders were trained to exhibit very positive democratic styles, while more directive styles were portrayed as negatively as possible (Gouran, 1970), resulting in a skewed and unfair comparison.

Underlying the stylistic approach is the notion that the leader's choice of a particular style of leadership depends upon his or her assumptions about human beings and what motivates them. Thus, the stylistic approach lies at the heart of several of the management theories discussed in Chapter 3. McGregor's Theory Y, for instance, posits certain critical beliefs about workers and their needs, abilities, and sources of motivation. Having embraced those assumptions, the Theory Y manager proceeds to exhibit a democratic, supportive, empowering style of leadership. In addition, leaders' style choices are often affected by their perceptions of what they can realistically do to influence others and their views of the resources over which they have some control (Pace, 1983).

Although the stylistic approach, with its emphasis on clusters of communication behaviors and underlying leader attitudes, represents an improvement over the trait approach, it still seeks to identify a "best" way to lead. Given the wide variety of organizations, types of workers, and tasks, the probability that one style of leadership will ever be found consistently superior to others seems remote. Situational factors will likely influence the success of any given leadership style.

Even so, it is important to recognize two things about the stylistic approach. First, whenever we attempt to profile or list the behavioral characteristics associated with effective leadership (as is common), we are embracing a stylistic view of leadership. Likert did it in the 1960s with his "participative manager profile" (see Chapter 3); more recently, Bennis (1989) published a list of what the next generation of leaders will have in common (see Table 6.2). Second, like the trait approach, the stylistic view of leadership can easily be translated into communication behaviors *or* values from which important communicated attitudes and communication characteristics can readily be derived. When Bennis points to *virtue,* for instance, we might logically assume that this quality would lead people to communicate honestly, or that a *belief in people and teamwork* would likely lead to supportive communicative behaviors, including active listening and encouraging others to be their best.

The Situational Approach

The futile quest for ideal leadership traits or styles inevitably led to questions about contextual or situational variables that might influence leadership. Perhaps the best-known proponent of this approach is Frederick Fiedler (1967; 1979) whose research efforts spanned nearly two decades and focused on such diverse groups as athletic teams, business management groups, bomber crews, surveying teams, and policy-making committees. Like many

TABLE 6.2

Common Characteristics of the Next Generation of Leaders

Broad education	Devotion to long-term growth rather than short-term profit
Boundless curiosity	Commitment to excellence
Boundless enthusiasm	Readiness
Belief in people and teamwork	Virtue
Willingness to take risks	Vision

SOURCE: Bennis, 1989.

others, Fiedler was interested in the extent to which leaders allowed others to participate in making decisions, especially comparing autocratic with democratic leadership styles. **Fiedler's contingency theory** concluded that the style of leadership most effective in any given situation depends upon three factors and the degree to which the leader has control over them:

1. *The power of the leader's position*—or the amount of social power or strength the leader holds in relation to other group or organizational members.

2. *The structure of the task being performed*—taking into account the clarity with which the group might measure success or failure, the number of avenues through which the goal might be achieved, and the number of correct decisions available.

3. *The social relationships between the leader and others*—or the degree to which the members like, are loyal to, and are willing to follow the leader. Of the three, Fiedler found this one to be the most important.

These factors in turn define the "favorability" of the situation to the leader. According to contingency theory, the ideal situation is one in which the leader has high position power, is confronted with a clearly structured task, and possesses good social relations with other group members. In these circumstances, a more directive, task-oriented leadership style (with attention directed to getting the job done) is most effective. The leader can exert considerable control without arousing negative sentiments. Productivity is achieved without losing group cohesiveness. Fiedler also argued that the task-oriented style is more effective when conditions are extremely unfavorable—that is, things are going badly for everyone, the group is unproductive, group members are hostile, and the organization is in danger of falling apart. The crisis nature of this low-control situation calls for firm and directive leadership supplied by a task-motivated leader. By way of contrast, the democratic style is most successful when the group is functioning under moderately favorable conditions.

In reality, most organizational settings present the leader with a mixed bag. The leader may have the necessary position power but be faced with a complex and ambiguous task; some interpersonal relationships may be good, while others are strained. In general, Fiedler's contingency theory leads to the conclusion that democratic leadership remains preferable in many organizational situations but that its effectiveness will always depend upon the peculiarities of the situation. To be effective across situations and over time, the good leader must remain vigilant. Although Fiedler's work has been the subject of considerable controversy (Ashour, 1973; Graen, Alveres, Orris, & Martella, 1970), the theory's predictions have received rather strong support from both laboratory and field investigations (Chemers, 1984; Strube & Garcia, 1981).

Other contingency-oriented leadership theories have addressed the relationship of leadership decision-making style to group performance and morale. One of the best-known theories is Vroom and Yetton's **normative decision theory** (1973), which presents a range of decision-making approaches, including autocratic, consultative, and group styles. The dimension underlying the range is the degree to which the leader allows subordinates to participate in the decision-making process. The model specifies which of the styles is most likely to yield effective decisions under varying circumstances. Like Fiedler's theory, this model assumes that there is no one best way to make decisions and that the most effective style will depend on the characteristics of the situation.

The situational characteristics considered most important from the perspective of normative decision theory are (1) the expected support, acceptance, and commitment to the decision by subordinates and (2) the amount of structured, clear, relevant information available to the leader. Vroom and Yetton supplied three rules for determining which styles will be most effective. First, other things being equal, autocratic decisions are less time-consuming and therefore more efficient. However, a leader who lacks sufficient structure and information to make a high-quality decision must consult with subordinates to gain that information and to enlist their assistance and advice. Finally, if the leader does not have sufficient support from subordinates to be assured that they will accept the decision, the leader must gain their acceptance and commitment through having them participate in decision making.

Despite the similarity of Fiedler's and Vroom and Yetton's theories, they diverge sharply on the question of individuals' ability to modify their decision styles. Vroom and Yetton's normative model assumes that leaders can quickly and easily change their behavior to fit the demands of the situation, whereas Fiedler sees leadership style arising out of stable, enduring, well-learned personality attributes that are quite resistant to change.

Of the human resources management theories discussed in Chapter 3, Hersey and Blanchard's life cycle theory (1972) most clearly exemplifies the contingency perspective. These scholars argued that the effectiveness of a leader's style depends upon how well it is adapted to the job and psychological maturity levels of subordinates. Different approaches work better with different kinds of workers—and workers' levels of maturity will change (as will their need for a particular style of supervision) over time.

Other factors besides the situational ones discussed above likely influence the effectiveness of any leadership style. For instance, *workers' self-confidence* should influence the style of leadership they are willing to tolerate or accept. If an organization is undergoing dramatic technological changes, for example, employees may feel overwhelmed and thus welcome a very directive, structured style of leadership that serves to train them in using the new technologies. If, however, they are dealing with a type of task with which they have dealt successfully in the past, they may insist on a fairly high level of self-management.

The leader's actual or perceived *competence* is another important situational variable. A leader who is exceedingly well informed, highly intelligent, and experienced at the kind of task confronting the group is quite likely to be accepted, regardless of the style of leadership she or he exhibits (within reasonable limits). This is especially true under conditions where group members lack experience or knowledge. These variables in turn interact with the perceived salience of getting the job done right, or on time, and the extent to which those involved with the work are *committed to the task* and the organization's goals. Finally, groups tend to accept styles of leadership that have allowed them to function successfully in the past. A task team that just received rave reviews or has experienced vast gains in productivity will be more accepting of the style of its leaders than will groups that have experienced continued or significant failure.

The situational approach to leadership clearly argues for the importance of identifying and acknowledging contingencies. Perhaps its most important message is the need for leaders thoughtfully and intelligently to assess their particular organizational situation in terms of culture, norms, values, group members and their needs, the task, and so forth—and then to choose a style of leadership that best "fits" the situation. Moreover, this thoughtful assessment is an ongoing process that must be repeated across tasks and time, with changing and maturing workers, and with evolving organizational needs. The situational approach offers no formula for leadership effectiveness. Instead, it seems to suggest that leaders must be both analytical and intuitive, flexible and innovative. Their communication skills must cover a wide range—from listening, prodding, and encouraging to confronting and soothing. From a situational perspective, leadership becomes more art than science.

The Functional Approach

Each of the leadership approaches discussed above focuses on either the behavior or traits of formally appointed leaders. The functional approach, however, conceives of leadership differently. From a functional perspective, the behavior of *any* group member that promotes the achievement of group or organizational goals is considered leadership behavior. In this view, leadership functions are typically performed by more than one group member, and all individuals in a group or organization could conceivably contribute to the achievement of mutual goals. In this hypothetical situation, all of these individuals would function as a leader; but the nature, quality, and extent of their leadership activity would likely vary considerably.

In the area of group communication research, it has long been acknowledged that different individuals may play varied communication task and socioemotional roles, many of which can make positive contributions to the group's endeavors—for instance, initiating new ideas, providing information, integrating diverse perspectives, and supporting others. These specific communication behaviors *may* function as leadership acts, depending upon the situation. For instance, providing information is a leadership behavior and assists goal accomplishment only if the information is accurate, if the group needs it, and if it is offered in a collaborative spirit. Many communicative roles identified in studies of small groups are fairly specific to group work and exclude the broader functions that effective leaders at the organizational level need to perform. Mintzberg's classic research (1990) on the nature of managerial work provided a broad sketch of some of these more general functions:

> My description of managerial work suggests a number of important managerial skills—developing peer relationships, carrying out negotiations, motivating subordinates, resolving conflicts, establishing information networks and subsequently disseminating information, making decisions in conditions of extreme ambiguity, and allocating resources. Above all, the manager needs to be introspective in order to continue to learn on the job (p. 175).

Clearly, research has not identified all potentially relevant leadership behaviors. Moreover, among the variables believed to be positively associated with the exertion of influence within a group, no one has actually identified the functions that are uniquely related to leadership. Someone could perform a number of different positive task and social functions during a single meeting or over time and yet not make a significant contribution toward the group or organization's goal accomplishment. From the functional perspective, then, leadership might most appropriately be viewed as a multidimensional characteristic that each member will likely exhibit in some form at some time. Perhaps only a few, however, will lead in a significant and enduring way.

The functional approach is the most inclusive of all the perspectives on leadership. It focuses more on the quality of interaction and the importance of getting the job done than on the need to identify formal leaders. Because it acknowledges the value of sharing leadership, it offers an intellectual framework for empowerment in which individuals are allowed to make contributions and, beyond that, are encouraged to act responsibly in considering the kind of contribution they might make.

As chairman and chief executive officer of Xerox, Paul Allaire's comments on organizations seem to reflect a functional approach to leadership. He has argued that organizations should think of themselves as communities rather than as hierarchies. "Our objective is to create natural work groups, organized around natural units of work, which develop as work communities—communities of practice, communities of work, communities of learning—communities that have communities within them" (Allaire, 1991). This philosophy seems to suggest the need and opportunity for everyone to make a contribution.

Consistent with the metaphor of community, the functional approach appears to bring a new set of values to the study of leadership, values that are quite in keeping with feminist views of power. Resisting the hierarchical structure of traditional organizations, feminists conceptualize organizations in terms of networks or webs of relationships, with leadership at the web's center, moving out throughout the group or organization in a dynamic, engaging way (Helgeson, 1990). We will return to feminist views of power in a later section of this chapter.

The Transactional Approach

Like the functional perspective, the transactional approach to leadership focuses less on identifying a particular leader's actions and attributes and more on describing the relationship between leaders and followers. For instance, through his studies of **leader legitimation,** or how individuals are acknowledged as leaders by their followers, Hollander (1958; 1970) made a significant contribution to this approach. At the foundation of Hollander's theory is the notion of "idiosyncrasy credit"—the freedom that valued group members are given to deviate somewhat from group norms, or to act idiosyncratically. Idiosyncratic credits are earned by demonstrating competence and shared values, thus serving to make the individual more indispensable to the group. The individual's achieved value (or status) then allows her or him to introduce new ideas and new ways of doing things to the group or organization, creating the potential for adaptability and change. From Hollander's perspective, the leader legitimation dynamic is viewed as a process of social exchange by which group members exchange their competence and loyalty for group-mediated rewards— ranging from tangibles such as income to intangibles such as honor, status, and influence.

Another transactional perspective, the **vertical dyad linkage model,** was advanced by Graen and his associates (Graen & Cashman, 1975; Graen & Ginsburgh, 1977). This research showed that the nature of the exchange processes between leaders and subordinates can have far-reaching effects on group performance and morale. Graen's studies demonstrated that a leader or manager develops a specific and unique exchange with each of his or her subordinates. These exchanges might range from a true partnership in which the subordinate is given considerable freedom and autonomy in defining and developing a work-related role to exchanges in which the subordinate is restrained and controlled. Not surprisingly, the more positive exchanges are associated with higher subordinate satisfaction, reduced turnover, and greater identification with the organization. Although this model does not explore the causes of positive and negative exchanges, it serves to redirect attention to the relationship between leader, follower, and situation, encouraging a broad and dynamic view of the study of leadership.

The Attributional Approach

Perception and cognition have played a major role in leadership research. Attribution theory, in particular, is concerned with the cognitive processes that underlie interpersonal judgments (Heider, 1958; Jones & Davis, 1965; Kelley, 1973). Some leadership theorists have applied attribution-based theories to judgments involved in the leadership process.

From an attribution perspective, one of the key features of interpersonal judgments is the strong tendency for an observer to develop causal explanations for another person's behavior. Explanations of a person's behavior often center on the question of whether the behavior was determined by factors internal to the actor (such as ability or effort) or by external factors (such as situational forces, task characteristics, or luck). Research has demonstrated that observers have a strong bias toward attributing an actor's behavior to internal causes (Jones & Davis, 1965). This tendency may result from the observer's desire for a sense of certainty and predictability about the actor's future behavior. In addition, if the observer might be responsible for the actor's behavior, attributions internal to the actor remove that responsibility. For instance, a parent might attribute his child's poor performance in schoolwork to a learning disability, thus relieving the parent of responsibility for that performance.

Green and Mitchell (1979) adapted some of the propositions of attribution theory to the processes that leaders use to make judgments about subordinates' performance. For instance, studies indicate that supervisors make more negative and more internal attributions when the negative outcomes of a subordinate's behavior are more severe (Mitchell & Kalb, 1981; Mitchell & Wood, 1980). In one study, nursing supervisors were asked to judge a hypothetical subordinate's performance. The supervisors' judgments of a nurse who left a railing down on a patient's bed were more negative if the patient fell out of bed than if the patient did not. Naturally, these judgments have important implications for later actions the supervisor might take with respect to promotion, termination, or salary.

Measuring Leadership: A Matter of Perception?   Some attribution theorists have pointed to problems or restrictions associated with measuring leadership. For example, Calder argued in his attribution theory of leadership (1977) that leadership processes and effects exist primarily as perceptual processes in the minds of followers and observers. In fact, most of the measuring instruments used in leadership research ask the respondent for *perceptions* of leadership processes. These perceptions, judgments, and attributions are thus distorted by the respondent's biases. Each individual may hold an implicit personal theory of leadership that serves as a cognitive filter to determine what the observer will notice, remember, and report about the leadership process. For instance, if individuals believe that good leaders are very considerate of others, they are more likely to notice and report the considerate behavior of a leader whose group they have been told performed quite well (Lord, Binning, Rush, & Thomas, 1978). Moreover, Ayman and Chemers (1983) found that the structure of leader-behavior ratings depends more on the culture of the raters than on the actual behavior of the leader. Thus, a leader who communicates with a domineering style might be rated quite positively in a culture that values this communication trait; the same leader would fare less well in a more democratically oriented culture.

In one sense these distortions in the observation of leadership effects are potentially disturbing. However, perception, judgment, and expectations form the core of interpersonal relationships. Behavior that is perceived or expected may be more important than actual behavior. And it is possible that the desire and expectations of subordinates may elicit or influence actual behaviors on the part of leaders.

Examined comparatively, these diverse approaches to leadership offer largely contrasting conceptualizations. Some see leadership embodied in a small number of individuals formally appointed to positions of authority in an organizational hierarchy; others suggest that leadership can spring up wherever someone facilitates the organization's progress toward its goals. Some believe that leadership is associated with personal style or skills; others point to the role of perception and context. In nearly every discussion, however, it is commonly assumed that notions of leadership are intertwined with notions of power and influence.

Conceptualizing Power

So long as organizations have hierarchies, questions concerning status and power will remain. Typically, those who occupy positions of high status in the organizational hierarchy also possess considerable power. Clearly, the two are practically interrelated and, at the same time, conceptually distinct. **Status** is the value, importance, or prestige associated with a given role or position. **Power,** in contrast, is the ability to influence others. Early conceptions of power focused on controlling others and maintaining and exploiting dependencies. More modern views focus less on control and more on process. However, one may still possess high status without exerting influence over others; conversely, one may be extremely influential without occupying a position carrying high status. Thus, the two remain theoretically distinct.

Power and communication are inextricably linked. Those who seek to influence others must rely on communication. Of course, how this communication manifests itself will differ greatly among those who seek to wield power. For instance, one manager known to one of the authors attempts to exert power by talking frequently and at length during meetings, by carefully controlling every meeting's agenda (thus restricting the sorts of issues that can be discussed), by telling those who disagree with him that they are "out of order" or "misinformed," by selectively sharing information with those who support him (thus controlling the amount and quality of information to which different members of the organization have access), and by promptly returning the e-mail messages and phone messages of his supporters while responding belatedly to those of others. In short, this manager communicates so as to control information, to reward and punish, to dominate, and to remind others constantly of the rewards associated with deferring appropriately to his authority. Although negative, this illustration demonstrates how power and communication are intertwined and introduces the notion that power possesses many dimensions.

Different Perspectives on Power

For many years power was viewed as a way for those in positions of authority to control others, to foster dependencies, to get people to do things they would not otherwise do, and essentially to accomplish goals the leader deemed important. Such control-based conceptualizations of power often incorporated coercion and threat, thus carrying negative connotations. Kanter (1979) expressed it compellingly:

> Power is America's last dirty word. It is easier to talk about money—and much easier to talk about sex—than it is to talk about power. People who have it deny it; people who want it do not want to appear to hunger for it; and people who engage in its machinations do so secretly (p. 65).

Kanter went on to argue that power, when properly conceptualized and understood, is potentially not only positive but essential if leaders are to be effective. She succinctly defined power as "the ability to mobilize resources (human and material) to get things done" (p. 66). She argued further that many organizational woes can be attributed to positions that foster powerlessness. Rejecting the notion that power resides in personal attributes or skills, she articulated the view that the sources of productive power reside in the position, rather than in the person. Kanter believes that power evolves from two kinds of capacities: (1) access to resources, information, and support needed to carry out a task; and (2) ability to get cooperation in doing what is necessary. Kanter's sociological perspective has received much attention and support. It does, however, devalue the role of personal attributes and skills. While some positions (including those of first-line supervisors and staff professionals) are often associated with powerlessness, examples abound of individuals who are sufficiently resourceful to rise above their position and exert considerable influence. Staff professionals, for instance, may have access to valuable information and influence their bosses significantly through both personal and professional ties.

Others have approached power from a psychological perspective. McClelland and Burnham (1979), for instance, argued that individuals bring different kinds of needs to their organizational experiences. They identified, in particular (1) *the need for affiliation*—having the desire to be with others, to belong, to be liked, and to interact socially; (2) *the need for achievement*—being driven to succeed, extremely hardworking, and desiring feedback; and (3) *the need for power*—having (in the negative sense) the need to dominate, or (in the positive sense) the ability to make subordinates feel inspired to excel and to work together (often as a team) in pursuit of organizational objectives. Based on their research, McClelland and Burnham (1979) concluded that excellent leaders possess a strong need for power in the positive sense, with lesser needs for achievement and affiliation. They described these leaders as mature, noting, "Above all, the good manager's motivation is not oriented toward personal aggrandizement but toward the institution which he or she serves" (p. 278).

Whether power resides in the individual or in the person (or, more likely, somewhere in between), virtually every scholar agrees that those organizational members who experience feelings of powerlessness suffer in a variety of ways. The powerless are likely to be molded (or perceive that they are molded) by their environment. If they have a good idea, they feel impotent as change agents. Responses to ongoing feelings of powerlessness include apathy, withdrawal, frustration, and hostility. Those who occupy official positions of leadership may display especially negative reactions to their own powerlessness. As Kanter (1979) argued, "In large organizations, at least, it is powerlessness that often creates ineffective, desultory management and petty, dictatorial, rules-minded managerial styles" (p. 65).

Although we commonly think of power and its manifestations as being quite visible, power is clearly exercised both on the surface of organizational activity and deep within the very structure of the organization. For instance, those who wield power are able, unchallenged, to leave contentious items off the agenda of decision-making meetings, forcing the discussion to remain focused on "safe" or uncontroversial issues (Bachrach & Baratz, 1962). In such cases the exercise of power is not seen; rather, its impact is revealed in the absence of challenge (Frost, 1987). In his reflections on the meetings of President Kennedy and his cabinet that produced the decision to invade Cuba at the Bay of Pigs in an ill-fated attempt to overthrow Castro, Arthur Schlesinger (1965) noted with some bitterness his own unwillingness to speak up, to raise the grave doubts he felt about the wisdom of such a venture. Schlesinger attributed his reticence to an unwillingness to create a disturbance of the consensus he assumed to have developed during the meeting. He was reluctant to challenge the situation, to make a nuisance of himself. His inaction appears to have been a consequence of the covert power commonly found in highly cohesive groups.

Hidden Structures of Power

Power, however, also exists on a far deeper level, where it is actually embedded in the structure of the organization. It resides in the "socially structured and culturally patterned behavior of groups and practices of institutions" (Lukes, 1974, p. 22). Gramsci (1971) used the word **hegemony** to refer to the all-encompassing power that is hidden and, consequently, taken for granted by those who are most controlled by it. It is the power of implicit norms, standard operating procedures, and routines. This hegemony is so deeply embedded in the organizational system that challenges to the power holders are unlikely to arise at all.

Of course, disenfranchised or exploited groups can attack the hegemony of the dominant culture or ideology and propose a different set of assumptions. Some feminists, for example, have argued against the underlying ideology of a patriarchal society. They have pointed to hidden aspects of male-dominated organizations that lead to pervasive discrimination against women (Calvert & Ramsey, 1992). Radical feminists, such as Starhawk (1987; 1988) have sought to reconceptualize notions of power in organizations, attempting to dismantle the notion of power as domination and control. Labeling control-oriented power as "power-over," Starhawk advocated two alternative conceptualizations: "power-from-within" (the notion that all persons are inherently empowered by virtue of their own intrinsic resources and worth as human beings) and "power-with," ("the power not to command, but to suggest and be listened to . . . The source of power-with is the willingness of others to listen to our ideas" (1987, p. 10). Those who band together within a power-with framework are further empowered by the energy of the group (Griffin & Andrews, 1993). Thus, the radical feminist's reconceptualization of power challenges power-over and its status as the only legitimate (or real) form of power. This reconceptualization is grounded not in control over others but in a belief that power is potentially creative and regenerative—and that there are enough power and opportunities to communicate to be shared by all.

Bases of Power

However power is conceptualized, its sources are widely acknowledged as diverse. French and Raven's (1959) early discussion of the bases, or sources, of social power is still considered a useful framework for examining relationships in organizations. In their original formulation, they discussed five power bases, adding others more recently. Altogether, power sources could be said to include the following types: reward, coercive, legitimate, referent, expert, informational, and connectional. Figure 6.1 depicts the multiple faces of power.

As noted above, early notions of power (Emerson, 1962) assumed that person A's power over person B was directly related to B's level of dependency

FIGURE 6.1

The Many Faces of Power

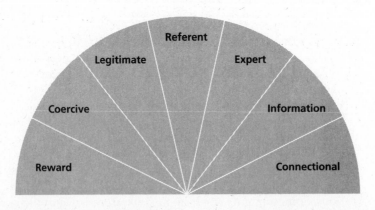

upon A. **Reward power** fits well within this framework, since it refers to an in-dividual's ability to elicit a desired response from another person by providing positive reinforcement. Since formally appointed leaders typically have the power to hire, promote, increase salaries, grant leaves, and so forth, they nearly always possess reward power. At the same time, of course, since they have the authority to fire, demote, downsize, and punish as well, they also have **coercive power,** or the ability to elicit a desired response by means of po-tential punishment. These "carrot and stick" faces of power are both prac-tically and conceptually linked—representing positive (reward) and negative (coercive) ways of getting others to comply with one's requests.

In their book *Corporate Cultures* (1982), Deal and Kennedy provided a memorable illustration of a manager whose approach to power relied heavily on carrots (rewards) and, especially in this passage, sticks (punishments). The manager in question is Harold Geneen, who took over a slow-moving, rather small company, ITT, and transformed it into one of the fastest-growing and most profitable companies in the country. Deal and Kennedy reported:

> The cornerstone of Geneen's management process was the monthly division-review meetings. In these mandatory meetings—held around a block-long conference table set up with microphones for about 150 people—division managers would report their results and then be subjected to intense, rapid-fire questioning from the sharp-eyed staffers around the table. Throughout the questioning, Geneen would sit quietly at the head of the table waiting for a sign of uncertainty or weakness on the part of the manager. At the first such sign, Geneen—in complete command of the facts because of his hard work and infallible memory—would take over the questioning and more often than not tear the manager's presentation to shreds (p. 42).

While not a pleasant scenario, it serves to illustrate the way communication might function from a coercive power orientation.

The third power base, represented by **legitimate power,** focuses on recog-nized authority. Those who respond to this kind of power do so not because of anticipated rewards or feared punishments but simply because they believe that the person making the request is fully authorized to do so. Thus, legiti-mate power is tied to the position occupied within the organizational hierar-chy or the formal role played in other social situations. The extent to which a particular position fosters power is related to the position's inherent character-istics (described below). Bosses, presidents, and department heads all possess some degree of legitimate power. If a request for information comes from a division head (even a division different from one's own), the subordinate is likely to cooperate because the request comes from someone formally empow-ered to ask for compliance. Similarly, employees regularly comply with the company security guard's request to sign in and out, even though their formal organizational status may be higher than that of the guard (who nonetheless is accorded the right to make such requests). Once again, the first three power bases are clearly interdependent since most individuals with legitimate power may also reward and coerce.

The fourth power base, **referent power,** functions most potently when one person strongly identifies with another, holds the individual in high esteem, and respects his or her judgment on appropriate values and modes of conduct. As the Hawthorne studies demonstrated several decades ago, informal work groups are often influential sources of referent power. Individuals may increase or decrease their productivity according to the behavior of other group members, rather than in keeping with the organization's formal reward system. Whether or not referent power functions positively depends partly upon the person or group with which the individual identifies and partly upon the values that the person or group embraces. In many organizations, for instance, upwardly mobile employees choose (or are chosen by) mentors who become constructive role models, supporters, and sponsors. The mentor's attractiveness often stems from referent power. Referent power may also grow from interpersonal attraction.

However, referent power may also have negative ramifications. Cult leaders, such as David Koresh of the Branch Davidians, for example, frequently rely on referent power to attract and retain their followers. Through strong attraction and identification, individuals like Koresh cause others to behave in ways that are quite contrary to their normal modes of conduct—including abandoning their families and homes and relinquishing their financial assets and other treasured possessions. Like other power bases, referent power often operates in tandem with other modes of power, involving rewards and punishments and, sometimes, perceived expertise. Koresh, for instance, was perceived by many as a Christlike figure with incredible expertise on the Bible and how to interpret it.

Clearly, another critical power base grows from **expert power**. Those with competence, experience, knowledge, and intelligence often wield expert power. As organizations move increasingly toward task-focused teams of specialists, expert power becomes especially salient. Team members who interact without formal differences in authority or position and without an official mechanism for rewarding or punishing (at least in the traditional sense) rely more on mutual perceptions of their expertise to establish dependencies and to exert and respond to influence. Expert power is a vital part of every organization. While some managers may feel threatened by employees who possess keen expertise, others purposely surround themselves with the best and the brightest. U.S. presidents have traditionally attempted to choose the best-educated, most experienced, and intelligent advisers they can find to fill key posts. Thus, unlike other sorts of power, expert power is often widely distributed throughout the organization. Moreover, as a personal attribute, expertise can lead to considerable power, regardless of one's formal position.

Still another power base, **information power,** refers to the power to control the availability and accuracy of information. Those who control the flow of information that others receive may influence their attitudes and behavior. Managers who keep their subordinates uninformed make it difficult for them to act or to make good decisions. Organizational gatekeepers are well positioned to control information flow. A secretary, for instance, may control when a manager receives certain reports, whose phone calls are forwarded promptly, and how much informal information the manager receives. However, it would be wrong to equate the possession of information with the possession of power. Information can overwhelm as well as empower. Individuals must know how to manage, organize, and interpret information if it is to operate as a source of power.

The final power source is **connectional power**. Of all the power bases, this is the most political. Based on social psychologists' notion that every exercise of power involves some form of social exchange (Secord & Backman, 1964), connectional power is the influence that leaders have as a result of who they know and the support they have from others in the organization. Although connectional power is often viewed as power emanating from those of greater status, it is also appropriately related to garnering support from subordinates and others whose cooperation and assistance are essential in getting the job done. Anyone in a formal position of authority can be made to "look bad" by those beneath them in the hierarchy, like the teacher whose students choose to behave badly on the day his teaching is being observed by the principal. More typically, however, connectional power is associated with a person's general connections with others whose knowledge, ideas, support, cooperation, and resources are needed to ensure effective leadership. More than the other power bases, connectional power is based on a norm of reciprocity. Anyone who wields power from this base should be prepared to cooperate with and support others.

Power bases stem from both personal and positional attributes. However, one personal attribute not commonly acknowledged in the literature is **effort**. Normally, one must exert effort to attain and maintain any position of authority. Acquiring and controlling information also requires effort, as does developing sufficient expertise to receive promotions and other rewards. Those who exert effort learn more and become more valuable (and, hence, more connected) to others. Achieving visibility necessitates effort. Thus, working hard, taking on extra responsibilities, and demonstrating diligence are all positively associated with organizational power.

Power as Related to Position Characteristics

Many of the sources of power just discussed are largely associated with personal characteristics. However, as Kanter's views make clear, the nature of an individual's position and task assignments also play an important role. Several characteristics of a position account for its power potential: centrality, criticality, flexibility, visibility, and relevance (Kanter, 1979; Whetton & Cameron, 1991).

A position's **centrality** and **criticality** work in tandem. The more central a position is to the flow of information throughout organizational networks and the more critical the function is to the performance of others in the network, the greater the power associated with that position. Strategic contingencies theory (Hickson, Hinings, Lee, Schneck, & Pennings, 1971) argues that power is distributed unevenly within organizations because units and positions differ in their ability to control strategic contingencies (information, expertise, financing) critical to the performance of others. Few important organizational activities occur in isolation. Within an organizational system, what happens to one unit affects what happens to others. The more pervasive the effect of a position's activities throughout the organization, the greater the power base.

An interesting aspect of this view of position power is its implication that positions of power may be widely distributed throughout the organization. Individuals need not move up the formal hierarchy to gain power. Instead, informal network power is available to individuals at all levels—and may, in fact, precede formally acknowledged power. A person is often promoted, for instance, because she or he has demonstrated the ability to accomplish a great deal using informal networks. Those who benefit from this approach to power avoid becoming isolated, often reaching out to those in other divisions of the organization, thus becoming part of the organization's networks rather than just the unit's. Organizational positions, whether formal or informal, become more critical as a function of the level of expertise they require, the extent to which they are crucially related to the performance of others' tasks, and their uniqueness. For instance, when the CEO's private secretary is ill for several weeks, the office quickly becomes dysfunctional. However, the file clerk who is similarly absent can easily be "covered."

Another important position characteristic associated with power is **flexibility**. Flexibility is related to discretion or the freedom to exercise judgment. Positions that offer their occupants some latitude to improvise, to innovate, and to demonstrate initiative carry opportunities for power. Flexible positions have few rules or established routines governing how work should be done. In addition, when a nonroutine decision needs to be made, seeking the approval of a superior is not required. Flexibility tends to be associated with certain types of work assignments, particularly tasks that are high in variety and novelty (Hinings, Hickson, Pennings, & Schneck, 1974). People in such positions are assigned several types of activities, each of which requires the use of considerable judgment. The more routine the work and the fewer the tasks the person is assigned, the easier it is to preprogram the job to eliminate or minimize the need for discretion.

Positions of high **visibility** also tend to foster power. One measure of visibility is the number of people with whom a person interacts within the organization. Although visibility and centrality are often associated, they remain functionally and conceptually distinct. Those who are centrally located in a broad communication network tap into a rich flow of information, allowing them to satisfy the information needs of others. In contrast, those in visible positions may have the opportunity to interact with a large number of influential people, thus increasing their power by making their accomplishments more evident to the people who allocate resources, including desirable jobs and promotions.

Finally, Kanter associates a position's **relevance** with its power. Powerful individuals in organizations are generally associated with activities that are directly related to central objectives and issues (Salancik & Pfeffer, 1977). Lawrence and Lorsch (1967) identified the "dominant competitive issue" for companies using different types of technology. These issues are the activities that most account for the organization's ability to compete effectively with other members of its industry. Lawrence and Lorsch found, for instance, that companies using a standard mass-production (assembly-line) form of technology with a stable line of products and established customers were especially dependent on the efficiency of their production process. In contrast, "high-tech" firms, or companies producing custom-designed products, were most successful when they had strong research and development departments.

These studies have significant implications for the notion of task relevance. Those who seek influential positions should be sensitive to the relevance of their department's activities to the organization's overall mission. Computer scientists are more likely to feel empowered if they work for a software development firm than if they are employed by an insurance company. Teachers are more likely to feel valued if they work for an academic institution whose mission is largely geared toward teaching excellence and learning outcomes than if they work for a university where teaching and learning are subordinate to the primary mission of research.

Although these position-related characteristics of power have been discussed separately, they are intertwined with personal dimensions of power. Individual expertise, for instance, is bound to influence the sort of position a person is given. Brighter, more informed, individuals will likely be given greater discretion (flexibility) in work assignments and decision-making authority. Those with greater centrality will receive more information. Employees with informational power (coupled with expertise) may reach positions of greater visibility. Thus, individuals can acquire power through personal skills and attributes. At the same time, certain organizational roles position individuals so that they are surrounded by abundant opportunities for communicating with, influencing, and empowering others.

Empowerment

Many have argued that the effective use of power is the single most critical element of leadership. One scholar, Warren Bennis, sought to identify the defining characteristics of excellent leaders by interviewing ninety individuals who had been nominated by their peers as the most influential leaders in all walks of society. Bennis reported that these individuals shared one significant characteristic: They made others feel powerful (Bennis & Namus, 1985). These leaders, together with others, were able to accomplish exceptional organizational objectives. Bennis concluded that empowering others consistently produced several important benefits. Those who felt empowered reported feeling important and valued by their fellow workers. They developed a conviction that learning and competence really matter and strove to behave in ways consistent with those convictions. They also perceived themselves as part of a team and/or embedded within a community. Finally, they came to view their work as more engaging and challenging than ever before.

Different Views of Empowerment

In the scholarly literature, empowerment has been conceptualized as both a relational and a motivational construct. From a *relational perspective,* empowerment is viewed as the process by which a leader or manager shares her or his power with subordinates. In this context, power is interpreted as the possession of formal authority or control over organizational resources. The emphasis is upon sharing authority. As Burke (1986) noted, "To empower implies the granting of power—delegation of authority" (p. 51). Thus, many management theorists equate empowerment with delegation and the decentralization of decision-making power, leading to an emphasis on participative management techniques, quality circles, self-managed teams, and mutual goal setting (Kanter, 1983). Although these practices are probably positively related to subordinates' perceptions of empowerment, leaders' intentions and subordinates' perceptions may on occasion differ. It is conceivable that an employee may not desire the responsibility of participating in the decision-making process; thus, sharing decision making with such a person would not necessarily result in employee empowerment.

As noted in Chapter 1, empowerment has also been viewed, perhaps more profitably, as a *motivational construct,* especially within the psychological literature. From this perspective, individuals are assumed to have a need for power where power connotes an internal urge to influence and control other people (McClelland, 1975). Within this conceptual framework, an individual's sense of empowerment grows from managerial strategies and techniques that serve to strengthen the employee's feelings of self-determination or self-efficacy. Thus, to empower is to enable. Embracing the notion of empowerment as a motivational construct, Conger (1986) defined it as "a process of enhancing feelings of self-efficacy among organizational members through the identification of conditions that foster powerlessness [and by eliminating those conditions]" (p. 474). According to Conger, factors that contribute to feelings of powerlessness may arise from several sources, including the organizational environment, supervisory style, reward systems, or job design. Figure 6.2 sum-

FIGURE 6.2

**Contextual Factors Leading to Feelings
of Powerlessness**

Organizational Factors	**Supervisory Style**
Significant changes	Authoritarianism (high control)
Start-up ventures	Negativism (emphasis on failures)
Competitive ventures	Lack of rationale for actions/consequences
Impersonal bureaucratic climate	
Poor communication networks	
Highly centralized organizational structure	
Reward System	**Job Design**
Arbitrary reward systems	Lack of role clarity
Low incentive value of rewards	Lack of training/support
Lack of competence-based rewards	Unrealistic goals
Lack of innovation-based rewards	Low task variety
	Limited participation in decisions affecting work
	Lack of needed resources
	Lack of network-forming opportunities
	Highly established routines
	High rule structure
	Low advancement opportunities
	Lack of meaningful tasks/goals
	Limited contact with upper management

marizes those factors potentially leading to lower self-efficacy or feelings of powerlessness (Conger, 1986). Others concur that the absence of empowerment is characterized by feelings of powerlessness, alienation, and helplessness (Rappaport, 1984).

Profiling the Empowering Organization

Several researchers have concentrated on describing the culture, practices, and behaviors that typify an empowering organization. Noller (1991), for instance, suggested four components of what he calls a "Weberian Ideal" model of empowerment, which he described as follows:

> We may speak of empowerment for an individual or a group of individuals in a given situation . . . when the individual(s) has (have): (1) Full decision-making ability. (2) Complete responsibility for implementation of any decisions. (3) Complete access to relevant tools for both making decisions and implementing them. (4) The complete right/responsibility to accept the consequences of any decisions made (p. 12).

Noller noted that these conditions represent an ideal not frequently encountered in organizational reality. A critical component of this definition is his emphasis on the individual's willingness to take responsibility for the consequences of actions taken and decisions made.

Other writers have offered advice to managers by articulating empowering managerial practices. For instance, Conger's (1989) discussion of managerial techniques and strategies included these suggestions:

Involve subordinates in the assignment of work. Normally, it is the manager who hands out work assignments. When subordinates are permitted to make decisions about which tasks they choose to tackle, they are sharing some of the manager's authority.

Provide a positive, collaborative work environment. Whenever individuals are able to set aside formal role relationships and focus on seeking mutually acceptable solutions to common problems, they move in the direction of reciprocal empowerment.

Reward and encourage others in visible and personal ways. For most individuals, the value of a reward is increased when it is given in public and when it is very personal (accompanied by professional good taste). Acknowledging someone's excellent performance during a public speech or reading aloud a letter praising someone's fine work during a staff meeting might serve as such visible recognition.

Express confidence. Managers who share a difficult task with others and who actually involve others in demanding, challenging problem solving communicate a message of confidence that their fellow workers are up to the challenge. While sentiments of confidence can be expressed verbally, taking actions that demonstrate this trust may communicate an even more powerful message.

Foster initiative and responsibility. One especially effective manager encouraged his subordinates to identify problems within the organization and come to him with ideas for how to solve them. He consistently expressed tremendous enthusiasm whenever a subordinate identified a legitimate problem and offered a sound, promising, or innovative solution.

This manager prodded subordinates into being problem detectors and problem solvers—thus encouraging energetic, intelligent, and responsible behavior.

Build on success. The wisest managers are those who applaud and celebrate others' accomplishments. Rather than being threatened by those beneath, they point to their successes with genuine enthusiasm, reward them generously, and challenge them to excel even more.

Other descriptive characteristics of empowering organizations stem from Pacanowsky's ethnographic study of W.L. Gore & Associates. Based on his research, Pacanowsky (1987) offered several "operating rules of the empowering organization," arguing that they might "be the basis for creating empowering organizational cultures elsewhere" (p. 372). His "rules" included the following:

Distribute power and opportunity widely. This approach advocates letting people "own" the problems they are interested in, decentralizing the process by which important decisions are made and emphasizing the power to accomplish, as opposed to the power to dominate.

Maintain a full, open, and decentralized communication system. Information in this sort of organization flows freely, with fewer distortions and less attention to impression management. Mistakes are tolerated as people learn, grow, take risks, and keep on working.

Use integrative problem solving. This approach distributes problem-solving responsibilities among functional work units. Power, information, and opportunity are genuinely and widely distributed. Task forces are used abundantly. With new configurations of people coming together to solve problems, the work climate encourages innovation and creativity, fostering visibility for many and nurturing a "we" attitude among everyone.

Practice challenge in an environment of trust. Individuals will be better problem solvers when they participate in debate and lively conversations about the relative strengths and weaknesses of competing courses of action. Ideas are to be challenged and concerns expressed—but criticism and challenge must be offered in a spirit of support and help rather than in a spirit of one-upmanship. Ultimately, after issues have been thoroughly discussed, people must be given the chance to act according to their best information and judgment.

Reward and recognize people so as to encourage a high-performance ethic and self-responsibility. The best rewards grow from giving others increased power and opportunity rather than from instituting "employee of the month" awards. Thus, the emphasis is upon internal rather than external incentives. As individuals are given greater responsibilities, their credibility is also enhanced.

Become wise by living through, and learning from, organizational ambiguity, inconsistency, contradiction, and paradox. Most organizations exist in complex, ambiguous environments where information is equivocal and decision making is shrouded in uncertainty. Organizational values are often characterized by inconsistencies. People are encouraged to excel as individuals, while cooperative teamwork is simultaneously praised and rewarded. Learning to live with these apparently conflicting realities is critical to empowerment and growth.

Pacanowsky concluded his article with this summarizing perspective on empowerment:

> The empowering organization would tend to encourage concern for accomplishment rather than for status. Power would be used to get the job done, rather than to stand over others. Being capable of initiating action, the individual could look at others as ends themselves—capable of initiating action and therefore as worthy collaborators. The disempowering organization considers work an amoral activity—a job's a job, somebody's got to do it, you're only following orders, you've got two kids to feed. The empowering organization would consider work a moral activity (p. 378).

One might argue, of course, that some types of work lend themselves more readily to empowerment than others. Case 2 at the end of this chapter presents an insightful essay by Tom Peters that thoughtfully engages this question.

Finally, some scholars have offered a more theoretical approach to defining empowerment. Based on their view of empowerment as a process that creates intrinsic task motivation by providing an environment and tasks conducive to feelings of greater self-efficacy and energy (Conger & Kanungo, 1988), Thomas and Velthouse (1990) developed a conceptual model that specifies four dimensions of empowerment: impact, choice, competence, and meaningfulness. *Impact* is related to whether accomplishing a particular task or job will make a difference in the scheme of things. Theoretically, the greater the impact employees believe themselves to have, the more internally motivated they should feel (Rotter, 1966). The second dimension, *choice*, means the degree to which personal behavior is self-determined. According to this model, the more individuals are given the opportunity to select tasks, decide how they should be accomplished, and take responsibility for their outcome, the more empowered they should feel.

The third dimension is *competence*. For empowerment to be possible, those to whom tasks are assigned must possess the necessary skills, knowledge, experience, and other qualifications to enable them to move forward with confidence. Finally, *meaningfulness* is crucial. This dimension points to the value of a task or job in relation to the individual's own beliefs, ideals, and standards. The more closely a task is consistent with someone's value system, the more conviction she or he brings to its accomplishment. Without perceived meaningfulness, a sense of empowerment is unlikely. Recent research by Shulman and his associates has offered empirical support for this conceptualization of empowerment (Schultz & Shulman, 1993; Shulman, Douglas, & Schultz, 1993).

Trying to define empowerment in any universal or completely generalizable way is probably a futile quest. Each organization offers its own contingencies. The challenge of empowerment is somewhat task- and person-specific. Even so, the sorts of general characteristics and dimensions of empowerment articulated by several different writers and scholars seem relatively consistent. Leaders cannot entirely orchestrate empowerment, even if they want to. Perhaps the best they can do is create conditions that enable those who seek opportunities for empowerment to find them. Focus On highlights several instances of companies that have created empowering options for employees, giving them visible alternatives from which to choose as they go about deciding how they want to balance their personal and professional lives.

Leadership and Technology

Drucker's (1988) new team-based, empowering organization changes the role of the manager. No longer are managers so absorbed with decision making, implementing procedures, and assigning responsibilities. Instead, they are concerned with the behaviors and activities that promote information, sharing, cooperation, and employee problem solving. Dumaine (1993) pointed out that traditionally, a manager in an organization is viewed as one who

- thinks of self as a manager or boss
- follows the chain-of-command
- works within a set organizational structure
- makes most decisions alone
- hoards information
- tries to master one major discipline, such as marketing or finance
- demands long hours

However, the new team-based organization incorporates an entirely new set of assumptions about the role of the manager. The new breed of "nonmanager manager" is seen less as a traditional manager or boss and more as a facilitator or sponsor for self-managed teams who can employ technology to store, manage, transform, and communicate information. Dumaine contended that the "new" manager

- deals with anyone to get the job done
- changes organizational structures in response to market change

FOCUS ON

Offering the Opportunity for a Balanced Personal and Professional Life: One Vehicle for Worker Empowerment

For years IBM has steadily increased its efforts to adapt to family needs. It pioneered child-care and elder-care assistance programs. In 1988, IBM expanded its flextime program to allow employees to adjust their workdays by as much as two hours in either direction and adopted an extended leave-of-absence policy permitting up to a three-year break from full-time employment with part-time work in the second and third years. The company has also been experimenting with work-at-home programs. It has instituted family sensitivity training programs for more than 25,000 managers.

Johnson & Johnson recently announced an extremely broad work-and-family initiative that includes support for elder care and child care, greater work-time flexibility, management training, and a change in its corporate credo.

AT&T recently negotiated a contract with two of its unions that established a dependent-care referral service and provided for leaves of up to one year, with guaranteed reinstatement for new parents and for workers with seriously ill dependents.

At NCNB a program called "Select Time" allows employees at all levels, including managers, to reduce their time and job commitments for dependent-care purposes without cutting off current and future advancement opportunities.

Apple Computer operates its own employee-staffed child-care center and gives "baby bonuses" of $500 to new parents.

Eastman Kodak has adopted new rules permitting part-time work, job sharing, and informal, situational flextime.

SOURCE: Based on Rodgers & Rodgers, 1989, and the *Herald Times*, 1994.

- invites others to join in decision making
- shares information
- tries to master a broad array of managerial disciplines
- demands results

To influence people and create a shared vision, the new manager can use technology-based communication channels to influence people, to solve problems, and to make decisions. Ironically, however, little thought has been given to training managers systematically to incorporate technology as a mechanism for channeling leadership efforts.

In fact, one fundamental problem facing managers is that they are generally not well educated in the use of technology as a leadership tool. Indeed, in a special *Wall Street Journal* technology supplement (June 27, 1994), William M. Buckeley noted, "Most of the executives are over 40, and went to college before computers became part of the curriculum" (p. R20). Moreover, in most commercial managerial leadership training programs in the United States, technology is usually not presented in a training context as potentially contributing to the acquisition, demonstration, or maintenance of leadership. Rather, leadership is typically portrayed as consisting of a certain set of influence and communication traits and behaviors that, when developed properly, can enable individuals to motivate and shape the behavior of others, to manage organizational diversity and conflict, and to promote positive team-building behaviors so as to maximize organizational task performance. Technology is not acknowledged as a viable method for implementing or supporting organizational leadership.

Nevertheless, managers are often attracted to computer technology by the advertised promises of faster and more efficient communication. Yet the use of technology in teamwork is quite new and still not fully understood (Dickson, Partridge, & Robinson, 1993). Sproull and Kiesler (1991) argued that the real potential of computer technology and network communication goes far beyond the scope of simply improving communication speed. They suggested that technology's real power is its ability to change the overall work environment and to empower by enhancing the capabilities of employees. Leaders can thus potentially use technology to foster new kinds of task structures and reporting relationships, given that computer networks can change the conventional patterns of who talks to whom and who knows what. Of course, this new technology fosters challenges for leaders now and increasingly in the future. Sproull and Kiesler (1991) put it this way:

> In today's organizations, executives generally know whom they manage and manage whom they know. In the future, however, managers of some electronic project groups will face the challenge of working with people they have never met. Allocating resources to projects and assigning credit and blame for performance will become more complex. People will often belong to many different groups and will be able to reach out and network to acquire resources without management intervention or perhaps without management knowledge (p. 123).

Many believe that decisions concerning technology are so important that those in positions of leadership at the highest levels of organizational hierarchies should be involved. Fulk and Boyd (1991) argued that ". . . technological choices are far from neutral in their effects on organizational design and functioning . . . such choices are important managerial and strategic decisions that demand the attention of top executives" (pp. 427–428).

In an increasingly technological society, influence and leadership behaviors are exhibited in settings where technology can impact the speed, delivery, content, structure, and form of communication—and therefore the very vehicles by which leadership is acquired and demonstrated. Technology affects to whom individuals can talk, the richness of their information exchange, and the timing and speed of information dissemination and feedback. As we discussed in Chapter 5, technology-based channels give leaders the potential to overcome communication barriers imposed by time and space, thereby fundamentally reshaping the nature of organizational design, intelligence, and decision making. We hold that mechanisms for acquiring, defining, demonstrating, maintaining, and distributing leadership are therefore also influenced.

In her book *Leadership and the Computer,* Mary Boone (1991) provided real-life case examples to show how a few top executives have, in fact, employed computer technology and networks to communicate, coach, convince, and compete—that is, to lead. She identified and described key benefits that technology contributes to executive leadership. They are described below.

Leverage Time

Groupware allows executives to become less dependent on the schedules of others, since technology creates new ways of channeling information into and out of executive suites. This enhanced communication flow improves executive accessibility and responsiveness. It also allows executives the opportunity to work independently of time and location. The quality of decision making is thereby enhanced, and productivity increased because executives have more flexibility and better control over their time.

Being Well Informed

Using spreadsheets, statistical packages, internal and external databases, groupware, outline editors, and commitment-tracking systems, executives can become better informed about a wide range of topics. Computer technology and networks can keep them up to date, increase their depth of knowledge, provide control over removing or constructing filters on the information they receive, and help them to absorb information more quickly.

Communicating Effectively

Executives need to link themselves with their organizations, communicating freely with others at various levels and locations in the organization. The use of technology such as groupware overcomes problems of accessibility caused by barriers of time and space. Groupware such as e-mail helps executives access information directly, eliminating layers of management filtering. It also gives these leaders the ability to receive and incorporate feedback from employees electronically, thereby enhancing their capacity to listen. Groupware and various database and analytical software tools can help executives stay well informed and also enhance their ability to think through complex organizational problems and issues, potentially making them more persuasive in advancing sound arguments. Executives can incorporate groupware, multimedia, word processing, desktop publishing, and other technologies so that the presentation, channeling, and dissemination of their views, opinions, and policies are both timely, effective, and visually appealing. Groupware can also be used to help link the organization more closely, improving feedback and assisting executives who want to stay more closely in tune with their organization—perhaps allowing them to respond to problems and opportunities more quickly than in the past. Using groupware such as e-mail and voice mail, executives may seek advice from trusted colleagues, overcoming the constraints of time and space for informal communicative exchanges.

Coaching

Executives do not run organizations alone. To get work done, they must delegate. If leaders use technology such as internal and external databases to be well informed, they thereby increase their credibility regarding their sense of strategic direction and command of the facts. They can also use databases to track the status of commitments they and others make. Many technologies, including groupware, can be used to share information and monitor performance. By sharing external and operational information with employees and reviewing the same information themselves, leaders can teach others to assess problems and issues more carefully and critically before passing the information on to higher levels of the organization. In addition to identifying critical issues, employees can use technology to help them articulate more sophisticated explanations of why problems occurred, what measures were taken to correct them, and how they can be avoided in the future.

Shaping Organizational Culture

Technology can be used by executives to shape corporate culture by helping them to focus the organization's attention on what is important. Information tools can be employed by executives to establish shared language, common perspectives, and consistent facts as a basis for discussing and agreeing on plans. Databases and computer analysis tools such as spreadsheets and statistical packages can be used to tell others what information is important to collect and how it might be measured, viewed, and valued relative to performance objectives—thereby promoting shared values and a shared vision. These technologies can be used to facilitate the collection and analysis of information relevant to the processes of picking, promoting, and rewarding people. Finally, groupware technology can help flatten organizational hierarchies and empower individuals; it mitigates hierarchy by opening new channels of communication and allowing open sharing of information throughout an organization, a pre-condition for employee empowerment.

Enhancing Thinking

Executives can use computer software for word processing, spreadsheets, personal information management, project management, and statistical analysis. They can use groupware to manage complexity, to think creatively, to balance logic and intuition, to clarify their thoughts, to make use of time in reflection, and to hold more effective group meetings.

According to Boone (1992), the computer's role is not to supplant the executive's leadership role but to augment it. She cautioned:

> Computers don't set the goals; they just make human goals easier to reach. Computers aren't inherently good or evil. Rather the people who use them are responsible for the goals they seek. Because computers constitute such a powerful leadership medium, it is essential that leaders assess their motives for designing and using them.
>
> . . . The combination of enlightened, ethical leadership and powerful technology [and networks] brings with it incredible possibilities (p. 336).

Many executive computing programs fail because the chief information officer of the organization (the individual responsible for all information services) is unable to reverse a general executive perception of the computer as an administrative or clerical tool. To reverse such perceptions, Boone believes that chief information officers (CIOs) must adopt a business-driven approach to the use of technology. To do this, they must understand what information the executive wants and needs, when and in what form the information is needed, the overall organizational culture relative to technology, the use and sharing of information, and organizational attitudes about employee empowerment. Moreover, when technology is to be incorporated in the leadership function, the organization must be able to provide effective training and support for the technology and to monitor and understand its potential impact on organizational culture.

Boone's work is being extended by a joint research effort currently being conducted in the United States and Canada by the University of North Carolina at Greensboro and the Center for Creative Leadership. The goal of this research is to document further the use of and value assigned to technology by leaders in leadership activities and to gather data that will help show how to incorporate technology awareness into leadership training programs.

We believe that the challenge for leaders is to understand and appreciate technology so as to maximize its potential value as an organizational tool for leadership and team building. Technology offers opportunities for empowerment and improved communication and enables an organization to learn from and respond to its environment. In an age of corporate downsizing and competitive global markets, it is especially important that organizations communicate as effectively as possible and that they learn about new channels for leading.

We also acknowledge that the use of technology is no panacea for improving leadership and organizational effectiveness. Indeed, in many cases technology has been implemented without a clear appreciation for organizational needs or preferences. For example, it is a well documented fact that innovations such as e-mail may cause problems in organizations where sharing of information is not valued and where communication is expected to follow the chain-of-command. Also, inadequate training can inhibit any benefit, no matter what potential the technology may offer.

Thus, the availability of technology is certainly no guarantee that its value may be realized. Indeed, in a special technology supplement to the *Wall Street Journal* (June 27, 1994), Dennis Kneale summed up the situation:

> For the past ten years, companies have been on a blind-faith buying binge, investing well over $1 trillion in new computer systems to embrace the future and gain a competitive edge. Now, many of them are awakening with a hangover, and wondering: What was it all for, and where did we go wrong? The evidence of their misadventure is everywhere, but it can be boiled down to a simple truth: Companies are a long way from unleashing the real power of the technology that they have so dearly put in place (p. R1).

Summarizing Perspective

In this chapter we have discussed empowerment and its increasing importance for effective organizational performance. Empowerment demands new approaches to managing employees. It involves leadership actions—for example, coaching, negotiating, sharing, and facilitating—as opposed to traditional management activities such as informing, deciding, demanding and hoarding. When promoting empowerment, management communication becomes development-oriented rather than control-oriented.

Technology creates new opportunities for facilitating and exercising leadership and empowerment. Technology offers new means for creating and distributing communication and new mechanisms for sharing organizational decision making. However, many senior managers lack the same level of technological literacy as their employees, often making it difficult for their organizations to understand how to integrate technology into the empowerment process. Nevertheless, technology needs to be incorporated into leadership training programs so that tomorrow's leaders learn both how to manage and communicate using technology and how technology creates innovative opportunities for organizational behavior and design.

CASES FOR DISCUSSION

CASE 1 *The Post Office*

Over the past decade, ten enraged U.S. Post Office employees have killed thirty-four coworkers and supervisors. These shocking figures have prompted widespread discussion about the organizational environment in which these tragedies took place.

Some have pointed an accusing finger at the nature of the job. Workers typically sort letters on machines at a rate of one per second. They lift and throw thousands of packages each day and make deliveries at a pace established by management. Injury rates run high—as do tensions. While conflicts are scarcely unique to this industry, postal employees claim that their tensions fester in a classically managed, military culture in which many top managers communicate by directive and front-line supervisors hover over workers waiting for mistakes and monitoring their every move.

Some postal employees acknowledge that supervisors can be helpful and are certainly needed in some situations. However, the *New York Times* reported that one out of every twenty workers they interviewed pointed to a recent clash that they or a close colleague had had with a supervisor whom they considered overbearing. They described these supervisors as "martinets whose badge, the necktie, empowered them to treat grown men and women like boot-camp recruits".

One incident on August 20, 1986, dramatized the nature of the problem. On that day Patrick Henry Sherrill, a part-time letter carrier facing disciplinary action, killed fourteen fellow employees in the Edmond, Oklahoma, post office before killing himself. After the tragedy, managers at this large mail-processing and distribution plant seemed committed to smoothing relations with workers. The top manager, Terry Wilson, was praised by leaders of the three unions—representing the letter carriers, the postal workers, and the mail handlers—for keeping tensions low. However, Mr. Wilson's plant is in every sense a factory. The two processing floors are open and windowless, with assembly lines moving the mail from the receiving dock through cancellation machines to sorting machines and hand sorters, and then to boxes for local letter carriers and bins for shipment out of town. Banners across the walls exhort workers, "Work Safely, Avoid Accidents" and "Keep Alert, Keep Alive."

The plant's busiest time is at night from 10:00 P.M. to 11:00 P.M., when two shifts overlap. Most of the 1,070 employees start their shifts in the afternoon between 1:00 P.M. and 4:00 P.M. At this point, the military culture takes over. Each employee slides a plastic time card through a "transactor," a sophisticated kind of time clock, calibrated in 24-hour military time. When workers go to lunch, they slide in their cards and punch the OL button for "out to lunch." They punch other buttons to indicate that they are back from lunch, leaving the work station, or ending their shift. Workers say that supervisors use the transactor's precise records against them. Those who are a few military seconds late returning from lunch, for instance, can be called AWOL—and the penalty for AWOL infractions is LWOP, meaning "leave without pay."

In general, military symbolism pervades the Postal Service. Mr. Wilson, like postmasters everywhere, sits at a large wooden desk flanked by American and Postal Service flags. In the military, however, soldiers may follow orders blindly in the belief that their lives (or the lives of others) might be saved as a result. In the post office, in contrast, workers want to understand why they are asked to do something.

Postal supervisors are typically former line workers. They have their own break room and preferred parking places. But unlike military officers who are trained to take command, they are often no better educated, no better schooled in human relations, and no better paid than the workers, who earn $24,000 to $36,000 a year and as much as $10,000 more with overtime.

Workers claim that supervisors are quick to suspend them. Through the union-management grievance resolution procedure, they can get the suspensions annulled, and the wages they lost during the suspension are then returned; but often there is a price. One worker, a distribution and window clerk, has been fired four times and suspended more. All of these actions were subsequently reversed. However, he is currently undergoing psychotherapy due to a high level of job uncertainty. He says he doesn't eat or sleep properly and easily becomes argumentative.

Due to recent cuts in the supervisory staff, each supervisor's span of control has increased from nine to fifteen employees since the beginning of 1993. After the most recent round of slayings, the postmaster general ordered regional managers to establish focus groups made up of volunteers from management and blue-collar ranks and coached by counselors to examine the causes of workplace violence. Workers, who are skeptical, say that talk is cheap—and besides, they've heard it all befre.

Questions for Discussion

1. The postal workers in this case clearly suffer from what we might call "disempowerment." What factors have contributed most to this condition?

2. To what extent are the leaders to blame?

3. How do you assess the response of the postmaster general described in the last paragraph? What other actions might be taken to create a more constructive organizational climate?

SOURCE: Based on a story reported in the *New York Times*, May 17, 1993, pp. A1, A7.

CASE 2 *Pride, Empowerment, and the Nature of Work: Tom Peters Reflects*

Little has given me more pleasure of late than spring barn cleaning. Sheep, goats, llamas, and horses have been feeding there for months. The job is smelly, muddy . . . exhausting. Still, after three agonizing days, I was singularly satisfied. No, you can't eat off the floor. But I'm proud of it.

Cleaning the barn got me wondering about the nature of work, and the fact that any task can become a source of pride.

The *New York Times* recently ran an offbeat article on Melvin Reich, Manhattan's premier buttonhole man. "Buttonholes are what we do. We do buttonholes and buttonholes and buttonholes. I am specialized, like the doctors," said Reich. "You think it's nothing." And the clincher: "Zippers are a totally different field. It's a different game. A man can do so much."

Thinking about buttonholes this way may explain, among other things, the obsessive Japanese demand for quality, which we often see as sinister. After all, in Japan such things as arranging flowers and serving tea properly can be lifetime occupations.

For instance, the neophyte pursuing the Way of Tea spends years learning the intricate rituals of presenting the beverage correctly—selecting and handling utensils, preparing the garden path to the teahouse, placing the charcoal so that the glowing coals beneath the pot form a perfect cone. The server works even more assiduously at developing a "sincere heart," according to tea-master Soshitsu Sen XV. . . .

Soshitsu Sen XV offers superb advice for the Way of Tea—and life. "It seems wise . . . to abandon any goal of achieving success. . . . Giving up this goal may in itself result in a successful experience."

What an un-American idea! But, then, consider quality. Beating the drum for top quality scores is a snare. Instead, we should patiently create processes and a culture that make every day for everyone an adventure in pursuit of improvement. The eventual measure of quality is almost incidental—a more or less natural outcome of a continuing passionate journey.

We Americans characteristically pay more attention to the destination than the journey. And our fixation has paid off. But we frequently miss the mark when it comes to true mastery—of barn cleaning, buttonholes or automaking.

But, praise be, there's Sal Gomez, an auto worker I met during a tour of NUMMI, the . . . Toyota-GM joint venture. He's a denizen of one of several "kaizen shops"—little nooks along the assembly line where gizmos of various sorts are constructed to abet productivity.

Sal's completed hundreds of projects . . . he *is* in love with his work. His enthusiasm and energy made my day. For me, NUMMI will always be Sal—the embodiment of a new spirit that also happens to be successful in the marketplace. . . .

There's lots that can be done by the powers that be to improve the workplace. Yet you and I have a chance to make our own work special. If we don't, after all, it's we who suffer.

"It's a matter of indifference what a person's occupation is, or at what job he works," wrote the German dramatist C. F. Hebbel. "The crucial thing is how he works, whether he . . . fills the place in which he happens to have landed. The radius of his activity is not important; important alone is whether he fills the circle of his tasks." Or as Soshitsu Sen XV put it, "A monk once asked his master, 'No matter what lies ahead, what is the Way?' The master quickly replied, 'The Way is your daily life.' "

Won't you join me for barn cleaning next spring?

Questions for Discussion

1. How do you react to Peters's views of work, especially "mundane work"?

2. Does American culture make it difficult for workers to view their work in such a positive way? Why or why not?

3. If people were able to take Peters's advice, they would essentially be empowering themselves. Do you think self-empowerment is possible? Why or why not?

4. Think of an organization with which you are very familiar. What might its managers and leaders do to "patiently create processes and a culture that make every day for everyone an adventure in pursuit of improvement?" Try to be as specific as possible.

SOURCE: Peters, 1993.

Small Group Communication in the Modern Organization

Almost every time there is a genuinely important decision to be made in an organization, a group is assigned to make it—or at least to counsel and advise the individual who must make it.
J.R. Hackman and R.E. Kaplan, "Interventions into Group Process: An Approach to Improving the Effectiveness of Groups," *Decision Sciences, 5,* 1974.

As the above quotation vividly illustrates, individuals have always assembled in formal and/or informal groups in organizational settings to seek personal as well as group goals. Only during the past few decades, however, have organization and management theorists centered their notions of effective decision making and worker empowerment on practicing widespread delegation to groups. Committees, quality circles, task forces, and teams have become the buzzwords of the 1970s, the 1980s, and the 1990s. With new technologies offering computer support for group endeavors and unprecedented ways of linking individuals within and across organizations, group work is likely to become increasingly common, diversified, and innovative as the United States moves into the twenty-first century.

Yet hundreds of group studies have convincingly demonstrated that groups are no panacea. The potential negatives associated with group work include wasted time; uneven participation (some dominate, others loaf); costly decision making; poor organization; poor listening; pressure for uniformity; and ineffective leadership. Moreover, some groups include members of unequal status and/or authority, potentially hampering the free expression of diverse points of view. Groups are given to ignoring problem analysis and jumping to solutions. Individual group members may play negative roles—perhaps by raising constant objections, by telling endless stories, or simply by coming to meetings unprepared. In some organizations groups may take greater risks than individuals, partly because responsibility for group actions is diffused. Whether this increased risk taking has negative or positive results depends upon the nature of the problem before the group and the organization's norms regarding risk and innovation.

To balance the potential negatives, group advocates point to the opportunities for social interaction to fulfill personal needs, the greater pool of ideas and information (compared to an individual acting alone), the diversity of approaches to problem solving offered by the group, employee involvement in the decision-making process (leading to greater commitment to decisions and a higher quality of implementation), and the opportunity for rigorously testing ideas through group interaction. Perhaps most important, groups are often seen as vehicles for empowerment.

Since some groups work quite effectively while others flounder, several scholars have attempted to differentiate the communicative behaviors, attitudes, and interaction patterns that might distinguish effective from ineffective groups. Based on their research, Hirokawa and Scheerhorn (1986) pointed to five factors that can lead a group to a poor decision. They note, in particular, the improper assessment of a choice-making situation, the establishment of inappropriate goals and objectives, the improper assessment of positive and negative qualities associated with various alternatives, the establishment of a flawed information base, and faulty reasoning based on the group's information base. Other research by Hirokawa and Pace (1983) suggests that the quality of a group's decision making depends on four things:

1. *The way in which group members attempt to evaluate the validity of opinions and assumptions advanced by fellow discussants.* In effective groups, evaluations tend to be more rigorous.

2. *The careful, rigorous manner in which groups try to evaluate alternative solutions or courses of action, measuring them against established criteria.* Thus, groups should establish criteria, make sure the criteria are appropriate, and then use them for examining alternative courses of action.

3. *The kind of premises on which decisions are made.* Effective groups are more likely to use high-quality information and analyses, whereas ineffective groups rely more on questionable data and assumptions.

4. *The sort of influence exerted by prominent group members.* In highly effective groups, leaders are more supportive and facilitating and less inhibiting. At the same time, they ask good questions, challenge invalid assumptions, clarify information, and keep the group from going off on irrelevant tangents.

In this chapter we will define the meaning and scope of group communication. After considering different kinds of small groups, we go on to examine some portion of the extensive literature on communication among small groups. Understanding what is known about groups (the pitfalls as well as the promises) establishes a foundation for enhancing group processes and outcomes. In theory, groups are empowering; whether they realize their empowerment potential, however, depends in large measure on how well they are understood by those who participate in them.

The Small Group: Meaning and Scope

Defining the Small Group

When we speak of small groups in organizations, we are referring to groups who perceive themselves as something other than a collection of independently functioning individuals. Many years ago, Bales (1950) pointed to the importance of group members developing a *psychological relationship,* a sense of mutual awareness and interdependence. This evolving sense of interdependence typically develops over time, and in the context of repeated interactions. *Communication,* then, is another defining element of a small group. Traditionally, communicative exchanges in groups have occurred face to face in a typical meeting environment. Technology, however, is changing that. Group members can now interact without face-to-face contact, over great distances, and even at different times. The necessity for communicative exchanges, however, is still crucial. Finally, members of small groups possess some degree of *shared interest.* This interest often manifests itself as a goal upon which there is mutual agreement, although that agreement must be examined over time and as group assignments change. Baird (1977) provided a good synthesizing definition of a group as "a collection of more than two persons who perceive themselves as a group, possess a common fate, have organizational structure, and communicate over time to achieve personal and group goals" (pp. 168–169).

Groups come in many sizes. Traditionally, "small" groups range from five to nine, although numbers of up to fifteen or twenty are not unusual. In general, the larger the group, the more complex the patterns of interaction and the more formalized the procedures needed for managing the group's interactions. Most researchers agree, however, that the salient characteristics of the small group are interaction, the feeling of interdependence, and some degree of shared interest rather than any particular number of group members.

Groups in organizations do not exist as isolated units. They are, rather, subsystems embedded within the larger organizational system. As Jablin (1980) noted, their members are part of "an interlocking network of organizational roles" (p. 5). Groups represent subcultures that may reflect the larger organizational culture but may also differ in important ways. Moreover, each individual typically has multiple group memberships and may be subjected to conflicting pressures. Organizational groups are embedded within formal hierarchies and often function with appointed leaders. Given these general defining characteristics, several different types of small groups can be distinguished.

Types of Small Groups

Since contemporary management theories emphasize empowerment through group work, groups play varied and increasingly significant roles in all sorts of organizations. Many groups are formally appointed by management and direct their energies toward *decision making* or *problem solving*. These groups are task-oriented and goal-directed. They are created and sustained for the purpose of responding to some organizational need. In some instances, these groups will work together over time and on diverse tasks that fall within their realm of expertise. In other cases, *ad hoc* groups may be created to address a specific problem or complete a particular project. When the problem is solved or the project completed, the group is disbanded.

Indiana University, for example, currently faces a dreadful parking problem. Students and faculty purchase outrageously expensive parking permits that are typically useless after 8:00 A.M. By 8:15, the permits function more as hunting licenses. To address this problem, the chancellor has appointed an ad hoc parking committee whose task is to study the situation and present a solution to the Faculty Council. Once the committee has presented its proposed solution, it will cease to exist, as the Faculty Council and its standing committees take over and concern themselves with the details of implementation.

Although task-oriented groups are crucial from a management perspective, other kinds of groups fulfill additional important functions. Some groups, for instance, are geared toward *learning*. As the information age unfolds, accompanied by changes in technology and the work environment, the need for learning becomes increasingly compelling. Some learning groups are formed as part of formal orientation and training programs. Others meet, both formally and informally, over time. At Motorola, for instance, every employee is given the opportunity to develop new skills and acquire new knowledge for two weeks out of every year. This is time spent away from the job at the company's expense. Much of this learning and training occurs in relatively small groups.

Still other groups, *casual* or *cathartic,* are geared toward fulfilling personal needs for social interaction. Coffee break groups, lunch groups, and support groups represent this broad group category. Some form spontaneously; others may be organized by organizational leaders. Support groups, for instance, may grow from the organization's counseling program to help employees deal with drug and alcohol abuse, midlife crisis, divorce, or aging parents. Traditionally, these groups have been very important. As early as the 1930s, the Hawthorne studies (Roethlisberger & Dickson, 1939) identified the informal work group and the social support, good humor, and fellowship it offered as a significant source of employee motivation. Arguably, when work itself seems enrichment-resistant, one way of enhancing the employee's sense of well-being is to enrich the social context in which the work is performed. Occasionally, casual or support group experiences can evolve into more lasting social interaction that occurs outside as well as inside the organizational setting. For instance, work-related relationships may grow into influential, satisfying, and lasting friendships. When this happens, those involved in the experience begin to function as a *primary group;* they share and influence one other's values, attitudes, and actions.

Teams

We have already discussed the teamwork philosophy of organization theory as well as the use of self-managing teams as a current application of human resources management. The Center for Effective Organizations at the University of Southern California recently conducted a survey of Fortune 1,000 companies. They found that 68 percent use self-managing or high-performance teams (Dumaine, 1994). As small groups within organizations, teams generally consist of either project or work teams.

Project teams have existed for many years in organizational settings. Typically consisting of employees representing an array of specialties (such as marketing, sales, and engineering), they coordinate the successful completion of a particular project, product, or service. Project teams have been part of the space program for many years and are common in electronic, computer, and other research-based industries. These teams typically work quickly to clarify goals, roles, and responsibilities. They often possess little history, are likely pressured by deadlines, and may have difficulty establishing mutually satisfying working relationships. Nevertheless, cross-functional project teams have the advantage of allowing individuals from different organizational divisions to keep communicating with and educating one other, while reminding them of the importance of customer needs and satisfaction.

The other, and most innovative, kind of team is the *work team.* Wellins, Byham, and Wilson (1991) defined the work team as "an intact group of employees who are responsible for a 'whole' work process or segment that delivers a product or service to an internal or external customer" (p. 3). Work teams, which have become increasingly popular, are used in such diverse organizations as 3M, General Electric, AT&T, and Corning. As discussed in Chapter 2, Apple Computer's Macintosh was invented by a work team. Each of the companies that has won the Malcolm Baldrige National Quality Award (among them, Millikin, Motorola, Westinghouse, and Xerox) fostered teamwork among employees as a crucial component of its improvement efforts (Whetten & Cameron, 1991).

Katzenbach and Smith (1993) studied fifty different teams in over thirty organizations. Based on their observations, they concluded that the critical factor in establishing successful teams is to assemble a small number of people with complementary skills who share a commitment to a common purpose and who set forth a set of performance goals for which they hold themselves mutually accountable. They argued that teams develop direction, momentum, and commitment by working to shape a meaningful purpose. Team members then translate their common purpose into specific performance goals, such as reducing the rejection rate from suppliers by 40 percent or increasing the math scores of graduates from the 60th to the 80th percentile. Moreover, when team members work together toward common objectives, trust and commitment follow.

Can teams be empowering? Indeed they can, in the right circumstances. Dumaine (1994) argued that the best teams "are truly empowered to organize their work and make decisions" (p. 67). Mutual accountability is also a key ingredient, as Katzenbach and Smith (1993) noted:

> This sense of mutual accountability . . . produces the rich rewards of mutual achievement in which all members share. What we heard over and over from members of effective teams is that they found the experience energizing and motivating in ways that their "normal" jobs never could match (p. 116).

There is an important distinction between being held accountable by one's boss and being accountable to oneself and one's team.

There are, however, no guarantees. Sometimes teams are "set up" to fail. They may be launched in a vacuum, with little or no training or support, no changes in the design of their work, and no new technologies like e-mail to foster communication within and between teams (Dumaine, 1994). Managers must make a commitment to empowerment by demonstrating a willingness to give teams the authority to get the job done. This means providing access to resources, information, and technical assistance and allowing the teams to make decisions about how to proceed, how to delegate responsibility, and so forth.

Whether or not a team is effective, then, depends upon its members' skills, mutual trust, sense of purpose, and commitment to objectives—as well as external factors. When managers are truly committed to empowerment through teamwork, however, and are willing to put aside traditional hierarchical constraints and to think in fresh, creative ways, work teams can serve as true vehicles of empowerment. In their Statement of Aspirations, Levi Strauss & Company defines empowering leadership as that which "increases the authority and responsibility of those closest to our products and customers. By actively pushing responsibility, trust, and recognition into the organization, we can harness and release the capabilities of all our people" (Lumsden & Lumsden, 1993). Not surprisingly, work teams are an intrinsic component of the Levi Strauss culture.

Critical Group Variables

Pressure for Uniformity

Human relations researchers were perhaps the first to recognize the powerful influence of informal work groups on individual behavior in organizational settings. Over the past half century, the collective efforts of social scientists have identified the small group as a foundational element of social influence across all kinds of organizational settings.

The classic social influence investigation was conducted by Solomon Asch, who performed a series of experiments involving simple line discrimination tasks (Asch, 1956). In fact, the perceptual task of comparing one of three comparison lines with a test line was so simple that Asch reported that any individual with normal vision could make the correct match nearly 100 percent of the time. Asch subsequently coached a group of confederates to announce deliberately erroneous judgments on these same perceptual tasks. When a naive subject was placed among Asch's group of confederates and made to listen to the announced judgments of others before stating his or her own estimates, the results were radically skewed in the direction of the majority. Approximately one-third of all estimates reported by the subjects were identical with or in the direction of the distorted majority estimates. Only one-fourth of all naive subjects remained completely independent over a series of trials. Asch's findings are especially striking given that the individuals in his study were not acquainted with one another before the experiment, nor would they be likely to meet again. Moreover, the confederates made no overt attempts to persuade or pressure the naive group member. Finally, the line discrimination tasks had no real intrinsic importance to the subjects, to their future relations with others, or to the fate of anyone in the room.

We have mentioned **norms** several times in the preceding discussion. Schein (1969) defined a norm as "a set of assumptions or expectations held by the members of a group or organization concerning what kind of behavior is right or wrong, good or bad, appropriate or inappropriate, allowed or not allowed" (p. 59). Wahrman (1972) described norms in even stronger terms when he argued that they are "beliefs which . . . members of a group share, are aware they share, and believe they have a right to demand that other people [in the group] abide by them" (p. 205). Norms may be either *implicit* (not actually articulated, but known and understood) or *explicit* (formally stated either orally, in writing, or both). Explicit norms may refer to the number of hours someone is expected to work, dress code specifications, or the frequency of group meetings. Implicit norms could refer to whether one discusses politics at work, how often to invite the boss to dinner, or the wisdom of disagreeing publicly with those of higher status.

Whether individuals adhere to a group's norms depends upon a variety of factors. Chief among them is the degree to which they value their membership in and identify strongly with the group or organization (Cheney, 1983). In addition, people possess different motives for conforming. In some instances they may listen to other group members' arguments and actually become convinced that the group is right. (This kind of agreement grows from persuasion rather than from group pressure or coercion.) In contrast, others may simply find it easier, less stressful, or more politically astute to mouth their agreement, even though they privately disagree.

Occasionally, a person may end up in a group with a widely shared belief that consensus is necessary for group survival. One of the authors once belonged to an administrative team at a small private college. The college had fallen upon hard financial times. At an emergency meeting, the president of the college made the announcement that the group needed to develop and articulate a compelling strategy for raising funds to ensure institutional survival. This strategic plan was to be presented to the college's Board of Trustees in a few weeks. The president commented that *every group member* should be willing to stand behind the plan. If the board members were not completely convinced that the plan was feasible, they were prepared to close the college permanently. As the discussion of the plan evolved, the author did not agree with other group members who saw it as the wisest course of action. Nevertheless, she went along with the others so that the team could assure the board that they were united in their support for the plan and their commitment to it. (The plan, by the way, was accepted by the board, and the college is thriving today!)

Failure to conform to the group can be psychologically uncomfortable. Conformity, on the other hand, can be viewed as strategic. One organizational leader recently disclosed that he always "cooperated" with others on issues that he perceived as insignificant in the grand scheme. He laughingly noted that when he voted with others, he always made them aware of it, sometimes by joking that they "owed him." However, he actually viewed the situation as demanding that others would reciprocate. He had scratched their backs, and he fully expected others to extend the same courtesy to him. Implicit in this approach to conformity is the idea that individuals may conform when an issue is not of central importance to them, while remaining quite independent on issues about which they care deeply (Sherif, Sherif, & Nebergall, 1965).

For years, scholars debated whether the tendency to conform should be viewed as a personality characteristic. For the most part, however, situational factors seem to have the most influence on the individual's tendency to conform (e.g., Andrews, 1985). In general, individuals appear to be more likely to conform when they are in situations in which: (1) ambiguity or confusion exists, (2) the members of the group are unanimous, (3) the group contains those of higher rank, (4) the group is highly cohesive, or (5) a state of crisis or emergency seems to demand uniformity (for example, jury deliberations).

Groups exert pressure for uniformity in a variety of ways. Human relations researchers noted the verbal and nonverbal methods informal work groups used to get deviates "back in line." Tactics such as teasing, ridiculing, punching, and shoving were not uncommon in factory settings (Roethlisberger & Dickson, 1939). Schachter's laboratory research (1951) pointed to increases in the quantity of communication as a major pressuring tactic. Subsequent research by Taylor (1969) found that the verbal behavior of majority group members was characterized by reasonableness, dominance, and hostility. More recently, Thameling and Andrews (1992) described the communication behavior of majority group members as cooperative, opinionated, and emotional. Finally, Wenburg and Wilmot (1973) identified five sequential steps that most groups take as they attempt to influence opinion deviates:

1. delaying action (doing little overtly and hoping the deviate will conform without pressure)
2. chatting among themselves (possibly joking with the deviate)
3. ridiculing the deviate (overtly recognizing his or her behavior as different or unacceptable)
4. engaging in severe criticism (possibly including threats)
5. rejecting the deviate (ignoring, isolating, and preventing future interaction with the group).

This is only a rough model, and it does not take into account unique group characteristics (for example, level of cohesiveness) or the relationship between the deviate and the group.

One of the most critical variables affecting the treatment of deviates is their position or status within the group. In general, groups tolerate more deviant behavior from those of high status (Gouran & Andrews, 1984), but there are exceptions. A person of high status may be treated more harshly by other group members if he or she commits an act perceived as extremely serious or damaging. Presumably, such individuals are perceived as being more responsible for their own behavior (the vice president who steals versus the custodian who does the same thing). Moreover, the deviant behavior of someone who occupies a high position is believed to reflect negatively on the entire organization significantly more than the behavior of someone near the bottom. In general, however, high status permits greater freedom. Hollander's early (1958) "idiosyncrasy credit" model offers an interesting explanation of how this works. An individual who conforms, according to Hollander, accumulates status in the form of positive impressions or "credit" awarded by others. This credit then permits greater latitude for nonconformity under certain conditions. A basic feature of this model is that there is no fixed norm or set of norms with which all members must comply equally. Rather the group defines nonconformity or deviant behavior according to how the individual group member is perceived. Thus, the same act may be seen as deviant when performed by A and as creatively innovative when performed by B. Perceived deviation from this vantage point becomes person-specific and functionally related to status.

How does one respond to group pressure? Both individual and situational variables play a role. For instance, some tend to "go with the flow" in most situations, preferring to fit in with the group than to be perceived as "making waves." That is, even if they disagree with the group, they will vote with or pretend to agree with others—perhaps because they fear rejection, lack courage, have insufficient ego involvement, or hope to ingratiate themselves with others. Others may change their minds and begin to agree with the group's perceptions—either because they are in fact genuinely persuaded or because they have forced themselves to deny the validity of their own views or senses. Of course, some respond to group pressure by refusing to yield. Such challenges to the group's authority may produce a variety of results. For instance, if the group or organization is threatened by the deviate's act, he or she may be punished severely. Tompkins recounted the story of Roger Boisjoly, one of the engineers who unsuccessfully argued against launching the space shuttle *Challenger*. Boisjoly subsequently "deviated" further by going against the advice of management and reporting his reservations to the Rogers Commission, which investigated the disaster. Tompkins (1993) noted:

> He [Boisjoly] then lost his job at Thiokol. Residents of the town he lived in, who had once elected him mayor, now began to shun him and his wife . . . and many members of his own church refused to speak to him. A dead rabbit was placed in his mailbox. On several occasions while taking long walks near his home, he said, vehicles swerved as if to hit him (p. 169).

Boisjoly's situation is complicated in that his unwillingness to conform also served to "blow the whistle" on a group of very important people with a very great deal to lose.

More common instances of deviation can also lead to unpleasant consequences, especially in circumstances in which those in positions of power are intolerant of dissent. One woman recently challenged her boss during a departmental meeting. She had just learned that he had withheld important information from the group and had also lied with regard to some important recruiting in which the department was engaged. When she challenged his version of affirmative action at the meeting, he told her (in a loud and forceful voice) that she was "out of order." Then, giving her a cold, sharklike stare, he told her that he would not forget what she had said during the meeting. The next day, she found a note on her desk informing her that she had been removed from two important committees (one of which she had founded) and reassigned to a task force whose mission was largely to plan social events. Although many of her coworkers were sympathetic (and sent her e-mail messages, cards, and flowers in support), none stood with her in opposing this department head. Apparently, they feared retaliation. Behind the boss's back, however, they began to refer to him as "Hitler," and some exchanged cartoons making fun of tyrants.

In a healthier organizational climate, expressions of disagreement or dissent may be more positively received. For instance, Moscovici (1985) argued that little is known of the influence the deviate might exercise upon members of the majority. One study demonstrated that an intelligent, articulate deviate might exert considerable influence on the views of the majority, particularly on topics about which the deviate knows much and the other group members know little (Bradley, Hamon, & Harris, 1976). However, when it is the majority of group members who are better informed, the deviate's influence is lessened. According to Moscovici, when the minority members's *behavioral style* reflects such qualities as consistency, conviction, autonomy, and competence, the members of the majority may as a result attribute some "truth" and give some serious consideration to the minority position. Apparently, the most effective way to achieve minority influence is to exhibit a confident and consistent nonconforming position from the outset (Moscovici, 1985; Moscovici & Faucheux, 1972; Moscovici, Lage, & Naffrechoux, 1969; Moscovici & Nemeth, 1974).

Considered by themselves, pressure for uniformity and conformity behavior are neither good nor bad. They are simply facts of group and organizational life. Every group has norms—some of which are quite constructive and empowering, such as tolerating and encouraging the exploration of diverse points of view, being supportive of others, and so forth. Groups must examine their norms with vigilance. Whenever majority members attempt to pressure opinion deviates into public compliance, they run the risk of depleted morale and impaired decision making.

Role Structure

The norms that develop in groups typically suggest (or require) appropriate modes of conduct for all group members. At the same time, however, groups need considerable role diversity among their membership to function effectively. Conceptually, roles include behaviors, as well as the way those behaviors *function* within the group. Group members perform different, although often interdependent, functions as they work together on varied tasks. For instance, a group member may use humor during a meeting. Her humor, however, may function in diverse ways: to relieve tension, to diminish someone else's ego (especially if the humor is sarcastic), to get the group off track by distracting members from the task at hand, or to build group cohesiveness. Clearly, some of these behaviors are more functionally related to accomplishing group goals than others. Similarly, asking a question can function as a simple request for information ("Do we have projected trends for next month yet?"), as a strategy for changing the subject, as a vehicle for introducing a new topic, or as a "put down" or challenge ("What would *you* know about working in a factory?").

Various classification schemes have been developed to describe the roles or behavioral functions that group members enact. As shown in Table 7.1, these roles are typically classified into one of two main categories: group task roles and group building and maintenance roles (Benne & Sheats, 1948; Bales, 1950).

Task roles include the communication functions necessary for a group to accomplish its task; these often involve problem solving, decision making, information exchange, or conflict resolution. Although early discussions of group task roles treated them as unified, the contemporary view suggests that they represent *two* task dimensions: those roles focusing on the substance or

Task Roles

Initiator   Proposes new ideas, procedures, goals, and solutions; gets the group started.

Information giver   Supplies evidence, opinions, goals, and related personal experiences relevant to the task.

Information seeker   Asks for information from other group members, seeks clarification when necessary, and makes sure that relevant evidence is not overlooked.

Opinion giver   States her own beliefs, attitudes, and judgments; is willing to take a position, although not without sensitivity to others' views.

Opinion seeker   Solicits the opinions and feelings of others and asks for clarification of positions. Ideally, those who give opinions will be equally willing to seek opinions.

Elaborator   Clarifies and expands the ideas of others through examples, illustrations, and explanations. This role is valuable as long as elaborations are task-relevant.

Integrator   Clarifies the relationship between various facts, opinions, and suggestions and integrates the ideas of other members.

Orienter   Keeps the group directed toward its goal, summarizes what has taken place, and clarifies the positions of the group.

Evaluator   Expresses judgments about the relative worth of information or ideas; proposes or applies criteria for weighing the quality of information or alternative courses of action.

Procedural specialist   Organizes the group's work; suggests an agenda, outline, or problem-solving sequence.

Consensus tester   Asks if the group has reached a decision acceptable to all; suggests, when appropriate, that agreement may have been reached.

Building and Maintenance Roles

Supporter   Praises and agrees with others, providing a warm, supportive interpersonal climate.

Harmonizer   Attempts to mediate differences, introduces compromise, and tries to reconcile differences.

Tension reliever   Encourages a relaxed atmosphere by reducing formality and interjecting appropriate humor.

Gatekeeper   Exerts some control over communication channels, encouraging reticent discussants, discouraging those who tend to monopolize the discussion, and seeking diversity of opinion.

Norm creator   Suggests rules of behavior for group members, challenges unproductive ways of behaving, and gives a negative response when someone violates an important group norm.

Solidarity builder   Expresses positive feelings toward other group members; reinforces a sense of group unity and cohesiveness.

Dramatist   Evokes fantasies about persons and places other than the present group and time; may test a tentative value or norm through hypothetical example or story; dreams, shows creativity, and articulates visions.

TABLE 7.1

Constructive Roles in Groups

content of the issue being discussed (like giving information) and another set of roles that deal with procedural matters (like orienting and organizing the group). These two dimensions may function in tandem if, for example, someone initiates the discussion (a procedural act) by tossing out an idea (a substantive move). Nevertheless, the distinction may be important, since research on ad hoc groups suggests that group task behaviors providing procedural guidance may be perceived as especially valuable. In one study, for instance, those who were viewed as having provided significant procedural guidance were most likely to emerge as group leaders (Bunyi & Andrews, 1985). The extent to which procedural acts are valued may also depend upon the characteristics of group members. Individuals have been shown to vary significantly in their need for procedural order in group communication settings (Putnam, 1979; Hirokawa, Ice, & Cook, 1988; Wheeler, Mennecke, & Scudder, 1993).

The second major category of group roles is **group building and maintenance roles**. These roles build and sustain the group's interpersonal relationships, helping everyone to feel more positive about the group's task and to interact constructively and harmoniously. By reducing the competition between group members and their ideas, these behaviors nurture an enhanced sense of cooperative deliberation (Gouran & Hirokawa, 1986).

Although these roles are presented as largely desirable and constructive, they must be evaluated as they are enacted in a specific group context. For instance, establishing and maintaining norms is quite valuable as long as the norms are sound. If the group is committed to encouraging dissent, for instance, and someone attempts to stifle a minority view, reminding the group of its norm (tolerance for diversity) would clearly function positively. However, the person who helps the group support an attitude of intolerance would, by promoting that norm, function counterproductively. Moreover, roles in the building and maintenance category are traditionally associated with pleasant, harmonious social interaction. However, enacting some of them could readily produce tension and conflict—for example, by discouraging those who are dominating the discussion or challenging someone who is behaving unproductively. It seems that if groups are, in fact, to maintain themselves over time, they will of necessity go through moments of conflict and norm testing.

As noted earlier, most group members will perform diverse roles, and often the roles can be grouped together to form broader role clusters (see Figure 7.1). Those who function largely as opinion leaders, for instance, are likely to give their opinions rather frequently; but they also seek the views of others, evaluate everyone's views, support ideas they like, and—occasionally— offer procedural guidance. Similarly, the supportive role cluster might include behavior ranging from supporting others to relieving tension to showing solidarity—while also offering information and opinions as task behaviors.

Finally, not all roles function constructively in groups. To be avoided are **self-centered roles** that tend to further self-interests over group interests and goals (see Table 7.2). In general, the more that positive roles are enacted and shared in groups (and negative roles minimized), the greater the likelihood of

FIGURE 7.1

Group Role Clusters

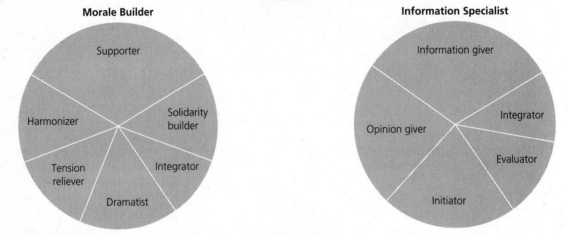

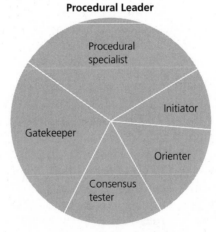

TABLE 7.2

Self-Centered Group Roles

Blocker Constantly objects to others' ideas and suggestions, insisting that nothing will work. May also repeatedly bring up the same topic or issue after the group has considered and rejected it.

Aggressor Insults and criticizes others; shows jealousy and ill will.

Storyteller Tells irrelevant, often time-consuming stories; enjoys discussing personal experiences.

Recognition seeker Interjects comments that call attention to his or her achievements and successes.

Dominator Tries to monopolize group interaction.

Noncontributor Is reticent and uncommunicative; refuses to cope with conflict or take a stand; fails to respond to others' comments.

Confessor Attempts to use the group as a therapeutic session; asks the group to listen to personal problems.

Special-interest pleader Represents the interests of a different group and pleads on their behalf.

positive group outcomes, such as enhanced morale and sound decision making. Moreover, from the functional approach to leadership (see Chapter 6), those who perform any positive roles are actually serving as group leaders, insofar as their behavior helps the group accomplish its goals.

Although much of the research on group roles has been conducted in laboratory settings, in actual organizations enacting roles may offer more challenge, as well as more opportunity. In effective teams, for instance, research has shown that during the commitment-building process, team members candidly explore both who is best suited to each task and how individual roles will come together (Katzenbach & Smith, 1993). In effect, the team establishes a social contract among members that relates to their purposes and guides and influences how they will communicate with one another. For example, companies such as Hewlett-Packard and Motorola have an ingrained performance ethic that enables teams to form "organically" whenever there is a clear performance challenge requiring collective rather than individual effort. As the teams form, they communicate specifically what sorts of roles need to be played and how the team will need to interact in order to reach performance goals. This approach to sharing roles in teams also serves to diminish some of the communication problems that often surface when individuals of unequal status attempt to collaborate in groups.

Status and Power

Historically, organizational groups have often been composed of members who possess varying levels of status and power and who therefore do not interact as equals, a fact that has sometimes served as an obstacle to effective interaction and decision making. As Gouran (1988) pointed out, "The differences that separate the members of a group into roles of varying importance can lead to a high ranking participant's having influence that is not commensurate with the worth of his or her contribution" (p. 200). Several studies have shown that fellow group members treat those who are perceived as possessing high status with greater deference than they do those of lower status. As noted earlier, high-status group members may be allowed to deviate more from group norms, again reinforcing the notion of unequal standards for individual group members (Gouran & Andrews, 1984).

Communication directed to those possessing high status is often distorted in significant ways. In general, upward communication is associated with approval-seeking behavior, although occasionally it may be characterized by aggression or hostility. Interacting with others who can influence one's career or can reward or punish in other ways apparently creates some ambivalence.

When those of lesser status defer to those of higher status, impaired decision making may also result. In his study of problem-solving groups, for instance, Torrance (1954) found that lower-status members who had the correct solution were prone to endorse the solution proposed by the highest-ranking member, even when it was incorrect. Thus, the privilege of holders of high status to influence the judgment and performance of others is difficult to overcome. Homans (1974) argued that individuals having high status are viewed as controlling scarce psychological and/or material resources. Compliance with their attempts to influence is motivated by a desire to share in the benefits these resources provide. John DeLorean's account of committee meetings inside General Motors provides a compelling illustration of the potential impact of high status on the behavior of those of lesser rank:

> Original ideas were often sacrificed in deference to what the boss wanted. Committee meetings . . . were either soliloquies by the top man, or conversations between a few top men with the rest of the meeting looking on. In meetings, often only three people . . . would have anything substantial to say, even though there were fourteen or fifteen executives present. The rest of the team would remain silent, speaking only when spoken to. When they did offer comment, in many cases, it was just to paraphrase what had already been said by one of the top guys (quoted in Wright, 1979, p. 47).

In every organization, even the most team-oriented and decentralized, status differentials exist. However, those of higher status have important choices to make. An executive can choose to wield influence either by stifling opinions and dissent or by insisting on hearing diverse points of view and encouraging all participants to think critically and voice their concerns. One executive refused to allow his board to make a decision until members had heard and fully discussed the arguments *against* the policy they were about to endorse (Drucker, 1968). Thus, the way in which status differentials affect the group depends in part on the existing organizational climate. For instance, Tjosvold (1985) found that when a cooperative climate existed, both low- and high-status superiors interacted far more constructively and supportively than they did in either individualistic or competitive climates. Clearly, those who are in positions of leadership, or who in other ways possess status and power, are ideally situated to empower others and to exert positive influence on the quality of the group's interactions. Moreover, the judicious use of authority to encourage the free expression of ideas and to reward initiative and innovative thinking can go far to eliminate the doubts and skepticism of less powerful group members.

Cohesiveness

Another significant variable that frequently affects group interaction is cohesiveness. As a group characteristic, **cohesiveness** is related to solidarity, the group's "stick-togetherness," and its ability to maintain itself over time and through crisis (Shepherd, 1964). Highly cohesive groups usually cling to their norms, attitudes, and values; not surprisingly, therefore, cohesiveness and conformity are closely related. Those who are a part of highly cohesive groups feel a strong sense of belonging, are proud of their group affiliation, and develop close friendships with other group members.

While it seems clear that the ambience in highly cohesive groups is pleasant, it is often erroneously assumed that these groups will therefore make excellent decisions or be extremely productive. From an organizational perspective, productivity is an especially sensitive issue. Yet research has demonstrated that cohesiveness neither increases nor decreases group productivity (Berkowitz, 1954). Instead, it serves to heighten the susceptibility of group members to mutual influence. Thus, if a highly cohesive group establishes a norm of low productivity, group members are likely to conform to the norm and produce little.

Sometimes cohesiveness can have an even darker side. Irving Janis (1982) recounted the story of the events that occurred a few days before disaster struck the small mining town of Pitcher, Oklahoma, in 1950. According to Janis, the local mining engineer had warned the town's citizens to leave immediately because the town had accidentally been undermined and was in danger of caving in at any moment. The day after the warning was issued, however, at a meeting of leading citizens belonging to the Lions Club, members joked about the warning and "laughed uproariously when someone arrived wearing a parachute" (p. 3). Complacency, born of cohesiveness, caused these men to reason that disasters of this sort just couldn't happen to fine folks like them in a nice little town like theirs. A few days later, this flawed reasoning cost several of these men and their families their lives.

Although this incident occurred over four decades ago, it is scarcely an isolated event. Groups and organizations often make poor decisions—in part because their cohesiveness contributes to a mindset that discourages dissent and the rational examination of alternative courses of action. The tragic decision to launch the *Challenger* was clearly influenced by the inability of those near the bottom of the organization to express to their superiors freely and fully their skepticism about the wisdom of launching the shuttle in extremely cold temperatures (Gouran, Hirokawa, & Martz, 1986; Browning, 1988; McConnell, 1987; Trento, 1987).

As noted earlier, pressure for uniformity often occurs in groups characterized by high cohesiveness. This pressure serves to reduce the range and quality of information and opinions presented and diminishes the advantages of having groups rather than individuals make decisions. We have already discussed some of the general problems associated with pressure for uniformity. In cohesive groups, group pressure can also gradually shift the group toward the position taken by the majority or by its most vocal members. Since such shifts depend more on intragroup pressures than on the quality of the arguments and information available, the group may end up making "extreme" decisions—ones that mindlessly continue existing policies, or are inordinately risky (Alderton & Frey, 1983; Cline & Cline, 1979; Siebold & Meyers, 1986). Moreover, since cohesiveness generates high levels of member commitment to group decisions and high levels of motivation to implement them, group members may do all they can to implement a poor or foolish decision, or to ignore or distort information that suggests their decision or proposed course of action might be unwise (Janis & Mann, 1977; Janis, 1985).

One of the most extensive investigations of the potentially negative impact of cohesiveness on a group's ability to make intelligent decisions was conducted by Irving Janis (1982). Janis examined the decision-making processes leading to several historic military and political fiascoes, including the 1941 decision to ignore warnings that Japan might attack Pearl Harbor; the 1961 decision to invade Cuba at the Bay of Pigs; and the 1974 decision by the Committee to Re-Elect the President to break into the Democratic party's headquarters at the Watergate complex, and then to engage in a cover-up. To explain how poor decisions were reached in each of these cases, Janis introduced the concept of **groupthink,** which he originally defined as "a model of thinking that people engage in when they are deeply involved in a cohesive in-group, when the members' striving for unanimity overrides their motivation to realistically appraise alternative courses of action. . . ." (p. 9). Later, Janis modified the groupthink construct to focus on "premature concurrence seeking," stressing the notion that although most groups strive for agreement over time, those truly engaged in "groupthink" seek consensus so swiftly and relentlessly that full and free discussion of alternative courses of action simply never occurs (Cline, 1990).

Janis identified eight negative qualities that commonly characterize groups plagued by groupthink (see Table 7.3). Janis did not argue that groupthink is invariably associated with group cohesiveness. He pointed out, rather, that strategies exist for counteracting it. According to Janis, the group's leader is in a position to insist on the open-minded pursuit of alternative courses of

TABLE 7.3

Groupthink Characteristics

Illusion of invulnerability   Creating excessive optimism and encouraging excessive risk taking.

Collective rationalization   Discounting warnings that might lead members to reconsider their assumptions.

Unquestioned belief in the group's inherent morality   Causing members to ignore the ethical consequences of their decisions.

Stereotyped views of opposition leaders   Presenting them as either too evil to warrant genuine attempts to negotiate or too weak or stupid to be a viable threat.

Direct pressure exerted on any member who expresses dissenting views Making clear that such dissent is unacceptable.

Self-censorship by group members   Attempting to minimize the importance of any doubts they might have.

Shared illusion of unanimity   Pretending that all opinions conform to the majority view.

Emergence of self-appointed "mindguards"   Protecting the group from conflicting information that might shatter their shared complacency.

SOURCE: Janis, 1982.

action. He suggested, in particular, that the leader might (1) assign to everyone the role of critical evaluator; (2) avoid stating personal views, especially at the outset; (3) bring in outsiders representing diverse interests to talk with and listen to the group; (4) play and ask others to take turns playing the devil's advocate; (5) let the group deliberate without the leader from time to time; and (6) after a tentative decision has been made, hold a "second chance" meeting at which each member is required to express as strongly as possible any residual doubts (Huseman & Driver, 1979). When leaders of highly cohesive groups endorse these kinds of norms, the groups should be able to function quite effectively. Cohesiveness need not doom a group. On the contrary, with appropriate vigilance, it can contribute to constructive, satisfying group communication.

Group Decision Process Models

Traditional Linear Models

The majority of groups in organizations participate in problem solving and decision making. The manner in which a group approaches the decision-making process is related to its success. Early research by Bales and Strodtbeck (1951) identified three clearly discernible stages of analysis in successful problem-solving groups: *orientation, evaluation,* and *control.* During the orientation stage, group members spent most of their time coordinating relevant information—exchanging information, orienting, repeating, and confirming. In the second stage, evaluative comments were predominant. Group members exchanged opinions, ideas, and feelings in an attempt to reconcile their differences over judgments of fact and the appropriateness of proposed courses of action. During the final control stage, individuals exchanged suggestions, considered alternative courses of action, and generally expressed considerable agreement and disagreement in arriving at a commonly accepted solution.

Another fairly linear model of task group development was proposed by Tuckman and Jensen (1977). Their group stages included *forming, storming, norming, performing,* and *adjourning.* Formative behavior involves establishing new relationships and seeking some sense of group spirit. In the next stage, group members begin to react to the demands of the situation. They may question the group's charge and the authority of others in the group, articulating some assertions of difference and independence. The norming stage sees the group agreeing on rules of behavior, criteria for decision making, and ways of doing things. Only during the fourth phase does the group really focus on the task or problem at hand. Finally, as the group's time together draws to a close, members strive for closure on both task and relationship issues, moving toward adjournment. This model emphasizes relationship development and thus is most appropriately applied to newly formed groups. It provides less specific information about ongoing groups' decision-making processes.

Process Models of Decision Making

As early as the 1960s, some researchers of small groups challenged the linear view of group decision making. Schiedel and Crowell (1964), for instance, began with the assumption that if group decision making were essentially linear, group members would make statements that initiated, extended, modified, and synthesized the topic under discussion. When they observed actual groups, however, they found that these kinds of statements accounted for only about 22 percent of the group's total interaction. Instead, Schiedel and Crowell observed a *reach-test* cycle, in which one participant would reach forward with a new idea that was then tested by elaboration, acceptance, or rejection by the other group members. A different member would then reach out with another idea, and the process would repeat itself. Far from a linear progression toward a decision, these groups followed a *spiraling* model, in which members bounced ideas back and forth as they moved toward consensus.

Fisher (1970) conducted yet another significant study of the interaction process leading to group consensus on decision-making tasks. He found that groups moved through four interrelated phases as they approached consensus: *orientation, conflict, emergence,* and *reinforcement.* During orientation, group members offer their ideas and opinions somewhat tentatively and perhaps ambiguously. As ideas are clarified and lines of disagreement drawn, they move into the conflict phase. Both positive and negative comments are offered, often with considerable assertiveness. Communication is typically persuasive or even argumentative in nature. During the third phase, a solution begins to emerge, and argument and disagreements decline. The final phase is a time of reinforcement, with group members confirming their emerging consensus and seeking to understand better the implications of their impending decision or action. Like Schiedel and Crowell, however, Fisher (1970; 1979) reported that groups do not progress steadily toward a final decision. Instead, they seem to move in jumps by offering amendments to different aspects of the proposal under consideration.

More recently, studies by Poole and associates suggested that groups develop according to a *multiple sequence model* (1981; 1983; 1985; 1988a; 1988b; 1990). That is, the groups studied tried to implement logical, orderly problem-solving sequences; but frequently, other factors—such as lack of information, task difficulty, and conflict—interfered. Moreover, Poole reported that periods of idea development and exploration were often broken by periods of integrating activity, like telling jokes, sharing personal stories, and exchanging compliments. In particular, Poole and Roth (1988b) found that groups go through periods of disorganization that are unpredictable and fail to follow a linear model. Taken as a whole, Poole's research suggested that group development is not as orderly as earlier models proposed. Figure 7.2 compares several decision-making models.

Distinguishing Effective from Ineffective Groups

Even though groups approach their problem-solving ventures with considerable diversity, researchers have continued to seek general factors that might distinguish effective from ineffective groups. In her longitudinal field study of eight project teams, for instance, Gersick (1988) reported that each team developed its own approaches during its early meetings and tended to stick with those until they reached a midpoint in the time available for completing the project. At this midpoint, each group experienced a transition, "a powerful opportunity to alter the course of its life midstream" (Gersick, 1988, p. 32). Depending upon whether or not the transition functioned constructively, the teams' final products or outcomes varied in quality. Successful groups used the transition as a time to examine and possibly change their basic operating assumptions. Unsuccessful groups tended to ignore the opportunity for self-examination and plowed ahead using the same, often self-defeating patterns.

FIGURE 7.2

Group Decision Models: A Comparison Over Time

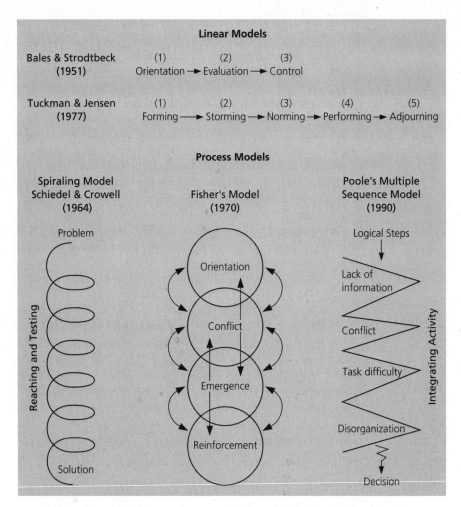

In general, Gersick's studies (1988; 1991) suggested that groups need to monitor their own interaction patterns and progress and be willing to make changes if they see they are not interacting constructively and productively.

Task group effectiveness was also studied in a laboratory investigation by Hirokawa (1983). He attempted to distinguish successful from unsuccessful problem-solving groups on the basis of the phases that characterized their discussions. His research indicated that no single uniform sequence of phases is necessarily associated with effective or ineffective problem solving. Rather, both kinds of groups take their own unique paths to solving their problems. One potentially important difference did emerge, however. Successful groups tend to begin their discussions by attempting to analyze the problem before trying to search for viable solutions.

Others believe that the attitudes group members bring to their deliberations may have a significant impact on the quality of their work. Some have argued that decision outcomes are mediated by vigilant information processing, wherein group members approach their work conscientiously and carefully (Janis & Mann, 1977; Gouran, 1982). As Gouran put it, "Although [procedures] can be very useful in keeping a decision-making discussion focused on the requirements of the question, you fall prey to the belief that the sequence itself rather than the qualities of mind it represents is what determines a group's effectiveness" (p. 30). Endorsing this view, Hirokawa and Rost (1992) advanced *vigilant interaction theory,* based on the belief that effective groups are more attentive than ineffective groups to the group process. They argued that effective groups are vigilant in their assessment of the nature of the task, their choice of criteria for evaluating alternatives, and their approach to weighing both positive and negative qualities associated with different decision options. Thus, the spirit in which the problem is tackled significantly influences the quality of the group's work.

Pragmatics of Problem-Solving Patterns

Some writers are skeptical of any approaches to problem solving or decision making that are based on the premise of rationality (Conrad, 1990). For instance, in Cohen, March, and Olson's (1972) *garbage can model,* decision making is seen as a garbage pail in which people, problems, alternatives, and solutions slush around until there is sufficient contact among these elements for a decision to emerge. According to these theorists, groups attempt to rationalize their decisions retroactively, but the decisions are really due to chance. They argued that the value of a decision should be judged according to group members' abilities to implement it and make it work, rather than by its intrinsic effectiveness.

While acknowledging that decision making is scarcely a completely rational process, most scholars agree that groups could benefit from adopting procedures that minimize the disadvantages associated with group interaction, such as looking at solutions before understanding the problem. For instance, Poole and Roth (1988a; 1988b) analyzed the sequences of activities in forty-seven decisions made by twenty-nine groups. They found that over half of the forty-seven decisions began with some form of solution focus. Fourteen of the groups never engaged in problem definition or other activities and spent the entire time focusing on solutions. Similarly, Nutt (1984) reviewed seventy-six cases of organizational decision making and reported that eighty-four percent of the cases used a solution-centered process. An initial focus on solutions may cause a truncated search and cursory consideration of alternatives. Even more serious, real problems may go unidentified in favor of problems that fit existing solutions. When this happens, the group actually formulates and attempts to solve the wrong problem.

In an attempt to address some of these problems and to encourage groups to examine problems more thoroughly and systematically, several writers and researchers have offered problem-solving patterns for groups to use. One of the most popular is John Dewey's (1910) *reflective-thinking sequence.* Particularly useful with questions of policy, this pattern consists of several questions:

1. How shall we define and limit the problem?
2. What are the causes and extent of the problem?
3. What are the criteria by which solutions should be judged?
4. What are the alternatives, and the strengths and weaknesses of each?
5. What solution can be agreed upon?
6. How can we put the solution into effect?

The value of the reflective-thinking sequence is its emphasis on careful problem assessment, thoughtful consideration of the criteria to be used in evaluating the competing solutions, and insistence on asking the group to grapple with the particulars of solution implementation.

Groups are notorious for making judgments about the quality or feasibility of members' ideas too early in the discussion. As a result, some researchers have proposed problem-solving strategies that encourage the generation of a maximum number of ideas without premature interpretation or analysis. For instance, some have advocated *brainstorming,* that is, proposing and listing ideas without passing any type of judgment or criticism. This procedure has been shown to produce fresher, better-quality ideas than do more ordinary problem-solving procedures (Dunnette, Campbell, & Jaastad, 1963). A related approach, the *nominal group procedure,* gives each group member an opportunity to brainstorm privately on paper. An appointed clerk then collects the lists of ideas and compiles a master list. Ultimately, group members vote on the items they consider most important (Mosley & Green, 1974).

Research comparing brainstorming groups with nominal groups has found that the nominal group procedure is more effective than brainstorming for groups composed of highly apprehensive members; it also appears better than brainstorming in terms of idea generation (Jablin, 1981). Its disadvantage (other than logistics) is that since the brainstorming is private, group members cannot be stimulated by hearing the ideas of others. Of course, group support systems allow groups to function as nominal groups by permitting members to brainstorm, organize, and evaluate their ideas anonymously using computers (see, for example, Gallupe, DeSanctis, & Dickson, 1988).

Leadership and Group Effectiveness

In Chapter 6 we discussed several different approaches to the study of leadership. From the functional perspective, any group might have as many leaders as there are group members, depending on how many make substantial contributions toward the group's goal. In organizational settings, groups typically operate with appointed leaders, many of whom hold positions of authority within the formal organization. Those leaders can choose to empower fellow group members by embracing a functional notion of leadership and encouraging others to share leadership, or they can make other, more restrictive choices. Tannenbaum and Schmidt (1958) suggested that the real measure of leadership style has to do with how leaders go about making decisions. They pointed to several options, ranging from the completely authoritarian (making a decision and announcing it) to the relatively democratic (defining some limits and asking the group to make the decision).

Although formally appointed leaders have special responsibilities for planning, conducting, and evaluating meetings, these functions can easily be shared with others. In a sense, common guidelines for responsible group membership apply to all group members, although arguably more so to the appointed leader, who should function as a positive role model for the other group members. Following are some widely accepted guidelines:

1. **Come to the meeting prepared to participate actively and constructively.** This guideline extends to having a positive attitude toward the group and its authority to make decisions and solve problems and being knowledgeable about the task before the group.

2. **Encourage the expression of diverse points of view.** Such qualities as open-mindedness and tolerance are critical.

3. **Establish and sustain norms of critical evaluation in a climate of mutual supportiveness.** Opinions and ideas should be argued and carefully scrutinized within a context of goodwill and personal respect.

4. **Work within the rules, criteria, and other established and agreed-upon limitations.** For instance, if criteria have been chosen to guide a decision, the group should use those criteria for weighing alternatives unless they are changed through mutual agreement.

5. **Interact ethically.** This guideline involves listening to one another with concern and respect, as well as consciously avoiding the negative roles cited earlier in this chapter. It also means communicating honestly and being willing to share responsibility for the group's collective decision once it is made.

By no means is this an exhaustive list of behavioral guidelines, but it does point to the sorts of behaviors and attitudes that both research and experience have shown to be positively associated with excellence in group endeavors. Those who lead groups should seek to model these kinds of behaviors and actively to encourage others to interact in these mutually empowering ways. And those who lead groups can only do so effectively in an organizational climate that promotes teamwork (see Focus On).

FOCUS ON   The Leader's Challenge: Building Team Performance

Establishing an organizational climate where teams and groups can thrive is a challenge facing almost every leader. Jon Katzenbach and Douglas Smith, coauthors of *The Wisdom of Teams: Creating the High-Performance Organization* (1993), offer this advice:

1. **Establish urgency, demanding performance standards, and direction.** All team members need to believe the team has urgent and worthwhile purposes, and they want to know what the expectations are. Teams work best in a compelling context. That is why companies with strong performance ethics usually form teams readily.

2. **Select members for skill and skill potential, not personality.** No team succeeds without all the skills needed to meet its purpose and performance goals. Yet most teams figure out the skills they will need after they are formed. The wise leader will choose people both for their existing skills and their potential to improve existing skills and learn new ones.

3. **Pay particular attention to first meetings and actions.** First impressions always mean a great deal. When potential teams first gather, everyone monitors the signals given by others to confirm, suspend, or dispel assumptions and concerns. They pay particular attention to those in authority: the team leader and any executives who set up, oversee, or otherwise influence the team. As always, what such leaders do is more important than what they say. If a senior executive leaves the team's kickoff to take a phone call ten minutes after the session has begun and never returns, people get the message.

4. **Set some clear rules of behavior.** All effective teams develop rules of conduct at the outset to help them achieve their purpose and performance goals. The most critical initial rules pertain to attendance, discussion (staying open-minded, encouraging diverse points of view), confidentiality, analytical approach, end-product orientation (everyone gets assignments and follows through on them), constructive confrontation, and, often the most important, contributions (everyone is empowered to do real work, something important).

5. **Set and seize upon a few immediate performance-oriented tasks and goals.** Most effective teams trace their advancement to key performance-oriented events. Such events can be set in motion by immediately establishing a few challenging goals that can be reached early on. There is no such thing as a real team without performance results, so the sooner such results occur, the sooner the team congeals.

6. **Challenge the group regularly with fresh facts and information.** A plant quality improvement team knew the cost of poor quality was high, but it wasn't until they researched the different types of defects and put a price

tag on each one that they knew where to go next. Conversely, teams err when they assume that all the information they need exists in the collective experience and knowledge of their members.

7. **Spend lots of time together.** Creative insights as well as personal bonding require impromptu and casual interactions just as much as analyzing spreadsheets and interviewing customers. Busy executives, managers, and team leaders may minimize the time they spend together. Yet, successful teams give themselves the time to learn to be a team. This time need not always be spent together physically; electronic, fax, and phone time can also count as time spent together.

8. **Exploit the power of positive feedback, recognition, and reward.** Positive feedback works as well in a team context as elsewhere. If everyone in the group, for example, is alert to a shy person's initial efforts to speak up and contribute, they can give the honest positive reinforcement that encourages continued contributions. There are many ways to recognize and reward team performance, from having a senior executive speak directly to the team about the urgency of its mission to using awards to recognize contributions. Ultimately, however, the satisfaction shared by a team in its own performance becomes the most cherished reward.

SOURCE: Katzenbach & Smith, 1993.

Small Group Networks

In Chapter 5 we examined the formal and informal communication networks that develop in organizations. All of the early research on *networks,* however, was conducted in laboratories using small groups. Most of the research was aimed at comparing the relative effectiveness of centralized and decentralized networks, especially in terms of decision making. The most frequent network configurations studied were the circle, the wheel, the Y, the chain, and the pinwheel (see Figure 7.3). In general, the early research (for instance, Leavitt, 1951) demonstrated that centralized networks were more efficient than decentralized networks in terms of speed, number of errors, and number of messages sent. Later research, however, (for example, Shaw, 1954) found that with complex tasks, the decentralized network was superior. Since most organizational problems with which groups grapple are relatively complex, decentralized networks should prove comparatively efficient. Moreover, in centralized networks, group members tend to be dissatisfied—those on the periphery feel only marginally involved in the process, while those in the central position suffer from information overload and may feel overly responsible for the group's work (Gilchrist, Shaw, & Walker, 1954). Finally, all other things being equal, those in central positions are most likely to emerge as

FIGURE 7.3

Network Configurations

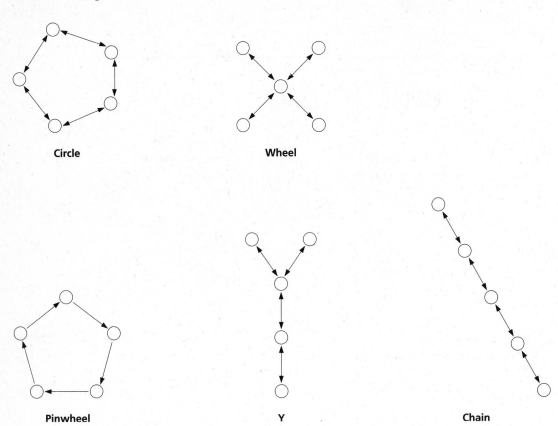

Circle

Wheel

Pinwheel

Y

Chain

leaders, probably because, by virtue of their position, they coordinate activities, distribute information, and control communication flow (Shaw, 1954).

Of course, in actual organizations not all things are equal. One of the problems with this early network research—referred to as the "cage studies" by Rogers and Agarwala-Rogers (1976)—was its artificiality. Assembled in a highly controlled laboratory environment, subjects were usually placed in cubicles with slots connecting the cubicles that could be opened or closed by the researcher to impose different communication patterns on the group. The subjects interacted only through exchanging cards and notes. This artificiality eradicated the influence of such factors as power relationships, the personalities and goals of group members, and nonverbal cues. Yet these and other political and social influences are salient realities of organizational life. More recently, network research (as discussed in Chapter 5) has moved beyond the confines of the small laboratory group to focus on the informal communication patterns that are integral parts of every organization. Moreover, the notion of networks has been broadened immensely in the wake of modern technology.

Using Technology for Collaborative Work

Technology affects the nature of group behavior and communication. Groups use technology to do work, and people in groups often differ in their levels of computer literacy, in their software and hardware knowledge and preferences, and in their awareness of how different technologies can be used to support group work. Hence, a group may be composed of individuals whose attitudes and skills differ with respect to technology.

Adaptive structuration theory (AST) attempts to explain why groups using the same technology may have very different experiences with it. AST (Poole, Siebold, & McPhee, 1985; Poole & DeSanctis, 1990) is a theory of technology adoption that contends that "social" or group technologies gain meaning only as they are used in team interactions. Groups adapt technology features to their needs to achieve certain outcomes. As a result, groups may use technology in a manner, or spirit, that the designers of the technology never intended (Poole & DeSanctis, 1990). What is important about this theory is that the features of the technology are not seen as determining group behavior. Instead, AST assumes that the impact of technologies comes from how people use and adapt to them. It allows for both intended and unintended consequences. Hence, whether a particular technology is empowering to a group or organization depends not only on the characteristics of the technology itself but also on how people actually use it.

This section explores some of the computer-based technologies that are available for group use in the mid-1990s. Computer networks and technologies are important to organizational communication in that they provide new means of access and voice for organizational members, thereby contributing to their empowerment. That is, an array of technologies allows people to communicate across time, place, and organizational boundaries and helps them to make timely and informed decisions. These technologies enable teams who are empowered to manage their own efforts, to share, coordinate, and control their work better.

As we will see, however, technologies differ in how information is captured, presented, and communicated. Technologies vary on a number of dimensions: the type of information that can be carried, the speed of the information transmission, and whether the message sender and recipient need to be available at the same time as the communication occurs. Understanding the trade-offs associated with choosing and using different technologies to communicate is crucial for the ability of group members to use and adapt technologies in a manner that best suits the group's objectives.

The Importance of Computer Networks: A Quick Primer

Any discussion of technologies supporting group work should include at least a brief discussion of **computer networks,** or the highways and superhighways that transmit digitized information—whether it be voice, data, or still or moving images. Networks enable the telecommunication of information, that is, the transfer of information electronically from one location to another. **Telecommunication channels** are the links by which information is transmitted in a network. They use various media, such as telephone lines, fiber optic cables, coaxial cables (the cable used for cable television at home), and microwave and satellite systems.

Networks can support both local and remote communication. The most common kinds of local networks employed in modern organizations are the *private branch exchanges* (*PBX*) and the *local area network* (*LAN*). The PBX connects incoming and outgoing telephone calls. It can store, forward, transfer, hold, and redial telephone calls. Moreover, it can carry both data and voice signals to create local networks, switching digital information among computers and office devices.

While PBXs use telephone lines, LANs use coaxial cables to connect network components. They are commonly used by organizations to link personal computers (PCs) for sharing computer peripherals and files. LANs are preferred over the PBX when high volumes of data and high transmission speeds are required. Hence, a LAN is preferable to a PBX for high-capacity network applications, such as e-mail, video conferencing, and graphics.

Wide area networks (*WANs*) span a wide geographical area, ranging from several miles to entire continents. Provided by carriers who are licensed by the government, WANs may consist of switched and dedicated telephone lines and microwave and satellite communications. WANs are what enable a retailer like J.C. Penney to link its 180,000 employees in 1,800 stores across the United States (Laudon & Laudon, 1993).

Taken together, these technologies represent the fundamental mechanisms for allowing internal and external organizational computer-based communication. They have become especially important now as organizations, especially businesses, seek to lower their costs and remain competitive. Indeed, the justification for meeting electronically rather than in person grows stronger every day. In 1990, for example, the typical U.S. firm spent $2,121 per employee per year for travel, according to Darome Teleconferencing. In contrast, the average video conference, with ten people conferring for fifty minutes, cost only $170 (Kleinschrod, 1991).

Technologies Supporting Group Communication

Groups can use technology to communicate with one another as well as with people outside their group. As mentioned earlier, a variety of technologies help team participants to communicate across space and time. Whenever these electronic media are used, certain communication channels—auditory, visual, nonverbal, and so on—may be precluded.

McGrath and Hollingshead (1993) provided a functional framework for assessing the comparative richness of group support technologies relative to the requirements they impose on groups. This framework takes into consideration the spatial and temporal distribution of group members, as well as the modes of communication available to them. In general, as the restrictiveness of a communication mode increases, the constraints on the amount and richness of information being transmitted also increase. Depending on the circumstances, these constraints may be good or bad for the group.

The technologies available to groups are typically divided into two broad categories. First, *distal, synchronous technologies* allow group members to communicate during the same period of time, whether they are physically together or apart. The term *distal* means that the technology allows communication across distances; *synchronous* means that communication is two-way and simultaneous. In contrast, *distal, asynchronous systems* permit group members to interact from different places (distal) and at different time periods (asynchronous).

McGrath and Hollingshead (1993) highlighted three types of distal, synchronous video systems:

1. Video walls or video windows, which provide continuous, interactive audio-video connections between two fixed locations.
2. Video conferences, which provide audio-video connections between people in two locations, but at a specific time rather than continuously.
3. Videophones, which link one individual with a second with both audio and video channels.

Video conferencing requires complex video conference facilities, technology to integrate images with data and voice transmissions, and appropriate technology and transmission media for relaying the massive volume of data required to transmit images. In 1992, only about ten thousand of America's two million conference rooms were wired for video meetings (Kupfer, 1992). However, recent advances in transmission technology have made video conferencing more affordable and easier to implement (Laudon & Laudon, 1993).

These systems offer the potential to reduce travel and increase group interaction. Apple Computer, for example, invested $6 million in video conferencing hardware, transmission, and staffing over four years. Apple has found video meetings to be cost-effective, saving $28 million in travel costs over the same four years. Hewlett-Packard's view is that while the travel savings are a benefit, the real value is the ability to make urgent decisions quickly and to get the right people involved. Hewlett-Packard leadership believes that video meetings have reduced the development time of some products by as much as 30 percent (Kupfer, 1992). Organizations can also use video conferencing to improve their corporate image and community relations, enhance

Video conferencing employs computers, networks, and television cameras to allow people in different locations to see and talk to each other and to share charts and other
meeting materials. (HMS Images/Image Bank)

management communication, perform market studies, plan worldwide networks, train employees, and coordinate the development and introduction of
new products (Powell, 1989). Ten to 15 percent of Fortune 1,000 companies
now use video conferencing for business meetings (Thuston, 1992).

McGrath and Hollingshead note, however, that this communication
medium does suffer some limitations. For example, while video meetings provide visual and auditory channels for interaction, they cannot yet support
other modes of communication (touch and smell) that are present when individuals meet face-to-face. In addition, audio and visual transmissions are often
not as clear or as rapid as face-to-face encounters. Finally, regulating the timing of who speaks to whom and when can present difficulties.

Michael Crowley, a director of information systems at PPG Industries, has
reported mixed results with video conferencing. He contends that video meetings are most efficient and effective for group work when participants already
know each other *and* are familiar with the material they are meeting to discuss.

Noninteractive (asynchronous) video systems include *videotape* or *video
broadcasts*. As evidenced by the evening news on television, these media can carry

substantial information from the sender to the receiver. Many corporations, such as Johnson & Johnson, IBM, Hewlett-Packard, and General Motors, have created their own internal video production facilities and networks. They use this medium to conduct sales meetings, introduce new products, educate customers, and conduct press conferences. Unfortunately, untimely delays in the sequence of transmission, reception, and feedback of organizational information are potential drawbacks (McGrath & Hollingshead, 1993).

Telephone calls/conferences are distal, synchronous technologies that allow several group members to confer via telephone. Ward (1990) suggested that this technology is fundamentally necessary for firms who want to remain competitive. He argued that teleconferencing uses input technology that is available most places worldwide—the telephone. With a teleconference, as many as sixty locations can be connected to share vital and pertinent information. Because of the simplicity of conducting meetings by telephone, Ward feels that the teleconference is a resource that allows communicators to take the initiative. About 60 percent of businesses now use teleconferencing on a daily basis (Thuston, 1992).

McGrath and Hollingshead (1993) suggested that telephone-based systems, while simple to use, eliminate not only the cues that accompany physical presence but also visual cues, such as nonverbal behavior and written information. Hence, while this technology provides an efficient medium for the exchange of ideas and verbal information, it is dramatically less rich than video conferencing.

Voice messaging systems allow for the creation, storage, and forwarding of voice messages, eliminating telephone tag. Unlike the passive answering machine, voice messaging systems allow users expanded options in message handling. The sender of a voice message can send a message to one or several recipients. The message recipient can delete the message, store it, and/or forward it to other users on the system. One of the strengths of voice messaging is that it allows "the expression of emotion and the interpretation of subtle meanings" (McGrath & Hollingshead, 1993, p. 83). Voice messaging systems are usually not appropriate for conveying extensive, detailed information, especially since the information cannot be visualized in textual or graphical forms.

Interactive (synchronous) *computer conferences* permit group discussions using computers. In a computer conference, individuals use personal computers to type in their ideas and thoughts, which are then broadcast electronically to other members of the group. For example, Caucus, a product of Camber-Roth, can support up to sixteen concurrent users in any given meeting. In this system, each electronic conference is linked to its own database, which can store prior group decisions, technical information, and data. Hiltz, Johnson and Turoff (1991) pointed out that computer conferences are designed to enable dispersed groups to communicate and work together effectively. They noted that these systems can be used either synchronously (with participants dispersed in separate locations) or asynchronously (with participants reading and writing at different times, as well as from different locations).

McGrath and Hollingshead (1993) argued that these systems have all the communication limitations of video and telephone systems, as well as others. Since there is no audio, it is difficult to express and interpret emotion, and almost impossible to detect subtle shades of meaning. Moreover, the production and reception of information is slower, since information is typed, not spoken. On the other hand, since composition and editing using this technology are separated from the transmission of information, the quality of the communication may increase. Also, unlike face-to-face meetings, everyone can talk (compose and send messages) at the same time. Thus, individuals can receive more input from fellow group members. There is, however, a substantial increase in the volume of information generated.

The last category in McGrath and Hollingshead's framework is the asynchronous, noninteractive system, such as e-mail and electronic bulletin boards. *E-mail* is the computer-to-computer exchange of messages via networking. Users with an e-mail account can send a message to one or many users at the same or other locations. These systems route and deliver messages, alert users that messages exist, and hold messages until they are read. Once read, messages can be filed, forwarded, or deleted. E-mail helps minimize team telephone tag and long-distance communication charges.

Electronic bulletin board systems are the electronic counterpart of a wall-mounted bulletin board. Individuals can use the electronic bulletin board to exchange ideas and information on special interest topics through a centralized database. Bulletin boards may be created internally or accessed through external subscription services, such as CompuServe or the Source. CompuServe has over one hundred bulletin board services on topics ranging from gardening to astrology, from PCs to the FBI's "most wanted" list.

McGrath and Hollingshead pointed out that these technologies raise questions concerning the timeliness of information since users are frequently dispersed in either time or space. They suggest that both the "natural order" of communication and the synchronized flow of communication may be disrupted.

To overcome an obvious lack of media richness, some e-mail users have devised unique methods for conveying emotions in electronic messages. "Smiley" dictionaries are lists of odd little punctuation sequences that allow users to embed emotional cues in their e-mail and bulletin board messages. They are called "smileys" because when the reader tilts her or his head to the left, the symbols look like little faces with a colon for eyes and a hyphen for a nose. When a message ends :-(, it means "I'm depressed." :-'| means the sender has a cold, and B-) means the person is "cool." One smiley dictionary [yes . . . there are many :-+] lists 664 distinct smiley variations (Miller, 1992).

Factors Influencing the Effectiveness of Technologies Available to Groups

Ultimately, the success of any group technology depends on two factors: *accessibility* and *use*. These factors in turn are influenced by the management style of those in positions of leadership, as well as by the general culture of the organization. Employees will use a technology to communicate with team members and significant others if the technology is readily accessible and if those with whom they need to communicate routinely use it. When multiple communication channels are available, team members may need to agree on which technologies will be used when and for what purposes. In addition, if the new technologies are to be empowering, team members must have some common understanding of mutual expectations and the "rules" for using such technologies. For instance, if one individual in the group fails to check his or her e-mail messages regularly, he or she may miss meetings, come poorly prepared, or simply end up being left out of many exchanges with fellow group members.

Some users of e-mail and voice mail complain that many individuals who send them messages do not use these technologies appropriately. For instance, they may receive long, detailed instructions in voice mail, which they will later need to reference when completing a task. In addition, other e-mail and voice-mail users claim that these technologies interfere with their productivity since they must (or feel they must) frequently check their electronic mailboxes for messages. Clearly, training in the appropriate use and application of electronic communication technologies is quite important.

Another problem associated with the use of electronic communication channels is the potential for becoming overwhelmed by junk mail. For example, groupware (which takes e-mail a step further by adding personal productivity tools and multiuser data management) forces organizations to cope with an increased flow of information. Giving employees access to networks also tends to increase the volume and speed of communication, some of which is inevitably unwanted. As David Daniels of MetLife argued, "If e-mail is like drinking from a straw, then groupware is like drinking from a firehose. There's definitely a risk of becoming overwhelmed by information that may be irrelevant" (Wreden, 1993, p. 55).

Depending on the circumstances, then, technology can either help or hinder group communication. In a series of experiments conducted at Carnegie Mellon University, Sproull and Kiesler (1991) compared how small groups make decisions through computer conferences, e-mail, and face-to-face discussion. They found that using an electronic medium caused participants to talk more frankly and more equally, and to make more proposals for actions, than they did in traditional meetings. In face-to-face discussions, usually a few people dominated the discussion. However, they also found that the increased democracy associated with electronic interactions interfered with decision making and increased conflict. In particular, decisions made via e-mail or computer conferences were made more slowly, and participants tended to express more extreme opinions and to vent their anger more openly (a phenomenon called "flaming") than when they sat together and talked.

When groups use technology to communicate, they need to be aware that different technologies affect the richness and speed of their communication in diverse ways. While technology can assist groups in overcoming the constraints of space and time, it also demands that groups learn and understand it so that they may faithfully appropriate its structures and realize its intended benefits.

Summarizing Perspective

Collaborative work is often viewed as the centerpiece of contemporary management theory. As we edge toward the end of the twentieth century, technology has assumed an increasingly significant role in group work. As Sproull and Kiesler observed, "Computer-based communication is extremely fast in comparison with telephone or postal services, designated 'snake mail' by electronic mail converts. People can send a message to the other side of the globe in minutes; each message can be directed to one person or many people. Networks . . . make time stand still" (1991, p. 116).

How computer-facilitated interaction will affect such critical group variables as pressure for uniformity and status and power structures is as yet largely unknown. Will individuals be more likely to share power as information and influence channels become more widely available? Will group pressure be diminished, since group members can interact with relative anonymity? What will happen to traditional views of leadership? How will group relationship development be affected, since some groups may make decisions without ever seeing or touching one another? What sorts of technological choices will groups make, and how will those choices influence the quality of their interaction processes, their productivity and creativity? Future research and experience with these technologies will help scholars and practitioners discover answers to these compelling questions.

CASES FOR DISCUSSION

CASE 1 *The Tenure Committee*

The Tenure Committee of the College of Arts and Sciences at Central World University (CWU) is one of the most powerful committees on campus. Composed of five tenured faculty and chaired by the dean of the college, Dean Mortonsen, the committee meets several times each year to decide on the fate of every faculty member who is under consideration for tenure. At CWU this is a critical moment in the life of the faculty member, since each may be considered for tenure only once. Faculty members who are granted tenure may stay at the university for the rest of their working lives, enjoying all of the security and stability that a successful academic life offers. If, however, the College Tenure Committee votes against a faculty member, he or she must leave the university at the end of the next year. Although appeals are possible and other committees exist to review the committee's procedures, it is widely known that in 98 percent of the cases, the tenure decisions made by the College Tenure Committee are binding.

The members of the CWU College Tenure Committee include the following individuals:

Professor Lewis Kingsly, distinguished professor of art history. As a Distinguished Professor, he has attained the highest possible rank for a faculty member. In his late fifties, Kingsly has an international reputation as a scholar and is known to have extremely high critical standards for judging tenure cases. This is his third year on the committee.

Professor Marlene Peterson, professor of English. Having served on the tenure committee for five years, she is the committee member with the most experience. A highly regarded poet in her early forties, she is known as a humane and caring teacher, as well as a gifted writer. One of her two sons is a junior honors student at CWU.

Professor Adolph Rudman, professor of chemistry. In his late thirties, Rudman has received more grants than any other faculty member in the Chemistry Department. Graduate students compete to work in his lab. He does little undergraduate teaching but has written over two hundred articles, many collaboratively with graduate students. Rudman's wife is also on the faculty. She is an assistant professor in the French Department, where she provides teacher training for new graduate students and is deeply involved with teaching un-dergraduates. She will be eligible for tenure in three years. Rudman is new to the committee.

Professor Eliot Sanderson, associate professor of psychology. Sanderson has not yet been promoted to full professor, but that is only because of his relative youth (early thirties). His academic credentials are impeccable. His scholarly expertise is in cognitive psychology; he has published groundbreaking research on artificial intelligence. He is also a popular teacher of the basic psychology course required of most undergraduates. This is Sanderson's second year on the committee.

Professor Cynthia Black, professor of anthropology. Black is a renowned anthropologist who has worked extensively with primitive societies and has published her findings in three award-winning books. She works mostly with doctoral students, who assist her with her field research. This is her third and final year on the committee, since her research and traveling make committee service difficult.

Dean George Mortonsen, dean of the college and professor of mathematics. The dean chairs the committee and has done so throughout his seven years as dean. Although he has worked in administrative posts for most of his years at the university, at the age of fifty-five Mortonsen remains proud of his Ivy League background and views himself as an intellectual leader. He takes the College Tenure Committee's work very seriously. After all, chairing this committee gives him the chance to carefully monitor (and hold high) the college's evaluation standards.

This year the committee is confronted with a particularly difficult situation. The president of the university, Earl Thomas, is a close friend of the dean. The president has made it clear on numerous occasions that he would like to see CWU become one of the top twenty research institutions in the country by the end of the decade. He believes (and the dean concurs) that only those faculty members whose research is truly outstanding should be tenured. At the same time, however, CWU is a large public institution, and as such is funded by the state legislature. In recent years, the state has become increasingly concerned over reports that the university is not taking its teaching mission very seriously. Reportedly, students are more likely to be taught by graduate students, many of whom have no teacher training or supervision, than by faculty members. When undergraduates are taught by faculty members, the classes are typically quite large (250 to 450 students). In this budget year, the state legislature has asked to see evidence that the university has renewed its commitment to teaching, especially teaching undergraduates. Finally, members of the Faculty Senate have passed (by a narrow margin) a resolution that tenure committees must consider excellence in teaching as grounds for granting tenure (as long as the applicant is also reasonably strong in research). This resolution stands in marked contrast to the dean's policy as leader of the College Tenure Committee during the past seven years, namely, requiring excellence in research and regarding teaching excellence, while laudable, as insufficient grounds for tenure. Those who served on the College Tenure Committee in the past strongly endorsed the dean's and the president's views of tenure criteria. The faculty in general are divided on this issue, as suggested by the debate and subsequent close vote in the Faculty Senate. The Senate's votes are formal recommendations to the administration but are not legally binding.

One of this year's candidates for tenure, Professor Sam Joseph, assistant professor of geography, possesses credentials that are likely to force the College Tenure Committee to confront the complex issue of tenure criteria. He comes to the committee with the strong support of his own department. Professor Joseph has served as director of undergraduate studies, and in that capacity, he has worked closely with other faculty members to develop a new (and much improved) academic advising system for undergraduate geography majors. He has received outstanding student evaluations across diverse courses. Joseph is as popular with freshmen when he teaches his huge lecture course on human geography as he is with graduate students. He has served on a large number of thesis and dissertation committees. A skilled statistician and methodologist, Professor Joseph devotes countless hours to assisting students with their research design, statistics, and other methodological problems. Joseph has also undertaken exceptional community service; he has developed geography modules for use by elementary and secondary teachers across the state. He has, moreover, worked closely with teachers to help them improve their ability to integrate geography into their social science program. In addition, he has coauthored a college-level geography textbook that has been widely adopted by colleges and universities across the United States. (It should be noted that a textbook is considered evidence of a teaching rather than a research contribution.) Thus, there is considerable evidence to substantiate Joseph's teaching excellence. In research, however, he has published one or two articles during each of the six years he has taught at CWU—a total of about ten publications. By past standards, this number of articles would be considered about average—normally considered adequate but not outstanding research. About half of his publications appear in really good geography journals; the others articles were published in less competitive journals.

Questions for Discussion

1. In what ways might the organizational and political environment of this particular small group influence its decision-making processes?

2. What socioemotional variables are likely to influence this group? In what ways?

3. How do you think the dean will approach his leadership role?

4. How do you think each member of the committee will vote? Why?

5. If you could advise the group on how to approach its task, what advice would you give? That is, how might the College Tenure Committee function as an effective group?

6. In your view, should Professor Joseph be given tenure? Why or why not?

CASE 2 *Reynolds and Reynolds Co.*

Like many companies, Reynolds and Reynolds Co. in Moraine, Ohio, was looking for ways to improve productivity without increasing costs. Its discovery? That the best results come from asking workers who actually do the jobs how those jobs can be done more efficiently.

One key Reynolds and Reynolds plant repairs computer and peripheral components, such as printers and monitors, that go into the company's automotive-dealer information system. While this plant is relatively small, employing only forty-five people, it plays a large role in the company's success. Specifically, repairing its own components costs Reynolds and Reynolds $35 per unit, while sending the parts outside for repairs costs $185 per unit. Thus, the Moraine plant saves the company nearly $8 million every year.

The company's approach to improving performance was to structure an employee-run problem-solving team that funneled ideas to management, to provide cross-training to most employees, and to put in place a series of small employee-suggested changes that ultimately resulted in large gains in efficiency.

An initial investigation of barriers to effective performance revealed conflict between the repair functions of the plant, which worked on a quota system, and the distribution function, which tried to be responsive to the needs of customers (people at other company locations). Since each function blamed the other for any problems, a five-person task force composed of people from both areas and one from internal engineering was formed and named ACT (Accomplishing Communications Team). This group then conducted a two-and-a-half hour plantwide meeting with all employees, with no supervisors or managers present. While some employees expressed skepticism during the meeting about management's true intentions for launching this effort, all eventually agreed to give the new system a try.

Over the next several months, the ACT members passed on to management a number of employee ideas, including proposed revisions in the weekly work schedules (which would be drawn up by employees themselves), a plan for cross-training repair technicians, and an improved method for labeling repair parts. All these measures, and many others, were implemented, resulting in significant savings to the company.

Ultimately, the approach increased productivity by nearly 40 percent, reduced the time parts wait for repairs from fourteen days to one day, and eliminated the need to recheck returned parts.

Questions for Discussion

1. What aspects of the group process probably helped the Reynolds and Reynolds performance improvement effort to succeed?

What factors probably impeded the effort's success?

2. What were the dangers of undertaking the effort described in this case, that is, what might have gone wrong?

3. Are there situations in which this sort of process probably should not be attempted? As a manager, what things would you consider when deciding whether or not to institute a process similar to that used by Reynolds and Reynolds?

SOURCE: Based on Narisetti, 1992.

Conflict and Organizational Communication

Good leadership frequently brings conflict to the fore—not for a fight, but to examine alternatives. Sometimes, you have to see how ideas, information, and values clash in order to make reasoned decisions.
Gay Lumsden and Donald Lumsden, *Communicating in Groups and Teams: Sharing Leadership*, 1993.

C onflict is an inevitable part of organizational life, as is the need to confront and manage it. Conflict arises as organizations change, and as individuals strive to cope with their mutual interdependency in a changing organizational environment. During the past several decades, theorists' views of conflict have changed dramatically. Classical organization theorists virtually ignored conflict, apparently convinced that rational managers would control their subordinates. If workers did create conflict, the manager's task was to eliminate it quickly and decisively, acting as a sort of firefighter, so as to redirect everyone's efforts toward the presumably shared goal of organizational productivity. In contrast, human relations theorists saw conflict as a threat to smooth interpersonal relations. In their view the presence of conflict suggested a breakdown in the organizational system of harmony and social support. From this perspective, then, the manager's job was to help everyone avoid conflict, a task that often meant simply "sweeping it under the rug," only to have it reappear later (often in an enlarged and more menacing form).

In recent years conflict has been viewed more realistically, and often more positively (Janis, 1982; Goldhaber, 1993). Contemporary scholars describe conflict as both inevitable and necessary. Some organizational leaders speak with conviction about the importance of dealing decisively with conflicts. For instance, Andrew Grove, president of INTEL, has argued:

> Many managers seem to think it is impossible to tackle anything or anyone head-on, even in business. By contrast, we . . . believe that it is the essence of corporate health to bring a problem out into the open as soon as possible, even if this entails a confrontation. Dealing with conflicts lies at the heart of managing any business. As a result,

confrontation—facing issues about which there is disagreement—can be avoided only at the manager's peril. Workplace politicking grows quietly in the dark, like mushrooms; neither can stand the light of day (1984, p. 74).

In spite of such compelling statements, our society remains highly ambivalent about the value of conflict. Maslow (1965) once noted that, on an intellectual level, managers appreciate the value of conflict and competition. Their actions, however, frequently demonstrate a personal preference for avoiding conflict whenever possible.

A classic study of decision making (Boulding, 1964) demonstrated the tension between intellectually accepting the notion that conflict can be useful and constructive and emotionally rejecting action based on this belief. In this study several groups of managers were assembled to solve a complex problem. They were told their performance would be judged by a panel of experts in terms of the quantity and quality of the solutions generated. The groups were identical in composition and size, except that half of them included a confederate who had been instructed by the researcher before the experiment to play the devil's advocate. The confederate's role was to challenge fellow group members' opinions and recommendations, forcing them to examine critically their assumptions and the logic of their arguments. At the end of the problem-solving period, the recommendations of both sets of groups were compared. Those groups with the devil's advocate had performed significantly better on the task. They had generated more alternatives, and their recommendations were judged superior. After a short break, the groups were reassembled and told that they would be performing a similar task during the next session. Before they began the discussion, however, they were given the opportunity to eliminate one member. In *every* group containing a confederate, he or she was the one asked to leave. As Whetten and Cameron (1991) pointed out, "The fact that every high-performance group expelled their unique competitive advantage because that member [apparently] made others feel uncomfortable demonstrates a widely shared reaction to conflict" (p. 396).

The fact that some conflicts are dysfunctional is indisputable. In general, sustained, unmanaged, or uncontrolled conflicts can lead to disastrous outcomes. However, conflict can be constructive and can serve several useful functions. For instance, through conflict, issues that would otherwise fester can be brought to the surface for resolution. Conflict can also function to relieve tension before it builds up and leads to volatile and destructive self-expression. As we noted in Chapter 7, many theorists believe that conflict is a necessary component of effective decision making. Without conflict, ideas and assumptions often go unchallenged (Hirokawa & Scheerhorn, 1986; Janis, 1982), leading to poor decisions. Similarly, conflict can bring forth creativity. As individuals interact to settle their differences, communication channels may open. Those who normally contribute little might be drawn out of their shells, engaged by the exciting, provocative exchange of ideas. Finally, conflict can facilitate problem solving. Since in many situations conflict proves stressful and intense, those involved are motivated to seek solutions that will reduce or lessen the tensions. Thus, conflict has the potential for serving a variety of fruitful functions.

The realization of constructive outcomes depends upon the quality of the ethical standards that guide the behavior of all those participating in the conflict resolution process. Kreps and Thornton (1984) called for several ethical conflict behaviors, including arguing with the specific issue at hand (and avoiding hidden agendas); refuting a person's position without resorting to character attacks; relying on substantive, logical arguments rather than overly emotional appeals; keeping an open mind; and replacing a win-lose attitude with a mutual-win orientation. Although somewhat lofty, these ethical guidelines can serve as the foundation for effective conflict processes and outcomes.

In this chapter we begin by describing several different types of conflict often encountered in organizational settings. Then we discuss some common sources of organizational conflict and explore the notion of conflict episodes, acknowledging the fact that conflicts go through stages and develop over time. Next we turn to an examination of conflict management styles; after describing them, we explore some of the situational factors that might favor one style over another. We also acknowledge that not all conflicts are resolved by individuals working directly with one another, and so we include a section on third-party methods of negotiation. After presenting a collaborative model of conflict management, we conclude the chapter by describing the ways in which technology might be used as a conflict management tool.

Conflict: Definition and Types

Conflict can be defined as "the interaction of interdependent people who perceive opposition of goals, aims, and values, and who see the other party as potentially interfering with the realization of these goals" (Putnam & Poole, 1987, p. 552). This definition emphasizes three basic characteristics of conflict: interaction, interdependence, and incompatible goals. Through social interaction, conflicts are formed and sustained (Folger & Poole, 1984). As individuals interact over time in groups and organizations, conflicts are shaped by their actions and reactions. Those involved in conflict situations are interdependent in that they cannot reach their goals alone—thus, each has the power to interfere with the other's goal accomplishment. Conflicts often grow from disagreements over the acquisition and use of resources and usually reflect perceived underlying differences in values and goals. Thus, an individual's perceptions, whether or not they are accurate, begin to shape the conflict.

Institutionalized Versus Emergent Conflicts

In organizational settings conflicts can be broadly classified as either institutionalized or emergent. **Institutionalized conflicts** grow from the nature of the particular organization and its purposes and goals. In most corporations conflict arises over the tension between profit and other aims, such as social responsibility or employee rights (see Chapter 10). Making a fuel-efficient automobile that meets the government's anti-pollution standards is clearly the legal and socially responsible action for a car manufacturer to take, but it may not be the most profitable. Similarly, major research universities confront the inevitable tension between the dual missions of teaching and research. The other major form of conflict is **emergent conflict,** arising from the formal and informal interactions of individuals on a day-to-day basis. Conflicts may emerge whenever people compete with one another for organizational resources or when individuals who do not particularly like one another have to work together on common ventures. Both kinds of conflict are challenging, since institutionalized conflicts are maddeningly predictable and tenacious, whereas emergent conflicts are potentially abundant and less predictable. Both can occur at several levels and/or in different settings: intrapersonal, interpersonal, intergroup, and interorganizational.

Intrapersonal Conflict.   **Intrapersonal conflict** occurs within individuals in organizations and commonly takes two forms, frustration and goal conflict. The simpler of the two, *frustration,* occurs whenever an individual's ability to attain a goal is hampered by the imposition of some barrier. For instance, Julie may have a desire to excel, but because of some barrier or limitation (such as inadequate education, limited talent, or a supervisor who doesn't like her), her performance evaluations remain average. Early responses to frustration are often constructive (for example, Julie may extend her education or request a transfer to another department). If these measures fail, however, prolonged frustration may result in less productive behaviors, such as withdrawal or aggression (Patton & Giffin, 1988).

The other type of intrapersonal conflict, *goal conflict,* is more complex. Here the attainment of one goal excludes the possibility of attaining another. Three principal types of goal conflict have been identified:

1. **Approach-approach.** The individual is caught up in trying to choose between two attractive, but mutually exclusive, goals. The MBA student with excellent job offers from Procter and Gamble and Xerox confronts this kind of goal conflict.

2. **Avoidance-avoidance.** The individual must choose between two mutually exclusive options, both of which are unattractive. The college graduate who receives job offers from companies located in Butte, Montana, and College Station, Texas, two of his least preferred locations, encounters conflict of this sort.

3. **Approach-avoidance.** An individual has both positive and negative feelings about trying to attain a goal because the goal possesses both attractive and unattractive characteristics. A successful manager who is also a devoted husband and father may be offered a tantalizing promotion that involves a huge pay and status increase. To accept the job, however, he must travel

about fifteen days each month, leaving his wife alone to care for their three young children. Thus, the job itself is attractive, but the personal sacrifice is not.

Each of these intrapersonal role conflicts requires the individual to make choices, some clearly more painful than others. Those confronted with avoidance-avoidance conflicts, for instance, may avoid choosing by rejecting both alternatives and continuing to seek new options. In either of the other role conflict situations, the individual will likely make a choice and then rationalize the decision by exaggerating the attractiveness of the chosen option while minimizing its potentially negative features.

Interpersonal Conflict. A second level at which conflict can occur is the *interpersonal* level. **Interpersonal conflict** typically occurs *between individuals* or between an individual and a group. Examples of the former are infinite: two managers competing for the same promotion, two coworkers who are interested in dating the same man, two athletes competing for the same trophy, two faculty members competing for the same research dollars, two teachers vying for the larger office, and so forth. In each instance, the competitors are striving for the possession of some finite resource available to only one of them. When organizational leaders become aware of interpersonal conflicts, they may strive to expand resources or divide or rotate them in some way (so that whoever gets some special resource this year will not get it next year). However, some resources cannot be divided (the desired date or the large office), and many interpersonal conflicts are outside the leader's realm of control.

The other main type of interpersonal conflict is *conflict within groups*. Many factors contribute to internal group conflict. Perceived changes, ranging from procedural change to changes in appointed leadership to changes in group composition, can provoke conflict. Sometimes conflict within groups can lead to negative group and individual outcomes, especially if one individual is in conflict with the rest of the group. As we pointed out in the preceding chapter, group pressure for uniformity is a reality of group work within organizations, especially in highly cohesive groups. Although in some circumstances those who depart from group norms may create constructive conflict and cause the group to think carefully and thoroughly, on other occasions sustained conflict between the individual and the group will lead to painful consequences, especially for the individual.

Conflict situations within groups are commonly classified as either *distributive* or *integrative*. A distributive situation is one in which a person can win only at someone else's expense, such as in a poker game. In an integrative situation, however, group members can integrate their resources toward a common task or goal, such as developing a joint grant proposal. The distributive approach creates many problems, including the development of a "we-they" orientation; inflated self-evaluations, accompanied by a diminished regard for the contributions of others; and perceptual distortions that falsify the sense of having responded adequately to each other's concerns (Blake & Mouton,

1961). Unfortunately, those who participate in labor-management negotiations characteristically use a distributive approach in their intergroup interactions. In contrast, integrative conflict can reap many group benefits, for example, genuine exploration of individual differences in opinions and values and identification of common ground where mutual goals can be achieved.

Intergroup Conflict.   The third level of conflict occurs between and among groups. **Intergroup conflict** has been associated with both positive and negative outcomes, including increased intragroup cohesiveness and solidarity; an exaggerated sense of the achievements of one's own group, coupled with an underestimation of other groups' efforts; hostility between groups; and generally negative and stereotyped attitudes toward other groups and their members. Many of the ways in which groups interact with and think about other groups are related to the development of a group ideology. The term *ideology* refers to the beliefs a group holds about the "structure of action" in the organizational system and about itself and other groups (Putnam & Poole, 1987). An ideology organizes a group's relationship with other groups, influences whether conflicts develop or not, and helps determine why groups choose the enemies they do.

The larger organization serves as the primary contextual determinant of intergroup conflict. As complexity (defined as the number of different units or specialties in the organization) increases, communication networks tend to fragment and lead to different perspectives within units. If this condition is combined with high interdependence, conflict between units increases (Lawrence & Lorsch, 1967; Putnam & Wilson, 1982; Thomas, 1976; Zald, 1962). Status differences among units also influence conflict. In general, the greater the status differences, the more interunit conflict (Dalton, 1959; Walton & Dutton, 1969). In an effort to gain control over their destinies, organizational units increase their concern for equity in the distribution of resources and rewards (Zald, 1981). Comparing rewards such as wages and hours can become a symbolic root of conflict among workers in different units (Whyte, 1955).

Depending upon how groups perceive the conflict situation, their conflict interactions will take different forms. In particular, those who see their relationship as competitive or distributive tend to withhold information, exhibit commitment to their position, and use threats in their intergroup interactions (Walton, Dutton, & Cafferty, 1969; Walton, Dutton, & Fitch, 1966). Those patterns often become rigid and formalized, fostering negative attitudes, suspicion, and disassociation between groups. Distributive patterns often lead to deterioration in relationships because of the emphasis on intergroup competition. Group members may go out of their way to proclaim their undying loyalty to the group. They may exaggerate the differences between themselves and members of other groups (while denying anything they might have in common with the others); and group members may make charges of disloyalty if any group member sees validity in the other group's position on key issues (Blake, Shepherd, & Mouton, 1964). In contrast, groups who perceive their relationship as cooperative or integrative employ problem solving, informality, openness, and flexibility in intergroup communication. These patterns clearly facilitate more positive and trusting intergroup attitudes than do distributive patterns (Putnam & Poole, 1987).

Although several types of intergroup conflict exist, two are especially common. **Functional conflicts** occur when organizational functions are divided into departments that often have entirely different perspectives on organizational processes. For instance, manufacturing divisions tend to have short-term perspectives and seek to maximize their own goals of long production runs and standardized products to meet unit cost goals. Marketing divisions, on the other hand, tend to have long-term perspectives and to evaluate products and services from the perspective of the consumer. Conflicts between these groups are common. *Line and staff conflicts* represent another common type of intergroup conflict. Staff groups are responsible for measuring, monitoring, analyzing, and projecting the work and results of the organization, while line groups are concerned only with the actual execution of the work. Line members often perceive staff as impractical, overeducated, inexperienced, or abstract, whereas staff may view line members as dull, narrow, inflexible, or unimaginative. Perceptual incongruities such as these are virtually guaranteed to produce conflict between these groups.

Interorganizational Conflict. Many of the same dynamics that operate in intergroup conflict also have an impact on the last conflict level, **interorganizational conflict**. However, the institutional environment in interorganizational conflict assumes a significant role since it is the arena in which conflict is played out (Van de Ven, Emmett, & Koenig, 1980). For instance, major automobile manufacturers regularly come into contact with a number of other organizations. General Motors (GM) may purchase automotive parts from Borg-Warner. Although those two corporations act cooperatively to build automobiles, they are also in a state of conflict: Borg-Warner wants to get the highest possible prices from GM for the parts it supplies, while GM seeks to pay the lowest prices possible. Similarly, advertising agencies handling the GM account want to charge the highest prices possible, whereas GM wants to keep its advertising budget as low as possible. The United Auto Workers (UAW) union wants as many of its members as possible employed by GM (since those individuals must pay union dues). Once union employees are hired by GM, the UAW will be eager to see them paid top wages, a goal that clearly conflicts with GM's need to keep its labor costs down. The federal government also imposes regulations concerning safety and pollution that are supposed to reflect the public interest. Since many of these regulations require considerable expense, they interfere with GM's desire to keep manufacturing costs down. Finally, consumers want a quality car at a low price, whereas GM wants to turn a profit. These examples are representative of the tensions between most organizations that either compete with or rely on each other in some important way. In each case, the organizations operate in a state of partial conflict and partial cooperation.

In most of these situations, conflict between organizations occurs primarily in the marketplace where organizations attempt to carve out and maintain "niches" or domains. As organizations compete for scarce resources, they must coordinate and control an uncertain environment. Thus, the processes and structures that organize market transactions influence the creation and monitoring of interorganizational conflict (Chatov, 1981). The management of interorganizational conflict usually focuses on regulating networks. Conflict management may also involve building integrative and cooperative networks between organizations and successfully moving through problem-solving, direction-setting, and structuring phases of interorganizational coordination (Gray, 1985).

Sources of Conflict

Implicit in our discussion of different conflict types is the notion that organizational conflict can be traced to diverse sources. Figure 8.1 highlights critical sources of organizational conflict. In almost every organization, for instance, *competition for rewards* is a potential source of conflict. Resources and rewards are always limited. Individuals compete for promotions, raises, grants, com-

FIGURE 8.1

Sources of Organizational Conflict

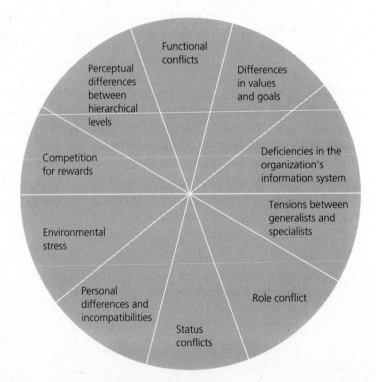

puter support, and status symbols; departments compete for budget alloca-
tions; and organizations compete for a larger share of the market. What one
competitor wins, another loses, so that if the amount won and the amount lost
are summed, they add to zero. This kind of "win-lose" or "zero-sum" competition is a clear illustration of distributive conflict. As competitive levels increase, conflict tends to escalate, and the motive for cooperation declines.

Another potential conflict source can be traced to *perceptual differences
between employees at different levels of the hierarchy.* Although organizations are
becoming flatter, most organizations are still composed of several hierarchical
layers. Research suggests that as workers move from one hierarchical level
to the next, their perceptions tend to change. Over thirty years ago, Likert
(1961) discovered that top staff, foremen, and line workers all felt that they
understood other people's problems but were themselves misunderstood. In
fact, none of them shared congruent perceptions of the others' problems and
priorities. In traditional, centralized organizations, where many organizational
levels prevail, those at the top and those at the bottom are especially likely to
misperceive one another's needs, aspirations, and problems.

Many organizational divisions have overlapping functions. Thus, *functional conflicts* can arise between departments, units, or individuals whose tasks
are interdependent but whose roles are incompatible. Sometimes the conflict
is over turf; on other occasions it is over values. Often the two are interrelated.
For instance, at most colleges and universities, promotion decisions are made
by three different units: the department (e.g., English), the school (for example,
College of Arts and Sciences), and the universitywide chancellor's committee.
Each unit has a promotions committee that votes on the faculty member's case,
beginning with the department and progressing to the college committee, and
then to the universitywide committee. Often, each of these committees feels
that it is the one best, and perhaps uniquely, equipped to make a binding, judicious promotion decision. Each may resent or challenge the authority of the
other committees. These functional conflicts are especially severe if the committees' values are incongruent. The department, for example, might seek to
promote based on solid performance in teaching and research, but the other
committees might hold out for research excellence as the sole criterion (as in
the case example at the end of Chapter 7).

As illustrated in the preceding example, individuals in any unit at any organizational level may come into conflict over *differences in values and goals.*
Production and sales units often conflict in this way, since sales is geared toward rapid production for high-volume business and speedy delivery, while
production prefers a slower pace that emphasizes quality. When the two values
of speed and quality clash (as they often do when the sales division puts in a
rush order or when production slows down), conflict is the likely result. Whenever groups or individuals within organizations possess different values, the
resulting conflicts can be quite difficult to resolve.

Less serious than conflicts over values are conflicts that grow from *deficiencies in the organization's information system.* An important message
may not be received, a supervisor's instructions may be misinterpreted, or

decision makers may arrive at different conclusions because they used different databases. Conflicts based on missing or incomplete information tend to be straightforward, in that clarifying previous messages or obtaining additional information generally resolves the dispute. Since value systems are not being challenged, these conflicts tend to be easily addressed by dealing directly with the information deficiency.

Another source of conflict stems from *tensions between generalists and specialists.* As jobs have become increasingly complex and science has made technology more intricate, specialists are needed more and more to perform those jobs and run those technological innovations. At the same time, however, management functions typically require generalists to perform them. In most traditional organizations, a relatively small number of generalists govern a much larger number of specialists, creating a host of potential conflicts. Because the generalist manager often knows considerably less about the job than the specialist worker does, that worker may find it frustrating or unproductive to communicate with his or her boss. Thus, the worker may choose to "short-circuit" the organization's formal communication lines, a practice frowned on by most supervisors. Moreover, conflicting loyalties may emerge. Among highly trained professionals, loyalty to a discipline or specialization may supersede loyalty to the organization, as when an engineer sees herself as an engineer first and an employee of Ford second. With further advances in technology and the increasing prominence of self-managed teams, conflicts between specialists and generalists may become less frequent (perhaps to be replaced by conflicts between specialists and other specialists).

One of the most pervasive sources of conflict in organizations is **role conflict**. If an individual's perception and enactment of a role differs significantly from the expectations of others, conflict is likely to develop over this discrepancy. One way this conflict may manifest itself is in *intrarole conflict,* in which an individual occupying a single role is subjected to stress. Those who surround the person may hold divergent expectations of how the role should be played. For instance, organizational forepersons are often subjected to contradictory expectations when management expects them to represent management interests during labor-management negotiations and labor expects them to act as representatives of labor. Sometimes individuals are placed in the position of having to make a choice between two or more competing roles that demand simultaneous performance. *Interrole conflict* is so common that virtually no one escapes it. Nearly every employee is also a spouse, a friend, a parent, and a member of the greater community. Conflict occurs when successful job performance requires a parent to miss a child's band concert, a son to leave an ailing parent in the hospital in a distant city, or a religious individual to miss attending services. Finally, *interpersonal role conflict* occurs when two or more individuals seek the same role or position, or when roles overlap so that two or more people are called upon to do the same things in different ways at the same time. Parents with two distinctly different approaches to disciplining a child are an example of the latter sort of interpersonal role conflict. Moreover, even though the organization designs a system to clarify and manage role assignments, conflict of this sort still may not be eliminated. A new department head once selected a particularly talented, but unpopular, person to assume a highly coveted position. Even though the manager justified his choice by explaining the system and criteria he used, fellow workers remained quietly irate. Whenever they had the opportunity, they proceeded to undermine their fellow worker's authority, leading to his ultimate removal from the job.

Since organizational roles are so significant, the ranking of those roles according to their importance or value can lead to **status conflicts**. Organizational members usually seek increases in status, accompanied by larger salaries, bigger officers, and more prestigious titles. Whatever symbolizes status, however, can also lead to conflict. Over the past few decades, Americans grew accustomed to entering an organization, working hard, and achieving promotions over time. Today, however, as people enter organizations with enhanced knowledge and specialization, they may move up quickly, jumping over those with seniority. Conflict can result when young, relatively inexperienced (although highly educated) employees are asked to supervise older, more experienced workers. Moreover, any individual in any kind of organization may develop an expectation for normal career development and achievement. If employees realize they will never attain the status they desire, they may become disillusioned, bitter, and hostile toward those who appear more successful.

Personal differences and incompatibilities are another common source of organizational conflict. Individuals may simply not like one another. Individual differences in background, education, socialization, age, and expectations can produce different needs, perceptions, and goals. As noted above, if those differences stem from different attitudes and values, the resulting conflicts can be severe. In communication involving individuals who are personally incompatible, discussions can become highly emotional and take on moral overtones.

Several of these conflict sources operate interdependently. For instance, personal differences members bring to an organization generally remain dormant until they are triggered by an organizational catalyst, such as interdependent task responsibilities. In addition, individuals may perceive that their organizational roles are incompatible because they are operating from different bases of information. They communicate with different sets of people, are tied into different reporting systems, and receive instructions from different supervisors.

Finally, from a systems perspective, a major source of conflict is **environmental stress**. Other conflict sources can only become more salient in a stressful environment. For instance, over the past few years, many large organizations have been "downsizing." A recent article in *Time* reports that "more than six million pink slips have been handed out since 1987, and layoffs are occurring at an even faster pace [now]. Despite signs of a brisker economy, at least 87 large firms announced major job cuts in the first two months of 1993 alone" (Baumohl, 1993, p. 55). When workers feel their jobs are threatened, and especially if there is much uncertainty about the rules by which the organization is operating, they will likely respond with frustration, hostility, and increased competitiveness. Focus On explores some of the frustration and confusion white males are feeling in an ever-increasing multicultural work environment, where the rules of promotion and advancement that once favored them are changing.

FOCUS ON

Increasing Diversity Can Be a Source of Conflict

For the most part, corporate boardrooms in major U.S. organizations remain a white man's world. But, in an increasing number of companies—especially those aggressively pushing diversity programs—some white males are arriving at a different conclusion. They are feeling frustrated, resentful, and most of all, afraid. There's a sense that, be it on the job or at home, the rules are changing faster than they can keep up with them. Thomas Kochman, a professor at the University of Illinois–Chicago who consults with companies on diversity issues, points out that "race and gender have become factors for white men, much the way they have been for other groups."

Although in some organizations diversity training is just window-dressing, in others it is taken very seriously, even though there is potential for conflict. At companies like AT&T, DuPont, and Motorola, the emotional landscape for white males is changing. White men must compete against people they may not have taken seriously as rivals—mainly women, Blacks, Hispanics, and Asians. White males sometimes say that diversity programs make them feel threatened or attacked. One vice-president noted that in the diversity group he was in, "there were some understandable reprisals against white males and, implicitly, the company." The reprisals "discounted all the good things white males have done."

Even in companies where diversity programs are new or haven't made much impact, white males are feeling pressure. Often for the first time in their lives, they're worried about their future because of widespread layoffs and corporate restructuring. Moreover, they know that with a more diverse population entering the work force, they are slowly becoming a minority. Through the year 2005, the U.S. Department of Labor estimates that half of all labor force entrants will be women, and more than one-third will be Hispanics, African-Americans, and members of other races.

In response to the realities of these shifting demographics, companies like AT&T have initiated serious diversity training efforts. For instance, AT&T sends employees through a course called "White Males: The Label and the Dilemma." The course profiles the future work force, then asks white males how they feel about being labeled a minority. The women and minorities in the class react to these men's views or challenge their conclusions. The one-day workshop is intense. One white male, a systems engineer said, "I didn't realize how much other white men felt attacked and how oblivious they were to the benefits that their race and gender bestowed." Minorities left the seminar with insights into white males. A black software designer pointed out that the seminar made him "more empathetic" to white males because it showed how deeply felt their concerns are. He learned that white men don't like being lumped together or blamed for "something their fathers and grandfathers might have done."

Tension and potential conflict over diversity, of course, are not resolved so easily. In fact, at AT&T, not all employees view the company's attention to white males favorably. Last year, at a conference that focused in part on the dilemma of white males in an increasingly diverse work place, some women and minorities complained. They wanted to know why an affirmative action workshop should devote *any* time at all to white men. One minority employee was so incensed that the worker didn't attend the workshop.

Clearly, organizational leaders will increasingly need to reflect on the best ways to approach the changing demographics of the work force and the potential conflicts that may arise from growing diversity.

SOURCE: Based on Galen, 1994.

Conflict Episodes

Regardless of the source or type, conflicts do not suddenly erupt full-blown. Rather, they develop over time as individuals and groups interact and as situational variables change (for instance, new leaders emerge, different tasks are assigned, or new rules are imposed). The complex interactions that surround the conflict process may be viewed as **conflict episodes**. Theorist Louis Pondy (1967) described these episodes as interactive conflict stages or phases: (1) latent conflict, (2) perceived conflict, (3) felt conflict, (4) manifest conflict, and (5) the conflict's aftermath. Pondy's model is depicted in Figure 8.2.

The first phase, **latent conflict,** occurs whenever the situation is ripe for conflict but those involved do not yet realize it. Whenever interdependent individuals interact on some joint task or venture, potential grounds for conflict exist. These are often mixed-motive situations in that people are motivated to cooperate for the sake of a shared goal but may also be competing for recognition or other rewards. Only under circumstances in which organizational members do not interact and share no common tasks are latent conflicts nonexistent.

In Pondy's model, the second conflict episode is **perceived conflict**. The notion of perception is extremely important in that latent conflicts may never progress until those who interact perceive not only that they are interdependent but also that their interests or values are incompatible. Their perception may or may not be accurate. It may grow from mutual awareness of a competitive feeling, or from someone outside the situation pointing out the grounds

FIGURE 8.2

**Pondy's Model
of Interactive
Conflict
Episodes**

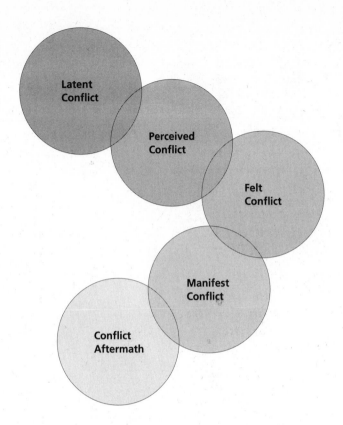

for conflict. A coworker may comment, "Why are you always helping him with his programming problems? Don't you realize you two are competing for the same promotion?" At this stage, no confrontation has occurred; there is only an awareness of frustrating differences or incompatible goals. Moreover, the conflict may be perceived by only one person, one group, or one side of those involved in the interaction. A manager may perceive that an employee is lazy, but the employee may see himself as hardworking. One worker may grow to perceive a competitive situation with her coworker (as in the illustration above); however, the latter may experience no feelings of competitiveness.

Finally, on occasion, perceived conflict can exist without latent conflict as a predecessor. For instance, we once worked with an organization in which several employees believed (erroneously) that they were competing with one another for promotions. In reality, each employee could be promoted if he or she met specific sales goals. Thus, they were competing with themselves, not with one another. Their interests were not incompatible. In fact, they could all benefit from sharing successful sales strategies with one another, so that each could be promoted. This notion is important from a communication perspective since communication that clarifies (in this instance, probably coming from a manager) can serve to extinguish the perceived conflict and restore cooperative motives.

Closely linked to perceived conflict is **felt conflict,** the point at which the parties begin to become emotionally involved with the conflict and to personalize it. Vague feelings of competitiveness or differences of opinion begin to mushroom. Perceptions and emotional reactions merge, but neither party takes action at this stage. However, those involved begin to focus on the conflict and to think about specific tactics, strategies, and possible courses of action. Since no action is initiated at this point, altered thinking and flexibility still exist. If any party to the conflict develops changed perceptions, leading to a diminished emotional reaction, no subsequent confrontation or other action will ensue. Fortunately, this "backpedaling" can be done without concern for saving face. If the conflict continues to be felt, however, those involved in it will likely move toward taking action.

The next conflict phase is **manifest conflict,** which occurs when those in conflict take overt action. Depending upon the organizational culture, the history and power relationship of the disputants, the salience of the issue and the feelings evoked, the extent to which external constraints exist, and the personal styles and ethical standards of the parties, this phase can be enacted in many different ways. For instance, action can be verbal or physical, overt or covert. Individuals can move into a problem-solving, constructive mode of interaction, or into an aggressive, hostile mode involving personal attacks. The way in which the conflicting parties have managed the earlier conflict stages will influence the overt behaviors associated with this stage. Manifest conflict is essentially communicative, comprising interactive cycles of messages, responses, and counterresponses. Once these cycles begin, no one person can control their development or outcomes (Kriegsberg, 1973). They tend to be self-perpetuating and to have a momentum all their own.

Structuring Strategies for Overt Conflict

Various structuring strategies can sometimes afford some control over the overt conflict stage. Many of the group decision-making procedures discussed in Chapter 7 can be usefully adapted to conflict situations. For instance, defining the problem and articulating the parameters of the felt conflict can be helpful. Establishing evaluative criteria can also prove valuable. Often the two work together. During a job search, two members of the search committee may have preferred candidates, George and Peter. After the first round of interviews, the committee members begin to argue vehemently about the comparative strengths and weaknesses of these two candidates. In this instance, the committee chair may attempt to structure the conflict by clarifying the job's critical requirements (that is, defining the "problem"), and based on that, prioritizing the criteria by which the respective candidates should be judged. Once all committee members have agreed (not necessarily without great debate), that the critical factors are successful sales experience, past work experience in a team-oriented organization, and a strong work ethic, they should be able to choose between George and Peter. If the committee chair possesses considerable status and power within the group and organization, he or she will be better equipped to employ these kinds of structuring strategies.

Sometimes conflicts escalate, either when conflict issues are expanded, when the parties become involved in face saving and preserving their self-esteem, or when rhetorical sensitivity is lost as emotional exchanges begin to dominate the interaction (Donohue, Diez, & Hamilton, 1984; Putnam & Jones, 1982). Conflict may arise over a specific issue. For instance, suppose the laser printer in an office is being used far too frequently. Since mostly secretaries have access to the printer in this office, the department head calls a meeting of the clerical workers to discuss the criteria governing the legitimate use of the printer. As the secretaries react to this specific problem, they soon *expand the conflict by bringing up all sorts of other issues* that have bothered them for some time. Before the meeting is over, the issue has grown to include who uses the copying machine more, why some secretaries take longer lunch breaks than others, why some arrive late while others leave early, what constitutes a valid excuse for a "sick leave," why one secretary often brings her grandchild to the office, and why another occasionally brings her ailing bulldog. Somewhere along the way, the laser printer issue has become embedded in a deeper, greater conflict.

Similarly, conflicts tend to escalate when they begin to involve *self-esteem* or *self-images*. For instance, in the meeting just described, one secretary might say, "Well, we wouldn't have these problems if everyone behaved more professionally. And what's more, everyone knows that no one is paying attention and so they think they can get away with whatever they want!" This sort of comment insults everyone's work ethic and likely brings forth defensiveness from the department chair, who is supposed to be in charge of this charming group. Such ego attacks lead to conflict escalation as everyone runs to his or her own defense.

Finally, conflicts may escalate because of *breakdowns in rhetorical sensitivity*. Somehow the realities of the situation are lost as self-interest becomes paramount and others' interests fade from view. Hostile expressions are reciprocated. Everyone forgets that some values are shared—such as the desire for maintaining a constructive working relationship and the need to find a mutually acceptable solution to the problem. In essence, winning the conflict becomes the main goal, taking on a symbolic significance that transcends all other considerations. Incentives to compete prevail, and incentives to cooperate are lost (Tegar, 1980). Clearly, then, conflicts during the overt stage can evolve either productively or destructively—and how they unfold can greatly influence the future of the disputants as well as the greater organization.

The final stage in Pondy's model is the **conflict aftermath**. This stage reflects the complex dynamics of the earlier phases. If a conflict was managed constructively, for instance, the aftermath might reflect improved relationships, creative solutions, and new tools for potential future conflicts. However, if the conflict led to a destructive, escalating interaction, the aftermath might circle back to the felt stage, but this time with perceptions and emotions more volatile and hostilities now open and likely to endure and grow.

Since conflict can function either productively or counterproductively, managing it effectively is crucial. The American Management Association has estimated that managers spend approximately 24 percent of their time dealing with conflict (Lippitt, 1982). The significance of conflict behaviors, however, is related more to their perceived salience than to their frequency. Many managers and other organizational members who excel in most facets of their jobs and communicate well under conditions of harmony perform far less effectively when they must cope with conflict. Moreover, when employees are dissatisfied with the way conflict is handled, they tend to feel less positively about other aspects of their jobs. Ideally, then, effective employees at any organizational level should be able to communicate appropriately under conditions of conflict. What is appropriate, however, depends upon the situation, including the conflict style preferences of the conflicting parties.

Conflict Styles

Researchers have discussed different conflict management styles since the mid-1960s. Among the first to do so were Blake and Mouton (1964), whose five-category Conflict Management Grid was soon replicated and refined by others (e.g., Rahim & Bonoma, 1979). Blake and Mouton conceptualized conflict style as a characteristic mode or habitual way in which a person handles a dispute. Style can also be viewed as an orientation toward conflict, or conflict tactics and strategies (either planned or enacted) (Folger & Poole, 1984). The styles generally studied emanate from a two-dimensional scheme based on concern for self (or task) and concern for others.

The first conflict style is **avoiding**. Although aware of conflict at a cognitive level, the person using this style may withdraw by removing herself or himself (psychologically or physically) from the conflict situation and either refraining from arguing or simply failing to confront. If the conflict is over serious or complex issues, avoidance behaviors may contribute to frustration, deny others' feelings, and generally aggravate the problem. Moreover, at a practical level, in organizational settings where interdependent tasks are commonly addressed, long-term avoidance is probably not an achievable strategy.

At the other extreme of managing conflict is **forcing**. Those who employ this style rely on coercion rather than on persuasion or collaboration. They use assertiveness, verbal dominance, and perseverance. When all else fails, they resort to their position power or formal authority, ordering others to comply simply because they are in charge. Less direct, manipulative forms of forcing are also possible, however. For instance, a manager with a forcing style might manipulate the composition of a committee so that the solution he prefers emerges through a "democratic" process. Although forcing may be an effective conflict style in some situations (when, for instance, quick action is required), it tends to breed hostility and resentment if used repeatedly.

The third conflict style is **accommodating**, an approach that glosses over differences, plays down disagreements, and generally trivializes conflict. In the ultimate sense, those who accommodate simply give in, setting aside their own concerns and surrendering to those of others, often with the goal of maintaining pleasant interpersonal relationships. Occasionally, accommodating is used strategically when someone sets aside his or her concerns on a particular issue, with the hope that the next time there is conflict, the other person will "owe me one." Whether or not this strategy is effective depends upon whether the terms of the accommodation are understood, as well as on the standards governing the other party's actions. Accommodating is most appropriately used when the person who chooses to accommodate truly perceives the issue as trivial.

As an even-handed approach to conflict, the **compromising** style carries considerable appeal. Compromising means searching for an intermediate position, splitting the difference, and meeting the opponent halfway. Thus, for both parties, partial satisfaction is achieved. Unlike the first three approaches, compromising appears fair and requires considerable effort and interaction (presumably involving both persuading and listening). The difficulty with compromising as a typical conflict style is that it is, above all, expedient. When used consistently, it sends the message that the individual is more interested in resolving the conflict than in actually finding an excellent solution to the problem. Moreover, no one is ever fully satisfied. While there are no real losers, neither are there any real winners. The feeling of accomplishment that can grow from working through a problem to consensus is never realized through compromise.

Finally, the preferred conflict style in many organizational contexts is **collaborating,** *or problem solving.* This style calls upon the disputants to face the conflict openly and directly, and to seek, by working together, an integrative solution. Collaboration grows from a trust-building process. It encourages those involved to express themselves assertively and reinforces the value of listening to others and approaching the problem constructively. Consistent with the supportive communication behaviors discussed in other chapters, the collaborative approach demands a focus on the problem and its thoughtful analysis rather than on the attribution of blame. It works best in organizational environments that foster openness, directness, and equality. With collaboration, the integrative approach to problem solving (as defined earlier) must prevail, and the "pie" is expanded by avoiding fixed, inflexible, incompatible positions. For complex, important issues the collaborative approach is preferable, both in the quality of the outcome achieved and in the feelings of empowerment that grow from people having successfully exercised their problem-solving skills in addressing a significant organizational issue.

Research on Conflict Styles

Theorists agree that no one style is the ideal way to manage all conflict situations (Rahim & Bonoma, 1979). The effectiveness of a particular strategy or style is contingent upon the situation and the way in which the disputants approach the conflict and communicate with one another (Phillips & Cheston, 1979). Nevertheless, some conflict management styles receive more emphasis and tend to be more favorably perceived than others. Clear differences exist, however, between the conflict styles that most typify managers' actual behavior and those preferred by subordinates. In general, supervisors rely on forcing as their most characteristic mode of handling conflicts (Howat & London, 1980; Morley & Shockey-Zalabak, 1986; Phillips & Cheston, 1979; Putnam & Wilson, 1982). Forcing based on position power is particularly characteristic of managers who demonstrate low levels of supervisory expertise (Conrad, 1983). Subordinates, in contrast, are much more likely to avoid (London & Howat, 1978), to smooth (Putnam & Wilson, 1982), or to compromise (Renwick, 1975) when placed in conflict situations with their superiors. These disparities probably reflect power and status differentials in handling conflicts (Putnam & Poole, 1987).

Moreover, conflict varies in frequency, acceptance, and style across organizational levels (Thomas & Schmidt, 1976). In general, the higher the position, the more frequent the occurrences of conflict and the more likely it is that disagreements will surface (Evan, 1965). Managers in high-level positions tend to view conflict more favorably than those in subordinate roles (Tompkins, Fisher, Infante, & Tompkins, 1974). These differences in frequency of and attitudes toward conflict suggest that hierarchical roles influence the use of communication strategies and conflict styles.

Subordinates prefer the collaborative conflict style, rating it as the most effective and satisfying approach to managing conflict (Burke, 1970; Lawrence & Lorsch, 1967; Wheeless & Reichel, 1990). In contrast, with rare exceptions, forcing correlates negatively with subordinate satisfaction (Putnam & Wilson, 1982; Robbins, 1978). The nonconfrontational style of avoidance has been shown to have the strongest negative relationship to subordinate satisfaction (Lawrence & Lorsch, 1967; Renwick, 1975). Wheeless and Reichel (1990) suggested that avoidance might be negatively perceived because conflict situations produce special needs for assistance "and the manager who avoids a subordinate in a time of need apparently becomes less attractive in task oriented environments" (p. 384).

Just as the collaborative style is most positively received by subordinates, managers too have acknowledged the strengths of this approach to managing conflict. In discussing incidents of effective and ineffective conflict resolution, Filley (1975) reported that managers described collaboration as a significant type of effective conflict management. In general, conflicts managed with this style tend to evoke intellectual rather than emotional intensity. In contrast to other methods, collaboration assumes that it is possible to find a solution that will benefit everyone.

Why is the collaborative style of conflict management not used with greater skill or frequency? Some argue that our society does not teach problem solving as a life skill. Instead, it emphasizes obeying authority figures, such as teachers and parents. When children mature and eventually become authority figures, they may expect to be obeyed or to dominate others. This power-oriented view inhibits the individual's ability to choose problem solving or collaboration as a natural conflict management style (Mayer, 1990). Moreover, in comparison with any other style, collaboration requires a greater degree of time, energy, and commitment (Blake & Mouton 1964; Derr, 1978). Thus, lack of skill in constructive confrontation combines with an unwillingness or inability to expend the necessary time, energy, or commitment to diminish the extent to which collaboration is used in conflict situations.

Situational and Perceptual Factors

While the collaborative approach is consistently hailed as effective in managing conflict, it is not necessarily the most appropriate conflict management style for every situation. For instance, collaboration is not appropriate when the conflict is trivial and quick decisions are required. Avoidance may be quite effective for handling less important and highly volatile issues, and forcing may be appropriate for crisis situations or for moving forward with unpopular courses of action (Rahim & Bonoma, 1979). Collaboration generally works well, however, in situations where parties are interdependent, where supporting and implementing the solution is required, and where the conflict stems from ambiguity or inadequate shared information.

Even though conflict styles can be described in theoretical terms, the precise relationship between those individual style preferences and actual communication behavior during a conflict remains unclear. For instance, Fairhurst, Green, and Snavely (1984) reported that although supervisors' conflict styles seemed to be consistent with their initial strategies for dealing with conflict, their subsequent strategies tended to be coercive no matter what their style. In addition, most research on conflict has focused on *perceived message behaviors* rather than on actual communication style. For instance, forcing is typically measured as the extent of reported verbal dominance—the extent to which one is perceived as using a loud voice, asserting opinions forcefully, prolonging the discussion of issues, holding firm on a preferred alternative, and using power and influence to win (Putnam & Wilson, 1982; Rahim, 1983; Riggs, 1983; Ross & DeWine, 1982).

Other research suggests that *disputants' perceptions of one another* also play a role when conflicts arise. For instance, individuals using forcing, avoiding, or collaborating conflict styles have a tendency to perceive the other party as using a similar strategy. Thus, *perceived reciprocity* is a key contributor to choice of conflict style (Thomas & Walton, 1971). In addition, perceptions and attributions concerning the cause of the conflict are also linked. Thomas and Pondy (1977) have pointed out that competitive intentions are often attributed to the other party, whereas collaborative and compromising causes are attributed to oneself. Unfortunately, this sort of *attributional process* may serve to polarize the disputants. Finally, research reveals that the choice of a conflict style or strategy hinges to a great extent on *the other party's tactics*. Specifically, disputants reciprocate their opponent's use of forcing, confronting, smoothing, and compromising behaviors in kind; avoiding tactics, however, typically follow a forcing style (Cosier & Ruble, 1981; Ruble & Cosier, 1982).

The *nature of the conflict issue* also plays a significant role in the choice of a conflict style. For instance, in conflicts caused by power struggles and incompatible values, disputants tend to rely on forcing strategies, whereas in controversies that stem from scarce resources, interpersonal incompatibility, and differing attitudes and opinions, individuals are more likely to choose compromising and smoothing tactics. The collaborative approach is most frequently used in the management of conflicts that stem from misunderstandings, ambiguous meanings, and discrepancies in reward allocation (Phillips & Cheston, 1979; Renwick, 1975). Other mitigating factors include the frequency and salience of the conflict. When a conflict issue is perceived as very important and agreement is likely, the collaborative approach is likely to be used. However, forcing strategies are more common in situations where conflict is characterized by high importance, low probability of agreement, and high frequency (Blake & Mouton, 1964; Howat & London, 1980). When issues are perceived as trivial and agreement is viewed as unlikely, organizational members often use avoidance (Rahim & Bonoma, 1979).

Whatever the conflict style or strategy chosen, its effective implementation will depend on the disputants' ability to adapt to the situation, their fairness and objectivity in approaching the conflict, and the way in which they communicate (Phillips & Cheston, 1979). There are many different ways of forcing, for instance—ranging from soft, persistent argument to unpleasant, loudly projected references to one's power and authority. Those at the receiving end will react differently, depending upon the specific verbal and nonverbal communication behaviors that make up the overall conflict style. Moreover, timing is important. Executives report that early intervention is critically related to effective conflict management (Phillips & Cheston, 1979)—the longer the delay, the more likely the conflict will escalate, perhaps out of control.

Structural Intervention in Managing Conflict: Third-Party Methods

When the conflicting parties are unwilling or unable to arrive at a resolution to their situation, they may resort to calling in a neutral third party for assistance. In this way, they extend or elaborate on the negotiation process. The third party could be a supervisor (in conflicts between employees), an upper-level manager (in conflicts between two departments), the chief executive officer (in conflicts between divisions), a government-appointed mediator (in labor-management disputes), or a judge in a courtroom (in conflicts between organizations). In these situations, the third party could play one of two roles: the **arbitrator,** who after hearing both sides of the issue, makes a decision that both parties must live by; or the **mediator,** who tries to facilitate communication between the parties so that they can work through their problems and arrive at a decision of their own. Although both processes rely on communication to manage information and exert social influence, mediation is a type of facilitation that hinges almost exclusively on communication for its success.

The mediator's task requires sensitivity. Striving to make logical decisions is only a small part of the mediator's role. Because conflicts have usually escalated before the mediator becomes involved, she or he often finds that the parties are no longer particularly logical. Thus, the mediator will have to deal with a number of irrational postures shaped by hurt feelings, a preoccupation with settling old scores, defensiveness, and distorted perceptions. Mediators, however, also have an advantage in this task. Because, unlike the disputants who are emotionally involved, mediators are usually much better able to maintain a proper perspective.

Mediators use varied tactics, including directive, nondirective, procedural, and reflexive techniques (Carnevale & Pegnetter, 1985). **Directive tactics** allow the mediator to exert substantive control over the negotiation by recommending proposals, giving opinions about positions, assessing the costs associated with demands, and occasionally inducing compliance (Kolb, 1983). In general, directive tactics are more effective in the latter stages of mediation than in early meetings—perhaps because near the end of a meeting, everyone is eager to reach some conclusion (Hilltrop, 1985). **Nondirective tactics** capitalize on the mediator's role in securing information for the disputants and in clarifying misunderstandings. Thus, the mediator may act as a conduit, passing information between the parties, or as a clarifier, paraphrasing messages and narrowing topics for discussion (Wall, 1981).

As **procedural tactics,** the mediator may organize separate or joint sessions, establish protocol for the sessions, regulate the agenda, and establish deadlines. Finally, mediators may use **reflexive tactics** to influence the affective tone of the mediation—developing rapport with participants, using humor, and speaking the language of both sides. Effective mediators use a combination of these tactics, although they report that reflexive tactics are more effective than directive and nondirective ones in facilitating joint collaboration (Carnevale & Pegnetter, 1985). Clearly, communication is central to the mediation process. As Kolb (1985) pointed out, mediators are like the directors of a drama; they set the scene, manage impressions, orchestrate the script, and maintain dramatic inquiry throughout the process.

Fortunately, most groups and organizations are able to manage their own conflict through negotiation and bargaining rather than having to call in third parties. Effective outcomes are more likely to be realized when individuals voluntarily solve their own disputes than when leaders or other third parties are asked to intervene. Thus, developing an understanding of productive, collaborative approaches to managing conflict is crucial.

Collaborative Conflict Management

Several integrative negotiation strategies have been shown to foster collaboration when it is possible and desirable to approach conflict from a problem-solving perspective (Northcraft & Neale, 1990). First, and perhaps most important, is establishing **superordinate goals**. The parties involved in the conflict should begin by focusing on what they share in common. As individuals become aware of the salience of their shared goals—greater productivity, a safer work environment, lower costs, a fairer evaluation system, or improved working relationships—they tend to realize the merits of resolving their differences so that these mutual goals will not be jeopardized. When consensus on common goals is achieved, the disputants can begin to move forward to examining their specific differences. Once established, superordinate goals must be referred to throughout the deliberations. Some researchers have cautioned, however, that superordinate goals are more likely to reduce perceived rather than underlying conflict (Hunger & Stern, 1976). Whether superordinate goals are helpful depends upon whether the groups develop a culture for mutual understanding and constructive interaction patterns (Deschamps & Brown, 1983).

Another important collaborative behavior involves *separating the people from the problem*. Having defined the mutual benefits to be gained by successfully resolving the conflict, the parties must direct their attention to the real issue at hand: solving a problem. As discussed in the section on supportive communication, negotiations are more likely to result in mutual satisfaction if the parties depersonalize the discussions. The participants might benefit from viewing each other as advocates for differing points of view rather than as rivals. They may need to suppress the desire for personal revenge or one-upmanship and avoid loaded language, such as labeling others' ideas stupid, crazy, naive, fascist, or ill-conceived.

In Chapter 7, we discussed the importance of groups identifying and using criteria for determining the quality of alternative solutions to a problem. In situations involving conflict, *articulating and using objective criteria* is equally crucial. No matter how many goals are shared, some incompatible interests are bound to exist. Rather than seizing on these as opportunities for testing wills, it is far more productive to determine what is fair. Doing so requires both parties to agree on how fairness should be judged. As objective criteria are discussed and agreed upon, individuals begin to shift their thinking from "getting what I want" to "deciding what makes most sense"—fostering an attitude of reasonableness and open-mindedness.

Also related to the open-minded pursuit of solutions is *focusing on interests, not positions*. In bargaining and negotiation settings, positions are thought of as bottom-line demands the negotiator makes. Interests, on the other hand, constitute the substructure of evidence and reasoning underlying the demands. Since interests tend to be broad and multifaceted, establishing agreement on them is easier. Achieving agreement, however, even on interests, involves a fair measure of creativity and requires redefining and broadening the problem to make it more tractable. Once a problem has been defined, there are a variety of ways to enlarge, alter, or replace it. If a problem such as sagging productivity has been defined in a specific way (for example, worker laziness), other contributing causes exist and can be articulated. Thus, one way to proceed is by generating at least two alternative hypotheses for every problem discussed. The purpose is to broaden the definition of the problem by thinking in plural rather than in singular terms. Thus, questions should be phrased, "What are the problems?" "What are the meanings of this?" "What are the results?"

Another possibility is to reverse the problem's definition by contradicting the currently accepted definition in order to expand the number of perspectives considered. For instance, a problem might be that morale is too high instead of too low, or that a work environment is characterized by too little rather than too much structure. Opposites and backward looks often enhance creativity. When a variety of interests and definitions of problems are examined, individuals are better able to understand one another's points of view and to place their own views in perspective. One party might say to the other, "Help me understand why you are advocating that position."

Another negotiation strategy requiring creativity is *inventing options for mutual gains*. Here, however, the creativity is focused on generating unusual solutions. While some negotiations may necessarily be distributive, negotiators should never begin by adopting a win-lose posture. Focusing both parties' attention on brainstorming alternative, mutually agreeable solutions naturally shifts the negotiation dynamics from being competitive to being collaborative. Moreover, the more options and combinations there are to explore, the greater the probability of reaching an integrative solution. Both goodwill and creativity are required as the parties ask, "What can we do that we haven't tried before?"

Several techniques used in small groups might prove useful, both in defining interests and problems and in generating solutions. Brainstorming (where ideas are tossed out without evaluation) is one potential technique. Another is the nominal group procedure, in which private brainstorming occurs (on paper) and ideas are collected and later shared and discussed. Finally, group support systems (GSS) allow for computer-assisted brainstorming, thus encouraging creativity and still preserving anonymity. Whatever approach to brainstorming is employed, those who participate in the process are basically asking, "Now that we better understand each other's underlying concerns and objectives, let's brainstorm ways of satisfying both our needs."

Finally, the parties' approach to the notion of "success" is critical. By maintaining a realistic, optimistic attitude, they can *define success in terms of gains, not losses.* For instance, suppose two coworkers, Anthony and David, share a rather crowded office. They both feel they need more privacy and a larger work space. They also feel they need new computers and printers since theirs are the oldest in the building. Several weeks after discussing their needs with their boss, they are given pleasant, private offices. However, they are told that they will have to keep their old computers and printers, at least for another year. How might Anthony and David react to this outcome? Their reactions will depend upon whether they are grateful for what they have gained or are focusing on what they failed to achieve. Individual reactions to an outcome are greatly influenced by the standards used to judge it. What were the most critical issues or criteria in this situation: privacy, space, or computer facilities? If gains are to be stressed over losses, the question to be asked is, "Does this outcome constitute a meaningful improvement over current conditions?"

An example of the collaborative approach to negotiations can be found in an examination of the 1978 Camp David Accords between Egypt and Israel (Fisher & Ury, 1981). When representatives from the two countries first sat down to discuss possession of the Sinai Peninsula, a collaborative agreement seemed impossible. Both parties demanded at least partial possession of the land that had been occupied by Israel since the 1967 Six-Day War. Both sides rejected an attempt at compromise that gave each country a portion of the

The Camp David Accords represents a historic illustration of the collaborative approach to resolving conflict. (UPI/Bettmann)

land. When the problem was framed in terms of the amount of land each country would occupy, potential solutions could only be distributive. Egypt demanded 100 percent, Israel demanded at least some significant portion of the land, and neither could be satisfied with anything less. Eventually, however, the seemingly single-issue conflict was reframed by examining the underlying interests behind the demands. Israel wanted possession of the land for security reasons, while Egypt actually wanted sovereignty over it. By agreeing to provide a demilitarized zone and to allow Israeli air bases in the Sinai, thereby assuring Israeli security, Egypt regained control of the Peninsula. The collaborative approach concluded with both sides "winning."

Using Technology as a Tool to Manage Conflict

We have already seen that technology provides extraordinary opportunities for channeling and supporting group work. Here, however, we examine how computer systems, particularly group support systems, negotiation support systems, and computer simulations can act as intervention mechanisms to address issues specifically related to group conflict management.

Argyris (1970) defines **intervention** as entering into a system of relationships to come between or among persons, groups, or objects for the purpose of helping them. The interventionist enters an ongoing system or set of relationships primarily to achieve three tasks:

1. To help generate valid and useful information.
2. To create conditions in which clients can make informed and free choices.
3. To help clients develop an internal commitment to their choice.

With regard to conflict management, group process interventions should consist of activities that help to promote

- a cooperative climate
- a focus on problems, not emotional issues
- an orderly and organized process
- consideration of a wide range of alternative solutions
- avoidance of artificial conflict-reducing techniques that rely on the leader to make the final decision (Fisher & Ury, 1981; Folger & Poole, 1984; Putnam & Poole, 1987; Walton, 1969).

Group Support Systems (GSS)

GSS employ software and hardware to promote and enforce these conditions. GSS act as a group process intervention by (1) providing an electronic meeting channel that can improve communication among group members and (2) delivering a structured, step-by-step series of activities to analyze the task.

GSS allow anonymous input and parallel and simultaneous processing, encouraging group member participation since views can be aired without inhibition or constraints. GSS facilitate the implementation of step-by-step procedures for decision making. They also help structure meeting activities, helping to keep groups on track as well as allowing them to work through conflict systematically. And the ability of GSS to provide an electronic record of meetings can help group members share a common understanding of what has transpired.

GSS appear to be especially conducive to situations in which the discussion focuses on conflicts of interest (McGrath & Hollingshead, 1993). In such situations the information richness of the communications media (GSS) appears effectively to match the information richness requirements for the negotiation aspects of the conflict management task, as depicted in Figure 8.3.

FIGURE 8.3

Task and Media Fit

Increasing potential richness required for task success / Task type(s)	Media for Group Communication System — Increasing potential richness of information			
	Computer systems	Audio systems	Video systems	Face-to-face communications
Generating ideas and plans	Good fit	Marginal fit Info too rich	Poor fit Info too rich	Poor fit Info too rich
Choosing correct answer: intellectual tasks	Marginal fit Medium too constrained	Good fit	Good fit	Poor fit Info too rich
Choosing preferred answer: judgment tasks	Poor fit Medium too constrained	Good fit	Good fit	Marginal fit Info too rich
Negotiating conflicts of interests	Poor fit Medium too constrained	Poor fit Medium too constrained	Marginal fit Info too lean	Good fit

SOURCE: McGrath & Hollingshead, 1993.

One of the earliest and most detailed studies of the impact of GSS on group conflict management was conducted by Poole, Holmes, and DeSanctis (1991). Given the attributes of the technology, they speculated that GSS should contribute to group conflict management in several ways:

1. Stimulate groups to explore a wide range of decision alternatives.
2. Provide a structured set of activities for the group to utilize during problem solving to help clarify group roles and procedures.
3. Provide voting schemes to encourage the use of polling to evaluate ideas.
4. Deemphasize personal relations through electronic input and display of ideas and positions by each group member.
5. Promote equalization of member participation.
6. Provide greater reliance on written media over spoken communication, given the electronic input and display of ideas.
7. Provide greater expression of affect, both positive and negative, during group discussion due to the electronic communication component of GSS.

They then conducted an experiment comparing groups using GSS with groups using only paper and pencils and groups using no support at all. Their findings indicated the following:

1. GSS groups explored fewer alternatives than groups using paper and pencil and groups with no support at all.
2. GSS groups did not understand group roles and procedures better than groups in the other two conditions.
3. GSS groups and paper-and-pencil groups voted more than groups with no support. GSS groups voted only somewhat more than paper-and-pencil groups, but voting tended to have a negative impact in GSS groups by cutting off or terminating discussions.
4. Compared with the other groups, GSS groups generated a greater proportion of statements that provided or sought information about conflicts in a nonconfrontational manner.
5. No differences were found in levels of member participation across group types.
6. GSS groups referred more to written material than did groups using no support at all.
7. Finally, in comparison with the other groups, GSS groups evidenced a slightly more positive working atmosphere.

In light of these mixed findings, Poole, Holmes, and DeSanctis argued that the impact of GSS on conflict management may depend on the attributes of the GSS employed and how the group applies them. For instance, the GSS used in this study had no specialized conflict management capabilities;

thus, GSS having advanced features such as problem-modeling capabilities could potentially offer better conflict management support. In addition, a group process facilitator was not used in this study. Yet a facilitator might have been able to help groups adapt GSS in a manner better designed to promote productive conflict management. Of course, users of any technology are influenced by expectations. So the way in which GSS is explained to users and the quality of training provided might well influence how they use the technology.

Other researchers have ventured into actual organizations to study the impact of GSS on conflict resolution. For instance, Nunamaker, Dennis, Valacich, and Vogel (1991) conducted an integrated series of laboratory and field studies that examined how groups used GSS when generating and discussing options during a negotiation process. They reported that GSS anonymity separated personalities from issues. They also discovered that anonymity promoted enhanced objectivity and improved the ability to generate options—particularly when issues were seen as critical or when power differences existed among the participants.

Other studies have supported the potential of GSS in conflict situations. For instance, when Sambamurthy and Poole (1992) explored the relative effects of communication and consensus support capabilities on the conflict management process for groups using GSS, they reached the following conclusions:

- Although groups used the same GSS, groups exhibited a variety of patterns of conflict management processes.

- Use of GSS to structure group meeting activities and communication helped groups to surface and resolve differences among group members, allowing higher post-meeting consensus on the group's decision.

- Groups using GSS were able to confront their conflict and resolve it more positively than groups provided with equivalent manual resources.

Based on these findings, these researchers concluded that ". . . decision support technologies which incorporate capabilities matching the demands imposed by the group decision-making process may heighten a group's ability to deal with conflict constructively and productively" (p. 246).

Finally, at Indiana University, GSS have been used to facilitate negotiations between administrative departments that are merging. GSS are used because managers know that in these meetings conflict may surface as a result of resistance to new management, new roles and responsibilities, or new assignments. The anonymity and simultaneity of the GSS provides people with a safe outlet for getting things off their chest so that issues and sentiments can be aired freely and addressed candidly without fear of repercussions. Participants in these sessions reported that using GSS also helps to break down communication barriers between new colleagues and to help managers surface and understand issues that may need to be negotiated both internally and with other departments.

Negotiation Support Systems

Negotiation support systems are decision support technologies that specifically focus on providing computerized assistance for situations in which strong disagreement on factual or value judgments exists among group members (Olson & Courtney, 1992). Negotiation support systems are interactive, computer-based tools specifically intended to help negotiating parties reach an agreement (Jelassi and Foroughi, 1989). These systems focus on enhancing the prospect of consensus, with the intent of making compromise possible.

Negotiation support systems may include decision support software with modeling capabilities such as decision trees, risk analysis, and forecasting methods, as well as software supporting structured group methods such as electronic brainstorming. Some of these systems even include artificial intelligence to help groups define and solve problems. Many commercial software products (including GSS) that encompass some or all of these features are available. Jelassi and Foroughi (1989) suggested that well-designed negotiation support systems take into account the following negotiation structuring issues:

- the behavioral characteristics and cognitive perspectives of negotiators
- the communication needs of different bargaining settings
- determination of each party's real interests
- generation of options for mutual gain
- data accuracy and consistency

Computer Simulations

In addition to the possibilities mentioned above, computers can also be used to simulate a negotiation process. Radlow (1995) pointed out that in most labor-management negotiations, disputes are usually settled by a compromise, and both sides win something. Thus, the inputs to the negotiation are the issues at hand, the outputs are the compromises, and the process is give and take. Based on this model, Radlow claimed, it is possible to develop computer simulations using a compromise-based model for labor-management and other negotiations. However, he acknowledged that such a system would actually resemble an elaborate expert system (a computer program that can solve problems from a specific knowledge base) rather than a typical simulation program. This is because the range of potential compromises requires programs with exceptionally long chains of IF . . . THEN statements for every possible negotiation contingency. Simpler models can be developed for more confrontational negotiations, in which neither labor nor management is interested in compromise but are both there to win.

Programs of the type described by Radlow are rare because a wide range of both known and unanticipated issues can develop during the negotiation process. However, in time, parties may be able to use commercial systems to conduct "what if?" analyses prior to or during an actual negotiation process.

Ironically, computer systems themselves have been a source of conflict in employee-management relations. Many labor unions were once vociferous in their crusade against office automation (Savage, 1990). They felt, with some justification, that technology threatened the loss of jobs for their members. However, many unions have come full circle and now offer training in computer use for their members' advantage. Instead of simply using technology to retrain members whose skills are being passed by, many unions have embraced technology to further their goals and to keep members abreast of computer skills. For example, the Air Line Pilots Association, whose pilots are already computer literate, has established services for members to access information about new technologies and to facilitate communication and negotiations with their employers.

In conclusion, we have seen that technology can be the source of and a potential remedy for conflict management. Computer technologies such as GSS, negotiation support systems, and computer simulation programs have unique features that can potentially facilitate the negotiation process. We have also seen, however, that realizing this value depends on the following key factors:

- how well the systems are designed
- how high are group member expectations of the technology
- how well group members are trained in the use of the technology
- what the nature of the technology is and how the group applies it
- how well the task and media fit on information richness

Summarizing Perspective

Conflict is a controversial subject. Even among those who herald its virtues, ambivalence persists. In organizations, however, the reality of interdependence, competition for scarce resources, and the necessity of coping with change while working together on all sorts of tasks create conditions in which conflict is inevitable. The types and sources of conflict are numerous, perplexing, and often tenacious. Even so, individuals at all organizational levels can, in the appropriate circumstances, learn to approach conflict cooperatively and collaboratively. On occasion, technology may function as a source of conflict, but it also offers new and ever-changing tools for groups to use in managing conflicts. With conflict comes the opportunity for growth and change, for innovation and empowerment, for problem solving and consensus building. Those who learn to confront their differences openly and honestly and to communicate about their differences with sensitivity and integrity can contribute to a constructive and satisfying organizational climate.

CASES FOR DISCUSSION

CASE 1   *"Win-Win Bargaining"*

Traditionally, labor-management relations in the United States have been largely adversarial in nature. Unions have viewed themselves as defenders of the "working class," or those who toil at the whim of a management structure more interested in company profits than employees' well-being. Conversely, management typically has viewed unions as unconcerned about company success or profitability, devoted instead to "protecting" marginal performers and maintaining restrictive work rules that maximize union membership even as they hamper company productivity. Not surprisingly, this adversarial relationship generally has dominated contract negotiations between unions and management. Company representatives have often aimed to minimize increases in "labor costs" (particularly increases in wages and benefits) and "beat the union"; unions for their part have sought to maximize wage and benefits increases and thus prove their value to their dues-paying members.

Changes in the nation's economy and rising competition from foreign firms have forced labor and management to change their approach and adopt a more cooperative stance. This change has in turn led to a new approach to contract negotiations: "win-win bargaining."

Among the earliest users of "win-win bargaining" were the United Paperworkers International Union Local 264 at the Waldorf Corporation's St. Paul, Minnesota, facility. Since previous negotiations had resulted in a strike and much continued dissension even after the contract had been settled, both parties felt that a new approach was needed. Nevertheless, there was some skepticism on both sides.

During their initial bargaining sessions, labor and management representatives agreed that their joint objectives in the contract talks were to reach a fair agreement, use contract language that would be understood by both parties, and keep everyone informed as the negotiations progressed.

Both sides also adopted a set of ground rules concerning the contract talks. These included the following:

▶ Discussion was to focus on issues, not personalities.

▶ Everyone was to be permitted to speak— and, moreover, to speak without interruption—not just the spokespersons for each side.

▶ Both sides would work at all times to maintain a "positive relationship."

▶ Agendas would be developed and followed for each bargaining session.

▶ Notes concerning each meeting would be kept jointly and approved by the participants at the beginning of the next session.

▶ Information would be shared and disseminated to employees through a jointly sponsored hotline and bulletin board communications.

Each issue was carefully explained and defined; brainstorming procedures were used to generate ideas; tentative resolutions were examined systematically and in accordance with agreed-upon objectives; all agreements were considered tentative and subject to final approval by the membership and senior company management. Participants were assigned specific roles, including discussion leader, spokesperson, participant, and facilitator.

The membership ratified the resulting contract almost unanimously, and with far less turmoil than had been the case three years earlier. Participants in the process also reported much higher levels of satisfaction both with the process itself and with the contract it produced. They claimed that the process was conducted in a more orderly manner than were previous negotiations, that caucuses were used less frequently and only for brief meetings, and that marathon bargaining sessions were avoided altogether.

A similar "win-win" approach has been used by the Chrysler Corporation and the United Auto Workers (UAW), who have worked cooperatively to develop "modern operating agreements" (or "MOAs") for some Chrysler plants. Generally, MOA plants have reported reduced operating costs, lower turnover, fewer grievances and lower absenteeism.

The MOA concept evolved in 1986–87 as a joint effort between Chrysler management and the UAW to improve quality and productivity on the assembly line. The MOAs were aimed at creating a more democratic work environment, and they served to eliminate superficial labor-management distinctions, reduce job classifications, eliminate inefficient practices, reduce the number of supervisory personnel

and union representatives, and establish self-directed work teams and a pay system that rewards workers for their job-related knowledge.

Each MOA has a team that participates in daily audits, assists in the development of work assignments, corrects minor and reports major tooling and maintenance problems, provides input regarding production standards, assists in methods planning, monitors and controls performance, coordinates overtime work, arranges vacation schedules, and performs other tasks. These teams are a key outgrowth of the cooperative bargaining undertaken by Chrysler and the UAW.

Questions for Discussion

1. What elements of effective conflict management seem to be present in "win-win bargaining" and "modern operating agreements"?

2. Are there situations in which "win-win bargaining" or "modern operating agreements" might not be effective? What factors must be present in order for these concepts to work?

3. To move a company away from the traditional "adversarial" labor-management approach toward more cooperative labor-management relations, what communication strategies might you use

CASE 2 *The Raise*

Mike Summers had a problem. In some ways, it was a good problem to have: Over the past year, his company, Argus Industries, had grown more than at any time since Mike had inherited the business from his father seven years earlier. His customer base

had doubled, the plant had grown from 185 to 270 employees, and the company's income had increased by 75 percent.

Much of the growth was directly attributable to one man, John Mardini, whom Mike had hired one year ago. John had worked for one of Argus Industries' largest competitors, but he had been laid off by that company and out of work for several months when he came to Mike's attention. After just a couple of interviews, Mike hired John to be the corporate vice president of production, with primary responsibility for overseeing and revamping the company's one manufacturing facility in a small Wisconsin town.

John proved to be everything Mike had hoped for—and more. Unlike the shy and reserved Mike, John was extremely outgoing and assertive, able to make profitable deals with suppliers and customers alike while restructuring the plant's organization and pay system. John's tough, aggressive style quickly won much support among the middle management group at Argus. He soon pushed aside the plant's general manager, Don Roper, and took over his responsibilities. In addition, John brought in several people he knew from his previous company, placing them in key positions within the plant.

Everything John did seemed to work. Despite some labor unrest among the plant's employees (some of whom were upset by the suddenly increased pace of change in the company), John's actions produced marked improvements in both quality and productivity. Everything seemed to be going in the right direction.

So what was Mike's problem? John's greatest strength—his assertiveness—was also the quality that Mike found most difficult to handle. Mike's personality was such that he preferred to avoid conflict, either by allowing others to have their way or by referring the conflict to some other party who would protect Mike's interests (his corporate attorney, for example). But now Mike was caught: John had gone directly to him to demand a significant increase in compensation.

Certainly, Mike was pleased with John's performance. But, in his view, John's demands were excessive: a 50 percent increase in salary, a 100 percent increase in his car allowance, a significant increase in his retirement benefits, and a percentage of the company's profits. Mike wanted to reward John for his contribution to the company and to keep John reasonably satisfied enough to remain in the organization, but he did not want to break the bank in doing so.

Mike called a consultant he had been using for a variety of other projects and asked for his advice.

Questions for Discussion

1. Imagine you are the consultant Mike called. What might you advise Mike to do? What things would you tell Mike to avoid doing?

2. Imagine you decided to facilitate a meeting between John and Mike to talk through this potential conflict. What things would you try to accomplish or avoid during that meeting? What topics would you want to discuss? What information would you collect before the meeting, if any? What would you want the outcome of the meeting to be?

9

Managing Diversity

*Managing cultural diversity effectively is a skill that can be learned. The key is realizing that cultural diversity is an **advantage** in the workplace. Diverse points of view, cultural orientations, insights, and perspectives breathe new life into your business. Valuing cultural diversity is clearly the way to keep your business competitive and productive.*
Sally J. Walton, *Cultural Diversity in the Workplace,* 1994.

The U.S. work force is increasingly characterized by diversity. In 1987 the Hudson Institute published its famous *Workforce 2000* report, projecting the character and needs of our work force at the turn of the century. The report showed that organizational homogeneity is rapidly diminishing as the standard ratios of sex, race, ethnicity, and age give way to ongoing and dramatic changes. Beginning in the 1970s, the U.S. organizational demographics on age, sex, education, and race began to change dramatically. This change was also reflected in the types of individuals entering the work force. No longer do organizational demographics mirror the composition of the top management team. Instead, it is more likely that top managers will be almost exclusively white and male while the work force they manage will be increasingly composed of women and people of color. In fact, by the year 2000, the U.S. work force will be significantly older and will contain a higher percentage of educationally disadvantaged workers. Only 30 percent of the new entrants to the labor force over the next ten years will be white males, compared with 47 percent in 1987. Almost two-thirds of the new entrants will be women. People of color will make up 29 percent of the new entrants—twice their share of the work force in 1987 (Johnston, *Workforce 2000,* 1987). By the middle of the twenty-first century, Anglo-Americans will be in a minority in the United States as the traditional minorities (African Americans, Hispanic Americans, and Asian Americans) assume majority status.

In March 1991, the U.S. Census Bureau released figures from its 1990 national census. During the last decade, the Asian-American population has more than doubled, the Hispanic-American population has grown by more

As organizational diversity grows, employees must learn to communicate effectively with those who differ from them in gender, race, and ethnicity. Accomplishing organizational goals increasingly depends on unleashing the creativity that may grow from culturally diverse groups engaged in common ventures. (Tom Stewart/The Stock Market)

than 53 percent, and the African-American population has increased by 13 percent. More than one-third of the nation's growth during the decade of the 1980s (from nearly 227 million to almost 249 million) came from immigration. For the first time, this growth is beginning to be reflected in all regions of the country (Walton, 1994).

In this chapter we explore cultural diversity broadly, examining issues related to race, ethnicity, age, and especially gender. Since understanding and creating organizational environments where *all* people can have a real chance of empowerment is so important, we begin by considering some examples of organizations grappling with managing diversity, including the aging work force. Then we consider multiculturalism in the context of the American educational experience because so many stereotypes, attitudes toward self, and learning outcomes begin in elementary, secondary, and college classrooms. What is learned at this level may serve to complicate later attempts to instill mutual respect and appreciation for diversity in the workplace. We move on to examine gender as a variable potentially affecting upward mobility and communication in organizational settings. Next we discuss discrimination and sexual harassment and consider ways in which organizations can provide opportunities for individuals to balance their personal and professional lives. We conclude this chapter, as we have most others, by discussing the potential role of technology in assisting organizations with cultural diversity and its management.

Managing Diversity as a Challenge to Organizational Leaders

Perhaps the primary task facing managers today is to create an environment in which each employee—regardless of race, age, ethnicity, or other factors irrelevant to level of performance—is motivated to perform and can experience a sense of empowerment. But it is not an easy task. For instance, research has shown that people who share experiences and attitudes and are similar to one another are also more likely to interact well with one another, like each other, and share a common bond (Pfeffer, 1985). People who are similar demographically (in age, sex, or race) are also more likely to have had common experiences, share similar values, and understand one another better. And such similarities make it easier for them to communicate with one another effectively. Organizations often experience greater turnover (both voluntary and involuntary) where there are large gaps in rank, and departments show greater turnover when there are large age differences among employees. Those most likely to leave are employees who are most different in age (Wagner, Pfeffer, & O'Reilly, 1984).

Other barriers exist. For instance, women and people of color may encounter negative gender or racial stereotypes, the pressure of the solo role (being the only woman or person of color), or the stereotype of incompetency stemming from the perception that they received their jobs because of affirmative action. People of color and female employees may also experience lower rates of promotion than do white males. Those who are married, especially those in dual career marriages, may find that their advancement options are limited since any geographical change requires two new jobs. Finally, those who are parents also face considerable transaction costs in making moves because of the difficulty in finding successful child care, the multiple constituencies to be satisfied, or the desire to maintain family stability (Northcraft & Neale, 1994).

In spite of the complexities of managing an increasingly diverse work force, organizations simply have no choice but to acknowledge the changes that are occurring and to take bold initiatives aimed at turning potential problems into advantages. Why? As organizations move toward the twenty-first century, they will experience increasing demands for creativity and innovation. A diverse work force has greater potential for creativity than a homogeneous one. Researchers into the creative process suggest that the most productive and creative individuals are those who have had a broad range of contacts and have interacted with a variety of individuals of diverse backgrounds (Kanter, 1988). Creativity is more likely to occur when basic beliefs or expectations are challenged. Over time, individuals working closely together tend to become more alike in their views, values, and perspectives. When this happens, people may become less sensitive to opportunities and more likely to stifle creativity. Arguably, then, when properly managed, diversity can give many organizations several advantages, among them the increased chance of an empowered work force. Focus On presents six arguments for cultural diversity in organizations.

Contemporary Organizations Grappling with Diversity

Adapting to the Aging Work Force

Between 1988 and 2000, the younger portion of the work force (ages twenty-five to thirty-four) will decrease by 11 percent. The number of workers between the ages of forty-five and fifty-four will increase by 61 percent, and this group will make up 22 percent of the work force by the year 2000. Couple this trend with both a decline in the quality of the education of the youngest entrants into the work force and the lifting of legally mandated retirement ages, and it is clear that organizations will have to rethink traditional ideas about older workers.

While labor force participation declines with increasing age, recent surveys suggest that this trend is not based on the desires of older employees. One-third of those currently retired would prefer to be working either part-time or full-time. Sixty-eight percent of all workers aged fifty or older say they never want to retire (Franklin, 1991). In fact, older workers will represent an increasingly larger pool of untapped talent for most employers.

One change that companies are likely to institute is in their benefits programs. For example, Aetna has recently overhauled its benefits program to include a graduated retirement plan that allows employees to cut back from full-time to part-time employment in the two to three years preceding retirement. Benefits are maintained, the company gains because the employee will have time to train his or her replacement, and the employee gains because he or she has more free time. Aetna also has a "return to work" program that hires retirees for temporary work assignments. Retirees can decide how long they want to work and whether they want to be retrained for job reentry if necessary. The plan also includes a fitness program designed for seniors and a redesigned pension plan. The same changes are occurring at Kentucky Fried Chicken and McDonald's, two other organizations that are adjusting their benefits for a new group of potential employees: the retired. For those who are part of this aging work force, such creative moves by organizations should foster a climate of goodwill and become another vehicle for employee empowerment.

FOCUS ON | ## Arguments for Cultural Diversity in Organizations

Cost Argument

As organizations become more diverse, costs of poor integration will increase. Companies that are able to integrate a culturally diverse work force will realize considerable cost savings over those companies that cannot or choose not to do so.

Resource-Acquisition Argument

Companies develop reputations as good places for women and minorities to work. Those with the best reputations will be able to attract the best people. As the labor pool shrinks and changes in composition, this advantage will become more important.

Marketing Argument

For multinational organizations, the insight and cultural sensitivity that employees with roots in other countries bring to marketing efforts should improve the effectiveness of such efforts. This reasoning also applies to ethnic groups within the United States.

Creativity Argument

Diversity of perspectives and less emphasis on conformity and adherence to past practices should improve the level of innovation and creativity among employees.

Problem-Solving Argument

Heterogeneous decision-making and problem-solving groups are likely to produce better solutions because they allow critical analysis from multiple perspectives.

System-Flexibility Argument

Organizations that are able to manage multicultural diversity effectively will necessarily become less standardized, more open, and more fluid. This fluidity should create greater flexibility to react to environmental changes more effectively.

Empowerment Argument

Individuals who work in organizational environments characterized by sensitivity and appreciation for diverse talents and perspectives grow to feel more valued and empowered, to relate better to their coworkers, and to gain more satisfaction from their jobs.

SOURCE: Based on Cox & Blake, 1991.

Technology, however, can present complications. New technologies require new skills. Thus, as retirees are offered opportunities to return to work, they must also be given the knowledge and skills needed to function effectively. Travelers Insurance, for instance, has already begun retraining its retirees. People who were knowledgeable clerks, formerly working in a paper-processing environment, have been trained to use computers to fulfill the same functions in new ways. Similarly, Chrysler and the United Auto Workers have created a Joint Skill Talent Program that provides a full range of education and training options to workers facing potential displacement.

Many believe that, when properly trained, older workers bring many advantages to the work force. Managers have found older workers to be dependable, polite, stable, and efficient. They may also serve as mentors or confidantes for younger, less experienced employees (Franklin, 1991). Although some companies have been leaders in using an older work force, changing demographics now demand that organizations more effectively use this particular talent pool.

Diversity Training

During a period of rapid growth in the late 1980s, GE Silicones in Waterford, New York, hired a number of chemical engineers and other professionals for several key initiatives, including the formation of a Total Quality Management department, expansion of the company's research and development function, and reorganization of the manufacturing operation. Nearly 30 percent of those hired were women and/or minorities. Some of the new staff objected to several of the company's practices, including the presence of pinup-style calendars in work areas, the lack of women's restrooms in the plant, managers' condescending attitudes toward women, managers' reluctance to give women work assignments that were considered "difficult" and therefore more suitable for men, lack of advancement opportunities for minorities, and lack of minority representation in the ranks of management.

Company managers quickly realized that they were not in tune with today's diverse work force and took steps to manage the diversity of their employees more effectively. They formed a steering committee of employee volunteers to help develop programs aimed at improving the quality of life for this culturally diverse employee population. Using that committee's recommendations, they then embarked on two major efforts: teamwork and diversity training.

Teams of volunteers representing a cross-section of the organization investigated a variety of cultural diversity issues raised by employees. These issues included family leave, flexible hours, working couples, minority recruitment, personal and professional development of employees, and mentoring. The teams worked to find ways to manage those issues and ultimately produced new company policies on family leave, child care services, job sharing and flextime, mentoring, and relocation.

The diversity training initiative began with top-level managers, who attended a three-day workshop discussing attitudes and stereotypes that impair communication with a diverse work force. Through role playing, group exercises, and written inventories, workshop participants were helped to understand themselves and their assumptions and biases more thoroughly, to develop skills for overcoming those stereotypes, and to communicate more effectively with others. Ultimately, diversity training was provided for all levels of the organization. The training program included a videotaped instructional presentation, question-and-answer sessions, reviews of organizational policies, and occasional role playing (Rice, 1994). Post-training surveys found that participants were highly satisfied with the quality of the training and optimistic about the organization's ongoing commitment to diversity.

The experience of GE Silicones is typical of many organizations. Realizing that the composition of today's work force has changed dramatically, companies are working to involve employees in developing ways to manage more effectively. Rather than focusing entirely on past practices and written procedures, these organizations seek to identify the needs of their employees and then to adapt their practices accordingly (Walton, 1994).

The Prudential Insurance Company, for example, surveyed its African-American workers in 1988 to determine why so many were leaving the company. The firm discovered that these individuals felt management was insensitive to diversity issues—a feeling shared by the company's female, Asian-American, and other minority employees, as Prudential later discovered. In response, the company initiated a policy of holding all managers accountable for improving diversity, formed diversity councils to monitor the effectiveness of diversity efforts, and required all senior-level managers to submit plans outlining how they would address diversity issues (Caudron, 1993).

Similarly, Hewlett-Packard found in 1988 that its minority employees had more negative attitudes than the rest of the employee population toward company pay and promotional practices. As a result, it too instituted new training, communication, accountability, and developmental programs (Caudron, 1993).

Ultimately, the key to managing diversity effectively is to value rather than suppress differences and to develop skills in listening and adapting to others (Thomas, 1991). Realizing, for example, that some cultures (such as Asian, Hispanic, Native American, or African-American) place great value on body language and other nonverbal cues, whereas others (such as Northern European, Swiss, or Anglo-American male) focus more on verbal behavior can help individuals to adapt their behavior accordingly (Kennedy & Everest, 1991). As the work force becomes increasingly diverse, such knowledge and communication skills will take on added importance.

One of the problems concerning many organizations' recent efforts to teach their employees about cultural diversity is that learning about other cultures is in many ways a lifelong process. It can be difficult, if not impossible, to alter individuals' attitudes and behaviors by exposing them to educational videos or one-shot training and development workshops (Murray, 1993).

In the section that follows we will examine some important research on the U.S. educational system and especially on interaction patterns in the classroom. The new IBM recruit fresh from an MBA program does not arrive at the firm a blank slate. All employees come into their business and professional lives carrying considerable "baggage." They bring not just what they have learned about accounting, finance, computers, or advertising, but also what they have learned about themselves, their fellow human beings, and those who occupy positions of authority. We believe that formal education, especially the early years of schooling, leaves an indelible imprint on the feelings, values, aspirations, and attitudes of each human being. Those who are treated with respect by teachers and peers will likely bring high self-esteem to their professional lives. However, those less fortunate, who have been made to feel inadequate, alienated, or marginalized, may bring defensiveness, low self-esteem, and self-defeating expectations to their jobs. *If* the business and professional world is to strive to create an equitable environment for all, at every level of the hierarchy, it must first grapple with the realization that people's past experiences have indeed been diverse. One way of seeking approaches to *affirming diversity* in the work force, then, is to examine the educational system. There we will find evidence of problems. At the same time, we may discern ways, largely through multicultural education, to teach individuals to understand, respect, and work creatively and constructively with cultural differences.

The Educational System: A Foundational Organizational Experience

In the foreword to Sonia Nieto's book, *Affirming Diversity: The Sociopolitical Context of Multicultural Education*, Jim Cummins of the Ontario Institute for Studies in Education pointed out that **multicultural education** entails

> . . . a direct challenge to the societal power structure that has historically subordinated certain groups and rationalized the educational failure of children from these groups as being the result of inherent deficiencies. Multicultural education as conceptualized here challenges all educators to make the schools a force for social justice in our society (xviii).

To realize this kind of educational experience, schools, as organizations that reflect society in general, must grapple with the persistence of discrimination. Discrimination, including sexism, racism, classism, and ethnocentrism, has a long history in our schools (Weinberg, 1977). Each of these forms of discrimination is based on the perception that one ethnic group, class, gender, or language is superior to all others. In the United States, the norm generally used to measure all others is European American, upper-middle class, English-speaking, and male. Based on perceptions of superiority, discrimination is part of the structure of schools, the curriculum, the education most teachers receive, and the interactions among teachers, students, and the community. As Nieto wrote:

> Overt expressions of racism [and other forms of discrimination] may be less frequent in the contemporary classroom than in the past. Nonetheless, no matter how infrequent, subtle, or unintentional, the effects of discriminatory attitudes and behaviors are always negative (p. 21).

Discrimination manifests itself in a variety of ways. For instance, according to *Barriers to Excellence: Our Children at Risk,* a 1985 report issued by the National Coalition of Advocates for Students, African-American children are three times more likely than European-American children to be placed in classes for the educable mentally retarded and only one-half as likely to be in classes for the gifted. Moreover, Latino students drop out of school at a rate higher than any other major group; in some places, that rate is as high as 80 percent.

School structures are in part to blame. In regard to gender, for instance, Shakeshaft (1986) argued that schools are organized to best meet the needs of white male students. Both policy and instruction are based on what is most effective for *their* needs, not the needs of either females or students of color. Shakeshaft pointed out that curricula follow the developmental level of males more closely than that of females and that instructional styles are largely geared toward competition as a preferred style of learning—even though it is far from the best learning environment for either females or most students of color. Commenting on gender, Treichler and Kramarae (1983) pointed out that "the general orientation among women is interactional, relational, participatory, and collaborative" (p. 120). Shakeshaft noted that high-achieving females receive the least attention of all from their teachers. Boys, in general, get more attention, both positive and negative, than girls do (Sadkar & Sadkar, 1984).

In their widely quoted paper "The Classroom Climate: A Chilly One for Women," Hall and Sandler (1982) summarized a large body of research that demonstrates significant differences in the way faculty treat male and female students respectively. For example, teachers ask males higher-order questions; make eye contact more often with boys than with girls; focus more on males' intellectual contributions and more on females' other attributes, such as neatness or good behavior; and generally pay less attention to girls. Girls, however, are not alone in being ignored or marginalized.

Ortiz (1988) found that teachers tended to avoid interaction with their Hispanic students, including eye contact and physical contact. A number of studies have documented that teachers tend to pay more attention to their white students than to their students of color (Jackson & Cosca, 1974;

McDermott, 1977). Teachers praise their white students more, direct more questions specifically to them, have higher expectations for their performance, and offer them more explicit encouragement.

The Power of Expectations

The impact of teacher expectations is critically important. As early as 1948, Merton coined the term *self-fulfilling prophecy* to suggest that students perform as teachers expect them to. Students' performance is based on subtle and sometimes not so subtle messages from teachers about their worth, intelligence, and abilities. In 1968, a controversial study by Rosenthal and Jacobson dramatized the importance of teacher expectations. Several classes of children were given a nonverbal intelligence test, which was said to measure the potential for intellectual growth. A random group of students was then selected by the researchers as "intellectual bloomers," and their names were given to their teachers. Although their test scores had nothing to do with their actual potential, the teachers were told that they should be alert for signs of intellectual growth in these children. Overall, these children, especially those in the lower grades, showed considerably greater gains in IQ during the following school year than did other students who were actually comparable in intelligence. They were also rated by their teachers as more interesting, more curious, happier, and more likely to succeed later in life (Rosenthal & Jacobson, 1968). Obviously, the ethics of this kind of research are highly questionable. Nevertheless, the results point to the power of teachers' expectations to influence student performance and growth.

What are teachers' expectations based on? Some scholars point to gender, race, or class. Based on a review of relevant research, Persell (1977) concluded that if race is not present as an issue (as in Rist's 1974 study that looked only at African-American students), then teachers' expectations are often based on social class. She found that expectations for poor children were lower than those for middle-class children, even when their respective IQ and other achievement scores were similar. Expectations for students in working-class schools are indeed minimal. One teacher in such a school was reportedly told by his principal, "Just do your best. If they learn to add and subtract, that's a bonus. If not, don't worry about it" (Anyon, 1980, p. 7). Teachers' assumptions that their students are "dumb" translate into an impetus for providing low-level work in the form of elementary facts, simple drills, and rote memorization.

Nieto (1992) was quick to point out that teachers' expectations are only one part of the problem. What influences students' ability to succeed is, more accurately, "a whole constellation of attitudes, behaviors, and structures" (p. 31). Moreover, teachers' expectations mirror those of the larger society. Societal expectations have an immense impact on student performance. For example, newly arrived Puerto Ricans and Mexican Americans tend to do better in school and have higher self-esteem than do those who were born in the United

States (Prewitt-Diaz, 1983). These students' self-esteem and lack of school success stem not from their ethnicity but rather from their interaction with U.S. society, which often scorns or devalues them (Matute-Bianchi, 1986).

Other problems have surfaced in such areas as testing and the curriculum. For instance, textbooks often serve to reinforce the dominance of the European-American perspective and to sustain stereotypes of any group perceived to be outside the mainstream. Although inequities are not as pronounced as they once were, a recent study by Sleeter and Grant (1991) reported the following:

- Whites still consistently dominate textbooks, although the margin of dominance varies.

- Whites still receive the most attention and dominate the story line and lists of accomplishments in most textbooks.

- Women and people of color are shown in a much more limited range of roles than are white males.

- Textbooks contain very little about contemporary race relations or the issues that concern women and people of color.

- Textbooks continue to convey an image of harmony among different groups and contentment with the status quo.

All in all, they found that although textbooks now include more women and people of color, they continue to legitimize the status of white males.

Interaction Patterns in the Classroom

Still other problems deal with pedagogy, in particular how teachers teach and generally interact with students. Britzman (1986) pointed to certain myths, widely held by teachers, that serve to perpetuate authoritarian practices in the schools (for example, the teacher as expert, self-made, and all-powerful in the classroom). Students are often profoundly uninvolved in their own learning since pedagogy is conceptualized as a one-way street. It is, as Freire (1970) once put it, the "banking" education, a process by which teachers "deposit" knowledge into students, who are seen as empty receptacles—an education for powerlessness.

Teachers are also sometimes woefully ignorant of differences in students' learning styles. In their research with children of various cultural backgrounds, Ramirez and Castaneda (1974) found that European-American students tended to be more field-independent learners—learning best in situations that emphasize analytic tasks and with materials void of a social context. By contrast, Mexican-American, American Indian, and African-American students tended to be more field-dependent or sensitive—learning best in highly social settings that involve cooperative work with others.

Finally, cultural influences are found in interactional or communication styles. For instance, Williams's ethnographic work (1981) in an inner-city school suggested that African-American students are skillful at manipulating the dynamics of their classrooms. Some teachers perceive this as delinquent behavior. However, other teachers found creative ways of using these skills in front-of-the-class performances related to instructional goals. Another issue has to do with the expectations of teachers as they ask students questions. Tharp (1989) explained how teachers' expectations of short "wait times" tend to be disadvantageous to American Indian students, who generally take longer to respond to teachers' questions because their culture tends to emphasize deliberate thought. Their cultural expectation is that one can make an informed and appropriate choice only when one has considered all the possible ramifications and implications of a decision. Thus, an American Indian student is unlikely to come forth with a quick response.

Other misunderstandings between teachers and students can grow from nonverbal behaviors. For instance, in Alaskan Native American cultures, raised eyebrows are often used to signify "yes," and a wrinkled nose means "no." Tensions have developed in classrooms where outside teachers have interacted with these students; the teachers interpreted these gestures as rude and preferred verbal responses to their questions (Nieto, 1992).

Still another dimension of cultural differences has to do with "rhythm." For example, African-American mothers and their children often use a "contest" style of speech that approximates the call and response patterns found in black music. Researchers have found that teachers using such rhythms in classrooms with African-American students often experience positive results (Tharp, 1989). Tharp's extensive review of culturally compatible education concluded that when schools change and are more attuned to children's cultures, the children's academic achievement invariably improves.

Although we might provide many more examples of the environments in which children of diverse cultural backgrounds are educated, the main points are rather straightforward. First, an appreciation of cultural diversity and knowledge of diverse cultures should grow from the individual's earliest organizational experiences in the classroom. Second, as leaders and classroom facilitators, teachers play a critical role in influencing students' perceptions of themselves and of one another. Teachers who understand and appreciate cultural diversity are more likely to establish learning environments that give every student a genuine chance to grow socially, emotionally, and intellectually. Finally, if students can take from their schooling lifelong lessons of mutual respect, tolerance for diverse styles of learning and interacting, and appreciation for diversity, the foundation for a fully functional, multicultural work force will exist. Until then, organizations will need to make up for the ignorance and biases that so many bring to their professional lives in order to cope with an increasingly culturally diverse work force. If McGregor's dream of "unlocking human potential" and empowering every employee is to be realized, understanding and managing diversity, with all of its complexities, is essential.

At the end of the chapter, we will examine the ways in which modern technology can help us manage diversity. In the next section, however, we turn our attention to the specific subject of gender, particularly leadership and communication in relation to gender.

Women in Positions of Leadership

Twenty-five years ago, only 5 percent of all management positions, at any level, were occupied by women. Today, the figure is closer to 37 percent (Spaid, 1993). Business journals regularly carry articles about women, who are increasingly moving into the ranks of corporate leadership (Konrad, 1990). In fact, recent years have witnessed substantial growth in leadership positions for women and minorities in general. Figure 9.1 summarizes management growth statistics for 1993. However, many writers have warned of obstacles and urge caution in viewing the kinds of statistics we have just quoted (Fierman, 1990).

The Glass Ceiling

First, the **glass ceiling** is very much intact. That is, there are organizational barriers that keep women from advancing, not because of an inability to

FIGURE 9.1

Women and Minorities in Management Positions

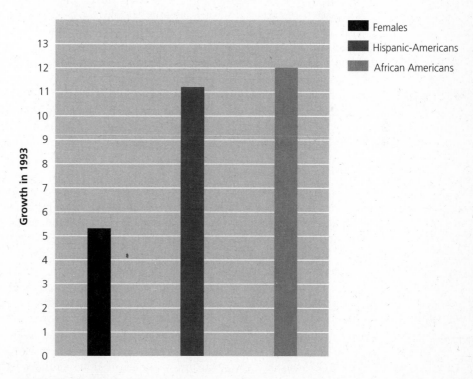

SOURCE: Data from Smith, 1994.

succeed at executive management but simply because they are women (Morrison, White, Van Velsor, & the Center for Creative Leadership, 1987). As we write this book, women are underrepresented in the higher ranks of management. Specifically, only 3 percent of top executive positions in U.S. businesses are held by women (Saltzman, 1991). The vast majority of women in positions of leadership are middle-level managers and lower-level supervisors. Moreover, women are dramatically underrepresented—indeed, almost invisible—in management positions of *any* kind in major corporations (Spaid, 1993). Less than 2 to 3 percent of Fortune 500 managers at any level are female. In some major organizations, the figures are even more dismal. Only 500 of 6,700 managers at IBM are women, and at AT&T, 26 of the top 880 executives are women (Northcraft & Neale, 1994).

While it may be difficult to prove that the glass ceiling exists, some forms of discrimination are clearly identifiable. Women still earn significantly less, (only 71 percent of men's salaries for comparable positions). Yet studies of managerial women (as well as studies of women in diverse group and organizational contexts) have confirmed that women do *not* have poorer skills, abilities, or motivations than their male counterparts. In fact, a recent survey of 25,000 workers in fifteen major U.S. corporations found that before children are born, women work an average of 44 hours per week at their jobs and men work an average of 41 hours per week. After children are born, women still average 44 hours per week, but the average time a male spends at the office increases to 47 hours per week (Pennar, 1991).

Nevertheless, the popular belief persists that women typically earn less than men because they leave the work force for family reasons; prefer styles of interacting, communicating, and leading that are suited to lower levels of management; select careers in lower-paying industries; or are less committed to their positions and their companies. To investigate these beliefs, Linda Stroh, Jeanne Brett, and Anne Reilly (1993) compared male and female managers and professionals who were equal in education, had shown commitment to their organization by having relocated within the previous two years at the company's request, were as economically powerful in their families (that is, earned more money than their spouses), and were as often employed in higher-paying industries. With this sample of women, we might expect that there would be no differences in earnings between men and women doing comparable work. Yet the results provided clear evidence that there was still a significant difference (11 percent) between the average salaries of women and men in this sample. Even these women were making only 89 percent of what their male counterparts earned.

The glass ceiling can be insidious primarily because it is not obvious. Managers and organizations may not even be aware that they are erecting and maintaining barriers for women and other minorities. In a study commissioned by the U.S. Department of Labor in 1990, nine Fortune 500 companies were randomly selected for review of their personnel policies and practices, specifically regarding promotion. The results were disturbing but not unexpected. While none of these nine companies had ever been cited for discrimination, a number of them failed to show good-faith efforts in meeting affirmative action requirements. Several findings applied to all the companies:

1. There was a point beyond which women and minorities did not advance.
2. Men of color plateaued at lower levels of the work force then women.
3. Monitoring for equal access and opportunity, especially as managers moved up the corporate ladder to senior levels, was almost never considered a corporate responsibility in terms of planning for developmental programs and policies.
4. Appraisal and total compensation systems that determine salaries, bonuses, and incentives for employees were not monitored. This situation is especially problematic, because research suggests that raters, especially when they are white, evaluate the job performance of African Americans less favorably than that of whites (Greenhouse, Parasuraman, & Wormley, 1990).

In general, 79 percent of Fortune 500 CEOs agreed that there were identifiable barriers preventing women from getting to the top.

Because of the underrepresentation of women in the upper ranks of management, women have had to face the challenge of trying to function effectively as "tokens." Harvard sociologist Rosabeth Moss Kanter has argued that those who are tokens (or in a distinct minority) in any group or organization will be subjected to particular pressures. Tokens stand out, are more carefully scrutinized, and are more likely to be stereotyped than are those in the majority (Kanter, 1977). In some organizations the underrepresentation of women has been linked with such problems as sexual harassment (see the section on sexual harassment later in this chapter).

As we try to understand the reasons women are underrepresented in management positions (especially at the highest levels of management), let us examine some of the research on the way in which women and men are perceived by others and communicate and interact with one other. Much of this research has taken place in small groups.

Leadership in Groups: Is Gender Relevant?

Over the past twenty years *some researchers have reported that men are more likely than women to emerge as leaders* in diverse communication settings involving group interaction. Men frequently receive higher group contribution and influence ratings and are more likely to be liked and sought after as future group partners than are their female counterparts (Andrews, 1992; Wolman & Frank, 1975). In one study, for instance, impartial observers rated men and women as similar in their interaction styles, but those participating in the groups rated the males more independent, rational, confident, and influential than the females, and they viewed males as leaders more often than they did females (Nemeth, Endicott, & Wachtler, 1976).

Some have argued that, at least historically, *women may have contributed to what appears to be a sex stereotype of female subordination* by demonstrating some reluctance to assume leadership positions. For instance, Megargee (1969) found that women were reluctant to take on leadership roles, even when they were paired with men who pretested low in dominance. Webber (1976) and Mamola (1979) reported similar findings. Of course, to some extent much of this literature must be considered in light of how leadership is most appropriately defined. For instance, some scholars have argued that men are more likely to engage in task-oriented acts in groups, whereas women are more inclined to perform socioemotional roles; for an interesting review of this controversy, see Anderson and Blanchard (1982). Scholars who report these kinds of distinctions have often noted that American social and cultural stereotypes associate the performance of task behaviors (especially initiating structure and direction) with the idea of being the group's leader (Bartol & Butterfield, 1976; Instone, Major, & Bunker, 1983). So, *if* it is true that women engage in fewer task behaviors than men, at least in U.S. culture, they would be less likely to be regarded as leaders.

Stereotypical perceptions of gender differences in speech may also plague women's attempts to ascend to leadership positions. Kramarae (1981) has pointed out that although women are perceived as speaking more "properly" than men, such speech is often unrelated to the possession of power (consider the case of female schoolteachers and secretaries). Kramarae's research on speech stereotypes suggests that women are perceived "to have control over grammatical forms and to desire non-combative interaction, but men are perceived to have control in a more basic sense over the speech situation" (p. 92). In general, stereotypic features of women's speech have long been viewed as "powerless"—including the use of tag questions and disclaimers. Table 9.1 provides examples of powerless speech.

In spite of the perceived differences noted above, *many argue that males and females are capable of performing equally effectively in leadership positions.* Some cite instances in which females are viewed as having outperformed males in leadership roles. For instance, in a study conducted at a human relations training conference, researchers noted that male participants who worked with female consultants reported higher levels of emotion, involvement, and learning and a greater ability to generalize what they had learned to other settings than did those who worked with male consultants (Correa et al., 1988). Goktepe and Schneier (1988) noted no significant differences between the effectiveness evaluations of male and female leaders; and Kushell and Newton (1986) reported that although subjects were more satisfied in democratically led groups, leader gender did not significantly affect their satisfaction with the group experience. Other factors, like the group's successful task completion, have also been acknowledged as critical determinants of group member satisfaction (Jurma & Wright, 1990).

Of course, *some research has emphasized the important distinction between biological sex and psychological gender,* advancing the argument that it is the

TABLE 9.1

Examples of
Powerless
Versus
Powerful
Speech

POWERLESS	POWERFUL
"Well, I'm no expert in this area, but I still think we ought to. . . ."	"I think we ought to do this."
"This seems like it would be a pretty good idea."	"This is a good idea."
"We ought to adopt that plan, don't you think?"	"We ought to adopt that plan."
"I kind of like that approach."	"I like that approach."
"I've never worked in that kind of organization, but it seems to me that we should go ahead and do it."	"We should go ahead and do it."
"These figures look excellent, right?"	"These figures look excellent!"
"Sounds good to me, but what do all of you think?"	"Sounds good to me!"
"Well, maybe we should consider this kind of option."	"We should consider this kind of option."

androgynous individual (a person possessing strengths in both the traditional masculine and the traditional feminine communication and behavioral categories) who is best suited for leadership. Hans and Eisenberg (1985) found, for instance, that androgynous persons were more willing than others to accommodate other group members' preferences. More important, androgynous individuals were more likely to express a preference for the leadership role; and when in the minority, they were more likely than stereotyped subjects (those who rate themselves either very traditionally feminine or very traditionally masculine) to be viewed by their peers as leaders. Finally, another study (Cann & Siegfried, 1987) reported subjects' overwhelming preference for human attributes not particularly associated with either gender (such as reliability, truthfulness, and efficiency) when rating both the kind of person they would like to work for and the kind of person they would hire to supervise others. However, when the same subjects were asked to indicate whether they would prefer a male or a female supervisor, 82 percent selected a male. These findings suggest that individuals are attempting to be fair-minded in choosing leaders but that they still prefer having males to supervise them.

As with any aspect of cultural diversity, many people, at least initially, believe that they prefer to work in familiar situations. Most have been supervised by males, and they continue to visualize themselves working in a male-dominated work environment. However, as work force demographics change and as people encounter more females and minorities in management positions, their attitudes, too, can begin to change. Evidence of this change was provided by the results of two surveys published in the *Harvard Business Review*. In 1965 the journal surveyed managers regarding their attitudes toward female managers. Nearly half (41 percent) were unfavorable, and another 6 percent were strongly opposed. Those most opposed were younger men who saw women as competitors; those least opposed were older men and men who had been supervisors or colleagues of female managers. Twenty years later, in 1985, the journal repeated the survey. This time only 5 percent of male executives viewed female managers unfavorably, and none was strongly opposed. In addition, the percentage who felt that businesspersons would never fully accept women had dropped from 61 percent to 20 percent (Bowman, Worthy, & Greyser, 1965; Sutton & Moore, 1985).

Communication Differences Between Men and Women?

When Robin Lakoff published her controversial work *Language and Women's Place* (1975) twenty years ago, it was widely believed that many, many communication differences existed between females and males, in both verbal and nonverbal behavior. For instance, women, according to Lakoff, asked more questions and used more tag questions and disclaimers than men. A few years later, Hennig and Jardim's best-selling book *The Managerial Woman* (1977) described women as being far less goal-oriented than men. These authors contended that most women were ten to fifteen years behind men of their age in career planning and goal setting.

Since then, much subsequent *research has revealed far greater gender-related similarities than differences in communication*. For instance, the research on tag questions and disclaimers remains mixed and inconsistent, with some studies reporting greater use by males, others reporting greater use by females, and many reporting no significant differences. Perhaps more important than the actual expressions used is whether they might be evaluated or perceived differently by others, depending upon the gender or status of those using them. A study by one of your authors (in Bradley, 1981) examined how fellow group members reacted to males and females who advanced arguments using varied linguistic and substantive techniques in decision-making groups. Qualifying expressions (like tag questions) were perceived as indicators of uncertainty and nonassertiveness when used by women but were seen as tools of politeness and other-directedness when used by men. In other words, the woman who said, "This study seems pretty conclusive. We really ought to do something about this problem, don't you think?" was seen as unsure of the appropriate course of action. The man who said exactly the same thing was regarded as showing concern for the views of others! If they persist, these differences in perception may prove problematic for women.

Other studies show men and women communicating and behaving similarly in some ways while maintaining differences in other areas. Sorcinelli and Andrews (1987) found, for instance, that female and male faculty members were equally capable of articulating appropriate career goals—both long- and short-term. However, differences persisted in the ways males and females talked about their goals. Women often pointed to barriers. One said, "I think about where I want to be, but I don't dwell on it. It's a way to set yourself up for disappointment. I don't think the system is set up for women to move through the usual channels." In striking contrast, a male faculty member said, "I've made all the right choices. I wanted to be a full professor and I did what I had to do for that to happen early in my career. My strategy now is to get funding and do even more of the kinds of things that will move me forward." While this particular statement may sound boastful, the overall tone of the interviews with dozens of faculty suggested that men simply were more confident that they would achieve the goals they had set forth. Women expressed a greater need to remain flexible and a far greater tendency to wonder about what the future might hold. About 30 percent of the male sample expressed some concerns about the future, whereas nearly 60 percent of the females expressed such uncertainties. In contrast to past research, women and men were equally realistic about the priorities and values of the organization, and both understood what was required to succeed in their organizational environment. However, women were less certain than men (40 percent uncertainty versus 15 percent uncertainty) that they would choose an academic career if they had it to do over again. Some, it seemed, had chosen their career due to limited options available to them at the time. One woman said, "I was conditioned (by my parents) to be a teacher. Women taught." Both men and women considered mentors to have played a significant role in shaping their expectations and behaviors during their years in graduate school. However, women were less likely than men to have turned to their professors for mentoring relationships.

Out of the extensive list of communication differences between the sexes that were widely reported over twenty years ago, only a few are consistently supported by current research. For instance, males speak more frequently and, once they get the floor, they tend to hold it for longer than women do (Eakins & Eakins, 1978). In addition, men tend to interrupt more, and they are especially inclined to interrupt women (Borisoff & Merrill, 1992). Some have argued that behavior such as interrupting others is more likely associated with the power of the individual occupying the position than with gender (Bradac & Mulac, 1984). Thus, since males are more likely to be in powerful positions, they are more likely (due to their role) to interrupt others—but the behavior should be attributed to their authority and power rather than to their gender. However, one study looked at individuals of equal power and reported relatively few interruptions when individuals were paired with those of the same sex. But, when men were paired with women, 96 percent of the recorded interruptions involved men interrupting women (see Pearson,

Turner, & Todd-Mancillas, 1991). Another study found that patients were more likely to interrupt a female than a male doctor. Psychologists have pointed out that fathers are more likely than mothers to interrupt their children, and both parents are more likely to interrupt their daughters than their sons.

Nonverbal differences also exist. In our culture, men are more likely than women to occupy large spaces by sprawling, stretching out their legs and arms; women tend to cross their legs and fold their arms and generally to occupy less space. These behaviors could be attributed to socialization and may be related to sex-specific attire and the sorts of gestures and movements either encouraged or impeded by wearing dresses or skirts as opposed to pants. Finally, women tend to smile more than men, and the smiles of women appear to be open to wide interpretation. Men seem to smile mostly when they are happy or pleased. Women, however, may smile as much when they are insecure, uncertain of what to do or say, or even when they are hostile as when they are happy. When small children are given photos of smiling men, they describe them with "happy/friendly" adjectives, but they describe similar photographs of smiling women as "hard to tell, can't say, or maybe happy" (Pearson, Turner, & Todd-Mancillas, 1991). Even children have learned that women's smiles may mean many different things.

Finally, differences between women and men have been exaggerated in much literature of the past. Reported differences may be attributable to an array of variables. Our sense of role-appropriate behavior, our expectations for one another, and our perceptions of others' potential and performance are surely influenced by what we absorb of societal beliefs about women and men during our formative years in the family and in the classroom. Thus, the seeds of discrimination are sown long before we graduate from college and acquire our first job. If we can seek ways to create a society that truly values diversity, that deflates stereotypes, and that socializes young people to think in terms of the value of human attributes regardless of race or gender or ethnicity, then we will discover that all individuals are potentially equally capable of functioning effectively in their professional lives. Creating an organizational environment where no one is placed in a token position at any level will move us in the direction of realizing empowerment for all.

Special Issues for Organizations: Discrimination and Sexual Harassment

Even when differences do exist, whether at the individual or the group level, they can function as sources of strength and creativity. Diversity in the work force provides the opportunity—and necessity—for everyone to grow and change. One goal of every organization should be to create a work environment in which every employee has a chance of performing at her or his maximum potential. However, some problems, such as discrimination and worker harassment, have thwarted this goal for many organizations.

Discrimination

Throughout this book we have stressed the importance of creating empowering organizational environments. We have asserted that communication plays a key role in establishing and maintaining such environments. In an earlier section, we noted the pervasive presence of **discrimination** in educational organizations. In other kinds of organizational contexts, discrimination is also a reality. An employer who asks some job candidates different questions from those she or he asks other candidates is communicating in a discriminatory manner. If an employer establishes evaluation and promotion policies with criteria so ambiguous that no one really understands the rules by which the "game" is being played, that employer is creating conditions where appraisal decisions may be made and communicated in ways that are poorly understood, resented, or resisted. Employers may simply fail to communicate with some employees, talk to them in demeaning ways, or say one thing officially and verbally and another different and often contradictory thing unofficially and nonverbally. Thus, communication often plays a major role in influencing the way employees feel about their organizational lives, their relationships with others, and their chances for succeeding on the job.

Legislation Aimed at Eliminating Discrimination.   In some cases, regulatory agencies have attempted to intervene to control certain organizational procedures and officially communicated policies. For instance, government regulations such as affirmative action policies require equitable procedures in screening, hiring, promoting, and terminating employees (Bergeson, 1991; Shaeffer, 1975; Stewart & Cash, 1994). Legislation in the United States that has made discrimination illegal includes the 1963 Equal Pay Act, which prohibits unequal pay for males and females with equal skills, effort, and responsibility who work under similar working conditions. Discrimination on the basis of color, race, religion, national origin, or sex is strictly forbidden by Title VII of the Civil Rights Act of 1964. Moreover, since 1972, the Equal Employment Opportunity Commission (EEOC) has had the power to take violators to court. In 1973, the Vocational Rehabilitation Act prohibited discrimination against persons with physical or mental handicaps and created the Office of Affirmative Action. Implemented in 1992, the Americans with Disabilities Act requires "reasonable accommodations" in existing structures (and all new structures) for job applicants with disabilities who request them, thus ensuring that a worker's disability is not an inherent barrier to effective job performance. Nevertheless, the problem of discrimination still exists, as evidenced by a recent study reported in the *Wall Street Journal*. Seventy percent of two hundred Fortune 500 recruiters falsely identified at least five of twelve unlawful questions as "safe to ask" in an interview (Woo, 1992).

In addition, the changes that have occurred as a result of legislation have primarily focused on the opportunities for individuals to be *hired* by organizations. While many more women and men of color now find positions in organizations, they subsequently experience (as we noted earlier) considerably more difficulty in advancing to executive management. A federally-funded report recently released by the Federal Glass Ceiling Commission, Washington D.C., reports that:

> African American[s] perceive this [ceiling] as virtually impenetrable . . . They view it not as a glass ceiling but as a *brick wall*. They believe that corporate America considers them a "necessary evil" because of the changing demographics of the marketplace, national and global . . . They believe that their talent, education and experiences are not valued. . . . At the same time, they feel they have no choice but to continue to fight against what they consider unfair and outright racist patterns in corporate advancement" (*Good for Business: Making Use of the Nation's Human Capital,* 1995, p. 69).

Levels of Discrimination.   For the most part, legislative attempts to regulate organizations have centered on the prevention of discrimination. However, organizations must confront two levels of discrimination. *Initial or overt discrimination* occurs at the time one is hired; *covert discrimination* occurs when a company is deciding whom to promote. This latter form of discrimination is the one that managers of the future will have to confront if they are serious in their commitment to a diverse and fully empowered work force.

In the wake of the legislation discussed above, overt discrimination against people of color, women, older workers, and the mentally and physically challenged has often been replaced by the more insidious covert discrimination. For African Americans in corporate America, discrimination make take the form of **colorism** (a predisposition to act in a certain manner because of a person's skin color). While about 15 percent of white Americans may be overtly racist, 60 percent are more or less neutral about African Americans (Jones, 1986). Managers in this group are not overtly racist, but they are the people who for a number of reasons either see discrimination take place and do nothing about it or inhibit the advancement of African-American managers, perhaps to avoid conflict within the organization.

Of course, discrimination can be aimed at many different groups. For instance, discrimination based on age is not uncommon. As the Bureau for National Affairs reported, "Age discrimination actions challenging employer decisions represent the hottest area of employment discrimination litigation today" ("Age Discrimination," 1989). In the bureau's view, the aging of the American work force, combined with employees' increased awareness of their rights under the Age Discrimination in Employment Act of 1967, should lead employers to anticipate being sued "whenever an employment decision—especially a termination decision—[appears] to be adverse to the interests of an older worker" (p. 1109). As we noted earlier in this chapter, some organizations have developed creative ways of dealing with the aging work force, but much work remains.

Discrimination Based on Sexual Orientation   Another form of potential *discrimination* is *based on sexual orientation or sexual lifestyle.* A 1987 Gallup poll revealed that 52 percent of the respondents preferred not to work with gays, 25 percent objected strongly to doing so, and two-thirds thought that gays should never be hired to teach in elementary schools (Kirk & Madsen, 1989). Another Gallup poll conducted in 1989 showed some change in attitudes, but at the same time, incidents of violence against gays rose sharply in some areas (*Newsweek,* 1990). Fitzgerald (1993) argued that homophobia is not just personal but is also institutionalized.

At the national level, heated debates over gays in the military and gay leadership in religious organizations have dramatized these tensions. On one of the authors' home campuses, a recent decision to create a modest advocacy office for gays and lesbians generated much controversy, including vehement protests from some student groups and members of the university's board of trustees—in spite of the fact that comparable offices for women, African Americans, and Latinos had been put in place on the campus some time before, without accompanying controversy. Discrimination against gays can take many forms. Using labels such as "fags," "queers," "fairies," and "dykes" is one. As Fitzgerald (1993) noted, "Such labels express the subordination of gays and lesbians and reinforce their status of 'strangers' in society" (p. 7). Like heterosexuals, gays may also be subjected to sexual harassment, although straight women remain the primary victims.

Homosexuals make up about 10 percent of the U.S. adult population and, regardless of stereotypes, they do not tend to work in certain industries. For example, a survey of over four thousand gay men and lesbians conducted by Overlooked Opinions, a Chicago market research firm, reported that 40 percent more homosexuals are employed in the finance and insurance industries than in the entertainment and arts industries, and that ten times as many homosexuals work in the computer industry as in the fashion industry. There are also more homosexuals working in science and engineering than in social services (Stewart, 1991).

One of the biggest concerns facing gays and lesbians in the workplace is the freedom to be themselves and to communicate honestly about who they are. In the Overlooked Opinions survey, about 67 percent reported that they had witnessed some form of hostility toward gays on the job. For instance, Ann Quenin had been working for a high-tech company for a few months and had received glowing performance reviews. But one day she was called into the boss's office and asked about her volunteer activities for an AIDS organization. Quenin's boss told her that her volunteer work was taking too much of her time and asked her to resign from her job. Quenin is now working for Lotus (the first major company to provide the same insurance and other benefits to homosexual partners that it accords to heterosexual spouses), where she was honored by the company for that same volunteer work (Hammonds, 1991).

The acceptance of gays and lesbians in the workplace is by no means universal. But, as in the case of Lotus, some organizations do actively encourage groups of gays and lesbians in the same way that they encourage other employee-based support groups. Organizations that provide this kind of support include Levi Strauss, AT&T, Boeing, DuPont, Hewlett-Packard, and Xerox. These companies view sexual orientation as simply another form of diversity. In addition, alienating a significant segment of the work force is not a sound strategy for any organization. An environment that is not empowering for everyone is not conducive to productivity in the long run. Moreover, gay students who are graduating and entering the job market are increasingly paying attention to the reputations for tolerance of the companies with which they seek interviews. In some cases, students with sought-after training and experience are actually turning down higher salaries to work for companies that are not homophobic. Companies such as Corning and Xerox are becoming more attractive because of their reputation for openness (Stewart, 1991).

Sexual Harassment

As women have entered the work force in increasing numbers, problems with **sexual harassment** have grown. The U.S. Air Force Academy, for instance, recently publicly acknowledged this problem. Following a February 1993 assault on a female freshman by several male cadets, new complaints led to the court martial and jailing of an instructor and a cadet for sexual misconduct. The academy's superintendent, General Bradley Hosmer, took decisive action after he learned that more than 50 percent of all female cadets said they knew of sexual harassment cases, but only 9 percent of the male cadets said they did (Schmidt, 1994).

Hosmer initiated a counseling system for harassment victims, aggressively examined all complaints, created focus groups of males and females to discuss sexual harassment and leadership ethics, and offered a course on "gender, race, and human dignity." Nevertheless, the academy, a tradition-bound, male-dominated institution that first admitted women only in 1976, faces a tough challenge. Just 13 percent of the current cadets are female, and only 13 percent of the faculty are women. Moreover, the academy lost 25 percent of its freshman women in two of its last three classes. Hosmer believes that female cadets may be leaving the school at higher rates due to the "pressures and tensions" of integrating women into a traditionally male environment (*Bloomington Sunday Herald-Times*, 1994).

Problems associated with sexual harassment received considerable attention in late 1991 when Clarence Thomas was accused of sexual harassment during hearings to confirm his appointment as a Supreme Court justice. Sexual harassment is a fact in the U.S. workplace. According to a *Newsweek* poll, 21 percent of women surveyed indicated they had been harassed at work, and 42 percent of working women knew someone who had been harassed. Fifty-three percent of the 1,300 members of the National Association for Female Executives reported that they had been sexually harassed or knew someone who had been sexually harassed (Kantrowitz, 1991). The situation is worse in male-dominated organizations. A Department of Defense study conducted in 1990 found that 64 percent of military women had faced abuse ranging from obscene jokes to outright assault (Northcraft & Neale, 1994).

The question of what exactly constitutes harassment has remained elusive. In its most obvious form, sexual harassment occurs when a person's supervisor requests sexual favors under the threat of denying promotion or pay increases, or even under the threat of termination. But this represents a narrow definition, describing only the most stereotypic cases.

In 1980, the EEOC issued guidelines that defined harassment as occurring when the following conditions apply:

1. Submission to the sexual conduct is made either implicitly or explicitly a term or condition of employment.

2. Employment decisions affecting the recipient are made on the basis of the recipient's acceptance or rejection of the sexual conduct.

3. The conduct has the purpose or effect of reasonably interfering with an individual's work performance or creating an intimidating, hostile, or offensive working environment (*Federal Register*, 1980).

This rather broad definition makes it clear that much sexual harassment is fairly subtle. It might, for instance, include nonverbal behaviors such as staring or leering, or verbal behaviors, such as sexual joking or using sexist language (e.g., referring to women as "girls"), or making sexist comments like "women just can't handle the pressure."

Apart from legal definitions of harassment, some researchers have studied the ways in which women themselves define harassment. One study found that while nearly 80 percent of women considered sexual propositions, touching, grabbing, and brushing as harassment, only 50 percent thought that sexual remarks and suggestive gestures were sexually harassing. Most believed that flirting and staring were the most frequent form of female-directed attention, but they did not, for the most part, view such behaviors as harassment (Powell, 1983). Moreover, there appear to be differences between the perceptions of men and women (see Figure 9.2). A *Harvard Business Review* survey reported that 24 percent of the women surveyed believed that a man giving a female worker a visual appraisal was harassment, while only 8 percent of men thought so (cited in Deutschman, 1991). While the definition of sexual harassment may vary from one individual to another, organizations must be increasingly aware that from a legal perspective, what constitutes harassing behavior is up to the person who feels harassed or threatened.

Although we have largely discussed the adverse effects of sexual harassment on women, it is important to recognize that the EEOC guidelines apply

FIGURE 9.2

**Female
Perceptions
of Sexually
Harassing
Behaviors**

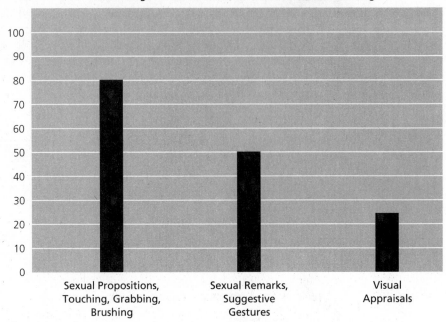

Percentage of Women Who View Behaviors as Harassing

SOURCE: Data from Deutschman, 1991.

equally to women and men. An early U.N. survey found that 50 percent of females and 31 percent of males had experienced some form of sexual harassment (Peterson & Massengill, 1982). An article in the *Wall Street Journal*
(1986) notes that sexual harassment can involve gay workers harassing others,
women harassing men, subordinates harassing managers, and outside vendors
harassing customers.

The odds are that sexual harassment is most likely to arise in the context
of an unequal power relationship (manager harassing subordinate; teacher harassing student). Moreover, certain types of individuals seem more likely to be
the victims of sexual harassment. For instance, Campbell (1986) pointed out
that in academic settings, the female students most likely to be harassed are
those who have either chosen a nontraditional field or do not conform to the
stereotypical feminine model (for instance, those who are assertive and independent and who actively engage in intellectual discussions with their male instructors). Of those men who report harassment, the majority are young
homosexuals, followed by an even smaller percentage of heterosexual males—
usually younger and from a lower socioeconomic background than their male
or female harasser.

The financial and human costs of sexual harassment can be great.
Financial costs include fines and other legal settlements, which can be sub-

stantial. Moreover, if the employer is a contractor with the federal government, it may lose its federal contracts. The human costs of sexual harassment include the victims' humiliation, embarrassment, helplessness, and anger (Dolecheck & Dolecheck, 1983). In many cases, victims live with these feelings rather than confront the offender for fear of retaliation. Several studies report that some victims eventually suffer from serious psychological problems requiring medical attention because of the harassment (Renick, 1980). More commonly, however, these emotional problems lead to increased absenteeism, reduced efficiency, and resignations (Dolecheck & Dolecheck, 1983). Thus, even in small businesses where EEOC guidelines are not binding (those with fewer than fifteen employees), employers should still be concerned about lowered morale and productivity. In many instances of harassment, both the victim and the perpetrator ultimately suffer. While the victim suffers throughout the harassment, the perpetrator may eventually be reprimanded, humiliated, demoted, or fired.

The EEOC clearly states that *proactive communication* aimed at preventing sexual harassment is the preferred method for eliminating such harassment. The commission offers these specific suggestions to employers:

1. Affirmatively raise the subject of sexual harassment.
2. Express strong disapproval.
3. Develop an appropriate sanction.
4. Inform employees of their right to raise the issue of harassment under Title VII and how to raise it.
5. Develop methods to sensitize all concerned (Peterson & Massengill, 1982).

Fortunately, many organizations have taken steps to avoid incidences of sexual harassment. While some efforts are comparatively minor (for example, including sexual harassment as a topic in supervisory training sessions), some firms have made major advances in addressing the problem. For example, DuPont recently invested $500,000 to develop a program designed to teach employees how to avert sexual harassment, rape, and other safety risks. In 1988, the company began offering its employees a four-hour workshop on harassment called "A Matter of Respect." Each workshop is led by specially trained teams of men and women, teams recruited from all areas of the company, not just from human relations. Small groups—always a balanced mix of men and women—watch videos portraying realistic incidents and then discuss appropriate responses. One workshop director pointed out that since the workshops began, the group leaders have heard about several subtle situations involving harassment—situations that the victims had little idea could be improved in any way (Deutschman, 1991). DuPont also runs a 24-hour hotline that offers advice on personal security and sexual harassment. Callers need not identify themselves, calling does not constitute bringing charges, and confidentiality is assured. Other organizations, like AT&T and Honeywell, have also made significant strides in creating effective sexual harassment programs and ensuring immediate investigation of any charges.

Some have argued that sexual harassment is less likely to occur in stable organizations where employees feel some sense of empowerment, loyalty to the organization, and respect for one another. In stable organizations, for instance, employees have the perception that they will be working together for a long time. Thus, how they relate to one another is likely to have long-term consequences. However, restructuring, downsizing, periods of recession, and the increased use of part-time employees are all factors conspiring to create environments that are less stable and therefore potentially more conducive to harassment.

Creating an Organizational Climate for Balancing Personal and Professional Lives

Having a clear policy statement on sexual or worker harassment is one step that every organization must take. However, as the composition of the work force and the nature of work change, additional steps are needed. Jamieson and O'Mara (1991) have argued that today's work force has embraced a set of values strikingly different from those held by workers of earlier generations. The pursuit of money and unwavering loyalty to the organization no longer form the heart of the contemporary value system. Instead, they have been replaced by such values as feelings of accomplishment, being treated with respect and dignity, involvement and pride in meaningful work, financial security (as opposed to wealth), and living a balanced life of good quality with opportunities for self-development and pursuing a healthy lifestyle. Any manager who embraces theories of empowerment through human resources management is likely to be sympathetic to seeking ways for employees to realize these kinds of goals.

For working mothers and fathers (or those who may be caregivers givers to the elderly), several organizational programs and policies can provide support. Rodgers and Rodgers (1989) argued that three broad areas require attention:

1. Dependent care, including infants, children, adolescents, and the elderly.
2. Greater flexibility in the organization, hours, and location of work, and creation of career paths that allow for family responsibility as well as professional ambition.
3. Validation of family issues as an organizational concern by means of company statements and manager training (p. 123).

Dependent Care

Among the options organizations might pursue with regard to *dependent care* are help in finding existing child care and efforts to increase the supply of care in the community (including care for sick children), financial assistance for child care, especially for entry-level and lower-level employees, involvement with schools and other community organizations to promote programs for school-age children whose parents work, and support for child-care centers in locations convenient to company employees. Although providing this kind of assistance can be expensive, some companies believe it is well worth the cost. For instance, SAS Institute, Inc., a North Carolina software company, provides child care at an on-site center at no cost to employees. The company, which reports that its turnover rates are less than half the industry average, feels that the center's extra expense is justified because it decreases the extremely high cost of training new workers (*National Report on Work and Family*, 1989).

Flexible Work Arrangements

Another issue has to do with *flexible work arrangements*. When employees have responsibilities for others, they frequently work far more than the traditional 40-hour work week. A study of two high-tech companies in New England showed that the average working mother logs in a total work week of 84 hours between her home and job, compared with 72 hours for male parents, and about 50 hours for married men and women with no children (Burden & Googins, 1986). It is little wonder that working parents are looking for new work arrangements. In some cases they are demanding them. Rodgers and Rodgers (1989) reported that up to 35 percent of working men and women with young children have told their bosses that they will *not* take jobs involving shift work, relocation, extensive travel, intense pressure, or lots of overtime. Some are turning down promotions that they think might put a strain on family life.

One way of responding to these expressed needs is through **flextime**— which can be designed either to make permanent alterations to a basically rigid work schedule or, more broadly, to allow variations from one day to the next. Flextime was pioneered in this country by Hewlett-Packard and is now used by about 12 percent of all U.S. workers. About half the country's large employers offer some kind of flextime arrangement. In 1988, Eastman Kodak announced a new work-schedule program that permits four kinds of alternative work arrangements: permanent changes in regular, scheduled hours; supervisory flexibility in adjusting daily schedules to accommodate family needs; temporary and permanent part-time schedules at all levels; and job sharing.

One of the greatest challenges for organizations that choose to offer flexible work arrangements is ensuring that those employees who take advantage of them will be viewed as committed workers and still have access to opportunities for upward mobility. For one thing, managers must find alternative ways of judging productivity. Time spent at work is not the only way to measure it. When motivated, some employees can produce a great deal in a limited period of time; in addition, they can take some work home and complete it after they have dealt with their family obligations. All workers (including those who are on the premises every day for eight hours) have periods of time when efficiency either rises or falls. Employers might think of productivity in terms of a completed piece of work (a report, a statistical analysis, or a book chapter—in the case of your authors) and focus above all on the work's quality.

Corporate mission statements must clearly articulate commitment to more flexible policies. Supervisors must be trained and educated to think in new ways and to become more flexible in their attitudes and techniques of assessment. Moreover, if flexible working arrangements are to enable those who use them to move upward in the organization, the company as a whole must be prepared to accept the notion that some managers will not be in the office on a regular or an entirely predictable basis.

While this notion may sound strange or unprofessional at first, the reality is that no supervisor is accessible all the time any way. Each has meetings, long phone calls and conferences, and periods of time when she or he needs the privacy to work without interruption. Supervisor accessibility, like other measures of effectiveness, is as much a matter of attitude, motivation, and hard work as it is physical presence in the building for a certain number of hours. The manager who acts too busy or is not eager to listen to candid feedback probably will not be effective in the long run, even if he or she is on the premises every day for long, regular hours. However, a supervisor who is in the office under some sort of flexible arrangement may still function quite effectively, encouraging employees to share their ideas and criticisms, keeping the door open, and showing enthusiasm for the achievements of those of diverse backgrounds and talents. But learning to think that such models of managerial effectiveness are possible and, perhaps in some instances, even preferable will require strong encouragement from those at the top, ongoing training, and no doubt some striking success stories.

Computers, Networks, and Gender Issues

We have already discussed sexual harassment in the workplace. However, computer-mediated interaction can also be afflicted by harassment and other diversity-related communication breakdowns. For instance, according to the popular press, diversity problems exist in cyberspace on the electronic freeway called the *Internet,* a loosely organized computer network that carries messages for an estimated 15 million users worldwide daily. Price (1993) reported numerous incidents in which women feel that they have been harassed, have received suggestive graphics, or have been stalked over computer networks.

Cheris Kramarae, a University of Illinois speech professor, observed that she initially believed cyberspace would be ". . . the ultimate bias-free workplace, where sexism, racism and age discrimination did not exist" (in Price, 1993, p. B1). However, after being the recipient of some sexually explicit graphics, she remarked, "[I was] surprised to see this on my computer screen uninvited. But I'm not surprised, given the problems in our culture, that when you get a new form of communication there's a gender hierarchy set up" (in Price, 1993, p. B1).

Kantrowitz (1994) pointed out that women complain of being subjected to many of the same harassment behaviors on computer networks and bulletin boards that irritate women in everyday face-to-face encounters. One response to electronic harassment has been the establishment of networks that are either coed and run by women or exist exclusively for women. For instance, ECHO (for East Coast Hang Out) and Women's Wire are coed and run by women. Rigdon (1994) noted that 40 percent of ECHO's 2,000 subscribers are female, and 90 percent of the 700 Women's Wire subscribers are female. Kantrowitz reported that harassment is nonexistent on both services.

Interestingly, when using on-line services, people sometimes "cross-dress" by assuming a name of the opposite sex. Rigdon claims that men do this more often, apparently in an attempt to crash women-only conferences.

It seems, then, that computer networks mirror real life. Some of the terrible things that transpire in traditional interactions also happen over networks. Cyberspace isn't Eden. It is marred by just as many sexist ruts and gender conflicts as the "real world."

Computer-industry experts say that on-line sexual harassment was predictable because of the huge number of people working and communicating via personal computers. As Price pointed out, "In the USA, there are 30,000 to 40,000 computer bulletin boards—databases where people can leave messages for each other. About 10 percent of those are on-line services you buy, like Prodigy. With millions of users, legal issues were sure to arise" (Price, 2B).

Many are concerned that sexually harassing comments will increasingly be sent electronically over bulletin boards and computer networks such as the Internet. Currently, no commission or government body oversees these transmissions. However, because most computer transmissions are carried out over telephone connections, the Federal Communications Commission has the authority to pursue harassment cases.

In addition to communication issues, there may be a fundamental difference in how men and women view computers. Kantrowitz (1994) argued, "Men think of machines as extensions of their physical power, as a way to 'transcend physical limitations.' That may be why they are more likely to come up with great leaps in technology, researchers say. Without that vision, the computer and its attendant industry would not exist" (p. 55).

Kantrowitz believes that women, in contrast to men, are less likely to be seduced by technology; they are much more practical, more interested in the computer's utility. Women may say, "I don't care about its innards. I just want to do the job" (Kantrowitz, p. 50).

The gender issue also permeates the computer industry itself. One of the biggest problems facing women in the computer industry is their small number. Zachary (1994) noted that in 1993, women accounted for only 16 percent of those with undergraduate engineering degrees. Also problematic for the computer industry is a recent study's finding that a significantly smaller percentage of women engineers are attracted to industry than to academic and government positions. Zachary reports that the study, conducted by the National Academy of Sciences, concluded that women find the climate in industry less favorable than elsewhere.

As a relatively new industry, the computer world might be expected to have more gender-diverse leadership. Yet Kantrowitz pointed out, "Wrong: few women have advanced beyond middle-management" (p. 2). She cited a study conducted in 1993 by the San Jose *Mercury News,* which found that there were no women CEOs running major computer manufacturing firms and only a handful running software companies.

To facilitate networking by women in technical fields, Kantrowitz identified the existence of an on-line network called "Systers." She noted, "There are now 1,740 women members from 19 countries representing 200 colleges and universities and 150 companies. Systers is part mentoring and part consciousness raising" (p. 52).

Finally, Herschel, Cooper, Smith, and Arrington (1994) reported the findings of one of the first research studies that explored whether group gender composition affects group behavior in a computer-mediated GSS meeting setting. They found no gender-related differences in the quality of computer-based brainstorming. However, in the oral discussions, they discovered that males gave a higher proportion of task-related answers than females, and uniform gender groups expressed more positive social behavior than groups consisting of mixed genders. They also found that uniform gender groups perceived greater participation in the decision-making process than did skewed groups.

Herschel et al. advanced two possible explanations for why using GSS might mitigate gender differences often reported in traditional group communication settings. First, it is plausible that the electronic communication channel used during the brainstorming process (featuring anonymity and simultaneity) masks certain differences in groups that become apparent only during oral discussions. Second, there may be a carry-over effect from the initial GSS brainstorming session, where access and voice are unrestricted, to the face-to-face interaction, so that everyone may feel more empowered to participate actively in the group activity. The latter possibility would support Jessup et al.'s (1990) theory of anonymous interaction, which contends that using GSS may help to reduce inner restraints on behavior by weakening immediate external social controls. Since these explanations remain speculative, we still have much to learn about how technology might help or hinder groups of varying gender configurations.

Of course, gender diversity is only one aspect of the broader diversity issues with which organizations must grapple. We now turn to a discussion of how technology, and especially the use of computers, might have an impact on how to manage cultural diversity in team and group organizational contexts.

Computers, Networks, and Cultural Diversity

Trompenaars' (1994) recent discussion of intercultural communication is useful for those organizations using technology to support same-time, same-place or same-time, different-place meetings for culturally diverse groups.

Trompenaars points out that Western society has a predominantly verbal culture. Traditionally, we communicate via paper, film, and conversation. Indeed, one could argue that word-processing and graphics software have been created expressly to support verbal communication.

In face-to-face meetings, cultural diversity often affects **discussion styles**. For instance, different cultures handle turn taking and interruptions quite differently. As Trompenaars explained:

> . . . For the Anglo-Saxon, when A stops, B starts. It is not polite to interrupt. The even more verbal Latins integrate slightly more than this; B will frequently interrupt A and vice versa to show how interested each is in what the other is saying.
>
> The pattern of communication for oriental languages frightens the westerner. The moment of silence is interpreted as a failure to communicate. But this is a misunderstanding. Let us reverse the roles; how can the westerner communicate clearly if the other person is not given time to finish his or her sentence, or to digest what the other has been saying? It is a sign of respect for the other person if you take time to process the information without talking yourself (pp. 74–75).

Cross-cultural problems can also arise from **tone of voice**. Trompenaars noted that for some societies, rising and falling inflectional speech patterns suggest that the speaker is not serious:

> . . . in most Latin societies, this exaggerated way of communicating shows that you have your heart in the matter. Oriental societies tend to have a much more monotonous style; self-controlled, it shows respect. Frequently, the higher the position a person holds, the lower and flatter the voice.
>
> A British manager posted to Nigeria found it was very effective to raise his voice for important issues. His Nigerian subordinate saw this unexpected explosion by a normally self-controlled manager as a sign of extra concern. After success in Nigeria, he [the British manager] was posted to Malaysia. Shouting there was a sign of loss of face; his colleagues did not take him seriously, and he was transferred (p. 75).

Relative to the spoken word, Trompenaars suggested that to express yourself in another language is a "necessary, if not a sufficient, condition for understanding another culture" (p. 76).

Of course, cultural diversity has implications for **nonverbal communication** as well, especially since so much communication (some estimates are as high as 75 percent) is nonverbal. Trompenaars illustrated the importance of grounding nonverbal communication within a specific cultural context:

> . . . In western societies, eye contact is crucial to confirm interest. However, the amount differs sharply from society to society. An Italian visiting professor at Wharton [School of Management, University of Pennsylvania] arrived on campus and was surprised to be greeted by a number of students. [He asked a student] if he knew who he was. The student said he was afraid he did not. "So why did you greet me?" "Because it seemed like you knew me, sir." The professor realized that, in America, eye contact between strangers is supposed to last for [only] a split second.
>
> Leonel Brug, a colleague at the Center for International Business Studies, was brought up in both Curaçao and Suriname. As a boy he would avoid eye contact, whereupon his Curaçao grandmother would slap him in the face (in some cultures body talk is very effective) and say, "Look me in the face." Respecting an elder involves eye contact. Leonel learned fast, and when in Suriname, looked his grandmother straight in the face to show respect. She slapped him too; respectful kids in Suriname do not make eye contact (p. 77).

Trompenaars remarked that habits of touching others, individuals' feelings about space and territory, and their assumptions about privacy are further manifestations of differences in cultures. He warned, "Never help an Arab lady out of a bus; it might cost you your [business] contract" (p. 77). Clearly, when people from diverse cultures meet, it is essential that they recognize their differences and refrain from making inappropriate judgments.

David Wigglesworth, president of a consulting firm, D.C.W. Research Associates International, (often referred to by his peers as a "dean of diversity") has told one author of this text that caution is especially needed when using different-time, different-place technologies. As he pointed out, "When I receive e-mail from clients in Saudi Arabia, for example, I can't simply read the text to understand their message. I have to ponder the message to figure out what it is they are really trying to say to me." That is, he attempts to ascertain the message within the message.

Wigglesworth's observations point to the limitations inherent in distant, one-way communication systems. In Chapter 7 we noted that McGrath and Hollingshead (1993) believe that technologies such as e-mail restrict the richness of the information being transmitted. Wigglesworth's experiences confirm this notion, suggesting that the loss of verbal and nonverbal signals creates ambiguity, especially where cultural diversity exists between the correspondents.

Researchers are increasingly interested in better understanding how technology either inhibits or empowers communicators of varying cultural backgrounds. For example, Chidambaram (1992) has reported that the research agenda for the Electronic Meeting Room (EMR) at the University of Hawaii is exploring the impact of computer support on multicultural communication. He noted that the primary objective of the EMR is to understand whether it can reduce barriers to multicultural communication and increase intercultural understanding.

Cultural differences affect group behavior in such areas as decision making, coordination, temporal orientation, and communication style. Chidambaram and his colleagues intend to use GSS to assess and understand how groups from different cultures adopt this technology and how they use GSS to make decisions, manage conflict, and formulate negotiation strategies in cross-cultural settings. The University of Hawaii's GSS research facility has already developed a tentative three-year plan to use technology specifically to support and enhance communication between American and Japanese managers and to increase intercultural understanding.

Other institutions are also beginning to study computer-mediated intercultural communication. For instance, the University of Hohenheim in Stuttgart, Germany is conducting GSS research in a multicultural context. The university has initiated two projects that focus on computerized teamwork and the use of coordination technology for business processes in multinational corporations. They are also engaged in working groups focused on group knowledge development and distributed meetings sponsored by the European Community in which European researchers cooperate to approach computer support for groupwork from a multidisciplinary perspective. Wagner, Wynne, and Mennecke (1993) noted that one of the interesting research issues these scholars face is whether results from empirical studies performed in the United States can be applied to Europe. Previous research should be replicated to access potential cultural differences.

Summarizing Perspective

Managing cultural diversity is challenging. But the potential benefits, both to the organization and to the individual, are well worth the time and sustained effort required to recruit and maintain a fully functioning, culturally diverse work force. The advantages of cultural diversity are numerous. As employees learn to value diversity, they may feel a sense of empowerment, as does anyone who has opportunities to learn and grow. Awareness of and appreciation of diversity can be liberating. Learning to interact effectively with those who differ from us in gender, color, race, or ethnicity enhances our skills, alters our attitudes, and educates us to be more sophisticated members of our own organizational communities and citizens of the world community.

Naturally, individuals differ. What a boring world it would be if we were all alike! If one of us differs in a specific way from others in our group or organization, an awareness of this difference need not become a cause of tension or shame, but rather a source of pride and a sense of power. Through a growing belief that we are unique individuals who can make a special contribution in our professional lives, each of us can experience empowerment.

The basis of an empowered, culturally diverse work force is organizational commitment to achieving it. Managers play a key role. Through their attitudes, policies, and communication practices, they set the pace and tone, contributing to an organizational culture where there is space and equal opportunity for all.

Technology can also play an important role in managing diversity. Some of the biases, attitudes, and experiences that people have had in the past can be difficult to confront face-to-face. However, some studies have shown that technological interventions can help. For instance, Herschel and Ehrhardt (in progress) have learned that complementing verbal discussions on diversity with the anonymity and simultaneity afforded by GSS helps many otherwise reticent participants to overcome both communication and evaluation apprehension on this potentially volatile topic. They have discovered that in this unique forum for discussion many issues surface that otherwise go unarticulated in face-to-face discussions, even when groups are supported by a trained process facilitator.

We believe that the lessons to be learned regarding the role of technology in managing diversity are many. In particular, we encourage students to do the following:

- Begin to explore and understand issues of diversity by attending seminars and reading texts on the subject.
- Consider how using technology creates problems and opportunities relative to diversity.
- Consider using technology to complement verbal discussions of diversity since people often feel empowered to speak more openly when they are not meeting face-to-face.

CASES FOR DISCUSSION

CASE 1 *Discrimination?*

When Dave was hired to be vice president of campus human resources at a major California university, he knew he was inheriting a difficult situation. Reporting to him would be a group of three directors, who, he was told, did not particularly want him to be hired.

In fact, this group did not particularly want anyone to be hired to fill the position of vice president. For the past two years, the position had been vacant; and the three had essentially managed the human resources function themselves without supervision. Indeed, for the eight years before that, they had reported to a vice president who spent most of his time on the golf course rather than in the office. Under his laissez-faire style of leadership, the directors had become powerful heads of one of the university's largest functions.

Unfortunately, under their leadership that function had also degenerated. Mistakes on university employees' paychecks had become commonplace; open positions took as long as eighteen months to fill; highly suspicious worker's compensation claims were paid without question or investigation, at a cost to the university of hundreds of thousands of dollars; employee grievances went months without a response from management; turnover among employees within human resources had reached unprecedented levels; and morale had fallen to an all-time low. Clearly, the department needed better leadership.

When Dave accepted the position, he left a good job at a major university in the Midwest, with assurances from his new boss, James, that he would have all the support he needed to straighten out his department. Indeed, had he not received such a commitment from James, he would not have made the move.

Shortly after taking the position, Dave hired a consulting firm to study the effectiveness of the campus human resources department and offer recommendations for improving its effectiveness. The study confirmed what he already knew: Dissatisfaction with the department was widespread, and change was needed immediately. But the consultants' report provided some unexpected information as well: The three directors were actively undermining Dave, spreading rumors that he was "mean," "vindictive," and "unreasonable" in dealings with his staff. Dave had been told to expect hostile actions by the directors; nevertheless, he was surprised and upset by the consultants' findings.

Dave went to James with the results of the consultants' study. "I want to make changes immediately," he said. "What kind of changes?" James asked. "I want to put the directors on probation, effective immediately, and terminate them if their performances do not improve within three months." In Dave's opinion, this approach would give the directors an opportunity to improve but still put them on notice that their employment was in jeopardy, as university regulations required.

"Hold on a minute," James said. "I can't support that." Dave was dumbfounded: "What do you mean?" "Think about it," James responded. "All three directors are female. All three are over forty years old. One is Hispanic. One is black. If we do what you're saying, they'll haul us all into court claiming discrimination. You've got to find some other way."

Reluctantly, Dave found another way. He reorganized the campus human resources department so that the managers below the three directors were put in charge of "special projects." No reduction in pay or benefits for the Directors was to occur. Nevertheless, all three of them filed grievances against Dave.

An attorney from the university met with Dave to discuss the impending grievance hearings. After Dave told him the reasons for the change, he responded, "You can't do that. The actions you took were for disciplinary reasons, and you can't reorganize under those circumstances. We'll lose the grievance, and you'll have to put everything back the way it was."

Following the attorney's advice, Dave changed his "reorganization" to a demotion, demoting all three directors to "special projects managers" for disciplinary reasons.

This time, all three directors filed charges of discrimination against Dave based on sex, age, and race. Ironically, James was named as a codefendant. In addition, all three directors immediately took paid medical leaves of absence, obtaining a doctor's assessment that they were too "stressed out" to continue working.

The university asked the consultants who had conducted the initial study to serve as witnesses in the grievance hearings. In preparation for those hearings, they met with the attorney who would be defending Dave. After discussing the facts of the case and the information the attorney could provide during the hearing, the consultants asked the attorney, "What do you think the outcome of this case will be?" "Well, it's hard to say for sure," the attorney replied, "but if I were a betting man, I would bet that Dave will be fired and the three directors reinstated."

Questions for Discussion

1. Could Dave have handled this situation better by involving a diverse group of employees? If he had asked you, what kind of advice might you have given him?

2. Should Dave be fired? Why or why not?

3. Should the directors be fired? Why or why not?

4. What principles regarding managing diversity might be drawn from this situation?

CASE 2 *"Homework"*

Until recently, Mary Lott drove a delivery truck for Parcels Unlimited. However, after having her second child in four years, she found that the demands of her family made full-time employment impossible. Since Parcels Unlimited does not provide benefits to employees working less than full-time, part-time work was undesirable; the rising cost of day care for her children made any absence from home expensive. Mary needed another way to make a living.

For extra income, Mary and her husband, Steve (a data-processing whiz), had been doing data entry and analysis for some friends whose employee relations consulting firm conducted employee opinion surveys for their clients. Mary approached her friends with a proposal: She would open her own business in her home, handle all of the survey data input and analysis for the consulting firm (which had been using another data-processing service occasionally as well), and take on any additional typing and report preparation the firm needed. The consultants would mail to her completed survey questionnaires for analysis and rough drafts of documents they needed typed, and she would mail back to their office completed materials.

The friends agreed, and initially, the arrangement worked well. Mary was able to care for her children during the day and enter survey data and type reports at night; Steve would program the computer and run data analyses during his spare time on evenings and weekends. But as the consulting firm's business expanded and the volume of work grew, some problems began to crop up:

▶ When one of the consulting firm's clients had questions about the data entry or analysis procedures, the consultants would give them Mary's home telephone number and suggest they call her directly. She began receiving calls almost daily, and often found herself answering the telephone with children screaming in the background—much to the puzzlement of the businesspeople on the other end of the line. She began to worry about the professionalism of her image.

▶ Other consulting firms learned about Mary's services and contacted her to request her assistance. Only after she had said yes too many times did she realize that she could not keep up with the demand.

▶ When Mary's neighbors learned that she was working at home, they asked if she would take care of their children as well— for a fee, of course. Sympathetic to the plight of working mothers, Mary inevitably said yes. The background noise during telephone calls from clients grew.

▶ Despite the telephone calls, most of Mary's day was spent interacting with children aged four and under. She found that she missed having contact with adults.

Mary liked the work she did, the time she spent with her children, the freedom to set her own schedule, and not having to commute to work. But she also realized that something had to be done differently.

Questions for Discussion

1. This case is a true story. Describe some of the tensions involved in balancing one's personal and professional life as portrayed in this situation.

2. What specific things would you do if you were Mary to gain more control over your life and to deal with your growing problems? What communication technologies might you use to cope more effectively with this situation?

3. Do you know of other individuals who have chosen to work in similar circumstances? What problems have they faced? How have they solved them?

CHAPTER 10

Ethics and Organizational Communication

Making ethical decisions is easy when the facts are clear and the choices black and white. But it is a different story when the situation is clouded by ambiguity, incomplete information, multiple points of view, and conflicting responsibilities. In such situations—which managers experience all the time—ethical decisions depend on both the decision-making process itself and on the experience, intelligence, and integrity of the decision maker.
Kenneth R. Andrews, "Ethics in Practice," *Harvard Business Review,* 1989.

Throughout our lives, and increasingly in organizational contexts, ethical questions abound. As we discuss and negotiate the answers to questions about meaning and purpose, profit and product quality, service and social responsibility, we inevitably make judgments about what is right, good, appropriate, and just. As individuals, we make decisions about how we will treat members of our families, how much we will work (during evenings and over weekends?), how we will spend our leisure time, whether or not to devote some of our time volunteering (perhaps at a soup kitchen or a center for abused women), and how to manage our multiple organizational identities. Similarly, the organizations with which we are affiliated will struggle with ethical concerns: How should products and services be advertised and priced, how should employees be treated, how responsible are we for protecting the environment, and how do the new technologies influence our work and our interactions with others? The ways in which we respond to these and other ethical questions, both as individuals and as organizations, provide considerable insight into our ethical character.

In this chapter we will define and discuss the importance of ethics and ethical communication. We will examine several different perspectives for making ethical judgments, perspectives among which individuals and organizations may choose. We will illustrate the pervasiveness of ethical questions in organizational contexts by briefly examining several specific ethical issues. Finally, we will consider the impact of technology on ethics and on organizational communication.

The Importance of Ethics

Unfortunately, in recent years an alarming number of "unethical" situations have arisen in American organizations. For example, the Ford Motor Company refused to alter the dangerous gas tank on its Pinto model because changing it would have cost the company $11 per car. In the end, the flaw cost Ford millions of dollars in lawsuits—and cost many people their lives. Chrysler was found to have disconnected the odometers in "new" cars that had been driven by its executives. Equity Funding tried to hide 64,000 phony insurance claims but went bankrupt when the truth came out. Ivan Boesky engaged in "insider trading," an illegal practice for investment counselors. A.H. Robbins knew of problems with its contraceptive Dalkon shield for years before they were caught and forced to inform the public. The billion dollars set aside for handling lawsuits against the company was dwarfed by the amount of claims—and the company filed for bankruptcy. A number of directors of savings and loan associations defrauded depositors, in many cases depriving people of their life savings. Phoenix financier Charles H. Keating, Jr., for instance, was condemned by a federal judge for "looting" the Lincoln Savings and Loan Association. It is little wonder that a large majority of the public think executives are dishonest, overly profit-oriented, and willing to step on other people to get what they want (Andrews, 1989). In addition, many believe that CEOs are ridiculously overpaid. An American CEO of a large company now makes $1 million to $2 million in annual salary and bonuses. This is 50 to 100 times the pay of the average worker. In Japan, comparable CEOs earn 16 times the average salary (Samuelson, 1991).

Whether or not everyone would agree that the behaviors described above are equally unethical (or even unethical at all), when considered together, they lead to a critical question: Why is ethical behavior important? In our view, there are several compelling reasons. First, *ethical behavior is usually associated with important positive consequences.* Honesty in one's professional dealings engenders trust and establishes the foundation for relationship development and positive future interactions. Business in particular depends on the acceptance of rules and expectations, mutual trust and fairness. Thus, ethical business is good business. In contrast, unethical behavior can cause serious damage affecting both the person committing the behavior and the people touched by it. In the cases described above, innocent people suffered serious financial losses, injury, or loss of life, and in some cases the perpetrators were sentenced to jail. But beyond that, the people and organizations (and indeed, entire industries) that were involved lost credibility. Once an organization's image is so tarnished that people are no longer willing to put their faith in it or its leaders, it is almost certain to fail.

Second, from a personal perspective, *ethical errors end careers* more quickly and with greater finality than any other errors of judgment. Lying, stealing, cheating, reneging on contracts, and so on undermine the very foundation upon which the business and professional world is built. Ethical behavior is especially important for organizational leaders because they influ-ence the ethical climate for everyone else. Leaders are role models. When they make ethical blunders, they are held especially accountable.

Third, *ethical behavior is empowering* for all parties. The manager who be-haves ethically establishes an organizational climate of supportiveness, hon-esty, and trust. This climate in turn empowers employees to try out new ideas, take risks, express dissent, and generally assume enhanced responsibility.

Finally, *ethical behavior is intrinsically valuable*. Those who know that they are honest, who behave humanely in their dealings with others, who are fair in their evaluations of others, and who are concerned for the welfare of the organization as a whole and the society it serves are rewarded with a peace of mind that carries no price tag.

Ultimately, the need for ethical behavior might best be expressed by the old maxim, "what goes around comes around." Managers who treat other people with unimpeachable integrity thereby earn those people's trust and make them more willing to support the organization. Conversely, managers who lack integrity promote mistrust among those with whom they deal and make their employees ashamed of their organization and the products and serv-ices they provide. Since workers feel their work is unworthy, they stop caring.

Values, Ethics and Ethical Communication

At the foundation of ethical behavior is a value system that serves as a guide for judging one's own and others' behavior and above all resists change. **Values** are among the most stable and enduring characteristics of individuals. They are the basis upon which attitudes and personal preferences are formed, as well as the basis for crucial decisions, life directions, and personal tastes. Organizations, too, have value systems (as we discussed in Chapter 2). They are perhaps the most critical component of the organizational culture. Increasing numbers of managers and scholars are stressing the importance of an organization's values and culture in building a strong, creative, and pro-ductive work force. As Aguilar (1994) pointed out, "When all is said and done, smart people who really like what they are doing, who like and respect their colleagues, who are prepared to take calculated risks, and who are mem-bers of a cohesive, well-run organization are what corporate excellence is all about. Business ethics is central to such an organization" (p. 157).

What are the most important values an organization can stress? A *Time* magazine survey suggests that managers at all levels place the highest value on *integrity* and *competence* in their superiors, peers, and subordinates (*Time*, 1987). Moreover, individuals thrive in organizations that stand for values they can embrace in their personal lives. Excellent companies have clearly stated values that make sense to their employees—and they reinforce these values through everything they do. As Tom Peters argued in *Thriving on Chaos* (1987), "Without a doubt, honesty has always been the best policy. The best firms on this score have long had the best track records overall—Johnson & Johnson, Hewlett-Packard, Merck, Digital Equipment" (p. 519). Peters pointed out that leaders should demand complete integrity from themselves and from their employees, "If a promise (even a minor one) is not kept, if ethics are compromised, and if management behaves inconsistently, then the strategies necessary to survival today simply can't be executed." Peters clearly links ethical behavior to organizational survival.

Almost every important issue discussed, assessed, and acted upon in organizations relates, directly or indirectly, to ethics. Johannesen (1992) defined **ethical issues** as those that "focus on value judgments concerning right and wrong, goodness and badness, in human conduct" (p. 30). The college president who must decide which department to eliminate to ensure the survival of the institution as a whole must grapple with ethical issues, as must the doctor who has to make a decision about putting a patient on a life support system, a supervisor who must determine the amount of work to be required of subordinates, and the division head who has to decide how to present financial data that reflect poorly on her own department. In each of these instances, *choice making* is central to the decision-making process. As we consider the choices individuals and organizations make when confronted with these kinds of situations, we obtain a clearer sense of their basic ethical posture.

Ethics go far beyond simple questions of legality or illegality—of bribery, theft, or collusion. The field of ethics considers what our relationships are and ought to be with our employers, coworkers, subordinates, customers, stockholders, suppliers, distributors, neighbors, and all other members of the communities in which we operate. As Solomon and Hanson (1985) noted, ethics are a "way of life. . . . It is the awareness that one is an intrinsic part of a social order, in which the interests of others and one's own interests are inevitably intertwined" (p. 5).

From a communication perspective, **ethical communication** facilitates the individual's ability to make sound choices. Ethical communication may include providing complete and accurate information upon which others can base their choices. It may involve establishing a supportive environment in which others feel comfortable making informed choices. One way to view ethical communication is in terms of supportive communication behaviors. In general, those who aspire to communicate ethically and supportively should espouse the following kinds of behavior:

- **Descriptive** (rather than evaluative)—being nonjudgmental, slow to question others' standards and values; willing to seek additional information.

- **Problem-oriented**—interested in defining mutual problems and cooperatively seeking solutions rather than pointing to people who can be blamed for problems.

- **Spontaneous**—straightforward, honest, and tactfully direct; unwilling to deal with others in manipulative ways.

- **Respectful**—interacting as an equal; demonstrating and seeking mutual trust and respect; encouraging participative planning while deemphasizing status, power, and formal role relationships.
- **Empathic**—attempting to see issues and problems from others' perspectives; identifying with others' needs, interests, and values.
- **Provisional**—willing to admit that one could be wrong; open to new ways of doing things; tentative in one's views (Gibb, 1961).

Ethical communication fosters conditions for human growth and development (Keller & Brown, 1968). It values the essential dignity of human beings and empowers them to realize their potential.

Ethical Perspectives

The way a person approaches choice making and communicative interactions depends largely upon the ethical perspective(s) from which she or he is operating. Ethics can be viewed from several different vantage points, each of which provides a different foundation for making moral judgments. The "best" approach or solution to a given ethical dilemma will vary depending upon the ethical perspective embraced. Among those most commonly cited are religious, economic, legal, utilitarian, universalist, humanist, dialogic, and situational perspectives. These ethical perspectives are summarized in Table 10.1.

Religious Perspective

Every world religion offers moral and spiritual injunctions that can be used to determine the degree to which a policy or course of action is right or wrong. The **religious perspective** teaches that behaviors such as lying, stealing, murdering, and treating others with disrespect are wrong. For instance, Christians are taught to treat others as they would like to be treated themselves while Taoists stress empathy and insight as roads to truth, deemphasizing logic and reason.

Some have attempted to apply religious standards to certain facets of organizational behavior. McMillan (1963), for instance, discussed the Golden Rule concept in terms of "multiple neighbors," holding organizations accountable to a constituency extending beyond employees to owners, clients, and the general public. Certainly, the systems school of organization theory embraces the accountability principle. At a more personal level, Alderson (1974) argued that much business conduct is controlled by rules of morality, many of which have the force of law. He contended that most businesspeople keep their word when they make a promise, devote many hours to civic institutions and social concerns, and try to influence others to give their best.

Others maintain, however, that moral leadership is sorely lacking, especially from those in the highest positions. For instance, Samuelson (1991)

TABLE 10.1

Ethical Perspectives

Religious	Follows moral and spiritual injunctions taught by a particular religion.
Economic	Strives to maximize revenues and minimize costs.
Legal	Stays within the boundaries of the law.
Utilitarian	Advocates whatever does the greatest good for the greatest number.
Universalist	Has good intentions; supports whatever maintains the dignity and worth of others.
Humanist	Endeavors to enhance unique human characteristics, such as reflective and rational thought and the motivation to serve others.
Dialogic	Promotes trust, concern for others, open-mindedness, empathy, humility, sincerity, and directness; is communication-focused.
Situational	Takes into account receiver expectations, crisis factors, and other situational variables when making ethical judgments.

argued "Too many chief executives share the ethics of a welfare cheat. The welfare cheat breaks the law to chisel the government [while] many a CEO twists company rules to raise his pay and bilk the company" (p. 55). Although these positions represent contrasting extremes, they both point to the importance of individual conduct and the personal standards (influenced by family, education, and religion) that those in key positions bring to the organizations for which they work.

Economic Perspective

The **economic perspective** bases ethical judgments on impersonal market forces. This school of thought holds that managers should consistently act to maximize revenues and minimize costs, and that this strategy itself will assure society of the greatest long-term benefit (Hosmer, 1987). This approach, however, does not take into consideration the well-being of some segments of society (for example, the poor and minorities, who do not or cannot participate in corporate ownership). Nor does it exclude the use of questionable practices (such as bribes, environmental pollution, or hazardous working conditions) that might serve to improve an organization's "bottom line." In effect, it is an impersonal approach that considers people a means to an end and considers their nature and well-being of little account. Some argue that an exclusive commitment to economic concerns is detrimental to the development of the organization's ethical culture. As Andrews (1989) wrote:

. . . management's total loyalty to the maximization of profits is the principal obstacle to achieving higher standards of ethical practice. Defining the purpose of the corporation as exclusively economic is a deadly oversimplification, which allows overemphasis on self-interest at the expense of consideration of others (p. 104).

Legal Perspective

Legal analysis reduces ethical judgments to a matter of law. Anything that is legal is ethical. Anything that is illegal is unethical. This approach has the advantage of facilitating simple ethical decisions: one has only to investigate the law, rule, or behavioral code governing a particular practice. The disadvantage of the **legal perspective** is that it often leads to oversimplification and superficiality. For instance, the law does not prohibit lying except under oath or in some formal contracts. Moreover, the law tends to focus on forbidding negative actions, but it does not require or even encourage positive actions (for instance, no law requires someone to go to the aid of a woman being raped). Finally, some laws in and of themselves are morally objectionable. Until the early 1960s, some areas of the United States legally required racial discrimination; and even now, existing laws concerning abortion, homosexuality, and religious observances in schools are repugnant to many.

Utilitarian Perspective

One of the classic cases of ethical tension exists between those who are concerned with the moral quality of an action independent of its consequences (deontologists) and those who believe that any action is right if it produces the greatest good for the greatest number of people (utilitarians). This tension is often dramatized by posing such hypothetical moral questions as, "Would you be willing to murder an innocent person if it would end hunger in the world?" Not surprisingly, the utilitarian would respond affirmatively, while the deontologist would surely reject the notion. Thus, from a **utilitarian perspective,** usefulness and expediency are the criteria used to make ethical judgments. Motives are considered insignificant. Only consequences matter. Thus, from a utilitarian point of view, the "goodness" of all sorts of organizational behaviors—from creating new products and advertising them to developing employee support programs—such as day care and counseling—can actually be measured. In marketing a new product, for instance, a major concern for a utilitarian is simply, "Will the product sell?"

The utilitarian perspective focuses on ends rather than means. Thus, its practical significance is great. Organizations must be concerned with the ultimate effects of their plans, policies, and rules. Laudable means that fail to promote important organizational goals will be subjected to criticism and likely replaced with more effective strategies. However, ends do not always justify means, and the rights of the minority must not be sacrificed for the "good" of the majority. Thus, this perspective shares some of the characteristics—and limitations—of the economic perspective.

Universalist Perspective

Whereas the utilitarian perspective considers the outcomes of an action, the universalist maintains that because outcomes are too difficult to predict or control, the more appropriate focus is on *intentions*. Thus, the morality of an action depends upon the intentions of the person making the decision or performing the act. If that person wishes the best for others, her or his actions are ethical even if, due to the person's clumsiness or ineptitude, another person is hurt.

At the heart of the **universalist perspective** is the belief that people have certain universal duties or responsibilities in their dealings with one another, such as telling the truth, not taking another's property, and adhering to agreements. So long as the individual's intent is to uphold these duties, he or she is behaving ethically. Using this approach, human beings are viewed as ends rather than means. They are inherently worthy of dignity and respect and are not resources or tools to be used to achieve others' purposes. Value resides in the persons themselves and in their relationships.

Like the other ethical perspectives, the universalist perspective introduces certain complexities. First, it is difficult to make judgments about others' (and even our own) intentions. Former President Richard Nixon was quick to embrace a universalist perspective when he argued that even though his actions in the Watergate cover-up had been unfortunate, his intentions or motives remained untainted. In organizational settings, and especially in business, people at times *do* serve as a means to an end. For example, customers are a means of allowing the company to make money and its employees to earn a living; employees in turn are a means of getting work done. However, an exclusive or primary focus upon others as a means to the desired ends fails to honor universalist criteria for ethical behavior.

Humanist Perspective

Some writers use the **humanistic perspective** by attempting to make ethical judgments philosophically, isolating certain unique characteristics of human nature that should be valued and enhanced. They then look at a particular technique, rule, policy, strategy, or behavior and attempt to determine the extent to which it either furthers or hampers these uniquely human attributes. Aristotle, for example, believed that truly human acts were performed by rational persons, that is, individuals who recognized what they were doing and freely chose to do it (Flynn, 1957). Modern writers have identified such uniquely human attributes as the individual's symbol-using capacity, the need for mutual understanding, the motivation to serve both self and others, and the capability for rational, reflective thought. Burke (1966) talked of the human need to transcend individual differences and to communicate cooperatively. In her book *The Worth Ethic,* Kate Ludeman (1989) argued, "The Worth Ethic is a belief in your indelible self-worth and the fundamental and potential worth of others. . . . Worth Ethic managers commit themselves to help employees develop and use their skills and talents" (p. xv).

From these statements about individual attitudes and behaviors, we might infer that the ethical organization would encourage its members to communicate fully, freely, and cooperatively. Thus, organizational incentives aimed at nurturing cooperation rather than competition would be emphasized. Arguably, from the humanist's perspective, some management theories, such as McGregor's Theory Y or Blake and Mouton's team approach, would be considered more inherently ethical than others.

Dialogic Perspective

A communication-centered approach to judging ethical behavior has emerged from the scholarship on communication as dialogue rather than monologue (Johannesen, 1971; 1992). According to the **dialogic perspective,** the attitudes that individuals in any communication transaction have toward one another are an index of the ethical level of that communication. Some attitudes are believed to be more fully human, more likely to encourage self-actualization, and more humane than others. According to Johannesen (1992), when people communicate from a dialogic perspective, their attitudes are characterized by honesty, trust, concern for others, open-mindedness, empathy, humility, sincerity, and directness. They are nonmanipulative, encourage free expression in others, and accept others as persons of intrinsic worth, regardless of differences that may exist between them. A dialogic ethic creates a climate in which people are empowered to be authentic about who they are and what they stand for, to confirm the worth of others, to be accessible and attentive, and to share a spirit of mutual equality. In contrast, unethical communication behavior is characterized by monologue and by such qualities as deception, superiority, exploitation and domination, insincerity and distrust. Freedom of expression is stifled, and other people are viewed as objects to be manipulated.

The dialogic perspective has much in common with both the humanist and the universalist ethical perspectives. It is unique, however, in its focus on communication as the primary means of examining the ethical level of human behavior. Like McGregor, dialogic theorists contend that individual behavior reflects underlying attitudes (Stewart, 1978). From an organizational perspective, one potential disadvantage of the dialogic perspective is that it focuses exclusively on processes, doing little to link them to tangible outcomes. Dialogic communication, for instance, may or may not yield greater efficiency or productivity—or even the greatest good for the majority.

Situational Perspective

Some theorists are less universal in their approach to ethics, believing it impossible to set definitive ethical guidelines except as they relate to a specific situation. Ethical criteria might vary as variables in the organizational situation change. In an organizational crisis involving genuine danger to human lives, for instance, the leader who uses emotional appeals or behaves autocratically might well not be judged harshly from a **situational perspective,** although the same behavior in ordinary circumstances would more likely be viewed as unethical. In addition, judgment of an individual's behavior may depend upon the political or cultural context in which the organization is embedded.

Perhaps the major advantage of the situational perspective is its flexibility and the extent to which it encourages thoughtful consideration of the particular context of each act of human behavior. However, the ethical judgment must be grounded in one or more of the general ethical perspectives discussed above; otherwise, problems of inconsistency and unfairness may result. That is, one might generally approach ethical decision making from a dialogic perspective, also embracing universalist ethical criteria; however, in a specific situation, economic or utilitarian concerns might take precedence. For example, one manager fired a first-line supervisor immediately when presented with decisive evidence that he was sexually harassing his subordinates. In this situation, the dialogic perspective was sacrificed so that the utilitarian principle of the greatest good for the greatest number could be upheld.

Ethical Issues

If organizational members try to ignore or minimize the ethical implications of their decisions and actions (perhaps by failing to talk about them), unhealthy, disempowering, and ultimately unproductive organizational climates are likely to develop. Ethical dilemmas cannot be avoided. Some ethical quandaries have existed for many years, such as how to manage the tension between service and profit; others have emerged relatively recently in the wake of the technological revolution, such as dealing with software piracy. In this section we will briefly examine some critical ethical issues.

Before we do, however, we want to emphasize *the centrality of communication to the ethics-building process.* For instance, organizational *codes of ethics formally communicate* the organization's views of ethical conduct. Because these ethical codes are often broad-based, they empower employees by challenging them to live up to their own best sense of ethical conduct. In addition, *organizational leaders* who *communicate informally, on a day-to-day basis, with employees* about their beliefs and the principles that inform their decisions and actions and who listen to the expressed values and beliefs of others also contribute to an ethical, empowering organizational culture. Kouzes and Posner (1993) pointed out, "By engaging in discourse and dialogue, people develop a sense of their own and others' moral language" (p. 65).

An excellent example of the way such open discussion might develop can be found in the comments of John Dubinsky, CEO of Mark Twain Banc-shares:

> I take every opportunity I can to talk to my people about this [ethics], especially those who have recently joined the firm. The best way to raise these issues, I find, is through specific examples. For example, if the bank were asked to lend money for the financing of a pornographic shop, would this be okay? What about an abortion clinic? As it is, the bank does have a policy against making a loan for a porno shop, but its position concerning the abortion clinic is undecided. In the discussions on abortion clinics, we get strong feelings both ways. I find that helpful. Indeed, the goals of these talks is not so much to state company policy as it is to make our officers—and that includes me—more sensitive to the ethical dimensions of our business (quoted in Aguilar, 1994, p. 36).

What is critical about developing codes of ethics and having ongoing conversations about ethics is that organizational leaders, through formal and informal communication channels, are heightening employee awareness of the importance of ethics and challenging them to empower themselves by thinking of the ethical implications of each organizational endeavor. We turn now to a consideration of some critical ethical issues.

Social Responsibility

To what extent do organizations have social responsibilities over and above their obligations to their stockholders? Many would argue that, indeed, organizations *are* responsible to society—not just to their stockholders and their employees but also to their customers, the general public, and the environment. However, the scope of that responsibility remains an area of controversy.

An increasingly significant issue involving organizational social responsibility is the environment. In the past, organizations have polluted the air and water, transported and dumped hazardous waste, and generally shown little respect for the earth or its inhabitants. The problems seem overwhelming—the burning and clearing of the tropical rain forests, the thousandfold increase in the rate at which living species become extinct, global warming, and stratospheric ozone depletion. In his book, *Earth in the Balance: Ecology and the Human Spirit* (1992), Vice President (then Senator) Al Gore illustrated one manifestation of the problem:

Small communities . . . throughout the Southeast and Midwest are being deluged with shipments of garbage from the Northeast. Rural areas of the western United States are receiving garbage from large cities on the Pacific coast. . . . One of the most bizarre and disturbing consequences of this considerable shipment of waste is the appearance of a new environmental threat called backhauling. Truckers take loads of chemical waste and garbage in one direction and food and bulk liquids (like fruit juice) in the opposite direction—in the same containers. . . . Although the trucks were typically washed between loads, drivers described lax inspections, totally inadequate washouts, and the use of liquid deodorizers, themselves dangerous, to mask left-over chemical smells (pp. 153–154).

Gore went on to note that although legislation has been passed prohibiting this practice, no legislation can stop the underlying problem. As one means of disposal is prohibited, the practice continues underground or a new method is found. The "unthinkable becomes commonplace because of the incredible pressure from the mounting volumes of waste" (p. 154). Clearly, the relationship between organizational systems and their environments will raise increasingly compelling ethical questions in the future.

Fortunately, several excellent examples of socially responsible organizations can be found. One is Control Data Corporation and its founder, chairman, and CEO, William C. Norris. During 1967, when riots erupted in a depressed area of Minneapolis and St. Paul not far from Control Data's headquarters, Norris responded in a manner that might be viewed as a model of social responsibility. "You can't do business with the town on fire," he said. "So you stop and think why this has happened. It happened because of inequities. The people felt so damn frustrated that this was their way of expressing themselves" (Solomon & Hanson, 1985, p. 184). Thus, in 1968, Norris and Control Data opened a new plant in the riot-torn area of Minneapolis and provided their new employees with a child-care center and intensive job training (including basic courses in computer skills). In 1970 they opened a second plant in St. Paul. Since that time, the company has launched programs to revitalize urban and rural areas, create jobs through business development, provide training to prison populations, and meet other social needs.

Another exemplary organization widely recognized for its strong ethical character and keen sense of social responsibility is Johnson & Johnson. In 1982, seven people died after ingesting one of the firm's products, Tylenol capsules, that had been laced with cyanide. Even though the poisoning had occurred outside Johnson & Johnson's premises and was limited to the Chicago area, the company withdrew all Tylenol capsules from the U.S. market, at an estimated cost of $100 million. At the same time, the company initiated a comprehensive communication effort, involving 2,500 employees throughout the organization, aimed at the medical and pharmaceutical communities. The company's handling of the tampering crisis (its second such crisis) prompted then President Ronald Reagan to applaud Johnson & Johnson's leadership in a speech to the Business Council in Washington D.C. Noting its commitment to socially responsible behavior, Reagan said, "Let me congratulate one of your members, someone who in recent days has lived up to the highest ideal of corporate responsibility and grace under pressure. Jim Burke of Johnson & Johnson, you have our deepest admiration" (Benson, 1988, p. 62). The *Washington Post* wrote of the incident, "Johnson & Johnson has succeeded in portraying itself to the public as a company willing to do what's right, regardless of cost" (quoted in Aguilar, 1994, p. 164).

Interestingly, James Burke gave considerable credit to the organization's code of ethics, a code originally formalized in the 1940s, prominently displayed in all managers' offices, and revitalized by Burke through extensive discussions with top management in the 1970s. In the aftermath of the Tylenol tamperings, Burke noted, "I think the Tylenol story is the most powerful thing that has occurred in American business to underline the value of a moral statement" (Aguilar, 1994, p. 68). Focus On presents Johnson & Johnson's current Credo.

Although it might seem that large corporations have the greatest opportunities and resources to demonstrate a social conscience, those who run smaller organizations have been known to make impressive contributions as well. One woman who runs a private communication consulting firm in Washington, D.C., for instance, became deeply concerned about the plight of single mothers who were trying to gain employment after the birth of a child but either could not find or could not afford child care. This woman bought and renovated a large house, identified five needy single mothers, and rented the house to them for $100 a month each. Then she found five elderly people who had no families but who were in relatively good health and loved young children. They, too, were brought to the house to live—and they cared for the children while the mothers went to work. Besides the initial cost of the house (over $250,000), this businesswoman spent an additional $5,000 each year, just to keep the house running and in good condition. Thus, through her effort and generosity, she helped meet the needs of single mothers, several young children, and the elderly—on a small scale, but in a truly significant and enduring way.

Of course, the ethical issues we have chosen to address in this chapter are often interdependent. For instance, the ethical and socially responsible action on occasion may lead to a (hopefully temporary) decline in profits, the next ethical issue we discuss.

Service Versus Profit

Most business theorists argue that good service means better profits—that maximizing the services provided to customers ultimately improves an organization's "bottom line." In certain kinds of industries, like health care, the

FOCUS ON   Johnson & Johnson *Our Credo*

We believe our first responsibility is to the doctors, nurses and patients, to mothers and fathers and all others who use our products and services. In meeting their needs everything we do must be of high quality. We must constantly strive to reduce our costs in order to maintain reasonable prices. Customers' orders must be serviced promptly and accurately. Our suppliers and distributors must have an opportunity to make a fair profit.

We are responsible to our employees, the men and women who work with us throughout the world. Everyone must be considered as an individual. We must respect their dignity and recognize their merit. They must have a sense of security in their jobs. Compensation must be fair and adequate, and working conditions clean, orderly and safe. We must be mindful of ways to help our employees fulfill their family responsibilities. Employees must feel free to make suggestions and complaints. There must be equal opportunity for employment, development and advancement for those qualified. We must provide competent management, and their actions must be just and ethical.

We are responsible to the communities in which we live and work and to the world community as well. We must be good citizens—support good works and charities and bear our fair share of taxes. We must encourage civic improvements and better health and education. We must maintain in good order the property we are privileged to use, protecting the environment and natural resources.

Our final responsibility is to our stockholders. Business must make a sound profit. We must experiment with new ideas. Research must be carried on, innovative programs developed and mistakes paid for. New equipment must be purchased, new facilities provided and new products launched. Reserves must be created to provide for adverse times. When we operate according to these principles, the stockholders should realize a fair return.

pharmaceutical industry, and academic institutions, however, this principle does not necessarily hold true.

In the mid-1980s, the federal government became increasingly concerned about rapidly rising health care costs. As a result, in 1983 Congress enacted the Medicare Prospective Payment System (PPS), which established fixed amounts that would be paid to hospitals for each of 468 different types of treatments. Medicare would henceforth pay a certain amount for a hip joint replacement, a certain amount for bypass surgery, and so on. (Prior to that time, Medicare and Medicaid had paid hospital charges regardless of the amount charged.) Under the new plan, hospitals whose actual costs fell below the fixed levels could keep the difference; those whose costs exceeded the established levels suffered losses. Since an average of 40 percent of all hospital patients are covered by Medicare, this step represented a significant change in health care funding. Soon after, other private insurers implemented similar plans of their own.

Hospitals responded to these financial pressures in several ways, most of which attempted to reduce the costs of providing care (Shortell, Morrison, & Friedman, 1990). Reducing patients' "length of stay" became a key element of cost reduction. For example, by reducing from five days to three the amount of time an appendectomy patient spent in the hospital, hospital administrators could reduce the cost of delivering care to that person. Other procedures that used to require a two- or three-day hospital stay were reevaluated and offered on an outpatient basis. Thus, cataract implant surgery is now typically performed in the early morning and the patient is released later the same day—even though most implant surgeries are performed on elderly patients who are often not in ideal health and require some assistance even in the best of circumstances—help that may or may not be available to them in the days following their surgery.

In other cases, health care organizations have begun marketing their services more aggressively, with ethical implications. One such instance involved a Chicago-based hospice (designed to provide home care for terminally ill patients believed to have six months or less to live). In a memo sent to employees, hospice management offered to pay cash bonuses to nurses to recruit patients, thereby increasing their business. A subsequent memo directed the nurses to immediately hospitalize all patients admitted to the hospice program during the weekend (despite federal regulations that no more than 20 percent of hospice care is to be in the hospital). Hospice care provided on an inpatient basis is more lucrative for the hospice organization. According to an article appearing in the *Chicago Tribune,* one memo from an administrator stated, "The low census in both inpatient units cannot continue to occur. Quite frankly, it is strangling us financially" (*Chicago Tribune,* 1990, sec. 4, p. 1). More than a dozen employees quit their jobs in this organization, saying they were disturbed by what they viewed as unethical practices.

Finally, many health care organizations are taking steps to lower costs and improve their financial strength by reducing the number of staff (including the number of people who provide care directly to patients), reducing or eliminating services and treatments that have proven unprofitable, conducting fewer routine tests, and attempting to control equipment and supply costs. Still, over one hundred hospitals have been forced to close each year, and financial pressures remain (*Hospitals,* 1989).

Health care administrators and managers thus face a variety of ethical choices, which are likely to become even more difficult as technological options exceed available resources. Among the compelling questions are the following: What level of health care is "good enough"? Should services offered be based on community needs, financial realities, or some compromise between the two? How far should a health care organization go in trying to increase its business volume? How much work can reasonably be demanded of hospital employees (a question relevant to every organization, as we will discuss below)? Ultimately, the responses to ethical issues like these will determine the quality and type of health care patients receive in the future.

Employee Rights

The treatment of employees by their superiors involves a myriad of ethical issues. Most theorists argue that employees have certain basic rights and that the ethics of management's treatment of employees can be judged, at least in part, by the extent to which those rights are upheld. We will consider four examples of those rights here. Others, such as the right to fair and equitable treatment for women and minorities, were addressed in Chapter 9.

The Right to a Safe and Healthful Work Environment.   The Occupational Safety and Health Administration (OSHA) was established to ensure that employers provide safe working conditions for their people. Yet abuses occur. The authors recently became aware of a situation involving a sheet metal company in the Midwest. After being hired by a hospital to replace its air conditioning ducts, the company hired a nineteen-year-old for $5.75 an hour to drive a truck and help unload materials. After a few weeks, however, the supervisor asked the young man to help install the ducts—a task for which specialists normally receive $30 per hour. Not only did the teenager feel unqualified for the job (and financially exploited), he also worried about the potent odors that seeped from the sealant used to "glue" the duct segments together. One day the young man was working above an office where a pregnant woman was employed as a secretary. She complained about the odor and asked him if he thought it was safe for her to work in the office while the ducts were being replaced. He therefore agreed to check the label on the sealant cans, and on doing so discovered to his horror that the sealant contained poisonous chemicals. Its label warned against inhaling or touching—particularly for children, pregnant women, and those with specific allergies. The young man returned to inform the woman of the danger and then, having breathed toxic chemicals for two weeks, quit the job. The company soon hired another teenager to replace him.

Clearly, the ethical questions posed by this example are numerous. Unqualified individuals were employed to perform a job that should have been reserved for experts (who could be expected to know enough to work only with gas masks)—apparently, to save money. Both employees and clients were exposed to dangerous chemicals without their knowledge. Finally, the quality of work could not have been guaranteed since untrained, inexperienced workers were doing it. The hospital administrators were not getting the service they paid for—and if the ducts turned out to be improperly installed, future health hazards would likely emerge.

Even more dramatic and tragic examples have been reported. Scientists from Argonne's Center for Human Radiobiology, for example, counted nine deaths from breast cancer among a group of 463 women who had all worked in a luminous processes plant in Ottawa, Illinois, painting clock and watch dials with radium. Given statistics available at the time, this breast cancer death rate was nearly three times higher than that of women working in comparable occupations. These women reported that safety precautions were almost nonexistent and that workers were constantly contaminated with the radioactive material. In fact, they stated that company officials told them that radium was safe to handle. Women at the plant sometimes painted their fingernails with radium paint; others took pots of radium paint home to paint light switches that would glow in the dark. Workers routinely contaminated their hair, arms, legs, and feet with the radioactive material accidentally while they worked, and they wiped paint-covered hands on the front of their work smocks. The plant closed in 1978 (Solomon & Hanson, 1985).

While the need to protect workers in the workplace would seem incontrovertible, many important issues remain. For instance, many major U.S. corporations (including General Motors, Gulf Oil, Dow Chemical, Union Carbide, and Monsanto) have policies concerning "fetal protection" that prohibit women from working in areas that might endanger their pregnancies. "I can't go anywhere," said Patricia Briner, who fills batteries with acid for Milwaukee-based Johnson Controls, Inc. "The good jobs are in departments where lead is used—and women aren't allowed to work in them. The company says it's too dangerous. That includes women who aren't pregnant and who don't ever intend to become pregnant" (Kleiman, *Chicago Tribune,* 1990, sec. 4, p. 2). A spokesman for the company said that according to company research, lead exposure "has a minor impact on men, but overwhelming evidence indicates risk to fetuses. It would be unconscionable to expose women to it. We're trying to do the right thing" (p. 2). Ultimately, the Supreme Court will have to determine whether OSHA regulations, which require companies to take steps to protect third parties (such as fetuses) from workplace dangers, take precedence over Title VII of the U.S. Civil Rights Act, which prohibits discrimination in job assignments.

The Right to Privacy.   Most people would agree that employee offices, lockers, files, telephone conversations, personnel data, outside activities, and so on should be not be invaded by their employers—that people have a right to privacy at work. Yet the limits of employee privacy are being pushed back almost daily. For example, employees are now being tested in a variety of ways by their employers—for drug and alcohol use, for AIDS, and for honesty—sometimes as part of the selection process (Greenberg, 1988). Employees subjected to such tests often object that what they do on their own time is their own business. Yet three Northwest Airlines pilots were convicted recently of flying under the influence of alcohol—the result of a party in which they had participated "on their own time," as they tried to argue, the night before the flight. Employees at a meatpacking plant in Monmouth, Illinois, objected to random drug and alcohol testing conducted by their employer, despite the fact that their jobs required them to use extremely sharp knives to butcher hogs and the testing was designed to improve safety. As one company foreman said, "We try to protect those who are too dumb to protect themselves."

Electronic monitoring of employee performance has also increased. An estimated 10 million workers in the United States have their work output measured electronically, or their phone conversations listened to during the workday. Those employees most frequently monitored include telephone operators; airline, auto rental, and hotel reservation clerks; insurance claims processors; and newspaper classified ad and circulation workers. Critics claim that such monitoring increases work stress (bringing about "electronic sweatshops") and may lead to a loss of freedom. However, others argue that monitoring is essential to ensure the quality of customer service work (*Chicago Tribune*, 1990, sec. 4). Legislation to limit employer monitoring of employees is pending.

The Right to Live a Balanced Life.   How much time and effort can an organization demand of its employees without making an unethical claim on their time? Should organizational commitment be measured in hours? What is

This computer-based active badge system was developed by Olivetti Research to help locate workers. Olivetti believes that the increased productivity achieved from the use of the devices will more than offset any concerns about worker privacy. (Olivetti Research Ltd.)

the relationship between having a work ethic and being a workaholic? These are questions that are not easily answered but that increasingly demand our attention.

If Americans are devoting too much time to their jobs, the problem may originate at the top with the CEOs and other executives who, through their actions, set the pace for those below them. In an article revealingly titled "Stop Whining and Get Back to Work," *Fortune* writer Sally Solo (1990) reported that CEOs expect between 54 and 60 hours a week from their upper-level executives. Moreover, these CEOs overwhelmingly believe that U.S. companies will have to push executives even harder in the future to keep up with global competition. In addition, when organizations undergo downsizing, workers at every level are adversely affected, especially in terms of overwork. Cameron's recent studies of downsizing at thirty auto-related industrial companies in the upper Midwest concluded that most carried out restructurings badly and gave little thought to rebalancing the workload among survivors of the layoffs. Cameron noted "There's a general approach of throwing a hand grenade at a bunch of employees, and whoever survives has to do all the work there was before" (O'Reilly, 1990, p. 41). "Working smarter" is often a euphemism for "working harder." In Japan, when a worker dies of exhaustion, they call it *karoshi*, or "death from overwork." At this point, Americans have no such word for this phenomenon. But will there soon be a need for one?

Some evidence suggests that younger American employees are beginning to take things into their own hands. As one writer put it, "With their personal and family lives in smithereens or a state of perpetual postponement, what seems a substantial contingent of the formerly ambitious have begun harboring seditious thoughts about the work ethic and the all-importance of a dazzling career" (O'Reilly, 1990, p. 39). Cathy Cook provided a compelling example. For eighteen months prior to the introduction of Steve Jobs's Next computer, Cook was responsible for fielding questions from hordes of reporters eager to learn about the new, largely secret machine. Cook often worked from 7:30 A.M. to 11:30 P.M. and then went home to an answering machine with several dozen messages to review before starting the next day. She lost her boyfriend and found herself unable to spend time with her seriously ill mother. Ultimately, she quit her job at Next and enrolled at Harvard's Kennedy School of Government. She plans to return to Silicon Valley eventually but vows to live a balanced life.

In 1990 *Fortune* interviewed thirty college-educated twenty-five-year-old business beginners who reported a strong need for balance in their lives (Deutschman, 1990). They uniformly stressed the importance to them of quality of life, although they defined the good life in diverse ways. Careers were described as being part—but not all—of those things adding meaning to life. Most expressed strong reservations about the lives of many upper-level, highly "successful" executives they observed—lives riddled with unhealthy habits, divorce, and workaholism. They were more likely than those ten years older to stress the value of flexible work schedules, leisure time, exercise, church membership, family life, and volunteerism.

What might organizations do to offer employees the opportunity for living more balanced lives? Apple Computer is more sensitive than many companies to the stress that comes with overwork. It offers a massage parlor on the premises, sponsors an equestrian club, and gives aikido lessons to help workers blow off steam. However, when one manager came to work two days after she gave birth last year, Apple executives did not send her home. They left the decision to her. As O'Reilly put it:

> It is easy to forget that hard work is not inherently good or moral, but only as noble as what you're striving to achieve. Working so hard that you're a dismal parent is wrong. Working hard so you can become filthy rich is merely greedy. Working overtime because your boss is too dim to let you do meaningful, efficient work is foolish, unless you are paid handsomely for the aggravation (p. 46).

The Right to Blow the Whistle. Despite traditional organizational rules prohibiting "insubordination," most would agree that employees should have the right to refuse orders that violate their principles (for instance, falsifying figures in a financial statement, giving or accepting bribes, lying to government agencies, and so on). Yet the acceptability of an employee "blowing the whistle" when she or he sees an organization engaging in unethical practices remains controversial. The **whistle-blower,** according to Walters (1975), "[has] decided at some point that the actions of the organization are immoral, illegal, or inefficient, . . . [and] acts on that belief by informing legal authorities or others outside the organization" (p. 26). In short, whistle-blowers put their duty to the public above their loyalty to the organization.

The prototypical case of a whistle-blower involved Dan Gellert, a pilot for Eastern Airlines, who became concerned about the safety of the Lockheed 1011 airplane. In flight simulations the automatic pilot would disengage without warning about 90 seconds before landing (or about 2,000 feet above the ground). Gellert reported his concerns to company management, which promised to look into it. On December 29, 1972, an Eastern Airlines L-1011 crashed, killing 103 people. Gellert took his report to the top of the company, where he was ignored. Then he sent his report to the National Transportation Safety Board. While his actions did prompt some needed adjustments in the automatic pilot (done quietly by the company), Gellert was demoted and then grounded. After going through a grievance procedure for seven months, Gellert sued Eastern. Ultimately, he won $1.6 million (more than he had sued for).

For years, organizations like the American Association for the Advancement of Science have encouraged acts of whistle-blowing. However, Dudar (1979) argued that "most people who wind up in the fraternity [of whistle-blowers] begin almost accidentally, expecting gratitude and encountering, instead, a stone wall of either indifference or hostility" (p. 52). However well justified the whistle-blower's charges, management in both industry and government have traditionally moved quickly to retaliate. As Hilts (1993) pointed out in the *New York Times,* "Often they are punished more harshly than the wrongdoers they catch" (p. E6). In 1965, for instance, General Motors hired private detectives to spy on Ralph Nader because he had evidence from a whistle-blower condemning the Corvair for safety reasons. The three engineers who testified before the Rogers Commission that they had voiced strong objections to launching the *Challenger* in 1986 (objections that were completely ignored by management) were unceremoniously stripped of their authority, deprived of their staffs, and prevented from seeing critical data concerning the *Challenger* disaster (Glazer & Glazer, 1989). In general, reprisals implemented by management range from personal harassment to blacklisting to dismissal. The strategies seem aimed at defining the dissident employee as the source of the problem, undermining his or her credibility and effectiveness as a potential witness, and demonstrating to other workers the high cost of nonconformity.

The practice of whistle-blowing emerged as a significant social force in the 1960s. Public concern about nuclear accidents, dangerous drugs, and toxic wastes eventually led to government regulation of private industry, spawning a host of new laws that explicitly protect workers who report unethical actions in the workplace. For example, in 1988, OSHA issued final rules outlining procedures the agency would use to investigate cases in which employees in the trucking industry alleged that they were fired or otherwise subjected to retaliation by their employers for voicing complaints about health or safety conditions. In 1990 the state of Wisconsin enacted new employment laws making employers liable for retaliation taken in the belief that an employee has filed a complaint, even if the employee has not actually filed. New Jersey had already enacted such legislation in 1986.

Once a perceived wrongdoing is discovered, the process that leads to blowing the whistle is inherently communicative. The employee may choose to try to remedy the situation by communicating his or her knowledge of the problem to someone in a position of authority within the organization. This communication may take place informally initially, but if the problem is not addressed following this initial attempt, the employee is likely to communicate more formally (meeting with official decision-making bodies or filing formal reports). If all attempts to communicate internally fall on deaf ears, the employee then must decide whether to seek an audience outside the organization, such as a government agency or the media.

The controversy over whistle-blowing brings into conflict two commonly held values: loyalty to the organization versus responsibility to society. Of course, in an organization characterized by a clear sense of social responsibility, incidents necessitating whistle-blowing may never arise. In a less ideal organizational environment, however, whistle-blowing requires deep convictions and the courage to do what one views as right even when confronted with potentially threatening consequences. Behavior consistent with one's ethical principles may lead to enhanced self-esteem and peace of mind, ends that are surely empowering.

In the second half of this chapter we consider ethical issues that relate to technology. Interestingly, some of the issues we have already addressed (such as employee rights to privacy and codes of ethics) are also critically intertwined with advances in technology. For the most part, in this book we have discussed technology as potentially empowering. In this chapter, however, we will emphasize the possible abuses of technology and, hence, the ongoing need for vigilance.

Technology: Boom or Bust?

Groupware and other technologies have had a dramatic effect on organizational design and behavior. We have seen how technology can bring about flattened organizational hierarchies, facilitate decision group making, help to coordinate self-managed teams, promote empowerment, and provide new channels for organizational leadership.

However, technology may be likened to a double-edged sword. Laudon and Laudon (1994) noted that with new information technology ". . . it will also be possible for you—but not necessary—to decentralize power in an organization, invade the privacy of your employees while you improve service to customers, reach markets served by your global competitors and cause widespread unemployment, engage in new kinds of criminal activity as your company seeks to protect itself from information disclosures, and create new kinds of products which eliminate older products and the employment of people who make those products" (p. 700).

Certainly it was not the intent of technology developers to corrupt organizational and societal behavior. Most technologies were simply designed to expedite the way we manage, store, handle, and communicate information. In particular, Oz (1994, pp. 18–19) pointed to the following functions:

1. **Data collection.** Computer terminals in the form of cash registers, ATMs, and other devices collect millions of data pieces daily. For example, whenever a customer buys something in a supermarket, the sale is recorded and channeled into one or more databases. The quantity purchased may be automatically recorded into an inventory file, and the total sale into a sales file; and if more data are supplied by the customer, they are channeled into a specific file for marketing purposes.

2. **Data processing.** Data are like raw material. They cannot be used unless processed and organized. With the proper programs, computers perform numerous arithmetic and logic operations that process data into useful information. Information is used to make decisions, create reports, and compile lists for marketing and other purposes. In a few seconds, a

computer can perform tedious calculations that would take humans days or weeks. A file containing millions of personal records can be reorganized in any prescribed order within seconds.

3. **Storage and retrieval.** The great capacity of storage media and the speed of the computer allow quick storage and retrieval of large amounts of data. A whole library can now be stored on a few optical disks. Thanks to computer networks, storage and retrieval can be carried out regardless of the physical location of the data.

4. **Communication.** Computer networks are used to transmit and receive information and to share computer resources. As long as an individual has access to a computer network, any resource that is part of the network is at the individual's disposal. A person can run a computer program from thousands of miles away and receive the results on his or her own monitor. Computer networks provide e-mail capabilities, replacing telephone and telex communication.

5. **Presentation.** Multimedia techniques allow the user to combine text, audio, and video information in the same presentation. The combination may present ideas in a manner clearer than conventional methods. Thus, computers are effectively used for educational and training purposes.

6. **Control.** Computers can be programmed to control processes that used to be monitored by humans. They can control manufacturing machines, nuclear reactors, and traffic lights.

7. **Dissemination of expertise.** Using artificial intelligence techniques, much of an expert's knowledge can be transformed into a computer program. The program later replaces human experts by providing a specialist's advice.

While these technologies certainly provide the ability to enhance organizational productivity, the real possibility exists that information technologies can and will be misused and abused. New communication channels and computer capabilities provide opportunities for some people to use technology in ways not intended or even anticipated by the systems' designers. Consider these actual occurrences in which ethical issues have surfaced in the everyday use of computers and networking technologies.

- A federal judge placed a twenty-four-year-old computer science student on three years' probation for intentionally disrupting a nationwide computer network. The student was also fined $10,000 and ordered to perform 400 hours of community service (Markoff, 1990).

- An America Online subscriber reportedly contacted several newspapers and television stations with claims that unsolicited pornographic photos of children had been sent to him via private e-mail on the service (Lindquist, 1991).

- When Alana Shoars arrived for work at Epson America, Inc., one morning in January 1990, she discovered her supervisor reading and printing out e-mail messages between other employees. As e-mail administrator, Ms. Shoars was appalled. When she had trained employees to use the computerized system, Ms. Shoars told them their mail was private. Now a company manager was violating that trust. When she questioned the practice, Ms. Shoars was told to mind her own business. A day later, she was fired for insubordination. She has since filed a $1 million wrongful termination suit (Rifkin, 1991).

- The receptionist at Chicago's Davy-McKee Corp. didn't quite get it. "Do you have an appointment?" she asked the battery of federal marshals and computer experts who barged into the construction engineering firm's office on a raid. When the Software Publishers Association lawyer flashed a court order permitting the search of the company's computers for illegally copied software, the receptionist asked if they would mind coming back Monday.

  "I know, are you from 'Candid Camera'?" she finally asked. Surprise drop-ins by the software industry's trade association have become a staple in the anti-piracy battle, as courts dole out search warrants and the software association increases its piracy police (Hendren, 1993).

- Employees at Crown gas stations from Florida to Maryland don't have to worry about the boss dropping in unannounced. But that's because Crown executives hundreds of miles away can monitor and talk to workers through an electronic surveillance system installed at 110 of the company's 450 stations. Crown Central Petroleum Corp. officials say the system helps ensure that the Slushie machine is full, gives workers a feeling of security, boosts morale, and prevents theft. Critics say Crown's surveillance system is just one in a growing stockpile of weapons employers are using to force improvements in worker productivity. The result, they say, is alienated, resentful employees (Dominguez, 1993).

- Intruders have broken into the giant Internet computer network, and users are being advised to protect themselves by changing their passwords. The Internet is an international system linking computer networks among universities, government agencies, corporations, and private users. The break-ins may jeopardize the work of tens of thousands of computer users, warned the Computer Emergency Response Team based at Carnegie Mellon University in Pittsburgh. Intruders can delete or remove other users' files (Wire Reports, 1994).

While Oz (1994) has documented the contributions of information technology to society, he has also acknowledged that technology virtually opens the door for new phenomena and ethical dilemmas. He identified a number of key issues surrounding the continuing use and growth of information technology:

- **Worker displacement.** Information-intensive industries like banks, insurance companies, and other service organizations are gradually replacing employees with computers that do the job "better and faster."

- **Computer illiteracy.** In our society, computer illiteracy increasingly handicaps workers and potentially hurts the audiences they serve. Computer skills are now seen to be a necessary and integral part of educational curricula, including the liberal arts. In both the service and the manufacturing sectors, computers are critical to providing effective products and services to the all-important customer.

- **Depersonalization.** Electronic communication, while often efficient, is sometimes impersonal and irritating. For example, many organizations have replaced customer service workers with voice messaging systems, which ask callers to choose their requirements from a tedious menu of options that take a disproportionate amount of time to negotiate and often end in frustration.

- **Overreliance on computers.** Computer-based systems can fail or make errors with dramatic consequences. For example, in 1990, a computer failure at AT&T severely slowed down the nationwide long-distance network for about eleven hours. Imagine the response if the IRS had computer problems that slowed the payment of refunds!

- **Health hazards.** It has been claimed that video display terminals may cause eye strain and reproductive problems, that printers may cause noise pollution, and that frequent use of computer workstations may cause musculoskeletal problems. Legal observers predict increasing litigation against computer product manufacturers.

- **Invasion of privacy.** As noted earlier, technology allows firms to monitor inexpensively the movement and the communication of employees; sell databases of customer information; send unsolicited fax messages; and violate copyright laws by illegally reproducing images, audio, software, text, and data.

- **Computer crime.** Criminal activities have entered the computer domain. Examples include the copying of software protected by trade secret, copyright, and/or patent law; information theft; service theft (unauthorized use of hardware and software); data alteration and data destruction; program damage due to a computer virus; hacking (gaining unauthorized access to a computer); computer fraud (the illegal transfer of funds electronically), the theft of computer equipment and supplies; the misuse and illegal possession of information; and the use of computer systems or information to violate free trade.

Laudon and Laudon (1994) identified four key trends that, in their view, provide the fundamental basis for ethical issues involving information technology. First, they noted that *computer power,* measured by the number of integers that a computer can process in a second, *has been doubling every eighteen months since the early 1980s,* making it possible for most organizations to use information systems for their core production processes. These organizations are, they argued, now more dependent on these systems and hence more vulnerable to system errors and poor or erroneous data. Laudon and Laudon stated that social rules and laws have not yet adjusted to this dependence and that standards for ensuring the accuracy and reliability of information systems are not universally accepted or enforced.

Second, *advances in data storage techniques and rapidly declining storage costs have been responsible for multiplying the databases on individuals* (employees, customers, and potential customers) maintained by private and public organizations. Laudon and Laudon suggested that these advances in data storage have made the routine violation of individual privacy both cheap and effective.

Third, *advances in data mining techniques for large databases is a technological trend that heightens ethical concerns.* Computers are used to identify buying patterns of customers and to suggest appropriate responses. Laudon and Laudon cited one instance in which a retailer analyzed customer buying patterns and found that if someone in the Midwest buys disposable diapers at 5 P.M., the most common item next purchased is a six-pack of beer. The retailer decided, therefore, to put beer and snacks next to the diaper rack!

Finally, these authors argued that *advances in the telecommunications infrastructure in the United States will allow vast amounts of data to be moved quickly and will enable remote databases to be mined using small desktop computers (PCs).* In particular, development of a national computer "superhighway" or communications network poses many ethical concerns for both individuals and businesses. For example

- who will account for the flow of information over these networks?
- will information collected about an individual be traceable to a source—can you find out who is collecting information about you?
- what will these networks do to the traditional relationships between family, work, and leisure?

Legislation

To curb the abuse of information contained on paper and/or electronic media, Congress has passed laws that try to govern record keeping in the United States. Some of the key pieces of legislation are listed in Table 10.2.

Since 1976, state legislatures have also started to consider laws relating to abuse of computers, data, and software for the purpose of committing crimes with the aid of, and against, computers. As of 1990, forty-nine states had statutes against computer-related crimes (Oz, 1994).

Technology Codes of Ethics

Often, firms take preemptive action to inhibit criminal behavior and prevent legislated mandates by drafting their own codes of ethical behavior. Noting that about 60 percent of Fortune 500 firms have a general information systems code of ethics, Laudon and Laudon (1994) urged managers to develop

Freedom of Information Act of 1966

Federal government records are accessible by nearly everyone with few exceptions. Although some information may be withheld due to issues relating to national security and/or foreign policy secrecy, this otherwise-guaranteed access to government information represents one of the most progressive laws in the world.

Fair Credit Reporting Act of 1970

This legislation was passed to control the propagation of personal credit information. It states that credit agencies cannot share credit information with anyone but authorized customers, and it gives citizens the right to inspect their credit records and be notified of their use for employment or credit.

Privacy Act of 1974

This legislation was enacted to protect individual privacy interests from government misuse of federal records containing personal information. It lays down conditions that federal agencies and their contractors must follow concerning how information about individuals may be collected, stored, accessed, and distributed.

Copyright Act of 1976

This act protects intellectual property (authored work) against copying. The Computer Software Protection Act of 1980 amended the Copyright Act by specifically including software among the works protected.

Right to Privacy Act of 1978

Enacted in response to the increasing use of computerized databases in financial institutions, which have become vast repositories of personal information, this statute limits the conditions under which the federal government may search an individual's bank records.

Electronic Communications Privacy Act of 1986

The purpose of this act is to prevent criminals from concealing illegal activity either by encrypting their communications about their activities or by taking advantage of security measures designed to defeat illegal tampering or eavesdropping.

Computer Security Act of 1987

As more and more information gathered by the federal government was handled by computers, Congress found it in the public interest to set up minimum security practices for federal computer systems.

Video Privacy Protection Act (1988)

This act prevents video rental records from being sold or released without a court order or the consent of the person renting the video.

TABLE 10.2

Legislation Affecting Access to Information

an *information systems–specific set of ethical standards* grounded in five moral dimensions:

- **Information rights and obligations.** A code should cover topics like employee e-mail privacy, workplace monitoring, treatment of corporate information, and policies on customer information.

- **Property rights and obligations.** A code should cover topics like software licenses, ownership of firm data and facilities, ownership of software created by employees on company hardware, and software copyrights. Specific guidelines for contractual relationships with third parties should be covered as well.

- **Accountability and control.** The code should specify a single individual responsible for all information systems, and underneath this individual others who are responsible for individual rights, the protection of property rights, systems quality, and quality of life (job design, ergonomics, employee satisfaction). Responsibilities for control of systems, audits, and management should be clearly defined. The potential liabilities of systems officers, and the corporation, should be detailed in a separate document.

- **System quality.** The code should describe the general levels of data quality and system error that can be tolerated, with detailed specifications left to specific projects. The code should require that all systems attempt to estimate data quality and system error probabilities.

- **Quality of life.** The code should state that the purpose of systems is to improve the quality of life for customers and for employees by achieving high levels of product quality, customer service, and employee satisfaction and human dignity through proper ergonomics, job and work flow design, and human resource development (p. 732).

DeMaio (1991) suggested that codes of ethics are important because, to the extent that an organization is dependent on the behavior of its members, those in charge must convey expectations and provide guidance on how to behave. According to him, it is a mistake to assume that people will automatically apply to information the same ethical norms that they apply to tangible assets. He argued that technology has made it more difficult for individuals to develop on their own an appropriate and sharply focused information code of ethics, for the following reasons:

1. Intangible property is different from physical assets, and the widespread use of electronics has increased the differences.

2. There is a conflict between the natural urge to communicate and the need to protect proprietary data.

Future Issues

"Downsizing, rightsizing, reengineering, empowering, TQM, and process redesign" are all terms used by business to describe processes whereby large corporations squeeze out inefficiencies so that they can respond to global competition and technological change while at the same time working to improve product quality and customer service. These changes, however, have not come without societal consequences. As Fierman (1994) put it:

> Like the tolling of an iron bell, a gloomy statistic has begun to resonate with many Americans: By some calculations, one out of four of us is now a member of a contingency work force, people hired by companies to cope with unexpected or temporary challenges. . . . such workers typically lead far riskier and more uncertain lives than permanent workers . . . by the year 2000 fully half of all working Americans—some 60 million people—will have joined the ranks of these freelance providers of skills and services. Does the bell toll for you? (pp. 30–31).

The social phenomenon of the "just-in-time" worker was certainly not planned. Indeed, many workers view the demise of the employee-employer marriage as being "un-American." To the surprise and anger of many U.S. workers, holding one or two jobs from cradle to grave is now the exceptional employment history, whereas only a few years ago it was the norm.

The need for organizational efficiency and flexibility also runs counter to the belief that competitive advantage depends upon keeping a stable and empowered work force. That is, empowerment assumes motivation, creativity, and independence—both in actions and in communication. The new practical and even ethical dilemma faced by organizations is whether the goal of an empowered work force can ever be achieved with employees who are also viewed by companies as disposable (see Case 1) and who have no reason necessarily to be loyal and make decisions in the firm's best interest. Indeed, Fierman (1994) noted that even CEOs appear split as to whether the trend toward using more contingent workers (workers hired for temporary periods) is good for the United States (see Table 10.3).

TABLE 10.3

CEO Poll

The Trend Toward Using More Contingent Workers is:	
Good for the U.S.	48%
Bad for the U.S.	25
Neither	20
Not sure	7

SOURCE: *Fortune*, January 24, 1994.

Summarizing Perspective

As organizations attempt to grapple with ethics, they increasingly seek varied routes for communicating their values. For instance, they may develop corporate mission statements to tell employees what the organization is about and where it is going. These statements may serve to separate an organization from its competition and provide it with a sense of identity, legitimacy, and direction. The mission statement may be accompanied by a code of ethics (a general code, as well as one that is technology-focused as discussed above), which speaks to activities that cannot be closely supervised by management, like honesty in dealing with clients or mutual respect among employees. Now adopted by more than 200 of the *Fortune 500* companies, ethical codes contribute to long-term organizational success only to the extent that they are upheld by *both* employers and employees; that is, they depend upon voluntary cooperation. Finally, and most important, *management behaviors* remain the real key to developing organizational ethics.

Managers can influence their organization's ethical climate in several ways. They may, for instance, emphasize and discuss ethics continually. A code of ethics becomes real only when a manager talks about it by encouraging subordinates to raise ethics-related issues, doubts, or concerns; by referring to it when answering questions or making decisions; and by keeping others' attention focused on it. Managers must also develop and articulate realistic goals. Employees who are confronted with goals they cannot achieve are tempted to cut corners, sacrificing ethics for achievement. By identifying areas that are vulnerable to unethical practices, managers may also avoid ethical problems by discussing with employees the sorts of temptations that might arise. Finally, by encouraging reporting of unethical activities, managers let all employees know that each of them has an important role in enforcing ethical standards; at the same time, they indicate their serious intent to ensure ethical behavior (Dolcheck, 1989).

Ultimately, values cannot be taught; they must be lived. People emulate what they see, not what they are told. If they see that unethical behaviors are practiced or tolerated, they will pay little attention to written codes of ethics or mission statements. Richard Zimmerman, chairman and CEO of Hershey Foods Corporation, refers to his company's value system as an "anchor" for the organization and asserts, "Each manager must have a grip on those clearly defined values and be able to demonstrate them through their own behavior to employee groups" (Blank, 1986, p. 33). Andrews (1989) argued that ethical decision making is the key to effective management, maintaining that ethical decisions require three qualities of those making them:

- *Competence* to recognize ethical issues and to think through the consequences of alternative resolutions.
- *Self-confidence* to seek out different points of view and then to decide what is right at a given time and place in a particular set of relationships and circumstances.

- *Tough-mindedness* or the willingness to make decisions when all that needs to be known cannot be known and when the questions that press for answers have no established and incontrovertible solutions (pp. 100–101).

In this chapter we have raised some important ethical questions with which all organizational members must grapple. They are especially compelling for those in positions of leadership who are committed to creating empowering organizational cultures. Clearly, many of the issues we have discussed focus on the use of technology. In the book's final chapter, we return to a more optimistic view—demonstrating technology's great potential for empowering, enhancing communication, and inspiring creativity and innovation.

CASES FOR DISCUSSION

CASE 1 *Disposable Workers*

The world's largest temporary employment agency is Manpower, Inc., with 560,000 employees. Every day, it sends people to American offices and factories to earn a day's work for a day's pay. The United States is increasingly becoming a nation of part-timers and freelancers, of temps and independent contractors. The notion of a temporary or "disposable" work force may be the most important trend in business today, and one that is fundamentally changing the relationship between Americans and their jobs. For companies of all sizes, the phenomenon provides a way to remain globally competitive while avoiding the growing burdens imposed by employment rules, antidiscrimination laws, health care costs, and pension plans. But for workers it often means an end to job security and the sense of meaning that comes from being a loyal employee associated with one organization.

Every day, agencies like Manpower and Kelly Services dispatch 1.5 million temps— nearly three times as many as ten years ago. An additional 34 million people start their day as other types of "contingent" workers. Some are part-timers with some benefits. Others work by the hour, by the day, or by the duration of the project, receiving a paycheck without benefits of any kind. Some fit the stereotype of temporary workers: secretaries, security guards, sales-clerks, and assembly-line workers. Others in this category, however, are far less likely: doctors, high school principals, lawyers, bank officers, X-ray technicians, biochemists, engineers, managers—even chief executives. For instance, a company that needs a tough boss who can clean up a bad situation might contact IMCOR, a Connecticut-based firm that boasts a roster of senior executives who are expert at turning companies around.

With surprising rapidity, companies are shedding a system of mutual obligations and expectations built up since the Great Depression—a tradition of employment that rewarded performance, valued loyalty, and viewed workers as a vital part of the enterprises served. For the growing ranks of contingent workers, the new ways mean no more pensions, health insurance, or paid vacations. Even worse, for millions of workers time-honored notions of fairness are being cast aside. Working as a temp often means being treated as a second-class citizen. It can also mean doing hazardous work without essential training, or being subjected to sexual and racial harassment. For highly trained professionals such as engineers, accountants, and financial managers, the new system may work well, since they can expect to thrive by providing highly compensated services to a variety of employers. Their loyalty is to their profession, rather than to General Motors or Boeing. They may perceive the new arrangement as more flexible and challenging. They can afford to pick and choose their employers if they are in high demand and good at what they do. Most Americans, however, work better under conditions of comfort and security.

Behind this profound change in the workplace are the impersonal market forces of the new global economy. Americans must now compete for jobs with the growing legions of skilled workers in developing economies from Asia to eastern Europe. U.S. executives have taken to talking about global "market prices" for employees, as if they were investing in cattle. Those who head organizations like Manpower argue they are not exploiting people. Rather, they are matching people with demands.

Critics argue, however, that the scramble to shed full-time workers (IBM has traded 10 percent of its staff for part-timers so far) may be as harmful to American industry as it is the American work force—as McGregor pointed out long ago, a well-trained, loyal work force is the greatest resource for any nation's industries. Moreover, far from being empowered, contingent workers labor under a cloud of uncertainty about the future. Secretary of Labor Robert Reich agrees, pointing out: "What we're seeing here is two trends on a collision course. One trend is empowerment, in which companies are revitalizing the core, strengthening relationships with workers. But the countertrend is the move toward contingent work, where there is always a question mark hanging over the relationship as to whether it will continue in the future. You can't do both".

Questions for Discussion

1. What sorts of ethical issues are involved in the situation described in this case?

2. What are the ethical perspectives that appear to guide businesses as they increasingly use temporary workers?

3. What are your ethical perspectives on this situation?

4. What are some possible ways of empowering a contingent work force?

SOURCE: Based on Castro, 1993

CASE 2 *E-Mail Ethics*

One communication technology rapidly growing in popularity is e-mail, the system whereby individuals send one another messages over a company's computer network. The e-mail recipient can, at his or her leisure, display the contents of his or her e-mail "box" (which typically lists the sender of each message and some indication of each message's content), and then decide which of those messages to read.

This method of communication can be extremely convenient. The sender can transmit messages whenever he or she wishes; the recipient can read messages and write responses as time allows.

However, the privacy of such messages has become a source of some controversy. In 1993, for example, *Macworld* magazine published a survey showing widespread eavesdropping by employers. Based on responses from 301 businesses employing over one million workers, *Macworld* estimated that as many as 20 million Americans may be subject to electronic monitoring on the job.

The *Macworld* survey found that more than 21 percent of the respondents had searched their employees' computer files, electronic mail, voice mail, or other networking communication. Of those who admitted to snooping, 74 percent had searched computer work files, 42 percent had searched electronic mail, and 15 percent had searched voice mail.

Why had these searches been conducted? To monitor work flow, investigate thefts, or prevent industrial espionage, some said. But whatever the purpose, there are no legal limits placed on employers "spying" on their employees in the workplace. They are free to view employees on closed-circuit television, tap their telephones, search their e-mail and network communication, and rummage through their computer files with or without employee knowledge or consent, twenty-four hours a day.

Georgia Jones learned this lesson the hard way. An e-mail expert, she was hired by a high-tech computer software firm in California to assist with the installation of a new e-mail system and to provide training to the company's 350 employees concerning how that system should be used.

After she had taken the job, she met with officials of the company to plan e-mail installation and training. Among the many questions she asked was, "Will employees' e-mail messages be confidential?" "Absolutely," she was assured.

During the training sessions, she repeated this information for the company's employees: She had been guaranteed that e-mail messages would be kept confidential, so that employees need not worry about the information they sent to one another.

A few months after the e-mail system had been installed and all employees had been trained, two first-line supervisors were fired by management. The rumor mill said they had been fired for "insubordination," and that the e-mail messages they had sent one another strongly criticizing management had somehow ended up "in the wrong hands." Because she was concerned about this rumor, Georgia decided she should meet with the company's president.

When she entered the president's office to keep their appointment, she noticed a stack of computer printouts on the credenza located along one wall of his office. A closer look revealed the contents of these printouts: employees' e-mail messages. When she asked, "What are those?" the president answered, "None of your business!"

Questions for Discussion

1. If you were Georgia, what would you do?

2. What breaches of ethics, if any, occurred in this case?

3. In your opinion, should employers have the right to inspect employees' e-mail files, voice mail messages, computer files, and so on? Why or why not?

4. If you were going to develop a code of ethics to address this issue, what rules and guidelines might you include?

SOURCE: Case based on information provided in *USA Today*, May 24, 1993.

Technological Innovation and Organizational Communication

The computer increasingly provides feedback and organizes interrelated information while continuously expanding the frontiers of interrelation. It expands the range and the scope of designated participation. It awakens possibilities of creation among the many, rather than just the minorities of past ages. After all, most of human achievement has been the anonymous assembly of discoveries and insights, from proverbs to building techniques, and their equally anonymous loss. The individuals within the great faceless creating mass of the human race can now relate to one another directly in real time, rather than over trade routes and centuries.

D. LeeBaert and T. Dickinson, "A world to understand: Technology and the awakening of human possibility," *Technology 2001: The future of computing and communication*, The MIT Press, 1991.

W e have seen that technology provides new channels for communication that fundamentally affect how work is done, how decisions are made, and how organizations are designed. Organizations use technology to improve communication and to coordinate people, resources, and work so that the firm is more efficient and effective and better able to survive in a rapidly changing environment.

Hotch (1993) argued "the next generations of technology will make current telecommunications look as awkward as the crank telephone of 1910. They will come by fits and starts, but they will transform the way business is done as surely as the telephone has" (p. 20). He noted that until this point in time, the kind of information transmitted was typically wed to a particular kind of technology hardware. For example, voice messages use telephone wires and phones, television and radio signals are broadcast via air waves or cable to television sets and radios. However, computer technology allows voice, text, images, sound, and video to be digitized into patterns of 1s and 0s that computers can receive, understand, process, copy, store, and transmit. Any information in this format can be delivered to any device that is capable of receiving, processing, and displaying it. Hence, Hotch argued, televisions equipped with digital technology can support computer text, a radio can receive a phone call, and computers equipped with multimedia capabilities can handle it all! Computers and networks allow many forms of communication to mesh on a single video display terminal.

Hotch noted that the major aim for technology manufacturers is to enable organizations to conduct business communication over long distances with the richness of face-to-face meetings. Moreover, he viewed wireless communication as making possible personal communication devices that combine voice, fax, electronic mail, and paging in a single unit.

In this, the final chapter, we will examine current technological innovations and preview some that are on the way. We will explore the information superhighway, noting its growth, future promise, and challenge. Then we will move to a consideration of reengineering and its implications (both positive and negative) for organizational communication. Next, we will examine a significant new market created by advances in technology: the home. We will conclude the chapter by reflecting on the relationship among technology, empowerment, and organizational communication.

The Information Superhighway

One of the most important technological developments of this decade may best be introduced by illustrating how it will change our lives:

> Imagine a day when you can get out of bed, take a shower, eat your breakfast, and get ready for work, but instead of leaving your house you stay home that day (the highway you *normally* take to work is under construction and traffic is a mess). You sit in your family room with a large screen (maybe it's your TV), and access the office and coworkers on the screen and have a video conference with them (some located in their office, some at home, your boss connected from a hotel room in Detroit).
>
> Sound like "the Jetsons"? That's just the tip of the iceberg. This is our future "data superhighway," and it's more than just a concept. It's slowly being constructed all around us, and someday, it will change much more than just your work day (Schindler, 1994).

In 1994, Vice President Al Gore unveiled the U.S. government's vision for the National Information Infrastructure—the information superhighway—a national broadband network that uses optic fibers rather than copper wires. The plan would overhaul longstanding communication laws, allowing head-to-head competition among telephone companies, cable firms, and other industry players for the right to provide an array of new information services. Services would range from movies delivered over telephone wires to interactive home shopping. The long-term goal is to provide two-way video, voice, and data communication to any school, home, or library that wants it. A senior citizen in a rural area state could undergo an on-line medical exam from a medical specialist located in a major urban medical center, or a student could browse the libraries of major universities for a homework assignment (Dentzer, 1994).

The information highway signifies the impending reality that consumer and computer technology will come together to produce a "communicopia" of interactive television and multimedia applications. Teresko (1994) contended that the information superhighway will provide new ways of doing business, advertising, and selling and delivering product. Indeed, he argued, products will no longer be defined by the industry offering them. For example, cable companies may provide telephone services, telephone companies may offer movies and video game devices, and computer companies may become software producers and publishers.

Technical advances that make this interactive communication possible include the ability to translate all audio and video communication into computer digital format, the ability to transmit digital signals over high-bandwidth fiber-optic lines or ultrahigh-frequency wireless channels, and new data compression and data storage methods to handle the sheer volume of information.

Current Organizational Applications

Freedman (1992) suggested four immediate applications for organizations:

1. **Videoconferencing**—the use of telecommunications technology to transmit voices and images in meetings whose participants are geographically dispersed.
2. **Multimedia**—technologies that facilitate the integration of two or more types of media, such as text, graphics, sound, voice, full-motion video, and/or animation into a computer-based application.
3. **Collaborative computing**—the use of computers and networks that enable groups and organizations to communicate and coordinate information across time and place.
4. **Local Area Network to Local Area Network communications**—bridges between networks that link personal computers to allow sharing of information and peripheral devices such as printers.

As corporate networks open up to customers, suppliers, and other outsiders, and as wireless and cellular communication becomes commonplace, entry into the organizational network will be accessible to anyone, anywhere. According to Freedman (1992), these developments will make it more important and more difficult to ensure the security, accuracy, and reliability of information.

Experts believe that by the end of the decade we will have access to shopping, movies, and other types of information on demand through some combination of interactive television, telephone, and computer (Dworetzky, 1994). Down the road another decade **virtual reality technology** will become more prevalent. This technology incorporates interactive graphics software and hardware to create computer-generated simulations that provide physical sensations emulating real-world experiences.

Although the technology is quite new, virtual reality is already being used for commercial purposes. Laudon and Laudon (1994) cited an instance:

> Matsushita Electric Works in Japan has put virtual reality to work in its department stores. . . . The stores sell kitchen appliances and cabinets. To promote these products Matsushita has created an application it calls Virtual Kitchen. The prospective buyers bring their kitchen layouts to the department store where trained staff enters a copy of the design into the computer. The customers then don a virtual reality headset and suddenly find themselves in their own kitchen. Now they can try out the appliances in various sizes, colors, and locations. They can test new cabinets, opening and closing the cabinet doors and drawers. They can place their existing table and chairs into the picture so that the scene will be very realistic. They can walk around and discover the feel and ambiance of the new kitchen. With this technology, the customer is able to buy with a great deal more

Created by Hines Illinois Veterans Administration Hospital, this virtual reality system is used to help design apartments for people in wheelchairs. Virtual reality uses computers to create artificial environments where users actually become an integral part of the computer-generated experience. (David Sutton)

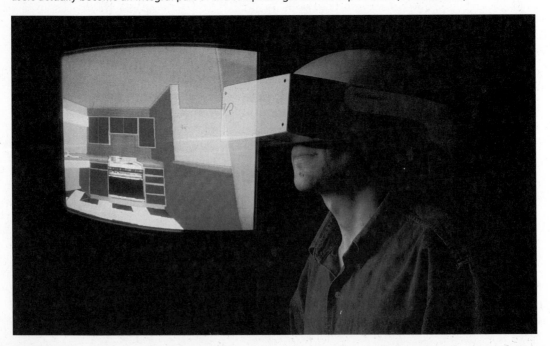

confidence. Matsushita is able to make many more on-the-spot sales (p. 537).

Negroponte (1994) argued that while technology will bring huge changes to our daily lives, technologies such as multimedia will be not the agent but the symptom of change. "What is changing our information and entertainment landscape is 'being digital'" (p. 27). Digitizing information (that is, storing and transmitting data via computers in 1s and 0s for speed and efficiency) will allow people both to have access to more information and to filter data to meet their personal information needs.

There are a number of examples in the application and research of new technologies that suggest both value and risk in the development and use of such technologies. For instance, Hiltz and Turoff (1992) explored educational applications in what they called the **virtual classroom (VC),** a teaching and learning environment located in a computer-mediated communication system.

According to Hiltz and Turoff, the objectives of the virtual classroom are (1) to improve access to advanced educational experiences by allowing students and instructors to participate in remote learning communities at times and places convenient to them, using personal computers at home, on a campus, or at work, and (2) to improve the quality and effectiveness of education by using the computer to support a collaborative learning process (p. 78).

Studies by Hiltz and Turoff pointed to the following outcomes when the VC is compared to the traditional classroom (TC) over the course of a semester:

- **Mastery** There were few significant differences in scores measuring the mastery of material taught in the virtual and traditional classrooms. In computer science and management courses, grades were significantly better in the VC section, but in others there was no significant difference.

- **Student preference** VC students perceived it to be superior to the TC on a number of dimensions: (1) convenient access to educational experiences, (2) increased participation in a course, (3) improved ability to apply the material of the course in new contexts and express their own independent ideas relating to the material, (4) improved access to their professor, (5) computer comfort: improved attitudes toward and greater knowledge of the use of computers, (6) improved overall quality, whereby the student assesses the experience as being better than the TC in some way (pp. 79–80).

In short, students who experienced group learning in the virtual classroom were likely to judge the outcomes of on-line courses superior to the outcomes of traditional courses. Furthermore, those students who experienced high levels of communication with other students and with their professor (who participated in a group learning approach to their coursework) were especially likely to judge the outcomes of VC learning superior to those of traditionally delivered courses.

In a different organizational context, Abel, Corey, Bulick, Schmidt, and Coffin (1992) reported on a project at US West Advanced Technologies, where a prototype multimedia communication service was developed to support dispersed teams. The rationale for the project was twofold. First, because of the planned information superhighway, US West felt it was an opportune time to investigate the use of multimedia to meet major marketplace needs. Second, as the company reasoned, ". . . major businesses are becoming more and more geographically dispersed because of the expanding global marketplace, the need to be near customers, the need to manufacture goods with the lowest possible labor cost, and the need to attract and retain skilled mobile workers by an attractive work location" (p. 127).

This project included twenty-four multimedia stations spread more or less evenly across two sites. The computer equipment was installed in private offices, common areas, and conference rooms interconnected by audio, data, and motion video networks. Users could place multimedia calls from their desks, participate in multilocation meetings, enter shared audio and video workspaces, look around remote spaces, and generally simulate many same-site interactions via the multimedia infrastructure. The project involved fifty staff members, twenty of whom were routine users of the technology, thirty of whom were occasional users.

US West found that multimedia station vendors should consider such issues as audio quality, the need for document sharing, the importance of eye contact, and the need for camera control in the development of integrated multimedia stations. In particular, any conferencing or multimedia collaboration environment that does not provide adequate audio quality is likely to fail. In addition, implementers should provide convenient access (e.g., desktop or laptop for traveling) for users, and make the system easy to use (Abel et al., 1992).

Perhaps the most important finding of this investigation was the importance and usefulness of video, especially as it supports various types of office-to-office and informal interaction. The researchers noted that "it enabled [them] to maintain much of the day-to-day life of an organization with about a fifth of its members physically separated by 45 miles from the others" (p. 138). Yet another intriguing finding was that multimedia calling was greatly preferred to "looking around" for remote office-to-office interaction. That is, out of respect for privacy, participants preferred placing a multimedia call than using a remote video camera to scan for the person they wanted to contact.

Support for Teams.   Jessup and Valacich (1993) predicted five important technological developments that will enhance support for organizational teams (see Table 11.1). Each of these developments will depend on further enhancements to network technology in order to carry the huge volume and assortment of information that teams will share. If realizing these opportunities seems less than plausible, Stewart (1994) has reminded us just how tangible and swift changes in technology and its application really are. Figures

TABLE 11.1

Technologies That Can Help Organizational Teams

Orchestrated Workflow

Technologies such as Electronic data interchange, e-mail, and on-line resource scheduling systems will be combined with new systems to further workflow automation.

Virtual Team Rooms

Teams communicate using various technologies, regardless of any member's physical location.

Cultural Mediation Systems

Technology will be used to help structure dialogues between cultures that diverge in terms of how they address issues.

Just-in-Time Learning

Technology will be used to provide quick access to information (text, data, video) or generate new information (interactive simulation).

Window to Anywhere

Technology similar to the multimedia concepts explored at US West will be used to simulate an across-the-table feeling for groups that are physically separated.

SOURCE: Jessup & Valauch (1993).

11.1, 11.2, and 11.3 support his contention that when a new technological infrastructure comes into existence (computers and communication devices), it rapidly changes how people conduct commerce and other aspects of their lives.

Indeed, some claim that in 1991 the industrial age gave way to the "information age." Stewart argued that 1991 was the first year in which ". . . companies spent more on computing and communications gear—the capital goods of the new era—than on industrial, mining, farm, and construction machines. Information technology is now as vital, and often as intangible, as the air we breathe, which is filled with radio waves. In an automobile you notice the $675 worth of steel around you, but not the $782 worth of microelectronics" (p. 75).

The Challenges of Technological Advancement

Accompanying advances in communication technology are new challenges. As mentioned in Chapter 10, one of the most important concerns will be

FIGURE 11.1

The Rise of the Information Economy

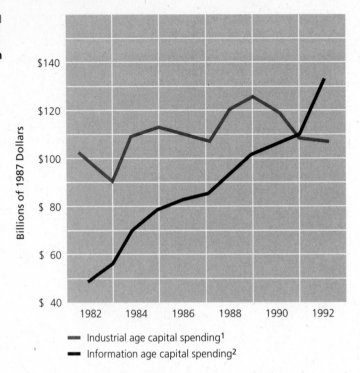

Billions of 1987 Dollars

— Industrial age capital spending[1]
— Information age capital spending[2]

[1]On industrial equipment, machinery for services, mining, oil fields, agriculture, and construction (except tractors).
[2]On computers and communications equipment.

SOURCE: Data from U.S. Department of Commerce, 1992.

controlling electronic crime. Information superhighways and wireless communication offer open invitations for information theft, copyright infractions, and other unethical and/or illegal actions.

Cellular technology has been shown to be especially susceptible to criminal activity. As Rosenthal (1994) noted, the cellular phone industry estimates that companies' losses from cellular fraud, which is a federal felony, range from $100 million to $300 million a year. To combat this fraud, companies have developed antipiracy software that recognizes unusual calling patterns (see Focus On).

What is significant about this development is that an industry is addressing the problem from the viewpoint of technology as well as law enforcement. As technology becomes more advanced and more complex, we expect that the technology used to monitor and control its use will also become more sophisticated.

Incremental changes to existing technology-based products and introductions of new technology to support and automate existing organizational processes are ongoing. Two recent product announcements by Lotus Corporation illustrate this trend.

FIGURE 11.2

**Companies
Exchanging
Data
Electronically**

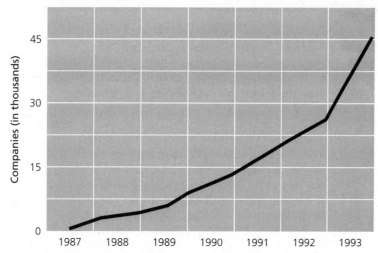

SOURCE: Data from EDI Yellow Pages, 1992.

First, Lotus announced that voice capabilities had been added to the Lotus Notes groupware product, which is currently used by approximately 750,000 employees at 3,200 companies (Stahl, 1994a). Now users of this product can add the capability to access data stored on computers with a phone call. "Phone" Notes users will be able to use a telephone to access information in Notes databases and e-mail, as well as to insert voice messages into documents. This groupware product thus allows anyone who has a telephone to use Notes

FIGURE 11.3

**Worldwide
Modern
Shipments**

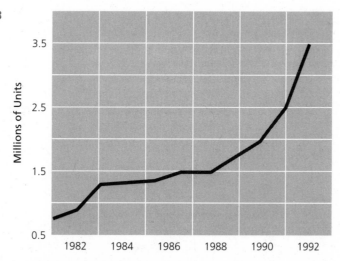

SOURCE: Data from International Data Corporation, 1992.

FOCUS ON

Technology Trials and Tribulations

Many times we have this inherent belief that the application of technology is a straightforward, rational process where the inputs are known and the outputs are predictable. Sometimes it is, sometimes it isn't. For example, you would think that e-mail is a rather noncontroversial technology. However, it turns out that in many states, e-mail use by government officials may be against the law, because it violates these states' open-meeting laws. The argument is that e-mail is public record and should be saved, archived, and not deleted because messages should be open to public scrutiny. Also, some doctors worry that use of e-mail by the gravely ill will promote the distribution of misleading information about drugs. Apparently, some patients are using e-mail to discuss untested treatments and cures for drugs that are under development. Doctors worry that such information sharing may skew drug-testing results.

Cellular phones have also suffered some unexpected maladies. For example, cellular bandits were pirating people's phones thanks to a simple security omission by the cellular phone companies. Every cellular phone emits a distinct serial number which updates the cellular network as to a user's location. Until recently, pirates were able to use scanners to pluck these serial numbers off the airways to create duplicate phones with these serial numbers that would bill calls to the original serial number owner's account. Cellular companies are now encrypting the serial numbers to prevent such piracy. Also, many people have purchased cellular phones because they thought they might be useful in case of emergencies while traveling. It turns out that so many cellular users have had trouble getting through to the cellular 911 service that the FCC may require improvement in service. Moreover, the FCC may also require cellular companies to develop new technology within five years to pinpoint the location of 911 cellular callers!

New technologies are being developed for your home that offer wonderful potential for solving unexpected problems. For example, AT&T recently shrank the electronic workings of a phone to a fingernail-sized computer chip costing just a few dollars. This means that phones could easily and cheaply be built into TVs, cars, and other appliances so that when leaving work, you might, for example, call your air conditioner to tell it to turn on. Just imagine if you got a busy signal? One computer company, Compaq, is promoting the concept of a central home PC into which people plug their appliances and other devices. Remember the movie "Home Alone?" Think what a child left alone might do with this PC!

to record messages, forward documents to fax machines, and interact with e-mail systems.

Second, Lotus announced that its new software product, Forms, allows users to design, route, and track business forms on personal computers (Stahl,

1994b). The annual cost of shuffling paper-based forms is more expensive than many people may realize:

- $6 billion spent on pre-printed paper forms
- $2 billion lost from waste and obsolescence
- $360 billion spent to distribute, sort, and update

Forms is intended to help people eliminate volumes of paper forms, saving filing space and preventing companies from being stuck with obsolete forms after new ones are ordered. Stahl suggests that the product can also play a role in business process reengineering because as corporations become more horizontal and streamlined around processes, fewer people are doing more work. To achieve this goal, organizations need to automate the mundane tasks that hinder productivity, such as filling out forms.

Reengineering and Organizational Communication

One the most fundamental management shifts in the twentieth century has been the change from emphasizing task management to focusing on continual reexamination of organizational processes so as to ensure maximum value to the organizational customer. In a sense, reengineering means that organizations start over, reevaluating ways in which they create products or services that deliver value to their customers. Hammer and Champy (1993) contended that organizations need to ask the question: "If I were starting over, what would I look like?" (p. 31). Reengineering means tossing aside old, established ways of conducting business and starting over, re-creating a company that incorporates the use of new ideas and current technologies.

Hammer and Champy formally defined reengineering as "... *the fundamental rethinking and radical design of business processes to achieve dramatic improvements in critical, contemporary measures of performance, such as cost, quality, service, and speed*" (p. 32). Understanding reengineering helps us comprehend how Drucker's (1988) "coming organization" can come into being. Hammer and Champy (1993, pp. 65–79) explained that in the "new world of work" the following changes occur when a company reengineers its business processes:

- **Work units change from functional departments to process teams—** units that naturally fall together to complete whole pieces of work (processes).

- **Jobs change from simple tasks to multidimensional, substantive work**—workers share joint responsibility for process results, requiring that each individual appreciates and understands the process as a whole.

- **People's roles change from controlled to empowered**—as management invests teams with the responsibility of completing an entire process, it must also give them the authority to make the decisions needed to get it done.
- **Job preparation changes from training to education**—training teaches "how" a job is done; education explains the "why."
- **There is a shift in emphasis from job activity to job results**—people are paid for the value they contribute, not simply for time spent on the job.
- **Job advancement is based on job ability, not performance**—advancement in one's position is seen as a change based on ability, not a reward (no longer is it assumed that top salespeople necessarily make the best sales managers).
- **Values change**—employees are expected to work for their customers, not for their bosses (employees are now rewarded for how well they create value for a customer, not for how well they are able to follow internal company policies and procedures).
- **Managers change from supervisors to coaches**—teams ask coaches for advice; coaches help teams solve problems.
- **Organizational structures change from hierarchical to flat**—process management is the responsibility of the process team, which minimizes the need for elaborate structures enabling management coordination and control.
- **Executives change from storekeepers to leaders**—flatter organizations move senior executives closer to the customers and to the people performing the company's value-adding work.

Technology allows these changes by enabling organizations to break the rules that heretofore have defined how work is conducted. The breaking of traditional rules has afforded innovative firms the opportunity to gain a competitive advantage at the expense of their competitors.

Illustrations of Reengineering

Some organizations have already used technology in a manner contrary to the traditional way of doing business. For example, Ford uses database and electronic data interchange technology in efficient and effective ways that eliminate overhead (especially excess inventories) for both Ford and its suppliers—violating the "rule" that vendors should be treated as adversaries. Also, Hammer and Champy (1993) showed how Wal-Mart and K Mart are using teleconferencing to allow headquarters-based merchandisers to provide store managers in the field with guidance and advice—enabling them to combine local initiative with corporate advice (p. 91). The use of teleconferencing undermines a traditional business belief that remotely located people can meet only infrequently and at great cost. Many other such situations can be identified where technology has changed the ground rules for organizing work (see Table 11.2).

TYPE OF TECHNOLOGY	RESULTING CHANGE
Shared Computer-based Databases	Allow information to appear in as many places as it is needed—breaking the old rule that information can appear in only one place at one time as it is captured.
Expert Systems	Help generalists do the work of an expert—breaking the old rule that only experts can perform complex work.
Technology Networks	Provide organizations the ability to simultaneously reap the benefits of centralization and decentralization (technology affords greater flexibility since its extends organizational communication and coordination across time and place)—breaking the old rule that firms must choose between centralization and decentralization.
Decision Support Software	Facilitates better decision making, which is now seen as part of everyone's job in team-based, flat organizational structures—breaking the old rule rooted in traditional hierarchical organizational structures that managers make all decisions.
Wireless Data Communication and Portable Computers	Enable field personnel to send and receive information wherever they are—breaking the old rule that field personnel need offices where they can receive, store, retrieve, and transmit information.
Interactive Videodisk Technology	Provides a novel and informative mechanism for communicating information to a potential buyer—breaking the old rule that the best contact with a potential buyer is always personal contact.
Automatic identification and Tracking Technologies	Help companies because things (a truck) can tell you where they are—breaking the old rule that you have to find out where things are.
High-performance Computing Technology	Helps organizations to revise plans instantaneously (using real-time data)—breaking the old rule that plans get revised only periodically (using historical data).

SOURCE: Hammer & Champy, 1993, pp. 92–99.

TABLE 11.2

How Technology Changes Work

However, technologies alone cannot work wonders. While information and information technology allow changes in organizational work, people also influence change in how work is done, since it is people who inevitably decide whether technology will be used to create an organizational culture of control or empowerment. As we have noted earlier in this text, organizational change is driven both by technology availability and by organizational need.

Technology Creates New Markets: The Home

The impact of technological change has been staggering. As of 1995, 9 million Americans subscribed to consumer on-line services such as Prodigy, Compuserve and America Online, and 39 million packages of multimedia software on CD-ROM had been shipped. *USA Today* (January 25, 1995, pp. B1–B2) reported that one-third of U.S. homes now have PCs and that half of all households will own a PC by 1997. In response to the shift in emphasis of PC sales from business to the home marketplace, new products are being developed and marketed to serve the home PC user.

For example, the real estate industry is creating on-line services for home buyers that provide access to real estate listings, maps, and information such as local school performance. Banks, aware of new opportunities made possible by home PCs with electronic communication capabilities, are working to develop new electronic services such as on-line banking and electronic bill paying. About 100,000 households bank from home, and that number could reach 7.5 million by the end of 1998 (*Wall Street Journal,* January 30, 1995, pp. A1–A3). American Express now offers ExpressNet, via which cardholders can pay bills, summon detailed billing histories, and list recent transactions. American Express also plans to allow users the ability to download such data into a PC's financial management software such as Quicken and MoneyCounts.

The development of secure PC-based credit card transactions is especially important to allow the development of interactive QVC-type transactions via on-line services using PCs. The *Wall Street Journal* also reported that though customers currently spend no more than $500 million annually on on-line consumer purchases, that number could reach $5.1 billion by the end of 1998.

USA Today also pointed out that the entertainment industry is now tuned into the potential business opportunities that exist with home PCs with Internet connections. Capital Cities/ABC has been experimenting with home PCs as a vehicle for interactive audiences. In one test of this technology, ABC put soap opera star Susan Lucci on an America Online "auditorium" where people could connect their PCs to an electronic service, type in their questions, and receive live answers, as if they were gathered in a room. Eight hundred people asked 2,000 questions in an hour. Also, the Discovery Channel is developing an on-line version of itself.

Is there room for interactive advertising? Certainly! Sony and McDonalds have already begun placing interactive advertisements on on-line services.

The Internet still has some commercial limitations, however. L.L. Bean, for example, found that although the Internet and commercial on-line services provide interactivity, they offer low-quality images and lack security for transactions.

Summarizing Perspective

All of the developments discussed in this and the previous ten chapters are rooted in the fact that new computer-based communication technologies have helped us to overcome barriers of place and time. This development in turn has promoted a new economy in which new, flexible, and team-based organizations that are customer-driven and service-oriented evolve on a continual basis. As we have also seen, in addition to facilitating changes in the economy and the nature of organizational design, technology impacts leadership, conflict management, employee empowerment, and ethical domains.

Technology is now permeating U.S. homes, allowing new opportunities for both business and pleasure. Because of the increased number of individuals with access to PCs and networks both at home and at work, many employers now expect employees to work at home more, either in lieu of or in addition to work performed at the office. With this increased work flexibility has also come increased electronic accessibility, and there is some question as to whether technology has invited employers to invade the privacy of their employees by encouraging, and even expecting, off-hour work and communication.

We continue to see instances where on-line services and the Internet suffer from issues relating to security and ethics. The inability to manage this problem has led to many violations of individual rights, and in many cases there is no way to trace the perpetrator. Computer networks and cellular communication have also spawned new opportunities for stealing corporate secrets and even products. And "viruses," much dreaded by living beings, now also afflict computers and computer networks.

Some are concerned about policy implications for the new technologies. Mitchell Kapor (1994), the creator of Lotus 1-2-3, suggested that interactive television and increased access to information may be problematic:

> Of course there's the potential downside: further depersonalization, lack of human contact—the kind of thing we have with couch-potatoes today. In the average household the television is on six to seven hours a day, and it's *not* interactive. You sit there while these electronic drugs are broadcast to you. But if we create the medium to be participatory, the opportunities are greater than the risks. We have to rely on society's ability to make intelligent choices (pp. 30–31).

Computers can enhance people's lives. Technology empowers individuals by providing access to information and voice in new and exciting ways. For, example, on-line services such as SeniorNet Online and AARP Online have become very popular because they allow seniors to keep in touch with family and friends when travel is prohibitive. Also many of these individuals have both the time and interest to explore and master the new world of cyberspace. Taylor (1994) noted that SeniorNet members ". . . in increasing numbers go on-line to discuss topics ranging from pets to sex after 70" (p. 28). On-line services were used to help locate victims of the 1994 Los Angeles earthquake, and they have allowed individuals with physical infirmities to make contact and engage in electronic discussions where relationships are not handicapped by awareness of an individual's physical limitations. Also reported in the press have been marriages between couples who met and initially developed a relationship via discussions on e-mail and electronic bulletin boards.

Multimedia technology, on-line services, and the Internet provide new and exciting opportunities for interactive learning. Enhanced graphic capabilities, easy-to-use software interfaces, sound capabilities, low software and hardware prices, and powerful communication capabilities have all helped the PC move quickly into the home. Imagine, in the comfort and privacy of your own home, you can now connect to Godiva Chocolatiers' on-line chocolate information service, day or night!

The implications for students of organizational communication are clear:

- Technology has altered, and will continue to alter, the very nature of organizational and interpersonal communication.
- Technology-based communication media vary in the nature of their information content and display capabilities (multimedia provides images, text and sound, whereas e-mail services simply offer textual messages).
- Information technology allows ongoing organizational reengineering, which similarly affects organizational design and communication.
- Because technology is continually changing, its capabilities and impact also evolve on an ongoing basis.
- Technology brings about both anticipated and unanticipated changes and opportunities.
- With change comes resistance to change; hence change must be managed, using effective communication.
- In the new high-tech, service-oriented economy, effective communication skills (both verbal and electronic) are especially valuable employee assets.
- Technology helps individuals to network with one another and to acquire information.
- Technology empowers by providing individuals with new and unique channels for access, voice, and action.

In writing this book, it has been our goal to examine organizational communication and empowerment within a technological context. Advances in technology have been both dramatic and swift, precipitating great changes in the way individuals interact within and between organizations. As technology evolves, so too will our need to reexamine and understand its evolving impact on organizational communication and empowerment.

CASES FOR DISCUSSION

CASE 1 *Managing by Computer*

Recently, Avantos Performance Systems, Inc., introduced "ManagePro," a new software program for supervisors and managers. The program combines some features from a "personal information manager" program (which is used to keep track of appointments, to generate lists, and so on) and some from project management software to produce a system for tracking time lines, projects, assignments, and employee performance.

The program keeps a running file on each person designated by the manager as the employee responsible for specific projects or assignments. It keeps a record of each employee's successes, failures, behavioral problems, performance against deadlines, and so forth. Within the program, each employee and each task are assigned a color-coded icon or symbol.

For example, imagine you have an employee named Dave. If he misses a deadline, you note that in his data file. If he arrives late for work, you note that as well. As Dave's performance continues to slip, his icon might change automatically from green to yellow to red.

As a manager using this system, you can easily spot trouble and take corrective action *before* a crisis occurs. And the computer program helps here as well: Built into the program are helpful hints on how to handle specific sit-

uations or disciplinary problems. When Dave's icon becomes red, for example, the program might suggest calling Dave in for a conference, giving him a negative performance evaluation, or assigning him to some form of remedial training.

The program also takes note of employees who perform well. If Dave's icon becomes or remains green, the program occasionally suggests giving him some form of reward or recognition, such as a bonus, a free lunch, a free ticket to a movie or baseball game, or a hearty "thank you" and handshake.

The suggestions offered by the program are derived from the management techniques of two consultants, William Benson and Edward Kappus, who operate a consulting company called Management Strategies International. A copy of their book, *Managing People: Your Competitive Edge in the 1990s,* is included with the software.

The president of Avantos Performance Systems, Inc., Norm Wu, argues that several advantages are provided by this program:

▶ Expenses for training supervisors and managers are reduced, since the computer in effect trains them day by day.

▶ The program enhances supervisory training seminars that the program users do attend.

Too often, Wu claims, supervisors and managers fail to apply the principles they are taught during training, or they lapse back into old habits when they return from seminars to the workplace. The computer program helps them to remember and apply the principles they are taught.

▶ The program ensures that managers and supervisors keep in touch with their employees and "keep everyone motivated," Wu claims. "It allows for steady, consistent and competent managing."

▶ When performance evaluations are provided (such appraisals are typically an annual exercise resisted by many supervisors and managers), the information recorded for each employee by this program should prove highly valuable.

The program is available for $395 directly from Mr. Wu's California-based company.

Questions for Discussion

1. Mr. Wu lists some of the advantages he perceives to be offered by this computer program. Do you also view these as advantageous? Why or why not?

2. What disadvantages or problems might this kind of program raise, both from the manager's and the employee's point of view?

3. If you were a manager, would you consider using this sort of program? Why or why not?

SOURCE: Coates, 1993.

CASE 2 *Planning for Future Leadership*

In a move that rocked the business world, Robert C. Stempel resigned his position as chairman of General Motors (GM) in October 1992. Many felt his style of management had become outdated and that his company had suffered as a result.

By most accounts, Mr. Stempel had been a competent manager who inspired loyalty from, and showed loyalty to, his staff. His grooming in the GM management system was thorough and carefully planned. But the failings of GM under his leadership and the circumstances surrounding his departure provide a dramatic lesson for today's corporation: Now more than ever, executives risk being the right leaders, but for the wrong times.

Boards often compound the problem by choosing CEOs groomed in yesterday's corporate cultures to solve today's problems. Yet as Warren Bennis, professor of business administration at the University of Southern California, pointed out, "With the galloping changes that are taking place—demographic, geopolitical, global—if you think you can run the business in the next ten years the way you did the last ten years, you are crazy."

According to John Cotter, president of John J. Cotter Associates, a Los Angeles-based consulting firm, the problem is "a reflection of the hiring, training and succession planning across the country." Indeed, situations similar to Stempel's arose recently when Tom H. Barrett resigned as chairman and CEO of Goodyear Tire & Rubber Co., and when Kenneth H. Olsen resigned the presidency of Digital Equipment Corp. Both had been longtime company men—Barrett had spent thirty-eight years with Goodyear and Olsen had founded and spent thirty-five years with Digital. Like GM, both organizations had faced significant changes in market demands, technology, and competition.

Some argue that the heart of the problem lies in the way organizations have traditionally developed managers. In many cases, CEOs of big companies are the products of long, ponderous, deliberate, and often very highly structured management succession systems. Many joined their companies right out of high school and worked their way up through the ranks, assuming greater and greater management responsibility along the way.

Among the flaws cited in the current system are these:

▶ The process takes too long.

▶ The system produces leaders who are too insular. Many lack outside contacts, however well respected they might be inside their organizations.

▶ The succession method ties the executives too closely to tradition. They may spend most of their adult lives in one set of market conditions. As a result, they often lack the ability to adapt to change, and in many cases, the ability or willingness to embrace innovative technologies.

Questions for Discussion

1. What, if anything, can organizations do to prepare their rising executives?

2. What kinds of challenges and opportunities resulting from advances in technology do aspiring organizational leaders face?

3. If someone seeking a leadership position in a major organization asked you how best to prepare for the future, what sorts of qualities, skills, attitudes, and learning experiences would you advise the person to develop and pursue? Why?

SOURCE: Based on Bennett, 1992.

WHAT IS THE INTERNET?

The Internet is a worldwide network of computer systems that connects businesses, organizations, government, and individuals. Using the Internet, you can send electronic mail (e-mail), chat electronically with others about issues, learn about companies, investigate university programs, and search for reference material when you need to research a paper for class. Topics relating to the Internet are now routinely covered by magazines, newspapers, and television, because many see it as a fundamental and dramatic shift in the way that we communicate and access information and entertainment.

What makes the Internet especially intriguing and attractive to commercial organizations is its accessibility to a worldwide audience and the ease with which an organization can maintain and change product information made available to Internet users. Moreover, the Internet offers the ability not only to convey textual information but also to communicate images, sound, and video—twenty-four hours a day.

There are 20 million daily users of the Internet, and this number is increasing rapidly. It is estimated that there will be 35 million people using the Internet by 1998. Why such growth?

- Students and faculty are hearing a lot about the Internet and are gaining access to it through their universities.

- Companies are increasingly putting their employees "on line" as they begin to recognize the new marketing and sales, research, and other communication opportunities that exist on the Internet.

- Anyone who has a computer at home equipped with a modem can gain access to the Internet by subscribing to an Internet access provider.

The only way to learn about the Internet is to dive right in and start "surfing" or "cruising" the Internet. Many people use the analogy that roaming through the Internet is like flipping through channels on your cable television. However, instead of wandering through forty or fifty channels, the Internet provides literally millions of "pages" of information on a vast array of topics that are created by people all over the world. Keep in mind that although the Internet is vast, so is the number of users who may be accessing the Internet at one time; sometimes you cannot access information due to high levels of demand.

Depending on the state of technology at your college or university, you will access and use the Internet either by typing in certain strings of characters or by using a computer mouse to click on certain highlighted words, objects, or images. This guide will help you get started, but it is by no means intended to be a comprehensive guide to how to use the Internet. Those of you who get hooked on the Internet will want to take advantage of a wide range of new books that are designed to help you navigate and explore cyberspace in depth (see the bibliography at the end of this appendix). Be prepared, however, to find that much of the resource material is complex, reflecting the complexity of the Internet itself.

Finally, we encourage classes to discuss issues raised by Internet capabilities and content. For example, what implications does the Internet have for training leaders or for empowering organizational teams? To what extent do you think that senior managers in many organizations are aware that their company may have a "home page" on the Internet? In what ways might use of the Internet by an organization's employees potentially expose the firm to new legal liabilities or distract employees from their real work? What should companies do about it? Can use of the Internet by students create new educational opportunities? Do some features of the Internet challenge the right to free speech? For example, should instructions for making a bomb be readily available on the Internet?

We hope that you will consider and discuss these issues as you progress through the text. The importance of the Internet and other computer technologies will continue to impact organizational communication in new and unique ways. Some of the effects will be expected, but other developments will not be anticipated. Our goal is to help you be aware of the dynamic relationship between technology and organizational communication, a relationship that is continually evolving.

Getting Started on the Internet

In this appendix we will cover a few of the more important features of the Internet. Determining what capabilities are available to you will depend a great deal on the networks, computer systems, and software that your college or university uses.

E-Mail

The most popular feature of the Internet is electronic mail (e-mail). While most university computer systems provide internal e-mail capabilities, use of the Internet allows students to send mail to students and faculty at other universities and to anyone who subscribes to America Online, CompuServe, Prodigy, or another Internet access provider. In fact, Internet e-mail has become a very popular way for parents to keep in touch with their children who attend institutions far away.

To use e-mail, you will need to get an e-mail account and password from your institution as well as instructions about how to log into your system and how to change your password. How you use e-mail depends on the software your university uses. You will need to obtain specific instructions regarding how to create, send, and display messages and how to navigate and manage your e-mail account. If you are going to use the Internet to send e-mail to remote locations, you will also need to know the account name, system, entity name, and domain name of the person to whom you want to send a message (entity names and domain names are collectively referred to as the **hostname**). For example, if I wanted to send a message to Bob Smith at the University of North Carolina at Greensboro, I would need to know Bob's e-mail account name. Let's say it is **bsmith**. With this information, I would do the following:

1. Log into my e-mail account
2. Type **send** at the mail prompt
3. Type **bsmith@iris.uncg.edu** after the prompt **To:**

In step 3 above, **bsmith** is the addressee or e-mail account name; **iris** is the system on which the account name resides; **uncg** is the entity where bsmith has an account; and **edu** tells us that bsmith's account resides at an educational organization. Everything after the @ symbol is the user address. Note that the letters after the last period are referred to as a *suffix*. If the suffix consists of three letters, it tells the computer the type of organization you are communicating with.

edu	educational institution
com	commercial institution
gov	government
int	international organizations such as NATO
mil	military
net	networking organizations
org	organizations that don't fit the other classifications (professional organizations, nonprofits)

If the suffix has two letters, it indicates that you are accessing an account in another country. These suffixes supplement the first set. For example, in the address **bsmith@iris.uncg.edu.us**, **bsmith** is the user name, **iris** is the host computer's name followed by the name of the network, called the **domain**. In this instance, the domain is **uncg**, which is further defined by the subdomain **edu**, which identifies the type of organization. The letters **us** are the top-level domain, indicating the country in which the system is located. The top-level domain name can be omitted from the address if the e-mail recipient's country is the same as the sender's.

au	Australia
ca	Canada
dk	Denmark
fr	France
de	Germany
il	Israel
va	Vatican

If you get mail from someone else on the Internet, you don't have to type all of the account information shown above to respond to the message. You only have to type **reply** because the system already knows the address of the person to whom you are responding. Some typical e-mail commands are listed in Table A.1.

Some account names are numbers; some are letters; some are both. Never guess, or your message may be returned to you as undeliverable. In fact, you must always be absolutely precise about an e-mail address! You must know the exact account and address information, as well as the exact format to which your e-mail system requires the message to conform.

Remember, the specific procedures for using your e-mail account and for creating and sending messages will depend on the type of computers and e-mail system that your institution uses.

Accessing LISTSERVE and USENET

You can use your e-mail account to subscribe to mailing lists or to converse with newsgroups on the Internet.

LISTSERVE allows you to subscribe to (be placed on an e-mail distribution list) or "unsubscribe to" (be removed from an e-mail distribution list) of Internet electronic discussion groups. For example, if you are a person who likes the blues, you could join a discussion simply by typing the words **subscribe blues-l [your first name] [your last name]** in the subject field of your e-mail memo and sending an e-mail message to **Listserv@brownvm.brown.edu**. You then simply send the e-mail memo. If later you decide to stop subscribing to this list, you send a memo to the same address but type **unsubscribe blues-l [your first name] [your last name]** in the subject field of your memo.

You can also subscribe to electronic journals. The procedure is the same as for discussion groups, except that instead of knowing the name of the discus-

TABLE A.1

E-Mail Commands

COMMAND	OUTCOME
Send	Sends a message or file to an individual or a whole distribution list
Reply	Answers a message you have received
Read [or Display]	Reads [or displays] a message
Delete	Deletes a message
Forward	Passes the message on to another e-mail user
Extract	Saves as a text file if, for example, you want to access the information with your word processor
Save	Saves a message
Print	Prints a hard copy of the message

TABLE A.2

Electronic News, Journals, and Discussion Groups

NAME	ADDRESS	DESCRIPTION
APP-ORGCOM	Address your e-mail message to **majordomo@creighton.edu** Then type the words **subscribe apporgcomm [your e-mail address]** in the message section	Discusses issues related to applied and organizational communication research
COMSERVE	Send an e-mail message to **comserve@vm.its.rpi.edu** In the message section, type *help*	Offers electronic discussion groups, access to the *Electronic Journal of Communication,* and searchable electronic databases of information
CRTNET NEWS	Address your e-mail message to **t3b@psuvm.psu.edu** Then type the words **subscribe crtnet [your first name] [your last name]** in the message section	Provides access to research on communication as well as announcements of interest to communication professionals
EDUPAGE	Address your e-mail message to **listserv@bitnic.educom.edu** Type the words **subscribe edupage [your first name] [your last name]** in the subject field	Provides a twice-weekly summary of news items on information technology
LAMBDAPIETA	Address your e-mail message to **lambdapieta-request@uamont.edu** Then type the words **subscribe lambdapieta [your first name] [your last name]** in the message section	Discusses topics related to being an undergraduate student in communication
NEWSLINE	Address your e-mail message to **comserv@vm.ecs.rpi.edu** Then type the words **Join Newsline [your first name] [your last name]** in the message section	An electronic newsletter describing Comserve, the electronic information and discussion service for communication faculty and students

sion list (Blues-L), you need to know the name of the electronic journal. Table A.2 lists news, journals, and discussion groups that relate to the study of communication.

To find out about more lists, you may want to subscribe to **newlists (info@vm1.nodak.edu)** where subscribers receive announcements of new

IDENTIFIER	CATEGORY
biz	business
comp	computers
news	general news items
rec	recreational
sci	scientific
soc	social
talk	debate-oriented
misc	others

lists. A word of caution though—if you decide to subscribe to newsgroups and discussions, be prepared for an onslaught of e-mail messages!

In USENET, an organized e-mail system, you don't send mail to one person; instead, your messages are sent to a newsgroup section, where they are available to anyone who accesses that newsgroup. In effect, your messages are posted to a newsgroup where people use *reader* software to look at newsgroup contents (this software must be installed either on the computer you are using or on the local host computer at your college or university). There are thousands of newsgroups covering a vast array of topics. To help you find groups that interest you, the USENET uses an identifier to categorize them. These identifiers are listed in Table A.3.

After the initial identifier comes the primary subject area. For example, **rec.audio** is about audio systems, **comp.os.ms-windows.app.wordproc** is about Windows word processors, and **news.pets.cats** is about cats.

The software needed to send and receive USENET newsgroups is in the public domain and is available to anyone who wants it, on any computer operating system. This software is necessary in order to download the articles (transfer files from another computer to your computer) and post articles to the newsgroup (transfer files from your computer to another computer). For more information, contact the people at your institution who provide computer support for faculty and students. To find out about more newsgroups, use USENET to request information about newsgroups from **news. announce.newuser.**

Other Features of the Internet

On the Internet, not only can you send mail to people on other computers, you can log into other computers to get information.

Telnet

Telnet provides a means for you to tap into remote computers and gain access to publicly available files as if you were directly connected to that computer. This capability is especially useful to students, teachers, and organizations in need of access to library card catalogs or large databases of information located elsewhere. Most university systems ask that you type the word **telnet** and an address at the prompt after you have logged into your computer network account. Once you press the ENTER key on your keyboard, the network will try to access the computer. Sample Telnet resources are listed in Table A.4. The three most important Telnet commands to remember are listed below:

OPEN — If you don't type the Telnet resource address right after the word Telnet (as described above), you will be left at a **telnet>** prompt. At the prompt, type the word **open,** followed by a space and the Resource address (for example, Telnet> Open 192.149.89.61)

CLOSE — To break a connection and then establish a new one, type **close** and then the **open** command

QUIT — Type **quit** to exit Telnet

File Transfer Protocol (FTP)

Telnet allows you to access another computer; FTP goes one step further. It allows you to get a file from another computer or to load one of your files onto another computer. Here's how it works. Imagine you are interested in cooking. Instead of typing the word telnet after logging into your network

RESOURCE ADDRESS	PROVIDES ACCESS TO	USERNAME/PASSWORD (IF ANY)
192.149.89.61	NASA Spacelink	newuser/newuser
fedix.fie.com	Federal Information Exchange	new/
library.dartmouth.edu	Dartmouth Library	
dra.com	Library of Congress records	
culine.colorado.edu	Major league sports schedules	
madlab.sprl.umich.edu	National weather forecast	
debra.dgbt.doc.ca	Technology	chat/

TABLE A.4

Sample Telnet Resources

computer account, type ftp and an address at the system prompt. Since you are interested in cooking, you might type ftp.gatekeeper.dec. Once connected to this computer, you can use the DOS command cd (change directory) to access the subdirectory /pub/recipes. To copy a file, use the get command followed by the file name. If the system allows you to add a recipe, type the PUT command, followed by the name of the file that you want copied to the remote computer's directory. One word of caution: Whenever you download files, you should use an antivirus program to check that new files do not contain an electronic virus that can cause problems for your computer.

As in Telnet, the most important commands in FTP are **OPEN, CLOSE,** and **QUIT**. And they work the same way as they do in Telnet. If you get stuck, you can also type **HELP**. Some useful FTP sites are listed in Table A.5.

Gopher

If you simply want to browse the Internet through a series of interconnected menus and don't want to have to log into a specific system through Telnet, you can use Gopher. How you get to Gopher depends again on the computer network at your college or university. The easiest way is to use your mouse and click on the Gopher icon when you use Microsoft's Windows (see Figure A.1). If that is not available, you should be able to connect to your school's UNIX computer, type **gopher,** and then press the ENTER key. If that doesn't work, access **Telnet** and type **open consultant.micro.umn.edu** at the **Telnet>** prompt. What Gopher will do is to "go for" the information you

SUBJECT AREA	ADDRESS	DIRECTORY PATH
Art	ftp.sunsite.unc.edu	/pub/multimedia/pictures/otis
Computers	ftp.casbah.acns.nwu.edu	/pub/bbs.lists
Guide to the Internet	ftp.eff.org	/pub/net__info/eff__net__guide
Literature	ftp.mrcnext.cso.uiuc.edu	/etext
Magazines	ftp.quartz.rutgers.edu	/pub/journals
Microsoft	ftp.microsoft.com	[login as anonymous]
Technology	ftp.u.washington.edu	/public/virtualreality
Television	ftp.nic.funet.fi	/pub/culture/tv+film

TABLE A.5

FTP Sites

want by providing you with menus that you can use to choose what you want to access (see Figure A.1). Gopher sites of interest to communication students are listed in Table A.6.

Veronica, Jughead, and Archie

Although Gopher can help you find information, it is not easy to wade through the vast quantity of information to find what you are looking for. Veronica, which can be accessed from the Gopher menu, allows you to search through an index of titles and directories from Gopher menus located all over the world (the GopherSpace). You can search for a broad topic like law using the Directories option, or for specific words like *multimedia* using the Search for Title Words option.

FIGURE A.1

A Sample Windows Gopher Menu

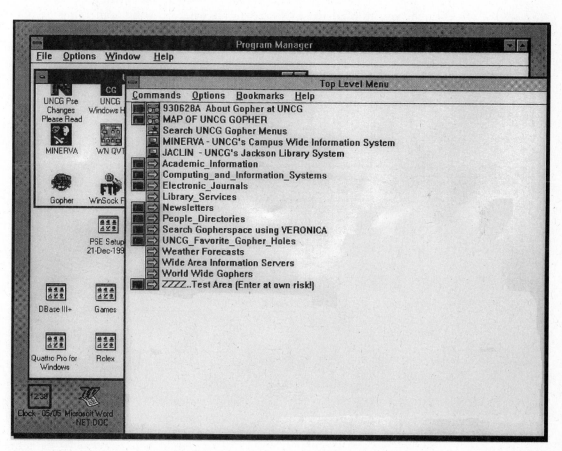

GOPHER SITES	ADDRESS
Wayne State Comm.	gopher.comm.wayne.edu
Iowa Comm	iam4l.arcade.uiowa.edu 2270
Utah Comm	[via Iowa Comm. gopher]
Comserve	cios.llc.rpi.edu
SCAP	gopher.esu.edu

Jughead is another add-on service for Gopher. It enables you to narrow your search more effectively to a few specific databases, thereby helping to eliminate possible redundancy in the search results.

Archie can be used to locate FTP files on the Internet. What Archie does is to maintain a list of available files at FTP sites. When you use Archie for a search, you don't have to worry about where to find something because Archie can tell you which FTP sites have the file you are looking for. There are a few ways to access Archie. One way is to use Gopher to connect to an Archie system (search for the word *Archie*). The other way is to use Telnet to connect to a system providing Archie services. Some Archie systems are listed in Table A.7.

WAIS

Archie is useful if you are trying to locate software or files available for FTP. Gopher is good if you are looking for something for which you suspect someone has built a Gopher menu. But when you are trying to search for documents by content, WAIS (the Wide Area Information Server) is the best choice. WAIS performs keyword searches of indexes, databases, and

SYSTEM TELNET ADDRESS	LOCATION
archie.ac.il	Israel
archie.ans.net	New York
archie.kuis.kyoto-u.ac.jp	Japan
archie.rutgers.edu	New Jersey
archie.sura.net	Maryland

archives on the Internet. It searches through indexes of topics stored in more than five hundred databases. First you tell WAIS where (in which databases) you want to look; then you tell it what to search for. WAIS then generates a list of matches. Since some versions of WAIS can be very difficult to use, it is often easier to use something called the World Wide Web (WWW) to perform a WAIS search. WAIS software is available for UNIX computers, IBM-compatible personal computers running Windows software, and the Apple Macintosh. Contact your institution's computer support personnel for more information.

World Wide Web (WWW)

WWW is easier to use than Gopher because it has a simplified interface. It employs a technology called hypertext (a method of linking words or graphics to other documents). Hypertext organizes Internet information onto a series of interconnected "pages" that may include text, graphics, sound, and video. To get from one page to another, you simply use your computer mouse to click on a word or image. While the first WWW programs provided simple text browsers for the Internet, newer programs provide sophisticated, easier-to-use interfaces that display graphics, images, and icons (see Figure A.2). Web pages are increasingly interactive, allowing, for example, feedback, exchange, and product orders. There are, however, real security issues on the Internet.

Netscape and Mosaic are two WWW browsers. They are both extremely easy to use, and they allow you to search for information either by entering a WWW address (http:\\www.cbs.com) or by stepping through the hypertext menus. Both Mosaic and Netscape offer access to a variety of search engines that can be used for topic searches. Figure A.3 presents a sample output screen generated by searching "organizational communication" using InfoSeek Search, a comprehensive and accurate WWW search engine available on Netscape.

There are many different and fascinating sites to access on WWW. A sampling is provided in Table A.8.

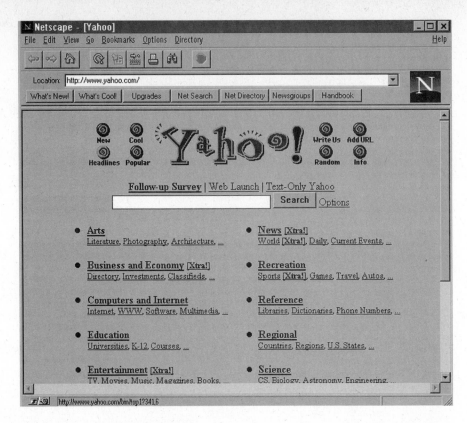

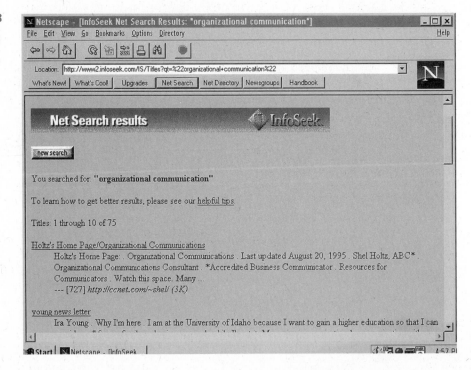

WEB SITE	UNIVERSAL RESOURCE LOCATOR (URL)*	SERVICE PROVIDED
American Communications Association	http://www.uark.edu/depts/comminfo/www/ACA.html	"One-stop shopping" for communication research information
American Universities	http://www.clas.ufl.edu/CLAS/american-universities.html	Home pages for American Universities
AT&T 800 Directory	http://att.net/dir800	Browsing and searching of 800 numbers by name and number
Branch Mall	http://branch.com/	Information service provider for businesses
City Net	http://www.city.net	Interactive guide to communities around the world for travel, entertainment, local business, and government and community services
Electronic Commerce Resources	http://www.premenos.com/Resources	Information on electronic commerce
Educom	http://www.educom.edu/	Information about Integrating technology into education
Edupage	http://www.educom.edu/edupage.new http://www.educom.edu/edupage.old (for back issues)	Summary of news items on information technology; issued three times a week.
FedEx	http://www.fedex.com/	Tracking of Fed Ex packages
GE	http://www.ge.com/	Company, product, and service information
Global Network Navigator	http://nearnet.gnn.com/gnn/GNNhome.html	An Internet service provider
Guide to NASA Online Resources	http://naic.nasa.gov/naic/guide/index.html	NASA's on-line information center
Houghton Mifflin Company	http://www.hmco.com/	Information about products and the company

TABLE A.8

Sample Internet Web Sites

WEB SITE	UNIVERSAL RESOURCE LOCATOR (URL)*	SERVICE PROVIDED
IBM	http://www.ibm.com/	Information about IBM and its products
InformationWeek	http://techweb.cmp.com/iwk	On-line magazine for information professionals
Internet Shopping Network	http://www.internet.net/	Interactive shopping for computer hardware and software
IRS	http://www.ustreas.gov/treasury/bureaus/irs/irs.html	Downloading and printing of tax forms
JP Morgan	http://www.jpmorgan.com/	Company, product, and service information
Library of Congress	http://lcweb.loc.gov/	On-line index and guide to the library
Louvre Museum, Paris	http://www.cnam.fr/louvre/ (Paris) http://sunsite.unc.edu/louvre/ (NC, USA)	Interactive guide to the Louvre Museum
Lycos Catalog of Web Resources	http://lycos.cs.cmu.edu	Carnegie Mellon has licensed this product to Microsoft for its Microsoft Network
MediaCity	http://www.mediacity.com/	News, resources, organizational information
Microsoft	http://www.microsoft.com	Downloading of programs to enable updating of computer systems
North Carolina State Univ.	http://www2.ncsu.edu/ncsu/chas/CIIT	Mass communication–oriented server
On-line Employment	http://www.espan.com http://www.careermosaic.com http://www.esc.state.nc.us	On-line job markets
The Princeton Review	http://www.review.com	Information about schools, tests, and financial aid

TABLE A.8

Sample Internet Web Sites (*Continued*)

WEB SITE	UNIVERSAL RESOURCE LOCATOR (URL)*	SERVICE PROVIDED
Security First Network Bank	http://www.sfnb.com	The nation's first Internet bank
Shopping 2000— Interactive Catalog	http://www.shopping2000.com/ shopping2000/shopping1.html	Interactive shopping guide to products and services of more than 40 direct merchants including JCPenney, Sears, Spiegel, Teleflora, and Hanes.
Time Warner	http://www.timeinc.com	Time Warner's on-line magazines
University of Texas Austin	http://www.utexas.edu/	Brief introduction to the Web and Web browsers via Learning Web section
US Postal Service	http://www.usps.gov/	Zip codes, postal rates, and other information
Weather	http://www.infi.net/nr/ weather/weather.html http://thunder.atms. purdue.edu/	Displays of the latest weather satellite photos
White House	http://www.whitehouse.gov	Information about the White House, Washington, D.C.
World Wide Yellow Pages	http://www.yellow.com/	Electronic Yellow Pages on Internet

URL is the Internet address

SOURCE: Compiled by Herschel & Chang Koh, 1995.

TABLE A.8

Sample Internet Web Sites (*Continued*)

In Summary

- Use e-mail to send or display electronic messages.
- Use LISTSERVE to subscribe to or unsubscribe to Internet electronic discussion lists.

- Use USENET to send and receive messages from newsgroups.
- Use TELNET to access remote computers in order to gain access to publicly available files.
- Use FTP to get a file from another computer or to load one of your files onto another computer.
- Use Gopher to browse the Internet through a series of interconnected menus.
- Use Veronica to search through an index of titles and directories from Gopher menus located all over the world.
- Use Jughead to narrow your Gopher search to a few specific databases, thereby helping to eliminate possible redundancy in the search results.
- Use Archie to search FTP sites for specific files.
- Use WAIS to search for documents by content.
- Use WWW to access Internet information as a series of interconnected "pages" that may include text, graphics, sound, and video.

GLOSSARY

Accommodating A conflict style that glosses over differences, plays down disagreements, and generally trivializes conflict.

Accountability A characteristic of an organizational system signifying that it produces output reflecting its goals.

Adaptive Structuration Theory (AST) An attempt to explain why groups using the same technology may have very different experiences with it. AST contends that social or group technologies gain meaning only as they are used in team interactions.

Affection A person's liking or attraction for another.

Arbitrator In a conflict situation, a third party who, after hearing both sides of the issue, makes a decision by which the disputants must live.

Avoiding A conflict style in which a person (although aware of conflict at a cognitive level) may withdraw by removing herself or himself (psychologically or physically) from the conflict situation, refraining from arguing, or simply failing to confront.

Bottom-up decision making An underlying principle of Japanese management according to which change and initiative within an organization should come from those closest to the problem and those who will feel a decision's impact should be involved in making it.

Boundary spanners Organizational members who interact extensively with individuals outside the organization.

Bureaucracy A type of organization, originally defined by Weber, that is typically characterized by formalized rules, regulations, and procedures; job specialization; a clearly defined hierarchy; rationality; and impersonality.

Cellular technology A wireless communication network that uses radio waves beamed from one antenna to another, with each antenna assigned to a specific geographic area called a cell.

Centrality The degree to which a position within an organization is fundamental to the flow of information throughout organizational networks.

Centralized form with decentralized management Management controls all major organizational functions, but lower-level managers are allowed some discretion in decision making and in their communication.

Charismatic authority In some cultures, the possession by leaders of authority because they are believed to have some "higher" power.

Coercive power The ability to elicit a desired response by means of potential punishment.

Cohesiveness A group's solidarity, closeness, and ability to maintain itself over time and through crisis.

Collaborating A conflict style, which grows from a trust-building process, that calls on disputants to face the conflict openly and directly and to seek, by working together, an integrative solution.

Colorism A predisposition for an individual to act in a certain manner because of another person's skin color.

Communication A mutually interdependent, dynamic process in which individuals exchange messages through diverse channels with the goal of formulating some shared meaning.

Communication network Informal channels of interaction, typically used for influencing organizational members' perceptions of reality and indoctrinating them to hold correct attitudes and behave in appropriate ways.

Competition for rewards A situation in which individuals or groups vie for resources; a potential source of conflict in organizations because resources and rewards are always limited.

Compromising A conflict style, widely perceived as evenhanded and thus appealing, in which disputants search for an intermediate position, split the difference, and meet each other halfway—thus achieving partial satisfaction for both parties.

Computer networks The highways and superhighways for transmitting digitized information, whether it be voice, data, images, or video, from one location to another.

Conflict aftermath In Pondy's conflict model, the final stage, which reflects the complex dynamics of the earlier phases; may be positive or negative.

Conflict episodes The complex interactions that surround the conflict process.

Congruence The matching of both verbal and nonverbal communication to what the communicator is thinking and feeling.

Conjunctive communication Message exchange that flows from previous statements or interactions. Conjunctive communicators make comments that are directly related to what others have said, wait for others to express their points of view before talking, and give a reasonably concise statement of opinion.

Connectional power The influence that individuals have as a result of who they know and the support they receive from others in the organization.

Corporatist environment An organizational habitat in which employees identify with the organization's values and find many of their most compelling needs fulfilled through their organizational experience.

Critical theory   Originating with the works of Marx, the view that organizations are vehicles of oppression and domination and that all workers (not just those in the minority) are oppressed by those in formal positions of power.

Criticality   The degree to which an organizational position's function is crucial to the performance of others in the network. Highly critical positions are associated with high power.

Culture   An organization's system of shared values and beliefs, which interacts with people, structures, and control systems to produce behavioral norms.

Decentralized approach   A method of management in which senior management controls all major organizational functions but lower-level managers are afforded some discretion in their decision making and communication.

Dependent care support   Organizational programs designed to provide assistance to working mothers and fathers and those who are care-givers to the elderly.

Dialogic perspective   A communication-centered approach for judging ethical behavior that views the attitudes of individuals in any communication transaction as an index of the ethical level of that communication.

Directive tactics   Techniques that mediators use to exert substantive control over a negotiation, including recommending proposals, giving opinions about positions, assessing the costs associated with demands, and occasionally inducing compliance.

Discrimination   The act of treating individuals differently, often based on their race, gender, class, or ethnicity.

Discussion styles   Ways of interacting in groups, such as taking turns and interrupting, that may differ from culture to culture.

Disjunctive communication   Message exchange that is disconnected from what was previously stated, occurring, for instance, when one person controls or dominates a conversation or meeting.

Divisional structure   An organizational design with a central coordinating entity as well as divisions that have their own management structure with direct responsibility for the divisions' operation and performance.

Dominance   The extent to which one person has power over or makes decisions that are followed by another.

Downward communication   Information flowing from the top of the organizational management hierarchy and telling people in the organization what is important (mission) and what is valued (policies).

Economic perspective   A point of view that bases ethical judgments on impersonal market forces and derives from the assumption that managers should consistently act to maximize revenues and minimize costs and that doing so will ensure the greatest benefit for society over the long term.

Effort   Expended energy that may lead to an individual's obtaining and maintaining authority or power in an organization.

Emergent conflict   A form of conflict that arises from the formal and informal interactions of individuals on a day-to-day basis.

Environmental stress   From a systems perspective, tensions or pressures generated from outside the organization; a major source of conflict, which may exacerbate other conflict sources.

Ethical communication   Message exchange that facilitates an individual's ability to make sound choices. Often includes establishing a supportive environment in which others feel comfortable making informed choices.

Ethical issues   Those matters that focus on value judgments concerning right and wrong, goodness and badness, in human conduct.

Expert power   A dimension of power having to do with an individual's competence, experience, knowledge, and intelligence.

Feedback   Output that is sent back into the organizational system from the environment or reactions, solicited and unsolicited, to something the organization has produced or an action it has taken.

Felt conflict   The point at which conflicting parties begin to become emotionally involved with the conflict and to personalize it through, for instance, escalating feelings of competitiveness or differences of opinion.

Fielder's Contingency Theory   A situational concept of leadership that argues that the style of leadership most effective in any given situation depends on three factors and the degree to which the leader has control over them: the power of the leader's position, the structure of the task being performed, and the social relationships between the leader and others.

Flexibility   The degree to which an organizational position permits its occupant to exercise discretion or judgment.

Flextime   Organizational programs designed to permit permanent alterations of basically rigid work schedules or, more broadly defined, to allow variations from one day to the next.

Forcing   A conflict style that involves the use of coercion rather than persuasion or collaboration.

Functional conflict   A type of conflict that occurs when organizational functions are divided into departments that often have entirely different values or perspectives on organizational processes.

Functionalist   One who approaches the study of organizational communication as if organizations were machines or objects to be studied. Functionalists tend to conceptualize an organization as a cooperative system in pursuit of common goals.

Glass ceiling   Organizational barriers that keep women (and other minorities) from advancing not because they cannot succeed at executive management but simply because they are women.

Group building and maintenance roles Parts played by individuals in a group that serve to build and sustain the group's interpersonal relationships, helping everyone feel more positive about the group's task and interact constructively and harmoniously. Such roles include supporter, harmonizer, and solidarity builder.

Group support systems (GSS) A technology that centers on computer-mediated group interaction and uses a local area network, individual personal computer workstations, and GSS software to support traditional, same-time, same-place group meeting activities.

Groupthink A way of thinking, originally defined by Janis, that people in highly cohesive groups may engage in when their striving for unanimity overrides their motivation to realistically appraise alternative courses of action.

Hawthorne studies Studies demonstrating the social nature of workers; emphasizing the value of democratic leadership, communication, and informal networks; and forming the empirical foundation of the human relations movement.

Hegemony The all-encompassing power that is hidden and taken for granted by those who are most controlled by it and therefore is unlikely to be challenged.

Heroes Organizational members (often leaders) who personify and illuminate an organization's values.

Horizontal communication Message exchange among peers to coordinate a task or to share their problems or message exchange between and among members of different organizational subunits.

Horizontal job loading A traditional approach to job enrichment that uses such techniques as job rotation and job enlargement.

Humanist perspective An approach to the making of ethical judgments that defines those characteristics of human nature that should be valued and enhanced and then looks at a particular technique, rule, policy, strategy, or behavior to determine if it either furthers or hampers these uniquely human attributes.

Hygiene factors Components of limited motivational value that are external to the actual job. Herzberg argues that such factors as salary and company policy are based on the work situation or environment and are not intrinsically motivating.

Impersonality A characteristic of interpersonal relationships in a bureaucracy whereby, according to Weber, managers maintain personal distance from employees and are thus more likely to make judicious judgments and to treat employees fairly and equitably.

Incongruence Communication that involves a mismatch between what the communicator is experiencing and what he or she is aware of at a conscious level.

Informal organization The informal network, often referred to as the grapevine, through which an individual communicates with someone else with whom he or she is not connected by a formal organizational channel.

Information environment The environment that people actively create through their perceptions, actions, and reactions and that they enact as they receive information and construct its meaning.

Information equivocality Messages that are ambiguous, complex, or obscure and hence difficult for organizational members to understand.

Information power An individual's ability to control the availability and accuracy of information.

Information sector Those who operate computer and information-processing technologies.

Input The energy an organization draws from its environment, including such resources as raw materials, buildings, and people.

Institutional isomorphism A view of organizational design that contends that historical changes shape organization structures such that organizations in related areas tend to resemble one another over time.

Institutionalized conflict A dispute that grows from the nature of a particular organization and its purposes and goals.

Interdependence The interrelatedness of various parts of the organization. From a systems perspective, no component of an organization, a living organism, or an economic system can be viewed in isolation; rather, it can be understood only in a dynamic, interdependent context.

Intergroup conflict A dispute between two of more groups or organizational subsystems that can lead to both positive and negative outcomes, ranging from increased intragroup cohesiveness and solidarity to negative and stereotyped attitudes toward other groups and their members.

Interorganizational conflict A dispute between organizations, the management of which usually focuses on regulation of networks.

Interpersonal conflict A dispute that occurs either between individuals or between an individual and a group.

Interpretivist One who views organizations as socially constructed entities, with communication as the process through which this social construction occurs. The interpretivist sees the organization as an array of factionalized groups with diverse purposes and goals.

Intervention The process of entering into a system of relationships between or among persons, groups, or objects for the purpose of helping them in some way.

Intrapersonal conflict Strife that occurs within individuals in organizations and commonly takes two forms: frustration and goal conflict.

Invalidating communication Message exchange that conveys an attitude of superiority, rigidity, or indifference.

Involvement The degree to which people identify or interact with each other.

Job enrichment   Making a job more intrinsically reward-ing; believed by human resources theorists to be criti-cally related to worker motivation and empowerment.

Job maturity   The ability or competence to carry out a task; the knowledge, experience, and skill needed to carry out work without the direction of others.

Job specialization   A characteristic of a bureaucracy re-quiring that job descriptions be carefully and clearly drawn and therefore that managers be clear in their ex-pectations, making worker behavior more predictable and leaving little to chance or interpretation.

Latent conflict   In Pondy's conflict model, the first phase which occurs whenever a situation is ripe for conflict but those involved do not yet realize it.

Leader legitimation   The process through which indi-viduals come to be acknowledged as leaders by their followers.

Legal authority   A kind of authority based on formal, impersonal, and therefore objective written codes of rules, according to Weber.

Legal perspective   An ethical approach that reduces eth-ical judgments to a matter of law, with anything legal being ethical and anything illegal being unethical.

Legitimate power   Recognized authority, tied to the importance of the position occupied within the organ-izational hierarchy or the formal role played in other social situations.

Life cycle theory of leadership   Hersey and Blanchard's notion that subordinates will change, grow, or mature over time and that in response to such changes, man-agers need to adjust their styles of leadership to meet employee needs.

Linchpins   Middle managers and lower-level supervi-sors who function as conduits between executives and workers.

Linear   Early models of communication that conceptu-alized communication as a largely one-way process in which information flowed from a source through a channel to a receiver.

Manifest conflict   The conflict phase in which those in conflict begin to take overt action.

Matrix structures   Organizational structures in which vertical and lateral channels of communication and au-thority operate simultaneously.

Mediator   A third party who tries to facilitate commu-nication between conflicting parties so that they can work through their problems and arrive at a decision of their own.

Member control perspective   A view of organizational design that argues that organizational structure results from management's desire to control workers and from the need to continually apply advancing technology to production.

Mind-work spectrum   A balance between jobs that re-quire the use and creation of information and those that are strictly manual.

Motivators   Intrinsically stimulating factors, such as a sense of achievement, responsibility, and work itself,

that derive from the nature of work, according to Herzberg.

Multicultural education   An approach to education that directly challenges the societal power structure that has historically subordinated certain groups and ratio-nalized the educational failure of children from these groups as being the result of inherent deficiencies.

Natural systems perspective   A view of the organiza-tion as a social entity whose purpose is to achieve nar-rowly defined goals through both formal and informal organizational structures.

Networks   Groupings of organizational members who engage in patterned interaction. Such networks exist at the organizational system, the group, and the per-sonal levels.

Nondirective tactics   Techniques used by a mediator in a conflict situation to secure information for dis-putants and to clarify misunderstandings.

Nonverbal communication   Diverse ways of commu-nicating/interacting without relying on the use of words—including eye contact, use of space, tone of voice, gestures, and movements.

Normative Decision Theory   A situational approach to leadership proposed by Vroom and Yetton that pre-sents a range of decision-making styles, including au-tocratic, consultative, and group, based on the degree to which the leader allows subordinates to participate in the decision-making process.

Norms   A set of beliefs or expectations mutually held by group/organizational members concerning the sorts of behaviors that are right or wrong, good or bad, or appropriate or inappropriate. Norms may be implicit or explicit.

Open systems perspective   A view of organizations that focuses on the arrangement of roles and responsi-bilities, internal operations, and boundary-spanning activities that enable the organization to persist and evolve over time.

Openness   A communication style, important between superior and subordinate, in which each party per-ceives the other as a willing and receptive listener and refrains from responses that might be perceived as dis-confirming.

Organization   A socially constructed entity in which human beings come together and often interact in purposive, goal-directed ways.

Organizational communication   That process wherein mutually interdependent human beings create and ex-change messages, and interpret and negotiate mean-ings, while striving to articulate and realize mutually held visions, purposes, and goals.

Output   The product or service that reflects the organ-ization's goals.

Participative decision making   A decision-making process championed by Likert in which those employ-ees who are most affected by a decision (especially those who have to implement it) are directly involved in making it.

Perceived conflict In Pondy's conflict model, the second stage, wherein those who interact perceive (accurately or inaccurately) not only that they are interdependent but also that their interests or values are incompatible.

Power In the traditional sense, an individual's ability to influence or control others because of their dependency on him or her; in the current sense, based more on the individual's ability to inspire trust and remain open to mutual influence.

Procedural tactics Techniques used by a mediator to organize separate or joint conflict resolution sessions, establish protocol for negotiation sessions, regulate the meeting's agenda, or establish deadlines for such meetings.

Psychological maturity An employee's willingness or motivation to do something constructive, a belief that responsibility is important, and the confidence to complete tasks without extensive encouragement.

Quality control circles Groups of employees, initially used by the Japanese in the early 1960s, who share some area of responsibility and who voluntarily discuss, analyze, and propose solutions to problems of quality that affect the area for which these employees are responsible.

Rational systems perspective A view of organizations as rational entities seeking efficiency.

Rationality The basis for exerting control in a bureaucracy.

Referent power Power that grows from one person strongly identifying with another, holding her or him in high esteem, and respecting the individual's judgment on appropriate values and modes of conduct.

Reflexive tactics Techniques used by mediators to influence the affective tone of a mediation, including developing rapport with participants, using humor, and speaking the language of both sides.

Relevance The extent to which a position in an organization is generally associated with activities that are directly related to central organizational objectives, issues, and goals.

Relevant environment Those physical and social factors outside the system's boundary that individuals within the system directly consider in their decision making.

Religious perspective A religiously based ethical perspective that offers moral and spiritual injunctions for determining the degree to which a policy or course of action is right or wrong.

Reward power An individual's ability to elicit a desired response from another person by providing positive reinforcement.

Rites/rituals Traditions, services, and ceremonies through which organizational members celebrate and reinforce their beliefs, applaud their heroes, and share their visions of the future.

Role conflict A dispute that may occur if an individual's perception and enactment of a role differ significantly from the expectations of others.

Self-centered roles Parts played by group members that tend to further self-interests over group interests and goals.

Self-managing teams Groups of employees who work together to assume such traditional management functions as preparing annual budgets, monitoring inventory, assigning jobs within groups, setting team goals, resolving internal conflicts, and evaluating team performance.

Semantic information distance A significant gap in information and understanding on certain issues that may exist between supervisors and subordinates because of differences in their experiences, hierarchical levels, and overall perspectives on the organization.

Service sector Businesses, such as education, that perform work for others that does not involve producing goods.

Sexual harassment Inappropriate/illegal conduct that may involve a person's supervisor requesting sexual favors under the threat of denying promotion or pay increases or even the threat of termination.

Situational perspective An ethical view that holds that definite ethical guidelines cannot be set apart from the specific situation. Thus, ethical criteria might alter as variables in the organizational situation change.

Status The value, importance, or prestige, often accompanied by power, associated with a given role or position.

Status conflict A dispute that grows from the ranking of group or organizational roles according to their importance or value.

Strategic choice perspective A view of organizations according to which the internal politics of an organization determines its structural form, affects how it relates to environmental constituencies, and influences its choice of relevant performance standards.

Subsystems Interdependent units within organizational systems.

Superordinate goals Common, overarching interests, objectives, or values that disputants might agree on as a step toward resolving their conflict.

Supportive communication Interaction that relies on the accurate exchange of messages and that therefore engenders feelings of support, understanding, and helpfulness, which can enhance the relationship between communicators.

Systemic distortion A type of communication distortion in which those in power create the false impression that management's interests are joined ideologically with subordinates' interests.

Task roles Communication functions taken on by group members that are necessary for a group to accomplish its task. These roles may be either substantive, such as giving information, or procedural, such as orienting the group toward its goal.

Telecommunication channels The links by which information is transmitted in a network, including telephone lines, microwaves, and satellite systems.

Theory X   A traditional approach to management based on direction and control through the exercise of authority.

Theory Y   An empowering philosophy of management championed by McGregor, and the theoretical foundation of human resources management, in which managers share decision making with workers at all levels of the organizational hierarchy and offer opportunities for workers to seek greater responsibility and achieve self-actualization.

Tone of voice   Inflectional speech patterns that vary from culture to culture (may range from exaggerated variations in rising and falling inflectional patterns to monotones).

Traditional authority   The kind of authority that is effective in cultures where many believe that hierarchies are proper because they have always existed.

Traditional centralized organizational form   Characterized by a high level of standardization where both management and organizational work are physically centralized.

Transactional   A modern model of communication that conceptualizes it as a two-way, reciprocal process of mutual message exchange. Sender and receiver roles are shared, feedback (both verbal and nonverbal) is crucial, and the receiver plays a key role in constructing the message's meaning.

Type-D organization   An organizational structure that supports distributed work arrangements by assigning work outside the core organization and by relying heavily on information technology.

Universalist perspective   An ethical outlook that maintains that because outcomes are too difficult to predict or control, the more appropriate focus is on intentions. Thus, the morality of an action depends on the intentions of the person making the decision or performing the act.

Upward communication   The communication flowing from subordinates to superiors, usually concerning employees' comments about themselves, their reactions about others, their reactions to practices and policies, and their thoughts about their work.

Upward distortion   A significant problem associated with superior-subordinate communication wherein those near the bottom of the organizational hierarchy are reluctant to communicate upward information that is unfavorable or that in any sense reflects on them negatively.

Upward influence   Subordinates' perceptions of a supervisor's ability to satisfy some of the subordinates' needs by influencing those higher in the organizational hierarchy.

Utilitarian perspective   An ethical viewpoint that holds any action to be right if it produces the greatest good for the greatest number of people.

Validating communication   Message exchange that helps others feel recognized, accepted, understood, and valued.

Values   The basis on which attitudes and personal preferences are formed; the basis for crucial decisions, life directions, and personal tastes; the foundation of ethical behavior; and an enduring and stable guide for judging one's own and others' behavior.

Vertical Dyad Linkage Model   A transactional perspective on leadership according to which the nature of the exchange processes between leaders and subordinates can have far-reaching effects on group performance and morale.

Vertical job loading   Herzberg's approach to job enrichment in which workers are given greater responsibility, assigned more challenging/difficult tasks, included in problem-solving sessions, and given opportunities to move upward and supervise others.

Virtual classroom   A teaching and learning environment in which groupware is used to support the dialogue between the instructor and students such that learning is not limited by time and place constraints.

Virtual reality technology   A technology that incorporates interactive graphics software and hardware to create computer-generated simulations that provide physical sensations emulating real-world experiences.

Visibility   The extent to which an individual's position allows him or her to interact with a large number of people within the organization.

Whistle-blower   An individual who has decided at some point that the actions of the organization are immoral, illegal, or inefficient and acts on that belief by informing legal authorities or others outside the organization, thus putting his or her duty to the public above loyalty to the organization.

REFERENCES

Chapter 1

Abramson, L.Y., Garber, J., and Seligman, M.E.P. (1980). Learned helplessness in humans: An attributional analysis. In J. Garber and M.E.P. Seligman (eds.), *Human helplessness: theory and applications,* pp. 3–34. New York: Academic Press.

Axley, S. (1984). Managerial and organizational communication in terms of the conduit metaphor. *Academy of Management Review, 9,* 428–437.

Baird, J.E., Jr. (1977). *The dynamics of organizational communication.* New York: Harper & Row.

Bavelas, A., and Barrett, D. (1951). An experimental approach to organizational communication. *Personnel, 28,* 366–371.

Bayless, A. (1986, October 16). Technology reshapes North America's lumber plants. *The Wall Street Journal, 6.*

Bennis, W., and Namus, B. (1985). *Leaders: Strategies for taking charge.* New York: HarperCollins.

Benson, G. (1983). On the campus: How well do business schools prepare graduates for the business world? *Personnel, 60,* 61–65.

Berger, S., Dertouzos, M., Lester, R., Solow, R., and Thurow, L. (1989). Toward a new industrial America. *Scientific American, 260,* 39–47.

Berlo, D.K. (1960). *The process of communication.* New York: Holt, Rinehart, & Winston.

Bernstein, A. (1994, August 15). *Inequality: How the gap between rich and poor hurts the economy: Business Week,* 78–83.

Block, P. (1987). *The empowered manager.* San Francisco: Jossey-Bass.

Burke, K. (1973). *The philosophy of literary form,* 3rd ed. Berkeley, CA: University of California Press.

Cetron, M.J., Rocha, W., and Luchins, R. (1988). Into the 21st century: Long-term trends affecting the United States. *The Futurist,* 29–40.

Cheney, G., and Tompkins, P.K. (1987). Coming to terms with organizational identification and commitment. *Central States Speech Journal, 38,* 1–15.

Clampitt, P.G. (1991). *Communicating for managerial effectiveness.* Newbury Park, CA: Sage Publications.

Conger, J.A. (1986). *Empowering leadership.* Working paper, McGill University, Montreal.

Conger, J.A. and Kanungo, R. (1988). The empowerment process: Integrating theory and practice. *Academy of Management Review, 13,* 471–482.

Curtis, D.B., Winsor, J.L., and Stephens, R.D. (1989). National preferences in business and communication education. *Communication Education, 38,* 6–15.

Dertouzos, M.L. (September 1991). Communications, computers and networks. *Scientific American, 265,* 62–69.

Drucker, P.F. (1959). *The practice of management.* New York: Harper & Row.

Drucker, P.F. (1988). The coming of the new organization. *Harvard Business Review, 66,* 45–53.

duPreez, P. (1980). *The politics of identity.* New York: St. Martin's Press.

Etzioni, A. (1964). *Modern organizations.* Englewood Cliffs, NJ: Prentice-Hall.

Galen, M. (1994, January 31). White, male, and worried. *Business Week,* 50–55.

Goldhaber, G.M. (1993). *Organizational communication,* 6th ed. Dubuque, IA: Brown and Benchmark.

Hafer, J.C., and Hoth, C.C. (1983). Selection characteristics: Your priorities and how students perceive them. *Personnel Administrator,* 25–28.

Hamilton, D. (1994, November 10). "White students learning what it is like to be a minority," *Bloomington Herald-Times,* D4. Originally printed in the *Los Angeles Times.*

Hunsicker, F.R. (1978). What successful managers say about their skills. *Personnel Journal,* 618–621.

Hyde, M.J. (1982). Introduction: The debate concerning technology. In M.J. Hyde (ed.), *Communication philosophy and the technological age,* p. 4. University of Alabama: University of Alabama Press.

Ivey, M. (1988, May 9). Long-distance learning gets an "A" at last. *Business Week,* 108–110.

Johansen, J. (1992). An introduction to computer-augmented teamwork. In R.P. Bostrom, R.T. Watson, and S.T. Kinney (eds.), *Computer-augmented teamwork* (pp. 5–15). New York: Van Nostrand Reinhold.

Kanter, R.M. (1989). The new managerial work. *Harvard Business Review, 67,* 85–92.

Katz, D., and Kahn, R.L. (1966). *The social psychology of organizations.* New York: John Wiley & Sons, Inc.

Laudon, K.C., and Laudon, J.P. (1993). *Business information systems: A problem-solving approach* (2nd ed.). Forth Worth, TX: The Dryden Press.

Luthans, F., Rosenkrantz, S.A., and Hennessey, H.W. (1985). What do successful managers really do? An observational study of managerial activities. *Journal of Applied Behavioral Science, 21,* 255–270.

Maccoby, M. (1976). *The gamesman: The new corporate leaders.* New York: Simon & Schuster.

Margerison, C., and Kakabadse, A. (1984). *How American chief executives succeed.* New York: AMA Publications.

McClelland, D.C. (1975). *Power: The inner experience.* New York: Irvington Press.

McGregor, D. (1960). *The human side of enterprise.* New York: McGraw-Hill.

McLuhan, M. (1964). *Understanding media.* New York: Signet Books.

Medhurst, M.J. (1990). Human values and the culture of technology. In M.J. Medhurst, A. Gonzalez, and T.R. Peterson (eds.), *Communication and the culture of technology,* pp. ix–xvi. Pullman, Washington: Washington State University Press.

Negroponte, N.P. (1991, September). Products and services for computer networks. *Scientific American, 265,* 106–114.

Neilsen, E. (1986). Empowerment strategies: Balancing authority and responsibility. In S. Srivasta (ed.), *Executive power,* pp. 78–110. San Francisco: Jossey-Bass.

Northcraft, G.B., and Neale, M.A. (1994). *Organizational behavior: A management challenge* (2nd ed.). Fort Worth, TX: The Dryden Press.

Offerman, L., and Gowing, M. (1990). Organizations of the future: Changes and challenges. *American Psychologist, 45,* 95–108.

Pacanowsky, M.E. (1987). Communication in the empowering organization. In J. Anderson (ed.), *Communication Yearbook 11,* pp. 356–379. Beverly Hills, CA: Sage Publications.

Pacanowsky, M.E., and O'Donnell-Trujillo, N. (1982). Communication and organizational cultures. *Western Journal of Speech Communication, 46,* 115–130.

Parsons, T. (1963). *Structure and process in modern societies.* New York: The Free Press.

Pelz, D.C., and Andrews, F.M. (1976). *Scientists in organizations,* rev. ed. Ann Arbor, MI: Institute for Social Research.

Peters, T., and Waterman, R.H. (1982). *In search of excellence.* New York: Harper & Row.

Peters, T. (1987). *Thriving on chaos.* New York: Harper & Row.

Prentice, M.G. (1984). An empirical search for a relevant management curriculum. *Collegiate News and Views,* 25–29.

Putnam, L.L. (1983). The interpretive perspective: An alternative to functionalism. In L.L. Putnam and M.E. Pacanowsky (eds.), *Communication and organizations: An interpretive approach,* pp. 31–54. Beverly Hills, CA: Sage Publications.

Putnam, L.L., and Pacanowsky, M.E. (1983). *Communication and organizations: An interpretive approach.* Beverly Hills, CA: Sage Publications.

Rogers, E. and Agarwala-Rogers, R. (1976). *Communication in organizations.* New York: The Free Press.

Schlender, B.R. (1991, August 26). Jobs and Gates together. *Fortune,* 50–54.

Schrage, M. (1990). *Shared minds: The new technologies of collaboration.* New York: Random House.

Sherman, S. (1993, June 14). The new computer revolution. *Fortune,* 56–80.

Simon, H.A. (1958). *Administrative Behavior,* 2nd ed. New York: Macmillan.

Solomon, J.S. (Fall 1987). Union responses to technological change: Protecting the past or looking to the future?, *Labor Studies Journal,* 51–65.

Sproull, L., and Kiesler, S. (1991, September). Computers, networks, and work. *Scientific American, 265,* 116–123.

Toffler, A. (1990). *Powershift.* New York: Bantam Books.

Tompkins, P.K. (1982). *Communication as action.* Belmont, CA: Wadsworth.

Tortoriello, T., Blatt, S., and DeWine, S. (1978). *Communication in the organization: An applied approach.* New York: McGraw-Hill.

Weick, K.E. (1969). *The social psychology of organizing.* Reading, MA: Addison-Wesley.

Wenburg, J., and Wilmot, W. (1973). *The personal communication process.* New York: John Wiley & Sons, Inc.

Whetton, D.A., and Cameron, K.S. (1991). *Developing management skills,* 2nd ed. New York: HarperCollins.

Whyte, W.H., Jr. (1957). *The organization man.* Garden City, NY: Doubleday.

Wilson, H., Goodall, H.L., and Waagen, C. (1986). *Organizational communication.* New York: Harper & Row.

Wriston, W.B. (1990). The state of American management. *Harvard Business Review, 68,* 78–83.

Chapter 2

Adams, P. (1975). *Organizations as bargaining and influence systems.* London: Heinemann.

Alavi, M., and Keen, P.G.W. (1989). Business teams in an information age. *The Information Society, 6,* 179–195.

Aldrich, H., and Herker, D. (1977). Boundary spanning roles and organizational structure. *Academy of Management Review, 2,* 217–230.

Barnard, C. (1938). *The functions of the executive.* Cambridge, MA: Harvard University Press.

Benjamin, R.I., and Blunt, J. (Summer 1992). Critical IT issues: The next ten years. *Sloan Management Review,* 7–19.

Bertalanffy, L.V. (1956). General systems theory. *General Systems, 1,* 1.

Boulding, K. (1956). General systems—The skeleton of a science. *Management Science, April,* 202–205.

Carnegie, D. (1936). *How to win friends and influence people.* New York: Simon & Schuster.

Clegg, S. (1990). *Modern organizations.* Newbury Park, CA: Sage Publications.

Coch, L., and French, J.R.P. (1948). Overcoming resistance to change. *Human Relations, 11,* 512–532.

Deal T.E., and Kennedy, A.A. (1982). *Corporate cultures.* Reading, MA: Addison-Wesley.

Dessler, G. (1980). *Organization theory: Integrating structure and behavior.* Englewood Cliffs, NJ: Prentice-Hall.

Drucker, P. (1988). The coming of the new organization. *Harvard Business Review, 66,* 45–53.

Duncan, R.B. (1972). Characteristics of organizational environments and perceived environmental uncertainty. *Administrative Science Quarterly, 17,* 313–327.

Fayol, H. (1949). *General and industrial management.* London: Pitman. (Originally published in 1916.)

Fleming, W. (1975). *Art, music, and ideas.* New York: Holt, Rinehart & Winston.

Franke, R.H., and Kaul, J.D. (1978). The Hawthorne experiments: First statistical reinterpretation. *American Sociological Review, 43,* 623–643.

George, C. (1972). *The history of management thought.* Englewood Cliffs, NJ: Prentice-Hall.

Jaques, E. (1990). In praise of hierarchy. *Harvard Business Review, 68,* 127–133.

Kanter, R.M. (1983). *The changemasters: Innovation for productivity in the American corporation.* New York: Simon & Schuster.

Katz, D., and Kahn, R.L. (1966). *The social psychology of organizations.* New York: John Wiley & Sons, Inc.

Koehler, J.W., Anatol, K.W.E., and Applbaum, R.L. (1981). *Organizational communication: Behavioral perspectives.* New York: Holt, Rinehart, & Winston.

Kreitner, R., and O'Grady, J.P. (1990). *Business,* 2nd ed. Boston: Houghton Mifflin.

Lewin, K., Lippitt, R., and White, R. (1939). Patterns of aggressive behavior in experimentally created "social climates." *Journal of Social Psychology, 10,* 271–299.

Lewin, K. (1947). Frontiers in group dynamics. *Human Relations, 1,* 2–42.

Laudon, K.C., and Laudon, J.P. (1993). *Business information systems: A problem-solving approach,* 2nd ed. Fort Worth, TX: Dryden Press.

Lawrence, P., and Lorsch, J. (1967). *Organization and environment: Managing differentiation and integration.* Boston: Harvard Business School.

Lohr, S. (1993, January 20). IBM posts $5.46 billion loss for 4th quarter. *New York Times,* pp. C1 & C5.

March, J.G., and Simon, H.A. (1958). *Organizations.* New York: John Wiley & Sons, Inc.

Mayo, E. (1947). *The human problems of an industrial civilization.* Boston: Harvard Business School.

McConnell, M. (1987). *Challenger: A major malfunction.* Garden City, NY: Doubleday.

McPhee, R. (1985). Four critical approaches to workplace power/control in organizational communication. Paper presented at the annual meeting of the International Communication Association, Chicago.

Miles, R. (1965). Keeping informed—Human relations or human resources? *Harvard Business Review, 43,* 148–163.

Mitchell, Russell (1989, April 10). Masters of innovation. *Business Week,* 58–63.

Mumby, D.K. (1987). The political function of narrative in organizations. *Communication Monographs, 54,* 113–127.

Noller, D. (1991). *Beyond a buzzword: An empowerment perspective.* Unpublished manuscript, University of Colorado, Boulder, CO.

Pacanowsky, M.E., and O'Donnell-Trujillo, N. (1982). Communication and organizational cultures. *Western Journal of Speech Communication, 46,* 115–130.

Pacanowsky, M.E., and O'Donnell-Trujillo, N. (1983). Organizational communication as cultural performance. *Communication Monographs, 50,* 126–147.

Pacanowsky, M.E. (1987). Communication in the empowering organization. In J. Anderson (ed.), *Communication Yearbook 11,* pp. 356–379. Beverly Hills, CA: Sage Publications.

Peters, T.J., and Waterman, R.H. (1982). *In search of excellence.* New York: Harper & Row.

Pride, W., Hughes, R., and Kapoor, J. (1993). *Business,* 4th ed. Boston: Houghton Mifflin.

Putnam, L.L. (1983). The interpretive perspective: an alternative to functionalism. In L.L. Putnam and M.E. Pacanowsky (eds.), *Communication and organizations: An interpretive approach,* pp. 31–54. Beverly Hills, CA: Sage Publications.

Rockart, J.F., and Short, J.E. (Winter 1989). IT in the 1990s: Managing organizational interdependence. *Sloan Management Review, 31,* 7–16.

Roethlisberger, F.J., and Dickson, W.J. (1939). *Management and the worker.* Cambridge, MA: Harvard University Press.

Rogers, E., and Agarwala-Rogers, R. (1976). *Communication in organizations.* New York: The Free Press.

Senn, J. (1995). *Information technology in business.* Englewood Cliffs, NJ: Prentice-Hall.

Sherman, S. (1993, June 14). The new computer revolution. *Fortune,* 56–80.

Smircich, L., and Calas, M. B. (1987). Organizational culture: A critical assessment. In F.M. Jablin, L.L. Putnam, K.H. Roberts, and L.W. Porter (eds.), *Handbook of organizational communication: An interdisciplinary perspective,* pp. 228–263. Newbury Park, CA: Sage Publications.

Smith, A. (1937). *The wealth of nations.* Vintage Books: Random House, (originally published in 1776).

Taylor, F. (1911). *Principles of scientific management.* New York: Harper & Row.

Tompkins, P., and Cheney, G. (1983). Communication and unobtrusive control in contemporary organizations. In L.L. Putnam and M.E. Pacanowsky (eds.), *Organizational communication: Traditional themes and new directions,* pp. 123–146. Beverly Hills, CA: Sage Publications.

Tompkins, P., and Redding, W.C. (1988). Organizational communication—past and present tenses. In G.M. Goldhaber and G.A. Barnett (eds.), *Handbook of organizational communication,* pp. 5–33. Norwood, NJ: Ablex.

Tortoriello, T., Blatt, S., and DeWine, S. (1978). *Communication in the organization: An applied approach.* New York: McGraw-Hill.

Tushman, M., and Scanlan, T. (1980). Boundary spanning individuals. *The Academy of Management Review, 5,* 123–138.

Uttal, B. (1983, October 17). The corporate culture vultures. *Fortune*, 66.

Weber, M. (1947). *The theory of social and economic organizations*. (A.M. Henderson and T. Parson, trans.; T. Parsons, ed.). New York: Oxford University Press.

Weick, K.E. (1969). *The social psychology of organizing*. Reading, MA: Addison-Wesley.

Weick, K.E. (1976). Educational organizations as loosely coupled systems. *Administrative Science Quarterly, 21*, 1–19.

Weick, K.E. (1987). Theorizing about organizational communication. In F.M. Jablin, L.L. Putnam, K.H. Roberts, and L.W. Porter (eds.), *Handbook of organizational communication: An interdisciplinary perspective*, pp. 97–122. Newbury Park, CA: Sage Publications.

White, R., and Lippitt, R. (1960). *Autocracy and democracy*. New York: Harper & Row.

Whyte, W.H., Jr. (1957). *The organization man*. Garden City, NY: Doubleday.

Chapter 3

Ballon, R.J. (1969). *The Japanese employee*. Rutland, VT: Charles E. Tuttle.

Bernstein, A. (1986, July 14). The difference Japanese management makes, *Business Week*, 47–50.

Blake, R., and Mouton, J. (1964). *The managerial grid*. Houston: Gulf Publishing.

Bowles, J.G. (1990, September 24). The human side of quality. *Fortune*, 24.

Brooks, B. (1991, November 11). Team approach helps keep Indiana Chrysler plant alive. *The Bloomington Herald-Times*, p. C4.

Causron, S. (1993, December). Are self-directed teams right for your company? *Personnel Journal, 72*, 81.

De Vries, M., and Miller, B. (1984). *The neurotic organization: Diagnosing and revitalizing unhealthy companies*. New York: HarperCollins.

Drucker, P. (1988). The coming of the new organization. *Harvard Business Review, 66*, 45–53.

Dumaine, B. (1990, May 7). Who needs a boss? *Fortune*, 52–60.

Graham, T. (1993, May 24). The Japanese culture inspires unique management practices. *The Bloomington Herald-Times*, p. B10.

Greiner, L. (1973). What managers think of participative leadership. *Harvard Business Review, 51*, 111–117.

Hackman, J.R., Oldham, G., Janson, R., and Purdy, K. (1975). A new strategy for job enrichment. *California Management Review, 17*, 57–71.

Herzberg, F. (1966). *Work and the nature of man*. Cleveland: World Publishing.

Herzberg, F. (1968). One more time: How do you motivate employees? *Harvard Business Review, 46*, 53–62.

Hersey, P., and Blanchard, K.H. (1969). Life cycle theory of leadership. *Training and Development Journal, 23*, 26–34.

Hersey, P., and Blanchard, K.H. (1977). *Management of organizational behavior: Utilizing human resources*, 3rd ed. Englewood Cliffs, NJ: Prentice-Hall.

Hersey, P., Blanchard, K.H., and Hambleton, R.K. (1977). *Contracting for leadership style: A process and instrumentation for building effective work relationships*. Columbus, OH: Ohio State University Center for Leadership Studies.

Hershey, G.L., and Kizzier, D.L. (1992). *Planning and implementing end-user information systems*. Cincinnati, OH: South-Western.

Herschel, R., and Andrews, P.H. (Spring 1993). Empowering employees in group work: A case for using group support systems. *Information strategy: The Executive's Journal, 9*, 36–42.

Herschel, R., Mennecke, B., and Wynne, B.E. (1991). Electronic meeting systems as a team building tool. Working paper, Indiana University, Bloomington, IN.

Hirokawa, R. (1981). Improving intra-organizational communication: A lesson from Japanese management. *Communication Quarterly, 30*, 35–40.

Hirokawa, R., and Miyahara, A. (1986). A comparison of influence strategies utilized by managers in American and Japanese organizations. *Communication Quarterly, 35*, 250–265.

Homans, G. (1950). *The human group*. New York: Harcourt Brace Jovanovich.

Johansen, J. (1992). Enhancing team performance with groupware. *Groupware Report*. Preview Issue. Athens, GA.

Kanter, R.M. (1989). The new managerial work. *Harvard Business Review, 67*, 85–92.

Keen, P.G.W. (1991). Computers and managerial choice. In H.J. Watson, A.B. Carroll, and R.I. Mann (eds.), *Information systems for management: A book of readings*, pp. 351–367. Homewood, IL: Richard D. Irwin.

Lawler, E.E. (1986). *High-involvement management: Participative strategies for improving organizational performance*. San Francisco: Jossey-Bass.

Likert, R. (1961). *New patterns of management*. New York: McGraw-Hill.

Likert, R. (1967). *The human organization*. New York: McGraw-Hill.

Madnick, S.E. (1991). The information technology platform. In M.S. Morton (ed.), *The corporation of the 1990s: Information technology and organizational transformation*, pp. 27–60. New York: Oxford University Press.

Maslow, A. (1954). *Motivation and personality*. New York: Harper & Row.

McCall, M.M., Jr., and Lombardo, M.M. (1983). What makes a top executive? *Psychology Today, 26*, 28–31.

McGregor, D. (1960). *The human side of enterprise*. New York: McGraw-Hill.

McGregor, D. (1967). *The professional manager*. New York: McGraw-Hill.

Ouchi, W.G. (1981). *Theory Z: How American business can meet the Japanese challenge.* Reading, MA: Addison-Wesley.

Pacanowsky, M.E. (1987). Communication in the empowering organization. In J. Anderson (ed.), *Communication Yearbook 11*, pp. 356–379. Beverly Hills, CA: Sage Publications.

Pascale, R., and Athos, A. (1981). *The art of Japanese management: Applications for American management.* New York: Simon & Schuster.

Peters, T.J., and Waterman, R.H. (1982). *In search of excellence.* New York: Harper & Row.

Preston, R. (1991). *American steel.* Englewood Cliffs, NJ: Prentice-Hall.

Sims, H.P., and Dean, J.W. (1985). Beyond quality circles: Self-managing teams. *Personnel, 62,* 26.

Stewart, L.P., Gudykunsz, W.B., Ting-Tomy, S., and Nishida, T. (1986). The effects of decision-making style on openness and satisfaction within Japanese organizations. *Communication Monographs, 53,* 236–251.

Takenoya, M. (1989). Communication practices in Japanese organizations. Unpublished manuscript, Indiana University.

Thornton, E. (1991, December 16). Fifty fateful years: From enemy to friend to——? *Fortune, 76,* 126–134.

Tompkins, P.K. (1993). *Organizational communication imperatives: Lessons of the space program.* Los Angeles, CA: Roxbury Publishing Co.

Werth, B. (1990, October 12). Quality leadership process, high-end strategy clicking at Thomson Consumer Electronics. *The Bloomington Herald-Times,* p. G1.

Wriston, W.B. (1990). The state of American management. *Harvard Business Review, 69,* 78–83.

Yang, C.Y. (1984). Demystifying Japanese management practices. *Harvard Business Review, 62,* 172–182.

Chapter 4

Andrews, P.H., and Baird, J.E., Jr. (1992). *Communication for business and the professions,* 5th ed. Dubuque, IA: Wm. C. Brown Publishers.

Anson, R. (1990). *Effects of computer support and facilitator support on group process and outcomes: An experimental assessment.* Unpublished doctoral dissertation, Indiana University, Bloomington.

Bales, R.F. (1971). *Personality and interpersonal behavior.* New York: Holt, Rinehart & Winston.

Baird, J.E., and Bradley, P.H. (1979). Styles of management and communication: A comparative study of men and women. *Communication Monographs, 46,* 101–111.

Bannister, B.D. (1986). Performance outcome feedback and attributional feedback: Interactive effects on recipient responses. *Journal of Applied Psychology, 71,* 203–210.

Beyer, J.M., and Trice, H.M. (1984). A field study of the use and perceived effects of discipline in controlling work performance. *Academy of Management Journal, 27,* 743–764.

Chidambaram, L., Bostrom, R., and Wynne, B. (1991). A longitudinal investigation of the impact of group decision support systems on group development. *Journal of Management Information Systems, 7,* 7–25.

Crocker, J. (1978). *Speech communication instruction based on employers' perceptions of the importance of selected communication skills for employees on the job.* Paper presented at the Speech Communication Association meeting, Minneapolis, MN.

Culnan, M.J., and Markus, M.L. (1987). Information technologies. In F.M. Jablin, L.L. Putnam, K.H. Roberts, and L.W. Porter, *Handbook of organizational communication: An interdisciplinary perspective,* pp. 420–443. Newbury Park, CA: Sage Publications.

Daniels, T.D., and Logan, L.L. (1983). Communication in women's career development relationships. In R.N. Bostrom (ed.), *Communication yearbook 7,* pp. 532–553. Beverly Hills, CA: Sage Publications.

Dansereau, F., Graen, G., and Haga, W.J. (1975). A vertical dyad linkage approach to leadership within formal organizations: A longitudinal investigation of the role-making process. *Organizational Behavior and Human Performance, 13,* 46–78.

Dansereau, F., and Markham, S. (1987). Superior-subordinate communication: Multiple levels of analysis. In F.M. Jablin, L.L. Putnam, K.H. Roberts, and L.L. Porter (eds.), *Handbook of organizational communication,* pp. 343–388. Newbury Park, CA: Sage Publications.

DeSanctis, G., D'Onofrio, M., Sambamurthy, V., and Poole, M.S. (1989). Comprehensiveness and restrictiveness in group decision heuristics: Effects of computer support on consensus decision making. *ICIS Proceedings.*

Dyer, W.G. (1972). Congruence. *The sensitive manipulator.* Provo, UT: Brigham Young University Press.

Fagenson, E.A. (1989). The mentor advantage: Perceived career/job experiences of proteges versus non-proteges. *Journal of Organizational Behavior, 10,* 309–320.

Fulk, J., and Mani, S. (1986). Distortion of communication in hierarchical relationships. In M.L. McLaughlin (ed.), *Communication yearbook 9,* pp. 483–510. Newbury Park, CA: Sage Publications.

Galbraith, J.K. (1975, December 9). Are you Mark Epernay? The literary Galbraith on the art of writing. *Christian Science Monitor,* 19.

Gibb, J.R. (1961). Defensive communication. *Journal of Communication, 11,* 141–148.

Hanson, G. (1986). *Determinants of firm performance: An integration of economic and organizational factors.* Unpublished doctoral dissertation, University of Michigan Business School, Ann Arbor, MI.

Harrison, T.M. (1985). Communication and participative decision making: An exploratory study. *Personnel Psychology, 38,* 93–116.

Hatfield, J., Huseman, R., and Miles, E. (1987). Perceptual differences in verbal recognition and relative job satisfaction. *Communication Research Reports, 4,* 8–13.

Herrick-Walker, S.J. (1991). *The effect of group decision support systems on decision-making groups containing high communication apprehensives: Satisfaction, participation, and productivity.* Unpublished master's thesis, Indiana University, Bloomington.

Hiltz, S.R., and Turoff, M. (1978). *The network nation: Human communication via computer.* Reading, MA: Addison-Wesley.

Hunt, G.T., and Cusella, L.P. (1983). A field study of listening needs in organizations. *Communication Education, 32,* 368–378.

Iaffaldano, M., and Muchinsky, P. (1985). Job satisfaction and job performance. *Psychological Bulletin, 97,* 271–273.

Infante, D.A., and Gordon, W.I. (1985). Superiors' argumentativeness and verbal aggressiveness as predictors of subordinates' satisfaction. *Human Communication Research, 12,* 117–125.

Jablin, F.M. (1979). Superior-subordinate communication: The state of the art. *Psychological Bulletin, 86,* 1201–1222.

Jablin, F.M. (1980). Superior's upward influence, satisfaction, and openness in superior-subordinate communication: A reexamination of the "Pelz effect." *Human Communication Research, 6,* 210–220.

Jablin, F.M. (1985). Task/work relationships: A life-span perspective. In M.L. Knapp and G.R. Miller (eds.) *Handbook of interpersonal communication,* pp. 615–654. Newbury Park, CA: Sage Publications.

Jessup, L., Connolly, T., and Tansik, D. (1990). Toward a theory of automated group work: The deindividuating effects of anonymity. *Small Group Research, 21,* 333–348.

Johannesen, R.L. (1971). The emerging concept of communication as dialogue. *Quarterly Journal of Speech, 57,* 373–382.

Kelly, M. (1993, January 30). Schools for leaders take more humanist approach. *The Bloomington Herald-Times,* p. B10.

Kelly, M.E. (1993). *An analysis of supervisor conflict management style and subordinate satisfaction with the performance appraisal interview.* Unpublished master's thesis, Indiana University, Bloomington.

Kram, K.E. (1985). *Mentoring at work: Developmental relationships in organizational life.* Glenview, IL: Scott, Foresman.

Larkin, T.J. (1980). Network analysis as an investigative tool for organizational communication. Paper presented at the International Communication Association Meeting, Acapulco, Mexico.

Liu, W., and Duff, R. (1972). The strength of weak ties. *Public Opinion Quarterly, 36,* 361–366.

Luthans, F., and Larsen, J.K. (1986). How managers really communicate. *Human Relations, 39,* 161–178.

Noe, R.A. (1988). An investigation of the determinants of successful assigned mentoring relationships. *Personnel Psychology, 41,* 457–479.

Noel, T. (1992). *Effect of anonymity on intact group performance and member attitudes in a group support system environment: An experimental assessment.* Unpublished doctoral dissertation, Indiana University, Bloomington.

Nunamaker, J., Dennis, A., Valacich, J., Vogel, D., and George, J. (1993). Group support systems research: Experience from the lab and field. In L.M. Jessup and J.S. Valacich (eds.), *Group support systems: New perspectives,* pp. 78–96. New York: Macmillan.

O'Reilly, C.A., and Anderson, J.C. (1980). Trust and the communication of performance appraisal information: The effect of feedback on performance and job satisfaction. *Human Communication Research, 6,* 290–298.

Pelz, D.S. (1952). Influence: A key to effective leadership in the first-line supervisor. *Personnel, 29,* 3–11.

Pincus, J.D. (1986). Communication satisfaction, job satisfaction, and job performance. *Human Communication Research, 12,* 395–419.

Ragins, B.R. (1989). Barriers to mentoring: The female manager's dilemma. *Human Relations, 42,* 1–22.

Read, W. (1962). Upward communication in industrial hierarchies. *Human Relations, 15,* 3–15.

Redding, W.C. (1972). *Communication within the organization: An interpretive review of theory and research.* New York: Industrial Communications Council.

Rice, R.E. (1984). Evaluating new media systems. In J. Johnstone (ed.), *Evaluating the new media technologies: New directions for program evaluation,* no. 23, pp. 53–71. San Francisco: Jossey-Bass.

Rice, R.E., Richards, W.D., and Cavalcanti. (1980). Communication network analysis methods. Paper presented at the International Communication Association Meeting, Acapulco, Mexico.

Rice, R.E., and Case, D. (1983). Electronic message systems in the university: A description of use and utility. *Journal of Communication, 33,* 131–152.

Richetto, G.M. (1969). *Source credibility and personal influence in three contexts: A study of dyadic communication in a complex aerospace organization.* Unpublished doctoral dissertation, Purdue University, Lafayette, IN.

Roberts, K., and O'Reilly, C. (1974). Failures in upward communication: Three possible culprits. *Academy of Management Journal, 17,* 205–215.

Rogers, C.W. (1961). *On becoming a person.* Boston: Houghton Mifflin.

Rogers, E., and Agarwala-Rogers, R. (1976). *Communication in organizations.* New York: The Free Press.

Romano, C. (December 1993). Fear of feedback. *Management Review, 82,* 38–41.

Schutz, W.C. (1966). *The interpersonal underworld.* Palo Alto, CA: Science and Behavior Books.

Scudder, J., Herschel, R., and Crossland, M. (1994). A test of a model linking cognitive motivation, idea generation, decision quality and group process satisfaction. *Small Group Research, 25,* 57–82.

Short, J., Williams, E., and Christie, B. (1976). *The social psychology of telecommunications.* New York: John Wiley & Sons.

Sieburg, E. (1978). *Confirming and disconfirming organizational communication.* Working paper, University of Denver, CO.

Smirich, L., and Chesser, R.J. (1981). Superiors' and subordinates' perceptions of performance: Beyond agreement. *Academy of Management Journal, 24,* 198–205.

Sproull, L., and Kiesler, S. (1985). Using electronic mail for data collection in organizational research. *Academy of Management Journal, 29,* 159–169.

Strickland, L.H., Guild, P.D., Barefoot, J.C., and Paterson, S.A. (1978). Teleconferencing and leadership emergence. *Human Relations, 31,* 583–596.

Sypher, B.D., and Zorn, T.E., Jr. (1987). Individual differences and construct system content in descriptions of liked and disliked coworkers. Paper presented to the Organizational Communication Division of the International Communication Association Convention, May, Montreal.

Tjosvold, D. (1984). Effects of leader warmth and directiveness on subordinate performance on a subsequent task. *Journal of Applied Psychology, 69,* 422–427.

Vroom, V. (1964). *Work and motivation.* New York: John Wiley & Sons, Inc.

Whetton, D.A., and Cameron, K.S. (1991). *Developing management skills,* 2nd ed. New York: HarperCollins.

Wienmann, J. (1977). Explication and test of a model of communicative competence. *Human Communication Research, 3,* 195–213.

Wreden, N. (1993, March/April). Regrouping for groupware. *Beyond Computing, 2,* 52–55.

Chapter 5

Aldrich, H. (1972). Technology and organization structure: A reexamination of the findings of the Aston Group. *Administrative Science Quarterly, 17, 1,* (Mar.), 26–43.

Argyris, C. (1972). *The applicability of organizational sociology.* London: Cambridge University Press.

Blau, P., and Scott, W.R. (1962). *Formal organizations.* San Francisco: Chandler.

Carlyle, R. (1990, February 1). The tomorrow organization. *Datamation,* 22–29.

Chandler, A.D., Jr. (1962). *Strategy and structure.* Cambridge, MA: MIT Press.

Child, J. (1972). Organizational structure, environment, and performance: The role of strategic choice. *Sociology, 6, 1* (Jan.), 1–22.

Davis, K. (1973). The care and cultivation of the corporate grapevine. In R.C. Huseman et al. (eds.), *Readings in interpersonal and organizational communication,* pp. 131–136. Boston: Holbrook Press.

Deal, T.E., and Kennedy, A.A. (1982). *Corporate cultures.* Reading, MA: Addison-Wesley.

Dominguez, C. (1991–92). The challenge of Workforce 2000. *Bureaucrat, 20, 4,* 15–18.

Drucker, P.F. (1988). The coming of the new organization. *Harvard Business Review, 66,* 45–53.

Etzioni, A. (1961). *A comparative analysis of complex organizations.* New York: The Free Press.

Fayol, H. (1949). *General and industrial management.* London: Sir Isaac Pitman & Sons.

Galagan, P. (1992, August). When the wall comes down: Views of Marvin Weisbord. *Training and Development, 46, 8,* 33–35.

Hage, J. (1965). An axiomatic theory of organizations. *Administrative Science Quarterly, 10, 3* (Dec.), 289–320.

Hage, J. (1980). *Theories of organizations.* New York: John Wiley & Sons, Inc.

Hage, J., and Aiken, M. (1967a). Relationship of centralization to other structural properties. *Administrative Science Quarterly, 12, 1* (June), 72–91.

Hage, J., and Aiken, M. (1967b). Program chance and organizational properties. *American Journal of Sociology, 72, 5* (Mar.), 503–19.

Hall, R. H. (1987). *Organizations: Structures, processes, and outcomes,* 4th ed. Englewood Cliffs, NJ: Prentice-Hall.

Hellweg, S. (1987). Organizational grapevines: A state of the art review. In B. Dervin and M. Voights (eds.), *Progress in the communication sciences 8.* Norwood, NJ: Ablex.

Hershey, G.L., and Kizzier, D.L. (1992). *Planning and implementing end-user information systems.* Cincinnati, OH: South-Western.

Huber, G.P. (1990). A theory of the effects of advanced information technologies on organizational design, intelligence, and decision making. *Academy of Management Review, 15,* 47–71.

Huber, G., Valacich, J., and Jessup, L. (1993). A theory of the effects of group support systems on an organization's nature and decisions. In L.M. Jessup and J.S. Valacich (eds.), *Group support systems: New perspectives,* pp. 255–269. New York: Macmillan.

Kanter, R.M. (1983). *The changemasters: Innovation for productivity in the American corporation.* New York: Simon & Schuster.

Katz, D., and Kahn, R. (1978). *The social psychology of organizations,* rev. ed. New York: John Wiley & Sons, Inc.

Kiechel, W. (1984, 25 June). Beat the clock. *Fortune,* 148.

Laudon, K.C. and Laudon, J.P. (1993). *Business information systems: A problem-solving approach,* 2nd ed. Fort Worth: Dryden Press.

Lewis, D.E. (1993, July 18). "Modem can link, or chain, worker to office," *Boston Sunday Globe,* pp. 1, 12.

Loveman, G. (1992, March 23). Here comes the payoff from PCs. *Fortune,* 96.

Malone, T., and Rockart, J. (1991, September). Computers, networks, and the corporation. *Scientific American, 265,* 128–136.

Mintzberg, H. (1979). *The structuring of organizations.* Englewood Cliffs, NJ: Prentice-Hall.

Mintzberg, H. (1981). Organization design: Fashion or fit? *Harvard Business Review, 59,* 103–116.

Parsons, T. (1960). *Structure and process in modern society.* New York: The Free Press.

Perrow, C. (1967). A framework for the comparative analysis of organizations. *American Sociological Review, 32,* 2 (Apr.), 194–208.

Peters, T., and Waterman, R. H. (1982). *In search of excellence.* New York: Harper & Row.

Pugh, D., Hickson, D., and Hinings, C.R. (1969). An empirical taxonomy of work organizations. *Administrative Science Quarterly, 14, 1* (Mar.), 115–26.

Ray, C., Palmer, J., and Wohl, A. (1991). Office automation: A systems approach, 2nd. ed. Cincinnati, OH: South-Western.

Roberts, K., and O'Reilly, C. (1978). Organizations as communication structures. *Human Communication Research, 4,* 283–293.

Scott, W.R. (1987). *Organizations: Rational, natural, and open systems,* 2nd ed. Englewood Cliffs, NJ: Prentice-Hall.

Simon, H. (1957). *Administrative behavior,* 2nd ed. New York: Macmillan.

Steiner, G., and Ryan, W. (1968). *Industrial project management.* New York: Crowell-Collier & Macmillan.

Taylor, F. W. (1911). *The principles of scientific management.* New York: Harper & Row.

Van De Ven, A., and Ferry, D. (1980). *Measuring and assessing organizations.* New York: John Wiley & Sons, Inc.

Vitalari, N. (1990). Exploring the Type-D organization: Distributed work arrangements, information technology and organizational design. In A.M. Jenkins, H.S. Siegel, W. Wojtkowski, and W.G. Wojtkowski (eds), *Research issues in information systems: An agenda for the 1990's,* pp. 101–129. Dubuque, IA: Wm. C. Brown.

Weick, K. (1976). Educational organizations as loosely coupled systems. *Administrative Science Quarterly, 21, 1* (Mar.), 1–19.

Weick, K. (1979). *The social psychology of organizing,* 2nd ed. Reading, MA: Addison-Wesley.

Wynne, B., Anson, R., Heminger, A., and Valacich, J. (1992). Support for organizational work groups: An applied research program of theory building and field testing. In R.P. Bostrom, R.T. Watson, and S.T. Kinney (eds.), *Computer augmented teamwork,* pp. 197–209. New York: Van Nostrand Reinhold.

Chapter 6

Ashour, A.S. (1973). Further discussion of Fiedler's contingency model of leadership effectiveness: An evaluation. *Organizational Behavior and Human Performance, 9,* 339–355.

Ayman, R., and Chemers, M.M. (1983). The relationship of leader behavior of managerial effectiveness and satisfaction in Iran. *Journal of Applied Psychology, 68,* 338–341.

Bachrach, P., and Baratz, M. (1962). Two faces of power. *American Political Science Review, 56,* 947–952.

Bennis, W., and Namus, B. (1985). *Leaders: Strategies for taking charge.* New York: Harper & Row.

Bennis, W. (1989). *On becoming a leader.* Reading, MA: Addison-Wesley.

Bird, C. (1940). *Social psychology.* New York: Appleton-Century.

Boone, M. (1991). *Leadership and the computer.* Rocklin, CA: Prima.

Boone, M. (Winter 1992). Taking an EIS health audit: Are your executives using EIS to augment their leadership? *Chief Information Officer Journal, 4,* 27–32.

Burke, W. (1986). Leadership as empowering others. In S. Srivastra (ed.), *Executive power,* pp. 51–77. San Francisco: Jossey-Bass.

Calder, B.J. (1977). An attribution theory of leadership. In B.M. Shaw and G.R. Salancik (eds.), *New directions in organizational behavior,* pp. 63–71. Chicago: St. Clair.

Calvert, L., and Ramsey, V. (1992). Bringing women's voice to research on women in management: A feminist perspective. *Journal of Management Inquiry, 1,* 79–88.

Clawson, V., and Bostrom, R. (July 1993). Facilitator role study: Take two. *Groupware Report,* Athens, GA, 4–6.

Chemers, M.M. (1984). The social, organizational, and cultural context of effective leadership. In B. Kellerman (ed.), *Leadership: Multidisciplinary perspectives,* pp. 95–112. Englewood Cliffs, NJ: Prentice-Hall.

Coch, L. and French, J.R.P., Jr. (1948). Overcoming resistance to change. *Human Relations, 11,* 512–532.

Conger, J.A. (1986). *Empowering leadership.* Working paper, McGill University, Montreal.

Conger, J.A. (1989). Leadership: The art of empowering others. *The Academy of Management Executive, 3,* 17–24.

Conger, J.A., and Kanungo, R.N. (1988). The empowerment process: Integrating theory and practice. *Academy of Management Review, 13,* 471–482.

Deal, T.E., and Kennedy, A.A. (1982). *Corporate cultures: The rites and rituals of corporate life.* Reading, MA: Addison-Wesley.

Dennis, A. (1992, September). Critical success factors for groupware implementation. *Groupware Report,* Athens, GA.

Dickson, G., Partridge, J., and Robinson, L. (1993). Exploring modes of facilitative support for GDSS technology. *MIS Quarterly, 17,* 173–194.

Drucker, P.F. (1988). The coming of the new organization. *Harvard Business Review, 66,* 45–53.

Dumaine, B. (1993, February 22). The new non-manager managers. *Fortune,* 80–84.

Emerson, R.M. (1962). Power-dependence relations. *American Sociological Review, 27,* 31–41.

Ends, E.J., and Page, C.W. (1977). *Organizational team building,* Cambridge, MA: Winthrop Publishers, Inc.

Fiedler, F.E. (1967). A theory of leadership effectiveness. New York: McGraw-Hill.

Fiedler, F.E. (1979). The leadership game: Matching the man to the situation. In R.C. Huseman and A.B. Carroll (eds.), *Readings in organizational behavior: Dimensions of management actions,* pp. 305–313. Boston: Allyn & Bacon.

French, J.R.P., Jr., and Raven, B. (1959). The bases of social power. In D. Cartwright (ed.), *Studies in social power,* pp. 65–84. Ann Arbor, MI: Institute for Social Research.

Frost, P. (1987). Power, politics, and influence. In F.M. Jablin, L.L. Putnam, K.H. Roberts, and L.W. Porter (eds.), *Handbook of organizational communication: An interdisciplinary perspective,* pp. 503–548. Newbury Park, CA: Sage Publications.

Fulk, J., and Boyd, B. (1991). Emerging theories of communication in organizations. *Journal of Management, 17,* 407–446.

Galbraith, J.R. (1967). Influencing the decision to produce. *Industrial Management Review, 9,* 97–107.

Gatewood, R. (1994, November 14). AT&T trains managers for the future. *The Bloomington Herald-Times,* p. A7.

Geier, J.G. (1967). A trait approach to the study of leadership in small groups. *Journal of Communication, 17,* 316–323.

George, J.F., Dennis, A.R., and Nunamaker, J.F. (1992, April). An experimental investigation of facilitation in an EMS decision room. *Group Decision and Negotiation, 1,* 57–70.

Gibb, J. (1961). Defensive communication. *Journal of Communication, 11,* 141–148.

Gouran, D.S. (1970). Conceptual and methodological approaches to the study of leadership. *Central States Speech Journal, 21,* 217–223.

Graen, G., Alveres, K.M., Orris, J.B., and Martella, J.A. (1970). Contingency model of leadership effectiveness: Antecedent and evidential results. *Psychological Bulletin, 74,* 285–296.

Graen, G., and Cashman, J.F. (1975). A role-making model of leadership in formal organizations: A developmental approach. In J.G. Hunt and L.L. Larsen (eds.), *Leadership frontiers,* pp. 23–36. Kent, OH: Kent State University Press.

Graen, G., and Ginsburgh, S. (1977). Job resignation as a function of role orientation and leaders acceptance: A longitudinal investigation of organizational assimilation. *Organizational Behavior and Human Performance, 19,* 1–17.

Gramsci, A. (1971). *Selections from the prison notebooks.* London: Lawrence & Wishart.

Green, S.G., and Mitchell, T.R. (1979). Attributional processes of leaders in leader-member interactions. *Organizational Behavior and Human Performance, 23,* 429–458.

Griffin, C., and Andrews, P.H. (1993). *Recasting power: A feminist perspective on organizations as structures of value.* Unpublished manuscript, Indiana University, Bloomington.

Heider, F. (1958). *The psychology of interpersonal relations.* New York: John Wiley & Sons, Inc.

Helgeson, S. (1990). *The female advantage: Women's ways of leadership.* New York: Doubleday.

Hersey, P., and Blanchard, K.H. (1972). *Management of organizational behavior.* Englewood Cliffs, NJ: Prentice-Hall.

Herschel, R., and Andrews, P. (Spring 1993). Empowering employees in group work: A case for using group support systems. *Information Strategy: The Executive's Journal, 9,* 36–42.

Hickson, D.J., Hinings, C.R., Lee, C.A., Schneck, R.E., and Pennings, J.M. (1971). Strategic contingencies theory of intraorganizational power. *Administrative Science Quarterly, 16,* 216–229.

Hinings, C.R., Hickson, D.J., Pennings, J.M., and Schneck, R.E. (1974). Structural conditions of intraorganizational power. *Administrative Science Quarterly, 21,* 22–44.

Hollander, E.P. (1958). Conformity, status, and idiosyncrasy credit. *Psychological Review, 65,* 117–127.

Hollander, E.P., and Julian, J.W. (1970). Studies in leader legitimacy, influence, and innovation. In L. Berkowitz (ed.), *Advances in experimental social psychology,* vol. 5, pp. 65–74. New York: Academic Press.

Huber, G.P. (1990). A theory of the effects of advanced information technologies on organizational design, intelligence, and decision making. *Academy of Management Review, 15,* 47–71.

Johansen, R. (Winter 1993). Teams for tomorrow. *GroupSystems V News, 3,* 2–3.

Jones, E.E., and Davis, K.E. (1965). From acts to dispositions. In L. Berkowitz (ed.), *Advances in experimental social psychology,* vol. 2, pp. 78–88. New York: Academic Press.

Kanter, R.M. (1979). Power failure in management circuits. *Harvard Business Review, 57,* 65–75.

Kanter, R.M. (1983). *The changemasters: Innovation for productivity in the American corporation.* New York: Simon & Schuster.

Kelley, H.H. (1973). The process of causal attribution. *American Psychologist, 28,* 107–128.

Kiely, T. (1993). Group Wary. *CIO,* 56–61.

Kilborn, P.T. (1993, May 17). Inside post offices, the mail is only part of the pressure. *The New York Times,* pp. A1 and A7.

Kouzes, J.M., and Posner, B.Z. (1993). *Credibility: How leaders gain and lose it, why people demand it.* San Francisco: Jossey-Bass.

Laudon, K.C., and Laudon, J.P. (1993). *Business information systems: A problem-solving approach,* 2nd ed. Fort Worth, TX: Dryden Press.

Lawrence, P.R., and Lorsch, J.W. (1967). *Organization and environment.* Boston: Harvard Business School, Division of Research.

Lord, R.G., Binning, J.F., Rush, M.C., and Thomas, J.C. (1978). The effect of performance cues and leader behavior in questionnaire rating of leadership behavior. *Organizational Behavior and Human Performance, 21,* 27–39.

Luke, S. (1974). *Power: A radical view.* London: Macmillan.

McClelland, D.C. (1975). *Power: The inner experience.* New York: Irvington Press.

McClelland, D.C., and Burnham, D.H. (1979). Power is the great motivator. In R.C. Huseman and A.B. Carroll (eds.), *Readings in organizational behavior: Dimensions of management actions,* pp. 275–286. Boston: Allyn & Bacon.

Mintzberg, H. (1990). The manager's job: Folklore and fact. *Harvard Business Review, 68,* 163–177. This article originally appeared in the *Harvard Business Review* in 1975.

Mitchell, T.R., and Kalb, L.S. (1981). Effects of outcome knowledge and outcome valence in supervisors' evaluations. *Journal of Applied Psychology, 66,* 604–612.

Mitchell, T.R., and Wood, R.E. (1980). Supervisors' responses to subordinate poor performance: A test of an attributional model. *Organizational Behavior and Human Performance, 25,* 123–138.

Noller, D. (1991). *Beyond a buzzword: An empowered perspective.* Unpublished manuscript.

Pace, R.W. (1983). *Organizational communication: Foundations for human resource development.* Englewood Cliffs, NJ: Prentice-Hall.

Pacanowsky, M. (1987). Communication in the empowering organization. In J. Anderson (ed.), *Communication yearbook 11,* pp. 356–379. Beverly Hills, CA: Sage Publications.

Peters, T. (1993, May 12). Even the most mundane work can become a source of pride. *The Bloomington Herald-Times,* p. B6.

Rappaport, J. (1984). Studies in empowerment: Introduction to the issue. *Prevention in Human Services, 3,* 1–7.

Rodgers, F.S., and Rodgers C. (1989). Business and the facts of family life. *Harvard Business Review, 67,* 121–129.

Rotter, J. (1966). Generalized experiment for internal versus external control of reinforcement. *Psychology Monograph 80.*

Russell, H.C. (1970). *An investigation of leadership maintenance behavior.* Unpublished doctoral dissertation, Indiana University, Bloomington.

Salancik, G.R., and Pfeffer, J. (1977). Who gets power— and how they hold on to it. A strategic-contingency model of power. *Organizational Dynamics, 5,* 3–21.

Schlesinger, A.M., Jr. (1965). *A thousand days: John F. Kennedy in the White House.* Boston: Houghton Mifflin.

Schrage, M. (1990). *Shared minds: The new technologies of collaboration.* New York: Random House.

Schultz, S.L., and Shulman G.M. (1993). *The development and assessment of the job empowerment instrument (JEI).* Unpublished manuscript, Miami University, Oxford, OH.

Secord, P.F., and Backman, C.W. (1964). *Social psychology.* New York: McGraw-Hill.

Shaw, M. (1955). A comparison of two types of leadership in various communication nets. *Journal of Abnormal and Social Psychology, 50,* 127–134.

Shulman, G.M., Douglas, J., and Schultz, S.L. (1993). *The job empowerment instrument (JEI): A replication.* Unpublished manuscript, Miami University, Oxford, OH.

Sproull, L., and Kiesler, S. (1991, September). Computers, networks, and work. *Scientific American, 265,* 116–132.

Starhawk. (1987). *Truth or dare: Encounters with power, authority, and mystery.* San Francisco: Harper & Row.

Starhawk. (1988). *Dreaming the dark: Magic, sex, and politics,* new edition. Boston: Beacon Press.

Stogdill, R. (1974). *Handbook of leadership.* New York: The Free Press.

Strube, M.J., and Garcia, J.E. (1981). A meta-analytical investigation of Fiedler's contingency model of leadership effectiveness. *Psychological Bulletin, 90,* 307–321.

Thomas, K., and Velthouse, B. (1990). Cognitive elements of empowerment: An "interpretive" model of intrinsic task motivation. *Academy of Management Review, 19,* 666–681.

Vroom, V.H., and Yetton, P.W. (1973). *Leadership and Decision-Making.* Pittsburgh: University of Pittsburgh Press.

Whetton, D.A., and Cameron, K.S. (1991). *Developing management skills,* 2nd ed. New York: HarperCollins.

White, R., and Lippitt, R. (1960). *Autocracy and democracy.* New York: Harper & Row.

Chapter 7

Alderton, S.M., and Frey, L. (1983). Effects of reactions to arguments on group outcomes. *Central States Speech Journal, 34,* 88–95.

Andrews, P.H. (1985). Ego-involvement, self-monitoring, and conformity in small groups: A communicative analysis. *Central States Speech Journal, 36,* 51–61.

Asch, S.E. (1956). Studies of independence and conformity: A minority of one against a unanimous majority. *Psychological Monographs, 70,* no. 416.

Baird, J.E., Jr. (1974). A comparison of distributional and sequential structure in cooperative and competitive group discussions. *Speech Monographs, 41,* 226–232.

Baird, J.E., Jr. (1977). *The dynamics of organizational communication.* New York: Harper & Row.

Bales, R.F. (1950). *Interaction process analysis: A method for the study of small groups.* Cambridge, MA: Addison-Wesley.

Bales, R.F., and Strodtbeck, F.L. (1951). Phases in group problem-solving. *Journal of Abnormal and Social Psychology, 46,* 485–495.

Benne, K.D., and Sheats, P. (1948). Functional roles of group members. *The Journal of Social Issues, 4,* 41–49.

Berkowitz, L. (1956). Group norms among bomber crews. *Sociometry, 19,* 141–153.

Bradley, P.H., Hamon, C.M., and Harris, A.M. (1976). Dissent in small groups. *Journal of Communication, 26,* 155–159.

Browning, L. (1988). Interpreting the Challenger disaster: Communication under conditions of risk and liability. *Industrial Crisis Quarterly, 2,* 211–227.

Bunyi, J.M., and Andrews, P.H. (1985). Gender and leadership emergence: An experimental study. *Southern Speech Communication Journal, 50,* 246–260.

Cheney, G. (1983). On the various and changing meanings of organizational membership: A field study of organizational identification. *Communication Monographs, 50,* 342–362.

Cline, R.J.W. (1990). Detecting groupthink: Methods for observing the illusion of unanimity. *Communication Quarterly, 38,* 112–126.

Cline, T., and Cline, R. (1979). Risky and cautious decision shifts in small groups. *Southern Speech Communication Journal, 44,* 252–263.

Cohen, M.D., March, J.G., and Olson, J.P. (1972). A garbage can model of organizational choice. *Administrative Science Quarterly, 17,* 1–25.

Conrad, C. (1990). *Strategic organizational communication: An integrated perspective,* 2nd ed. Orlando, FL: Harcourt Brace Jovanovich.

Dewey, J. (1910). *How we think.* Boston, MA: D.C. Heath.

Drucker, P.F. (1968). *Effective decisions.* Effective Executive Series.

Dumaine, B. (1994, September 5). The trouble with teams. *Fortune,* 65–70.

Dunnette, M.D., Campbell, J., and Jaastad, K. (1963). The effect of group participation on brainstorming effectiveness for two industrial samples. *Journal of Applied Psychology, 47,* 30–37.

Fisher, B.A. (1970). Decision emergence: Phases in group decision-making. *Speech Monographs, 37,* 53–66.

Fisher, B.A. (1979). Content and relationship dimensions of communication in decision-making groups. *Communication Quarterly, 27,* 3–11.

Gallupe, B., DeSanctis, G., and Dickson, G. (1988). The impact of computer-based support on the process and outcomes of group decision making. *MIS Quarterly, 12,* 277–298.

Gersick, C. (1988). Time and transition in work teams: Toward a new model of group development. *Academy of Management Journal, 31,* 9–41.

Gersick, C. (1991). Revolutionary change theories: A multiple-level explanation of the punctuated equilibrium paradigm. *Academy of Management Review, 16,* 10–36.

Gilchrist, J.M., Shaw, M., and Walker, L. (1954). Some effects of unequal distribution of information in a wheel group structure. *Journal of Abnormal and Social Psychology, 49,* 554–556.

Gouran, D.S. (1982). *Making decisions in groups: Choices and consequences.* Prospect Heights, IL: Waveland.

Gouran, D.S. (1988). Principles of counteractive influence in decision-making and problem-solving groups. In R.S. Cathcart and L.A. Samovar (eds.), *Small group communication: A reader,* 5th ed., pp. 192–208. Dubuque, IA: Wm. C. Brown Publishers.

Gouran, D.S., and Andrews, P.H. (1984). Determinants of punitive responses to socially proscribed behavior: Seriousness, attribution of responsibility, and status of offender. *Small Group Behavior, 15,* 524–544.

Gouran, D.S., and Hirokawa, R.Y. (1986). Counteractive functions of communication in effective group decision-making. In R.Y. Hirokawa and M.S. Poole (eds.), *Communication and group decision-making,* pp. 81–90. Beverly Hills, CA: Sage Publications.

Gouran, D.S., Hirokawa, R.Y., and Martz, A.E. (1986). A critical analysis of factors related to decisional processes involved in the Challenger disaster. *Central States Speech Journal, 37,* 119–135.

Hackman, J.R., and Kaplan, R.E. (1974). Interventions into group process: An approach to improving the effectiveness of groups. *Decision Sciences, 5,* 459–480.

Hiltz, S.R., Johnson, K., and Turoff, M. (1991). Group decision support: The effects of designated human leaders and statistical feedback in computerized conferences. *Journal of Management Information Systems, 8,* 81–108.

Hirokawa, R.Y. (1983). Group communication and problem-solving effectiveness: An investigation of group phases. *Human Communication Research, 9,* 291–305.

Hirokawa, R.Y., Ice, R., and Cook, J. (1988). Preference for procedural order, discussion structure and group decision performance. *Communication Quarterly, 36,* 217–226.

Hirokawa, R.Y., and Pace, R. (1983). A descriptive investigation of the possible communication-based reasons for effective and ineffective group decision making. *Communication Monographs, 50,* 363–379.

Hirokawa, R.Y., and Rost, K. (1992). Effective group decision making in organizations. *Management Communication Quarterly, 5,* 267–288.

Hirokawa, R.Y., and Scheerhorn, D.R. (1986). Communication in faulty group decision-making. In R.Y. Hirokawa and M.S. Poole (eds.), *Communication and group decision-making,* pp. 63–80. Beverly Hills, CA: Sage Publications.

Hollander, R.P. (1958). Conformity, status, and idiosyncrasy credit. *Psychological Review, 65,* 117–127.

Homans, G.C. (1974). *Social behavior: Its elementary forms,* 2nd ed. New York: Harcourt Brace Jovanovich.

Huseman, R.C., and Driver, R.W. (1979). Groupthink: Implications for small group decision making in business. In R.C. Huseman and A.B. Carroll (eds.), *Readings in organizational behavior: Dimensions of management actions,* pp. 100–110. Boston: Allyn & Bacon.

Jablin, F.M. (1980). *Groups within organizations: Current issues and directions for future research.* Unpublished manuscript, University of Texas at Austin.

Jablin, F.M. (1981). Cultivating imagination: Factors that enhance and inhibit creativity in brainstorming groups. *Human Communication Research, 7,* 245–258.

Janis, I.L. (1982). *Groupthink,* 2nd ed. Boston, MA: Houghton Mifflin.

Janis, I.L. (1985). Sources of error in strategic decision-making. In Johannes Pennings and associates (eds.), *Organizational strategy and change,* pp. 63–75. San Francisco, CA: Jossey-Bass.

Janis, I.L., and Mann, L. (1977). *Decision making: A psychological analysis of conflict, choice, and commitment.* New York: The Free Press.

Katzenbach, J.R., and Smith, D.K. (1993, March–April). The discipline of teams. *Harvard Business Review,* 111–120.

Kleinschrod, W.A. (1991, December). Video and audio conferencing: A better kind of meeting? *Office Technology Management, 26,* 54–58.

Kupfer, A. (1992, December 28). Prime time for video-conferences. *Fortune,* 90–94.

Laudon, K.C., and Laudon, J.P. (1993). *Business information systems: A problem-solving approach,* 2nd ed. Fort Worth, TX: Dryden Press.

Leavitt, H. (1951). Some effects of certain communication patterns on group performance. *Journal of Abnormal and Social Psychology, 46,* 38–50.

Lumsden, G., and Lumsden, D. (1993). *Communicating in groups and teams: Sharing leadership.* Belmont, CA: Wadsworth Publishing Company.

McConnell, M. (1987). *Challenger: A major malfunction.* Garden City, NY: Doubleday.

McGrath, J.E. (1984). *Groups: Interaction and performance.* Englewood Cliffs, NJ: Prentice-Hall.

McGrath, J.E., and Hollingshead, A.B. (1993). Putting the "group" in group support systems: Some theoretical issues about dynamic processes. In L.M. Jessup and J.S. Valacich (eds.), *Group support systems: New perspectives,* pp. 78–96. New York: Macmillan.

Miller, M.W. (1992, September 9). A story of the type that turns heads in computer circles. *The Wall Street Journal.*

Moscovici, S. (1985). Social influence and conformity. In G. Lindzey and E. Aronson (eds.), *Handbook of social psychology,* Vol. 2, pp. 347–412. New York: Random House.

Moscovici, S., and Faucheux, C. (1972). Social influence, conformity bias, and the study of active minorities. In L. Berkowitz (ed.), *Advances in social psychology,* Vol. 6, pp. 150–202. New York: Academic Press.

Moscovici, S., Lage, E., and Naffrechoux, M. (1969). Insistence of a consistent minority on the responses of a majority in a color perception task. *Sociometry, 32,* 365–380.

Moscovici, S., and Nemeth, C. (1974). Social influence II: Minority influence. In C. Nemeth (ed.), *Social psychology: Classic and contemporary integrations,* pp. 217–249. Chicago: Rand McNally.

Mosley, D.C., and Green, T.B. (1974). Nominal grouping as an organization development intervention technique. *Training and Development Journal,* 30–37.

Narisetti, R. (1992, November 29). "Bottom-up approach pushes plant's performance to the top," *Chicago Tribune,* Sec. 7, p. 13.

Nutt, P.C. (1984). Types of organizational decision processes. *Administrative Science Quarterly, 29,* 414–450.

Poole, M.S. (1981). Decision development in small groups I: A comparison of two models. *Communication Monographs, 48,* 1–24.

Poole, M.S. (1983). Decision development in small groups II: A study of multiple sequences in decision making. *Communication Monographs, 50,* 206–232.

Poole, M.S., and DeSanctis, G. (1990). Understanding the use of group decision support systems: The theory of adaptive structuration. In J. Fulk and C. Steinfeld (eds.), *Organizations and communication technology,* pp. 173–193. Beverly Hills, CA: Sage Publications.

Poole, M.S., and Roth, J. (1988a). Decision development in small groups IV: A typology of group decision paths. *Human Communication Research, 15,* 323–356.

Poole, M.S., and Roth, J. (1988b). Decision development in small groups V: Test of a contingency model. *Human Communication Research, 15,* 549–589.

Poole, M.S., Siebold, D.R., and McPhee, R.D. (1985). Group decision making as a structurational process. *Quarterly Journal of Speech, 71,* 74–102.

Powell, D. (1989, December). Videoconferencing: A wise strategy. *Networking Management, 7,* 28–38.

Putnam, L.L. (1979). Preference for procedural order in task-oriented small groups. *Communication Monographs, 46,* 193–218.

Rogers, E., and Agarwala-Rogers, R. (1976). *Communication in organizations.* New York: The Free Press.

Roethlisberger, F.J., and Dickson, W.J. (1939). *Management and the worker.* Cambridge, MA: Harvard University Press.

Schachter, S. (1951). Deviation, rejection, and communication. *Journal of Abnormal and Social Psychology, 46,* 190–207.

Schiedel, T.M., and Crowell, L. (1964). Idea development in small groups. *Quarterly Journal of Speech, 50,* 140–145.

Schein, E. (1969). *Process consultation.* Reading, MA: Addison-Wesley.

Shaw, M. (1954). Some effects of problem complexity upon problem solution efficiency in different communication networks. *Journal of Experimental Psychology, 48,* 211–271.

Shepherd, C.R. (1964). *Small groups.* Scranton, PA: Chandler.

Sherif, C.W., Sherif, M., and Nebergall, R.E. (1965). *Attitude and attitude change: The social judgment-involvement approach.* Philadelphia, PA: Saunders.

Siebold, D., and Meyers, R. (1986). Communication and influence in group decision-making. In R.Y. Hirokawa and M.S. Poole (eds.), *Communication and group decision-making,* pp. 96–115. Beverly Hills, CA: Sage Publications.

Sproull, L., and Kiesler, S. (1991, September). Computers, networks, and work. *Scientific American, 265,* 116–123.

Tannenbaum, R., and Schmidt, W. (1958). How to choose a leadership pattern. *Harvard Business Review, 36,* 95–101.

Taylor, K.P. (1969). *An investigation of majority verbal behavior toward opinions of deviant group members in group discussions of policy.* Unpublished doctoral dissertation, Indiana University, Bloomington.

Thameling, C.L., and Andrews, P.H. (1992). Majority responses to opinion deviates: A communicative analysis. *Small Group Research, 23,* 475–502.

Thuston, F. (1992, January). Video teleconferencing: The state of the art. *Telecommunications* (North American edition), *26,* 63–65.

Tjosvold, D. (1985). Power and social context in superior-subordinate interaction. *Organizational Behavior and Human Decision Processes, 35,* 281–293.

Tompkins, P.K. (1993). *Organizational communication imperatives: Lessons of the space program.* Los Angeles, CA: Roxbury Publishing Co.

Torrance, E.P. (1954). Some consequences of power differences on decision making in permanent three-man groups. *Research Studies, Washington State College, 22,* 130–140.

Trento, J. (1987). *Prescription for disaster: From the glory of Apollo to the betrayal of the shuttle.* New York: Crown Publishers.

Tuckman, B.W., and Jensen, M.A.C. (1977). Stages of small-group development. *Group and Organizational Studies, 2,* 419–427.

Wahrman, R. (1972). Status, deviance, and sanctions: A critical review. *Comparative Group Studies, 3,* 203–224.

Ward, J.R. (1990, March). Meetings by telephone. *Communications World, 7,* 14–15.

Wellins, R., Byham, W., and Wilson, J. (1991). *Empowered teams.* San Francisco: Jossey-Bass.

Wenburg, J.R., and Wilmot, W. (1973). *The personal communication process.* New York: John Wiley & Sons, Inc.

Wheeler, B.C., Mennecke, R., and Scudder, J.N. (1993). Restrictive group support systems as a source of process structure for high and low procedural order groups. Unpublished manuscript, Indiana University, Bloomington.

Whetten, D.A., and Cameron, K.S. (1991). *Developing management skills,* 2nd ed. New York: HarperCollins Publishers.

Wreden, N. (1993, March/April). Regrouping for groupware. *Beyond Computing, 2,* pp. 52–55.

Wright, J.P. (1979). *On a clear day you can see General Motors.* New York: Avon Books.

Chapter 8

Argyris, C. (1970). *Intervention theory and method.* Reading, MA: Addison-Wesley.

Baumohl, B. (1993, March 15). When downsizing becomes "dumbsizing." *Time,* 55.

Blake, R.R., and Mouton, J.S. (1961). Reactions to intergroup competition under win-lose conditions. *Management Science, 26,* 17–28.

Blake, R.R., and Mouton, J.S. (1964). *The managerial grid.* Houston: Gulf Publishing.

Blake, R.R., Shepard, H., and Mouton, J.S. (1964). *Managing intergroup conflict in industry.* Houston: Gulf Publishing.

Boulding, E. (1964). Further reflections on conflict management. In R.L. Kahn and E. Boulding (eds.), *Power and conflict in organizations,* pp. 47–64. New York: Basic Books.

Burke, R.J. (1970). Methods of resolving superior-subordinate conflict: The constructive use of subordinate differences and disagreements. *Organizational Behavior and Human Performance, 5,* 393–411.

Carnevale, P.J.D., and Pegnetter, R. (1985). The selection of mediation tactics in public sector disputes: A contingency analysis. *Journal of Social Issues, 41,* 65–81.

Chatov, R. (1981). Cooperation between government and business. In W. Starbuck and S. Nystrom (eds.), *Handbook of organization design,* vol. 1, pp. 409–437. Oxford: Oxford University Press.

Conrad, C. (1983). Power and performance as correlates of supervisors' choice of modes of managing conflict: A preliminary investigation. *Western Journal of Speech Communication, 47,* 218–228.

Cosier, R.A., and Ruble, T.L. (1981). Research on conflict-handling behavior: An experimental approach. *Academy of Management Journal, 24,* 816–831.

Dalton, M. (1959). Conflicts between staff and line managerial officers. *American Sociological Review, 15,* 342–351.

Derr, C. (1978). Managing organizational conflict: Collaboration, bargaining and power approaches. *California Management Review, 21* (2), 76–83.

Deschamps, J.C., and Brown, R. (1983). Superordinate goals and intergroup conflict. *British Journal of Social Psychology, 22,* 189–195.

Donohue, W., Diez, M., and Hamilton, M. (1984). Coding naturalistic negotiation interaction. *Human Communication Research, 10,* 403–445.

Evan, W.M. (1965). Superior-subordinate conflict in research organizations. *Administrative Science Quarterly, 10,* 52–64.

Fairhurst, G.L., Green, S., and Snavely, B.K. (1984). Managerial control and discipline. In B. Bostrom (ed.),

Communication yearbook 8. Beverly Hills, CA: Sage Publications.

Filley, A. (1975). *Interpersonal conflict resolution.* Glenview, IL: Scott, Foresman.

Fisher, R., and Ury, W. (1981). *Getting to yes.* Hammondworth: Penguin.

Folger, J.P., Hewes, D.E., and Poole, M.S. (1984). Coding social interaction. In B. Dervin and M. Voight (eds.), *Progress in the communications sciences, 4,* pp. 114–161. Northwood: Ablex.

Folger, J.P., and Poole, M.S. (1984). *Working through conflict.* Glenview, IL: Scott, Foresman.

Galen, M. (1994, January–February). White, male, and worried. *Business Week,* 50–55.

Goldhaber, G.M. (1993). *Organizational communication,* 6th ed. Dubuque, IA: Brown and Benchmark.

Gray, B. (1985). Conditions facilitating interorganizational collaboration. *Human Relations, 10,* 911–936.

Hilltrop, J.M. (1985). Mediator behavior and the settlement of collective bargaining disputes in Britain. *Journal of Social Issues, 41,* 83–99.

Hirokawa, R.Y., and Scheerhorn, D.R. (1986). Communication in faulty group decision-making. In R.Y. Hirokawa and M.S. Poole (eds.), *Communication and group decision-making,* pp. 63–80. Beverly Hills, CA: Sage Publications.

Howat, G., and London, M. (1980). Attributions of conflict management strategies in supervisor-subordinate dyads. *Journal of Applied Psychology, 65,* 172–175.

Hunger, R., and Stern, L.W. (1976). Assessment of the functionality of superordinate goals in reducing conflict. *Academy of Management Journal, 16,* 591–605.

Janis, I. (1982). *Victims of groupthink,* 2nd ed. Boston: Houghton Mifflin.

Jelassi, M.T., and Foroughi, A. (1989). Negotiation support systems: An overview of design issues and existing software. *Decision Support Systems, 5,* 167–181.

Kolb, D.M. (1983). *The mediators.* Cambridge: MIT Press.

Kolb, D.M. (1985). To be a mediator: Expressive tactics in mediation. *Journal of Social Issues, 41,* 11–26.

Kreps, G.L., and Thornton, B.C. (1984). *Health communication: Theory and practice.* White Plains, NY: Longman.

Kriegsberg, L. (1973). *The sociology of social conflicts.* Englewood Cliffs, NJ: Prentice-Hall.

Lawrence, P.R., and Lorsch, J.W. (1967). *Organization and environment.* Boston: Harvard University Press.

Likert, R. (1961). *New patterns of management.* New York: McGraw-Hill.

Lippitt, G. (1982, July). Managing conflict in today's organizations. *Training and Development Journal,* 67–74.

London, M., and Howat, G. (1978). The relationships between employee commitment and conflict resolution behavior. *Journal of Vocational Behavior, 13,* 1–14.

Lumsden, G., and Lumsden, D. (1993). *Communicating in groups and teams: Sharing leadership.* Belmont, CA: Wadsworth.

Maslow, A. (1965). *Eupsychian management.* Homewood, IL: Irwin.

Mayer, R.J. (1990). *Conflict management: The courage to confront.* Columbus, OH: Batelle Press.

McGrath, J.E. (1984). *Groups: Interaction and performance.* Englewood Cliffs, NJ: Prentice-Hall.

McGrath, J.E., and Hollingshead, A.B. (1993). Putting the "group" in group support systems: Some theoretical issues about dynamic processes. In L.M. Jessup and J.S. Valacich (eds.), *Group support systems: New perspectives,* pp. 78–96. New York: Macmillan.

Morley, D.M., and Shockley-Zalabak, P. (1986). Conflict avoiders and compromisers: Toward an understanding of their organizational communication style. *Group and Organizational Behavior, 11* (4), 387–402.

Northcraft, G., and Neale, M. (1990). *Organizational behavior.* Chicago: Dryden Press.

Nunamaker, J., Dennis, A., Valacich, J., and Vogel, D. (1991). Technology for negotiating groups: Generating options for mutual gain. *Management Science, 37* (10), 1325–1346.

Olson, D.L., and Courtney, J.F. (1992). Decision support models and expert systems. New York: Macmillan.

Patton, B.R., and Giffin, K. (1988). Conflict and its resolution. In R.S. Cathcart and L.A. Samovar (eds.), *Small group communication: A reader,* 5th ed., pp. 429–441. Dubuque, IA: Wm. C. Brown.

Phillips, E., and Cheston, R. (1979). Conflict resolution: What works? *California Management Review, 21,* 76–83.

Pondy, L. (1967). Organizational conflict: Concepts and models. *Administrative Science Quarterly, 12,* 296–320.

Poole, M.S., Holmes, M., and Desanctis, G. (1991). Conflict management in a computer-supported meeting environment. *Management Science, 8,* 926–953.

Putnam, L.L., and Jones, T. (1982). Reciprocity in negotiations. *Communication Monographs, 49,* 171–191.

Putnam, L.L., and Poole, M.S. (1987). Conflict and negotiation. In F.M. Jablin, L.L. Putnam, K.H. Roberts, and L.W. Porter (eds.), *Handbook of organizational communication: An interdisciplinary perspective,* pp. 549–599. Newbury Park, CA: Sage Publications.

Putnam, L.L., and Wilson, C.E. (1982). Communicative strategies in organizational conflicts: Reliability and validity of a measurement scale. In M. Burgoon (ed.), *Communication yearbook 6,* pp. 629–652. Newbury Park, CA: Sage Publications.

Radlow, J. (1995). *Computers and the information society.* Danvers, Mass: Boyd and Fraser.

Rahim, A. (1983). A measure of styles of handling interpersonal conflict. *Journal of Social Psychology, 126,* 79–86.

Rahim, A., and Bonoma, T.V. (1979). Managing organizational conflict: A model for diagnosis and intervention. *Psychological Reports, 44,* 1323–1344.

Renwick, P.A. (1975). Perception and management of superior-subordinate conflict. *Organizational Behavior and Human Performance, 13,* 444–456.

Riggs, C.J. (1983). Dimensions of organizational conflict: A functional analysis of communication tactics. *Communication yearbook 7,* pp. 517–531, Newbury Park: Sage Publications.

Robbins, S.P. (1978). "Conflict management" and "conflict resolution" are not synonymous terms. *California Management Review, 21* (2), 67–75.

Ross, R., and DeWine, S. (1982). *Interpersonal conflict: Measurement and validation.* Paper presented at the annual meeting of the Speech Communication Association, Washington, D.C.

Ruble, T.L., and Cosier, R.A. (1982). A laboratory study of five conflict-handling modes. In G.B.J. Bomers and R.B. Peterson (eds.), *Organizational behavior,* pp. 456–485. St. Paul, MN: West.

Sambamurthy, V., and Poole, M.S. (1992). The effects of variations in capabilities of GDSS designs on management conflict in groups. *Information Systems Research, 3,* 224–251.

Savage, J.A. (1990, July 23). Unions cutting bargain with high-technology "Devil", *Computerworld, 24* 1,115.

Tegar, A. (1980). *Too much invested to quit.* New York: Pergamon.

Thomas, K.W. (1976). Conflict and conflict management. In M. Dunnette (ed.), *Handbook of industrial and organizational psychology,* pp. 889–936. Chicago: Rand McNally.

Thomas, K.W., and Pondy, L.R. (1977). Toward an "intent" model of conflict management among principal parties. *Human Relations, 30,* 1089–1102.

Thomas, K.W., and Schmidt, W.H. (1976). A survey of managerial interests with respect to conflict. *Academy of Management Journal, 19,* 315–318.

Thomas, K.W., and Walton, R.E. (1971). *Conflict-handling behavior in interdepartmental relations* (Research Paper No. 38, Division of Research, Graduate School of Business Administration, UCLA). Los Angeles, CA: University of California.

Thompson, L. (1992). A method for examining learning in negotiation. *Group Decision and Negotiation, 1,* 71–85.

Tompkins, P.K., Fisher, J.Y., Infante, D.A., and Tompkins, E.L. (1974). Conflict and communication within the university. In G.R. Miller and H.W. Simons (eds.), *Perspectives on communication in social conflict,* pp. 153–171. Englewood Cliffs, NJ: Prentice-Hall.

Van de Ven, A.H., Emmett, D., and Koenig, R. (1980). Frameworks for interorganizational analysis. In A.R. Negandhi (ed.), *Interorganizational theory,* pp. 19–28. Kent, OH: Kent State University Press.

Wall, J.A. (1981). Mediation: An analysis, review, and proposed research. *Journal of Conflict Resolution, 25,* 157–181.

Walton, R.E. (1969). *Interpersonal peacemaking: Confrontations and third party consultations,* Reading, MA: Addison-Wesley.

Walton, R.E., and Dutton, J.M. (1969). The management of interdepartmental conflict: A model and review. *Administrative Science Quarterly, 14,* 73–84.

Walton, R.E., Dutton, J.M., and Cafferty, T.P. (1969). Organizational context and interdepartmental conflict. *Administrative Science Quarterly, 14,* 522–542.

Walton, R.E., Dutton, J.M., and Fitch, H.G. (1966). A study of conflict in the process, structure, and attitudes of lateral relationships. In A.H. Rubenstein, S. Haberstroh, and J. Chadwick (eds.), *Some theories of organization,* pp. 444–465. Homewood, IL: Irwin.

Wheeless, L., and Reichel, L. (1990). A reinforcement model of the relationship of supervisors' general communication styles to task attraction. *Communication Quarterly, 34* (4), 372–387.

Whetten, D.A., and Cameron, K.S. (1991). *Developing management skills,* 2nd ed. New York: HarperCollins.

Whyte, W.F. (1955). *Money and motivation.* New York: Harper & Brothers.

Zald, M. (1962). Organizational and control structures in five correctional institutions. *American Journal of Sociology, 68,* 335–345.

Zald, M. (1981). Political economy: A framework for comparative analysis. In M. Zey-Ferrell and M. Aiken (eds.), *Complex organizations: Critical perspectives,* pp. 237–262. Glenview, IL: Scott Foresman.

Chapter 9

Age discrimination actions flooding courts, new BNA special report finds. (1989). *Labor Relations Week, 3,* 1109.

Anderson, L.R., and Blanchard, P.N. (1982). Sex differences in task and social-emotional behavior. *Basic and Applied Social Psychology, 3,* 109–139.

Andrews, P.H. (1992). Sex and gender differences in group communication: Impact on the facilitation process. *Small Group Behavior, 23, 1,* 74–94.

Anyon, J. (1980). Social class and the hidden curriculum of work. *Journal of Education, 162, 1,* 67–92.

Barriers to excellence: Our children at risk. (1985). Boston: National Coalition of Advocates for Students.

Bartol, K.M., and Butterfield, D.A. (1976). Sex effects in evaluating leaders. *Journal of Applied Psychology, 61,* 446–454.

Bergeson, P.T. (1991). *The Americans with Disabilities Act (ADA): Practical considerations for employers.* Chicago: Pope, Ballard, Shepard & Fowle, Std.

Borisoff, D., and Merrill, L. (1992). *The power to communicate: Gender differences as barriers,* 2nd ed. Prospect Heights, IL: Waveland.

Bowman, G.W., Worthy, N.B., and Greyser, S.A. (1965, July-August). Are women executives people? *Harvard Business Review, 43,* 15–28.

Bradac, J.J., and Mulac, A. (1984). A molecular view of powerful and powerless speech: Attributional consequences of specific language features and communicator intentions. *Communication Monographs, 51,* 307–319.

Bradley, P.H. (1981). The folk-linguistics of women's speech: An empirical examination. *Communication Monographs, 48,* 73–90.

Britzman, D.P. (1986). Cultural myths in the making of a teacher: Biography and social structure in teacher education. *Harvard Educational Review, 56, 4,* 442–456.

Burden, D., and Googins, B. (1986). *Boston University balancing job and homelife study.* Boston University School of Social Work.

Campbell, D. (1986, December). Sexual harassment in education. *Notes on teaching and learning.* Teaching Resources Center, College of Arts and Sciences, Indiana University, Bloomington, Indiana.

Cann, A., and Siegfried, W.D. (1987). Sex stereotypes and the leadership role. *Sex Roles, 17,* 401–408.

Caudron, S. (1993, April). Training can damage diversity efforts. *Personnel Journal, 72,* 148–153.

Chidambaram, L. (1992). The electronic meeting room with an international view. In R.P. Bostrom, R.T. Watson, and S.T. Kinney (eds.), *Computer augmented teamwork,* pp. 285–294. New York: Van Nostrand Reinhold.

Correa, M.E., Klein, E.D., Stone, W.N., Astrachan, J.H., Kossek, E.E., and Komarraju, M. (1988). Reactions to women in authority: The impact of gender on learning in group relations conferences. *Journal of Applied Behavioral Science, 24,* 219–233.

Cox, T., and Blake, S. (1991). Managing cultural diversity: Implications for organizational competitiveness, *Academy of Management Executive, 5, 3,* 45–56.

Deutschman, A. (1991, November 4). Dealing with sexual harassment. *Fortune,* 145–148.

Dolecheck, C.C., and Dolecheck, M.M. (1983). Sexual harassment: A problem for small businesses. *American Journal of Small Business, 7,* 45–50.

Dropout rate for air force women soaring. (1994, May 22). *Bloomington Sunday Herald-Times,* p. A9.

Eakins, B.W., and Eakins, R.G. (1978). *Sex differences in human communication.* Boston: Houghton Mifflin Co.

Federal Register. (1980, November), vol. *45,* no. 219.

Fierman, J. (1990, July 30). Why women still don't hit the top. *Fortune,* 40–62.

Fitzgerald, T.K. (1993). *Homophobia and the cultural construction of the social stranger.* Unpublished manuscript.

Franklin, S. (1991, November 11). Job fair's motto: The more gray hair, all the more able. *Chicago Tribune,* section 3, 6.

Freire, P. (1970). *Pedagogy of the oppressed.* New York: Seabury Press.

Future of gay America, (1990, March 12). *Newsweek,* 21–22.

Goktepe, J.R., and Schneier, C.E. (1988). Sex and gender effects in evaluating emergent leaders in small groups. *Sex Roles, 19,* 29–36.

Good for business: Making full use of the nation's human capital (1995). A fact-finding report of the Federal Glass Ceiling Commission, Washington, D.C.

Greenhouse, J., Parasuraman, S., and Wormley, W. (1990). Effects of race on organizational experiences, job performance evaluations, and career outcomes. *Academy of Management Journal, 33,* 64–86.

Hall, R.M., and Sandler, B.R. (1982). The classroom climate: A chilly one for women? Washington, D.C.: Project on the Status and Education of Women, Association of American Colleges.

Hammonds, K. (1991, November 4). Lotus opens a door for gay partners. *Business Week,* 80–81.

Hans, V.P., and Eisenberg, N. (1985). The effects of sex-role attitudes and group composition on men and women in groups. *Sex Roles, 12,* 477–490.

Hennig, M., and Jardim, A. (1977). *The managerial woman.* Garden City, NY: Anchor Press.

Herschel, R., Cooper, T., Smith, L., and Arrington, L. (1994). Exploring numerical proportions in a unique context: The group support systems meeting environment. *Sex Roles, 31* (1–2), 99–123.

Herschel, R., and Ehrhardt, R. (in progress). The importance of providing anonymity and simultaneity in discussions of diversity.

Instone, D., Major, B., and Bunker, B. (1983). Gender, self-confidence, and social strategies: An organizational simulation. *Journal of Personality and Social Psychology, 44,* 322–333.

Jackson, G., and Cosca, C. (1974). The inequality of educational opportunity in the Southwest: An observational study of ethnically mixed classrooms. *American Educational Research Journal, 11,* 219–229.

Jamieson, D., and O'Mara, J. (1991). *Managing workforce 2000.* San Francisco: Jossey-Bass.

Jessup, L., Connolly, T., and Tansik, D. (1990). Toward a theory of automated group work: The deindividuating effects of anonymity. *Small Group Research, 21,* 333–348.

Johnston, W. (1987). *Workforce 2000.* Indianapolis: Hudson Institute.

Jones, E.W., Jr. (1986, May–June). Black managers: The dream deferred. *Harvard Business Review,* 84–93.

Jurma, W.E., and Wright, B.C. (1990). Follower reactions to male and female leaders who maintain or lose reward power. *Small Group Research, 21,* 97–112.

Kanter, R.M. (1977). *Men and women of the corporation.* New York: Basic Books.

Kanter, R.M. (1988). When a thousand flowers bloom: Structural, collective, and social conditions for innovation in organizations. In L.L. Cummings, and B.M. Shaw (eds.), *Research in Organizational Behavior, 10,* pp. 169–211. Greenwich, CT: JAI Press.

Kantrowitz, B. (1994, May 16). Men, women and computers. *Newsweek,* 48–55.

Kennedy, J., and Everest, A. (1991, September). Put diversity in context. *Personnel Journal, 70,* 50–54.

Kirk, M., and Madsen. (1989). *After the ball: How America will conquer its fear and hatred of gays in the 90s.* New York: Doubleday.

Konrad, W. (1990, August 16). Welcome to the woman-friendly company. *Business Week,* 48–55.

Kramerae, C. (1981). *Women and men speaking*. Rowley, MA: Newbury House.

Kushell, E., and Newton, R. (1986). Gender, leadership style, and subordinate satisfaction: An experiment. *Sex Roles, 14,* 203–209.

Lakoff, R. (1975). *Language and women's place.* New York: Harper & Row.

Mamola, C.F. (1979). Women in mixed groups: Some research findings. *Small Group Behavior, 10,* 431–440.

Matute-Bianchi, M.E. (1986). Ethnic identities and patterns of school success and failure among Mexican-descent and Japanese-American students in a California high school: An ethnographic analysis. *American Journal of Education, 95, 1,* 223–255.

McDermott, R.P. (1977). Achieving school failure: An anthropological approach to illiteracy and social stratification. In G.D. Spindler (ed.), *Education and cultural process: Anthropological approaches,* 2nd ed., pp. 40–53. Prospect Heights, IL: Waveland Press.

McGrath, J.E., and Hollingshead, A.B. (1993). Putting the "group" in group support systems: Some theoretical issues about dynamic processes. In L.M. Jessup and J.S. Valacich (eds.), *Group support systems: New perspectives,* pp. 78–96. New York: Macmillan.

Megargee, E. (1969). Influence of sex roles on the manifestation of leadership. *Journal of Applied Psychology, 53,* 377–382.

Morrison, A.M., White, R.P., Van Velsor, E., and the Center for Creative Leadership. (1987). *Breaking the glass ceiling: Can women reach the top of America's largest corporations?* Reading, MA: Addison-Wesley.

Murray, K. (1993, September 13). Companies rethink one-shot diversity training as new problems are created. *Chicago Tribune,* sections 4, 6.

Nieto, S. (1992). *Affirming diversity: The sociopolitical context of multicultural education.* New York: Longman.

Nemeth, C., Endicott, J., and Wachtler, J. (1976). From the '50s to the '70s: Women in jury deliberations. *Sociometry, 39,* 293–304.

Northcraft, G., and Neale, M. (1994). *Organizational Behavior: A Management Challenge,* 2nd ed. Fort Worth, TX: The Dryden Press.

On-site child care results in low turnover at computer firm. (1989, June 9). *National report on work and family, 2, 13.* Washington, D.C.: Buraff Publications.

Ortiz, F.I. (1988). Hispanic American children's experiences in classrooms: A comparison between Hispanic and non-Hispanic children. In L. Weis (ed.), *Class, race, and gender in American education,* pp. 198–212. Albany: State University of New York Press.

Pearson, J.C., Turner, L.H., and Todd-Mancillas, W. (1991). *Gender and communication,* 2nd ed. Dubuque, IA: Wm. C. Brown.

Pennar, K. (1991, October 28). Commentary: Women are still paid the wages of discrimination. *Business Week,* 35.

Persell, C.H. (1977). *Education and inequality: The results of stratification in America's schools.* New York: The Free Press.

Peterson, D.J., and Massengill, D. (1982, October). Sexual harassment—a growing problem in the workplace. *Personnel Administrator,* 79.

Pfeffer, J. (1985). Organizational demography: Implications for management. *California Management Review, 28,* 67–81.

Powell, G.N. (1983). Sexual harassment: Confronting the issue of definition. *Business Horizons, 26,* 24–28.

Prewitt-Diaz, J.O. (1983). A study of self-esteem and school sentiment in two groups of Puerto Rican students. *Educational and Psychological Research, 3,* 161–167.

Price, W. (1993, August 6). Harassment goes online: Low-tech problem hits PC networks. *USA Today,* B1–B2.

Ramirez, M., and Castaneda, A. (1974). *Cultural democracy, bicognitive development and education.* New York: Academic Press.

Renick, J.C. (1980). Sexual harassment at work: Why it happens, what to do about it. *Personnel Journal, 57,* 63–70.

Rice, F. (1994, August 8). How to make diversity pay. *Fortune,* 78–86.

Rigdon, J. (1994, March 18). Now women in cyberspace can be themselves. *The Wall Street Journal,* B1 & B4.

Rodgers, F.S., and Rodgers, C. (1989, November–December). Business and the facts of family life. *Harvard Business Review,* 121–129.

Rosenthal, R., and Jacobson, L. (1968). *Pygmalion in the classroom.* New York: Holt, Rinehart & Winston.

Sadker, D., and Sadker, M. (1984, March). *Year 111: Final report, promoting effectiveness in classroom instruction.* Washington, DC: National Institute of Education.

Saltzman, A. (1991, June 17). Trouble at the top. *U.S. News & World Report, 110,* 40–48.

Schmidt, E. (1994, May 1). Air force academy zooms in on sex cases. *The New York Times,* pp. 1, 3.

Shaeffer, R.G. (1975). *Nondiscrimination in employment, 1973–1975: A broadening and deepening national effort.* New York: The Conference Board.

Shakeshaft, C. (1986, March). A gender at risk. *Phi Delta Kappan,* 499–503.

Sleeter, C.E., and Grant, C.A. (1991). Race, class, gender, and disability in current textbooks. In M.W. Apple and L.K. Christian-Smith (eds.), *The politics of the textbook,* pp. 79–92. New York: Routledge & Chapman Hall.

Smith, K. (1994, December 31). "Women minorities in management up," *Bloomington Herald-Times,* C10.

Sorcinelli, M.D., and Andrews, P.H. (1987). Articulating career goals: A comparison of male and female university faculty. *Journal of the National Association for Women Deans, Administrators, and Counselors, 50,* 11–19.

Spaid, E.L. (1993, July 13). Glass ceiling remains thick at companies' top levels. *The Christian Science Monitor, 85 (158),* 9, 12.

Stewart, C.J., and Cash, W.B. (1994). *Interviewing: Principles and Practices,* 7th ed. Dubuque, IA: Brown & Benchmark Publishers.

Stewart, T.A. (1991, December 6). Gay in corporate America. *Fortune*, 43–56.

Stroh, L., Brett, J., and Reilly, A. (1993). All the right stuff: A comparison of female and male managers' career progression. *Journal of Applied Psychology*.

Sutton, C.D., and Moore, K.K. (1985, September–October). Executive women—twenty years later. *Harvard Business Review*, 63, 43–66.

Tharp, R.G. (1989). Psychocultural variables and constants: Effects on teaching and learning in schools. *American Psychologist*, 44, 2, 349–359.

Thomas, R.R., Jr. (1991). *Beyond race and gender*. New York: American Management Association.

Treichler, P.A., and Kramarae, C. (1983). Women's talk in the ivory tower. *Communication Quarterly*, 31, 2, 118–132.

Trompenaars, F. (1994). *Riding the waves of culture: Understanding diversity in global business*. New York: Irwin.

Wagner, G., Pfeffer, J., and O'Reilly, C. (1984). Organizational demography and turnover in top management groups. *Administrative Science Quarterly*, 29, 74–92.

Wagner, G., Wynne, B., and Mennecke, B. (1993). Group support systems facilities and software. In L.M. Jessup and J.S. Valacich (eds.), *Group support systems: New perspectives*, pp. 8–55. New York: Macmillan.

Walton, S.J. (1994). *Cultural Diversity in the Workplace*. New York: Irwin Professional Publishing.

Webber, R. (1976). Perceptions and behaviors in mixed sex work teams. *Industrial Relations*, 15, 121–129.

Weinberg, M. (1977). *A chance to learn: A history of race and education in the U.S.* Cambridge: Cambridge University Press.

Williams, M.D. (1981). Observations in Pittsburgh ghetto schools. *Anthropology and Education Quarterly*, 12, 211–220.

With problem more visible, firms crack down on sexual harassment. (1986, August 8). *The Wall Street Journal*, 12.

Wolman, C., and Frank, H. (1975). The solo woman in a professional peer group. *American Journal of Orthopsychiatry*, 41, 164–170.

Woo, J. (1992, March 11). Job interviews pose risks to employers. *The Wall Street Journal*, B1, B5.

Zachary, G.P. (1994). High-tech culture still impedes women. *The Wall Street Journal*, B1–B2.

Chapter 10

Aguilar, F.J. (1994). *Managing corporate ethics: Learning from America's ethical companies how to supercharge business performance*. New York: Oxford University Press.

Alderson, W. (1974). The American economy and Christian ethics. In J.S. Wright and J.E. Mertes (eds.), *Advertising's role in society*, pp. 163–175. St. Paul, MN: West.

Andrews, K.R. (1989). Ethics in practice. *Harvard Business Review*, 67, 99–104.

Benson, J.A. (1988). Crisis revisited: An analysis of strategies used by Tylenol in the second tampering episode. *Central States Speech Journal*, 39, 62.

Blank, S. (1986). Hershey: A company driven by values. *Management Review*, 75, 31–35.

Bosses peek at E-mail. (1993, May 24). *USA Today*, Sec B, p. 1.

Burke, K. (1966). *Language as symbolic action*. Berkeley, CA: University of California Press.

Castro, J. (1993, March 29). Disposable workers. *Time*, 43–47.

DeMaio, H. (1991). Your organization needs an information ethics program! *Management Accounting*, 73, 22–23.

Deutschman, A. (1990, August 27). What 25-year-olds want. *Fortune*, 42–50.

Dolecheck, M.M. (1989). Doing justice to ethics. *Supervisory Management*, 10, 35–39.

Dominguez, A. (1993, August 15). Has corporate Big Brother arrived? *Greensboro News and Record*, p. E1.

Dudar, H. (1979, October 30). The price of blowing the whistle. *The New York Times Magazine*, 41–54.

Fierman, J. (1994, January 24). The contingency workforce. *Fortune*, 30–36.

Flynn. (1957). The Aristotelian basis for the ethics of speaking. *Speech Teacher*, 6, 179–187.

Gibb, J. (1961). Defensive communication. *Journal of Communication*, 11, 141–148.

Glazer, M.P., and Glazer, P.M. (1989). *The whistleblowers: Exposing corruption in government and industry*. New York: Basic Books.

Gore, A. (1992). *Earth in the Balance: Ecology and the human spirit*. New York: Penguin Books.

Greenberg, E.R. (1988). Workplace testing: Results of a new AMA survey. *Personnel*, 65, 36–44.

Health care in the 1990s: Forecasts by top analysts. (1989, July 20). *Hospitals*. 34–40.

Hendren, J. (1993, January 10). "Software police" crack down on piracy. *Greensboro News and Record*, p. E3.

Hilts, D.J. (1993, June 13). Why whistleblowers can seem a little crazy. *The New York Times*, p. E3.

Hosmer, L.T. (1987). *The ethics of management*. Homewood, IL: Richard D. Irwin.

Hospice firm pays nurses to recruit patients. (1990, August 26). *Chicago Tribune*, sec. 7, p. 1.

Johannesen, R.L. (1971). The emerging concept of communication as dialogue. *Quarterly Journal of Speech*, 57, 378–382.

Johannesen, R.L. (1992). Perspectives on ethics in persuasion. In C.U. Larson (ed.), *Persuasion: Reception and responsibility*, 6th ed., pp. 28–53. Belmont, CA.

Keller, P.W., and Brown, C.T. (1968). An interpersonal ethic for communication. *Journal of Communication*, 18, 73–81.

Kleiman, C. (1990, August 27). 20 million industrial jobs hinge on "fetal protection" court case. *Chicago Tribune*, sec. 4, p. 2.

Kouzes, J.M., and Posner, B.Z. (1993). *Credibility: How leaders gain and lose it, why people demand it.* San Francisco: Jossey-Bass.

Laudon, K.C., and Laudon, J.P. (1994). *Management information systems: Organization and technology,* 3rd ed. New York: Macmillan.

Lindquist, C. (1991, December 9). "Child Porn" sent on America On-Line. *Computerworld, 25,* 7.

Looking to its roots. (1987, May 25). *Time,* 27.

Ludeman, K. (1989). *The worth ethic.* New York: E.P. Dutton.

Magazine Lists 100 Best Companies for Working Mothers. (1994, September 12). *Herald Times,* p. A6

Markoff, J. (1990, May 5). Computer intruder put on probation and fined $10,000. *The New York Times,* p. A1.

McMillan, J.E. (1963). Ethics and advertising. In J.S. Wright, and S.S. Warner (eds.), *Speaking of advertising,* pp. 453–458. New York: McGraw-Hill.

O'Reilly, B. (1990, March 12). Is your company asking too much? *Fortune,* 38–46.

Oz, E. (1994). *Ethics for the information age.* Dubuque, IA: Wm. C. Brown.

Peters, T.J. (1987). *Thriving on chaos.* New York: Knopf.

Phone monitoring: A fairness, privacy call. (1990, August 27). *Chicago Tribune,* sec. 4, p. 1.

Rifkin, G. (1991, December 8). Do employees have a right to electronic privacy? *New York Times,* p. 3, 8.

Rodgers, F.S., and Rogers, C. (November/December 1989). "Business and the facts of family life," *Harvard Business Review,* 121–129.

Samuelson, R.J. (1991, November 11). The boss as welfare cheat. *Newsweek,* 55.

Shortell, S.M., Morrison, E.M., and Friedman, B. (1990). *Strategic choices for America's hospitals.* San Francisco: Jossey-Bass.

Solo, S. (1990, November 16). Stop whining and get back to work. *Fortune,* 27–32.

Solomon, R.C., and Hanson, K. (1985). *It's good business.* New York: Harper & Row.

Stewart, J. (1978). Foundations of dialogic communication. *Quarterly Journal of Speech, 64,* 183–201.

Szwergold, J. (April, 1993). The great hi-tech threat. *Management Review, 82,* 9.

Walters, K.D. (1975). Your employees' right to blow the whistle. *Harvard Business Review, 53,* 26–34 and 161–162.

Wire Reports. (1994, February 5). Computer net intruders threaten work of users. *Greensboro News & Record,* p. A4.

Chapter 11

Abel, M., Corey, D., Bulick, S., Schmidt, J., and Coffin, S. (1992). Telecollaboration research project. In R.P. Bostrom, R.T. Watson, and S.T. Kinney (eds.), *Computer augmented teamwork,* pp. 67–85. New York: Van Nostrand Reinhold.

Baum, D. (1993, August 16). The convergence of TV and computers. *Computerworld, 27,* 89–90.

Bennett, A. (1992, October 27). Many of today's top corporate officers are the right people for the wrong time. *Wall Street Journal,* pp. B1–B3.

Coates, J. (1993, July 11). Place a management expert in your computer. *Chicago Tribune,* section 7, p.7

Cornish, E. (1992). Social and technological forecasts for the next 25 years. *World future society* (publisher of *The Futurist:* A journal of forecasts, trends and ideas about the future).

Davenport, T. (1993). *Process innovation: Reengineering works through information technology.* Cambridge: Harvard Business School Press.

Dentzer, S. (1994, January 24). Bypass on the information highway. *U.S. News & World Report,* 63.

Deutschman, A. (1992, October 5). America's fastest-growing companies. *Fortune,* 59–82.

Drucker, P.F. (1988, January–February). The coming of the new organization. *Harvard Business Review,* 45–53.

Dworetzky, T.A. (1994, February–March). Roadmap to the information highway. *Modern Maturity,* 24–31.

Freedman, D. (1992, May 15). The big band era: The band plays on. *CIO, 5,* 38–49.

Grupe, F.H. (1992, Summer). Can a geographic information system give your business its competitive edge? *Information Strategy: The Executive's Journal,* 41–48.

Hammer, M., and Champy, J. (1993). *Reengineering the corporation: A manifesto for business revolution.* New York: HarperCollins.

Henkoff, R. (1994, June 27). Service is everybody's business. *Fortune,* 48–60.

Hiltz, S.R., and Turoff, M. (1992). Virtual meetings: Computer conferencing and distributed group support. In R.P. Bostrom, R.T. Watson, and S.T. Kinney (eds.), *Computer augmented teamwork,* pp. 67–85. New York: Van Nostrand Reinhold.

Hotch, R. (1993, May). Communications revolution. *Nation's Business,* 20–28.

Huey, J. (1994, June 27). Waking up to the new economy. *Fortune,* 36–46.

Jessup, L., and Valacich, J. (1993). Future challenges in the evolution of group support systems. In L. M. Jessup and J.S. Valacich (eds.), *Group support systems: New perspectives,* pp. 78–96. New York: Macmillan.

Johansen, R. (1993). Groupware: Future directions and wild cards. In R.H. Sprague and H.J. Watson (eds.), *Decision support systems: Putting theory into practice,* 3rd ed., pp. 355–362. Englewood Cliffs: Prentice-Hall.

Kapor, M. (1994, February–March). Will I have control? *Modern Maturity,* 30–31.

Laudon, K.C., and Laudon, J.P. (1994). *Management information systems: Organization and technology,* 3rd ed. New York: Macmillan.

LeeBaert, D. and Dickinson, T. (1991). A world to understand: Technology and the awakening of human possibility. In D. LeeBaert (ed.), *Technology 2001: The future of computing and communication,* pp. 293–321. Cambridge, MA: The MIT Press.

Negroponte, N. (1994, February–March). What's in it for me? *Modern Maturity,* 27.

Rosenthal, L. (1994, February 20). Cellular carriers use software to stop thefts. *Greensboro News & Record,* p. E6.

Schindler, J. (Spring 1994). The data superhighway. *Gateway Monitor,* 3.

Schlender, B.R. (1991, August 26). The future of the PC. *Fortune,* 40–48.

Sprout, A. (1994, May 2). Moving into the virtual office. *Fortune,* 103.

Stahl, S. (1994a, May 16). Notes gets a voice. *Informationweek,* 86.

Stahl, S. (1994b, May 16). Lotus: Form is function. *Informationweek,* 86.

Stewart, T.A. (1994, April 4). The information age in charts. *Fortune,* 75–79.

Taylor, S. (1994, February–March). Can computing change my life? *Modern Maturity,* 28.

Teresko, J. (1993, August 2). Tripping down the information superhighway. *Industry Week, 242,* 32–40.

Ziegler, B. (1993, September 27). Calling all channels. *Business Week,* 130–135.

What Is the Internet?

Armbruster, L. (1994). *Internet essentials: A jump-start to getting on the Internet.* Indianapolis: Prentice-Hall.

Bradley, J.C. (1995). *A quick guide to the Internet.* Belmont, MA: Wadsworth Publishing.

Levine, J.R. and Baroudi, C. (1994). *The Internet for dummies.* San Mateo, CA: IDG Books Worldwide.

Manrique, C. (1995). *The Houghton Mifflin guide to the Internet for political science.* Boston: Houghton-Mifflin.

Pike, M.A. (1995). *Using the Internet.* Indianapolis: Que Corporation.

Pitter K., Amato S., Callahan J., Kerr N., and Tilton E. (1995). *Every student's guide to the Internet.* New York: McGraw-Hill.

Salkind, N. (1995). *Hands-on Internet.* Danvers, MA: Boyd & Fraser.

Wyatt, A.L. (1994). *Navigating the Internet.* Las Vegas: Jama Press.

Wyatt, A.L. (1995). *Success with the Internet.* Danvers, MA: Boyd & Fraser.

NAME INDEX

SUBJECT INDEX